A BUDGET OF PARADOXES

VOLUME I

BY

AUGUSTUS DE MO

PREFACE TO THE FIRST EDITION

(1872)

It is not without hesitation that I have taken upon myself the editorship of a work left avowedly imperfect by the author, and, from its miscellaneous and discursive character, difficult of completion with due regard to editorial limitations by a less able hand.

Had the author lived to carry out his purpose he would have looked through his Budget again, amplifying and probably rearranging some of its contents. He had collected materials for further illustration of Paradox of the kind treated of in this book; and he meant to write a second part, in which the contradictions and inconsistencies of orthodox learning would have been subjected to the same scrutiny and castigation as heterodox ignorance had already received.

It will be seen that the present volume contains more than the Athenæum Budget. Some of the additions formed a Supplement to the original articles. These supplementary paragraphs were, by the author, placed after those to which they respectively referred, being distinguished from the rest of the text by brackets. I have omitted these brackets as useless, except where they were needed to indicate subsequent writing.

Another and a larger portion of the work consists of discussion of matters of contemporary interest, for the Budget was in some degree a receptacle for the author's thoughts on any literary, scientific, or social question.

Having grown thus gradually to its present size, the book as it was left was not quite in a fit condition for publication, but the alterations which have been made are slight and few, being in most cases verbal, and such as the sense absolutely required, or transpositions of sentences to secure coherence with the rest, in places where the author, in his more recent insertion of them, had overlooked the connection in which they stood. In no case has the meaning been in any degree modified or interfered with.

One rather large omission must be mentioned here. It is an account of the quarrel between Sir James South and Mr. Troughton on the mounting, etc. of the equatorial telescope at Campden Hill. At some future time when the affair has passed entirely out of the memory of living Astronomers, the appreciative sketch, which is omitted in this edition of the Budget, will be an interesting piece of history and study of character.[1]

A very small portion of Mr. James Smith's circle-squaring has been left out, with a still smaller portion of Mr. De Morgan's answers to that Cyclometrical Paradoxer.

In more than one place repetitions, which would have disappeared under the author's revision, have been allowed to remain, because they could not have been taken away without leaving a hiatus, not easy to fill up without damage to the author's meaning.

I give these explanations in obedience to the rules laid down for the guidance of editors at page 15.[2] If any apology for the fragmentary character of the book be thought necessary, it may be found in the author's own words at page 281 of the second volume.[3]

The publication of the Budget could not have been delayed without lessening the interest attaching to the writer's thoughts upon questions of our own day. I trust that, incomplete as the work is compared with what it might have been, I shall not be held mistaken in giving it to the world.

Rather let me hope that it will be welcomed as an old friend returning under great disadvantages, but bringing a pleasant remembrance of the amusement which its weekly appearance in the Athenæum gave to both writer and reader.

The Paradoxes are dealt with in chronological order. This will be a guide to the reader, and with the alphabetical Index of Names, etc., will, I trust, obviate all difficulty of reference.

SOPHIA DE MORGAN.

6 MERTON ROAD, PRIMROSE HILL.

PREFACE TO THE SECOND EDITION

If Mrs. De Morgan felt called upon to confess her hesitation at taking upon herself the labor of editing these Paradoxes, much more should one who was born two generations later, who lives in another land and who was reared amid different influences, confess to the same feeling when undertaking to revise this curious medley. But when we consider the nature of the work, the fact that its present rarity deprives so many readers of the enjoyment of its delicious satire, and the further fact that allusions that were commonplace a half century ago are now forgotten, it is evident that some one should take up the work and perform it con amore.

Having long been an admirer of De Morgan, having continued his work in the bibliography of early arithmetics, and having worked in his library among the books of which he was so fond, it is possible that the present editor, whatever may be his other shortcomings, may undertake the labor with as much of sympathy as any one who is in a position to perform it.

With this thought in mind, two definite rules were laid down at the beginning of the task: (1) That no alteration in the text should be made, save in slightly modernizing spelling and punctuation and in the case of manifest typographical errors; (2) That whenever a note appeared it should show at once its authorship, to the end that the material of the original edition might appear intact.

In considering, however, the unbroken sequence of items that form the Budget, it seems clear that readers would be greatly aided if the various leading topics were separated in some convenient manner. After considerable thought it was decided to insert brief captions from time to time that might aid the eye in selecting the larger subjects of the text. In some parts of the work these could easily be taken from the original folio heads, but usually they had to be written anew. While, therefore, the present editor accepts the responsibility for the captions of the various subdivisions, he has endeavored to insert them in harmony with the original text.

As to the footnotes, the first edition had only a few, some due to De Morgan himself and others to Mrs. De Morgan. In the present edition those due to the former are signed A. De M., and those due to Mrs. De Morgan appear with her initials, S. E. De M. For all other footnotes the present editor is responsible. In preparing them the effort has been made to elucidate the text by supplying such information as the casual reader might wish as he passes over the pages. Hundreds of names are referred to in the text that were more or less known in England half a century ago, but are now forgotten there and were never familiar elsewhere. Many books that were then current have now passed out of memory, and much that agitated England in De Morgan's prime seems now like ancient history. Even with respect to well-known names, a little information as to dates and publications will often be welcome, although the editor recognizes that it will quite as often be superfluous. In order, therefore, to derive the pleasure that should come from reading the Budget, the reader should have easy access to the information that the notes are intended to supply. That they furnish too much here and too little there is to be expected. They are a human product, and if they fail to serve their purpose in all respects it is hoped that this failure will not seriously interfere with the reader's pleasure.

In general the present editor has refrained from expressing any opinions that would strike a discordant note in the reading of the text as De Morgan left it. The temptation is great to add to the discussion at various points, but it is a temptation to be resisted. To furnish such information as shall make the reading more pleasant, rather than to attempt to improve upon one of the most delicious bits of satire of the nineteenth century, has been the editor's wish. It would have been an agreeable task to review the history of circle squaring, of the trisection problem, and of the duplication of the cube. This, however, would be to go too far afield. For the benefit of those who wish to investigate the subject the editor can only refer to such works and articles as the following: F. Rudio, Archimedes, Huygens, Lambert, Legendre,--mit einer Uebersicht über die Geschichte des Problemes von der Quadratur des Zirkels, Leipsic, 1892; Thomas Muir, "Circle," in the eleventh edition of the Encyclopædia Britannica; the various histories of mathematics; and to his own article on "The Incommensurability of [pi]" in Prof. J. W. A. Young's Monographs on Topics of Modern Mathematics, New York, 1911.

The editor wishes to express his appreciation and thanks to Dr. Paul Carus, editor of The Monist and The Open Court for the opportunity of undertaking this work; to James Earl Russell, LL.D., Dean of Teachers College, Columbia University, for his encouragement in its prosecution; to Miss Caroline Eustis Seely for her intelligent and painstaking assistance in securing material for the notes; and to Miss Lydia G. Robinson and Miss Anna A. Kugler for their aid and helpful suggestions in connection with the proof-sheets. Without the generous help of all five this work would have been impossible.

DAVID EUGENE SMITH.

TEACHERS COLLEGE, COLUMBIA UNIVERSITY.

* * * * *

INTRODUCTORY

If I had before me a fly and an elephant, having never seen more than one such magnitude of either kind; and if the fly were to endeavor to persuade me that he was larger than the elephant, I might by possibility be placed in a difficulty. The apparently little creature might use such arguments about the effect of distance, and might appeal to such laws of sight and hearing as I, if unlearned in those things, might be unable wholly to reject. But if there were a thousand flies, all buzzing, to appearance, about the great creature; and, to a fly, declaring, each one for himself, that he was bigger than the quadruped; and all giving different and frequently contradictory reasons; and each one despising and opposing the reasons of the others--I should feel quite at my ease. I should certainly say, My little friends, the case of each one of you is destroyed by the rest. I intend to show flies in the swarm, with a few larger animals, for reasons to be given.

In every age of the world there has been an established system, which has been opposed from time to time by isolated and dissentient reformers. The established system has sometimes fallen, slowly and gradually: it has either been upset by the rising influence of some one man, or it has been sapped by gradual change of opinion in the many.

I have insisted on the isolated character of the dissentients, as an element of the a priori probabilities of the case. Show me a schism, especially a growing schism, and it is another thing. The homeopathists, for instance, shall be, if any one so think, as wrong as St. John Long; but an {2} organized opposition, supported by the efforts of many acting in concert, appealing to common arguments and experience, with perpetual succession and a common seal, as the Queen says in the charter, is, be the merit of the schism what it may, a thing wholly different from the case of the isolated opponent in the mode of opposition to it which reason points out.

During the last two centuries and a half, physical knowledge has been gradually made to rest upon a basis which it had not before. It has become mathematical. The question now is, not whether this or that hypothesis is better or worse to the pure thought, but whether it accords with observed phenomena in those consequences which can be shown necessarily to follow from it, if it be true. Even in those sciences which are not yet under the dominion of mathematics, and perhaps never will be, a working copy of the mathematical process has been made. This is not known to the followers of those sciences who are not themselves mathematicians and who very often exalt their horns against the mathematics in consequence.

They might as well be squaring the circle, for any sense they show in this particular.

A great many individuals, ever since the rise of the mathematical method, have, each for himself, attacked its direct and indirect consequences. I shall not here stop to point out how the very accuracy of exact science gives better aim than the preceding state of things could give. I shall call each of these persons a paradoxer, and his system a paradox. I use the word in the old sense: a paradox is something which is apart from general opinion, either in subject-matter, method, or conclusion.

Many of the things brought forward would now be called crotchets, which is the nearest word we have to old paradox. But there is this difference, that by calling a thing a crotchet we mean to speak lightly of it; which was not the necessary sense of paradox. Thus in the sixteenth century many spoke of the earth's motion as the paradox of {3} Copernicus, who held the ingenuity of that theory in very high esteem, and some, I think, who even inclined towards it. In the seventeenth century, the depravation of meaning took place, in England at least. Phillips says paradox is "a thing which seemeth strange"--here is the old meaning: after a colon he proceeds--"and absurd, and is contrary to common opinion," which is an addition due to his own time.

Some of my readers are hardly inclined to think that the word paradox could once have had no disparagement in its meaning; still less that persons could have applied it to themselves. I chance to have met with a case in point against them. It is Spinoza's Philosophia Scripturæ Interpres, Exercitatio Paradoxa, printed anonymously at Eleutheropolis, in 1666.

This place was one of several cities in the clouds, to which the cuckoos resorted who were driven away by the other birds; that is, a feigned place of printing, adopted by those who would have caught it if orthodoxy could have caught them. Thus, in 1656, the works of Socinus could only be printed at Irenopolis. The author deserves his self-imposed title, as in the following:[4]

"Quanto sane satius fuisset illam [Trinitatem] pro mysterio non habuisse, et Philosophiæ ope, antequam quod esset statuerent, secundum veræ logices præcepta quid esset cum Cl. Kleckermanno investigasse; tanto fervore ac labore in profundissimas speluncas et obscurissimos metaphysicarum speculationum atque fictionum recessus se recipere ut ab adversariorum telis sententiam suam in tuto collocarent. {4} Profecto magnus ille vir ... dogma illud, quamvis apud theologos eo nomine non multum gratiæ iniverit, ita ex immotis Philosophiæ fundamentis explicat ac demonstrat, ut paucis tantum immutatis, atque additis, nihil amplius animus veritate sincere deditus desiderare possit."

This is properly paradox, though also heterodox. It supposes, contrary to all opinion, orthodox and heterodox, that philosophy can, with slight changes, explain the Athanasian doctrine so as to be at least compatible with orthodoxy. The author would stand almost alone, if not quite; and this is what he meant. I have met with the counter-paradox. I have heard it maintained that the doctrine as it stands, in all its mystery is a priori more likely than any other to have been Revelation, if such a thing were to be; and that it might almost have been predicted.

After looking into books of paradoxes for more than thirty years, and holding conversation with many persons who have written them, and many who might have done so, there is one point on which my mind is fully made up. The manner in which a paradoxer will show himself, as to sense or nonsense, will not depend upon what he maintains, but upon whether he has or has not made a sufficient knowledge of what has been done by others, especially as to the mode of doing it, a preliminary to inventing knowledge for himself. That a little knowledge is a dangerous thing is one of the most fallacious of proverbs. A person of small knowledge is in danger of trying to make his little do the work of more; but a person without any is in more danger of making his no knowledge do the work of some. Take the speculations on the tides as an instance. Persons with nothing but a little geometry have certainly exposed themselves in their modes of objecting to results which require the higher mathematics to be known before an independent opinion can be formed on sufficient grounds. But persons with no geometry at all have done the same thing much more completely. {5}

There is a line to be drawn which is constantly put aside in the arguments held by paradoxers in favor of their right to instruct the world. Most persons must, or at least will, like the lady in Cadogan Place,[5] form and express an immense variety of opinions on an immense variety of subjects; and all persons must be their own guides in many things. So far all is well. But there are many who, in carrying the expression of their own opinions beyond the usual tone of private conversation, whether they go no further than attempts at oral proselytism, or whether they commit themselves to the press, do not reflect that they have ceased to stand upon the ground on which their process is defensible. Aspiring to lead others, they have never given themselves the fair chance of being first led by other others into something better than they can start for themselves; and that they should first do this is what both those classes of others have a fair right to expect.

New knowledge, when to any purpose, must come by contemplation of old knowledge in every matter which concerns thought; mechanical contrivance sometimes, not very often, escapes this rule. All the men who are now called discoverers, in every matter ruled by thought, have been men versed in the minds of their predecessors, and learned in what had been before them. There is not one exception. I do not say that every man has made direct acquaintance with the whole of his mental ancestry; many have, as I may say, only known their grandfathers by the report of their fathers. But even on this point it is remarkable how many of the greatest names in all departments of knowledge have been real antiquaries in their several subjects.

I may cite, among those who have wrought strongly upon opinion or practice in science, Aristotle, Plato, Ptolemy, Euclid, Archimedes, Roger Bacon, Copernicus, Francis Bacon, Ramus, Tycho Brahé, Galileo, Napier, Descartes, Leibnitz, Newton, Locke. I take none but names known out of their {6} fields of work; and all were learned as well as sagacious. I have chosen my instances: if any one will undertake to show a person of little or no knowledge who has established himself in a great matter of pure thought, let him bring forward his man, and we shall see.

This is the true way of putting off those who plague others with their great discoveries. The first demand made should be--Mr. Moses, before I allow you to lead me over the Red Sea, I must have you show that you are learned in all the wisdom of the Egyptians upon your own subject. The plea that it is unlikely that this or that unknown person should succeed where Newton, etc. have failed, or should show Newton, etc. to be wrong, is utterly null and void. It was worthily versified by Sylvanus Morgan (the great herald who in his Sphere of Gentry gave coat armor to "Gentleman Jesus," as he said), who sang of Copernicus as follows (1652):

"If Tellus winged be, The earth a motion round; Then much deceived are they Who nere before it found. Solomon was the wisest, His wit nere this attained; Cease, then, Copernicus, Thy hypothesis is vain."

Newton, etc. were once unknown; but they made themselves known by what they knew, and then brought forward what they could do; which I see is as good verse as that of Herald Sylvanus. The demand for previous knowledge disposes of twenty-nine cases out of thirty, and the thirtieth is worth listening to.

I have not set down Copernicus, Galileo, etc. among the paradoxers, merely because everybody knows them; if my list were quite complete, they would have been in it. But the reader will find Gilbert, the great precursor of sound magnetical theory; and several others on whom no censure can be cast, though some of their paradoxes are inadmissible, {7} some unprovoked, and some capital jokes, true or false: the author of Vestiges of Creation is an instance. I expect that my old correspondent, General Perronet Thompson, will admit that his geometry is part and parcel of my plan; and also that, if that plan embraced politics, he would claim a place for his Catechism on the Corn Laws, a work at one time paradoxical, but which had more to do with the abolition of the bread-tax than Sir Robert Peel.

My intention in publishing this Budget in the Athenæum is to enable those who have been puzzled by one or two discoverers to see how they look in a lump. The only question is, has the selection been fairly made? To this my answer is, that no selection at all has been made. The books are, without exception, those which I have in my own library; and I have taken all--I mean all of the kind: Heaven forbid that I should be supposed to have no other books! But I may have been a collector, influenced in choice by bias? I answer that I never have collected books of this sort--that is, I have never searched for them, never made up my mind to look out for this book or that. I have bought what happened to come in my way at show or auction; I have retained what came in as part of the undescribed portion of miscellaneous auction lots; I have received a few from friends who found them among what they called their rubbish; and I have preserved books sent to me for review. In not a few instances the books have been bound up with others, unmentioned at the back; and for years I knew no more I had them than I knew I had Lord Macclesfield's speech on moving the change of Style, which, after I had searched shops, etc. for it in vain, I found had been reposing on my own shelves for many years, at the end of a summary of Leibnitz's philosophy. Consequently, I may positively affirm that the following list is formed by accident and circumstance alone, and that it truly represents the casualties of about a third of a century. For instance, the large proportion of works {8} on the quadrature of the circle is not my doing: it is the natural share of this subject in the actual run of events.

[I keep to my plan of inserting only such books as I possessed in 1863, except by casual notice in aid of my remarks. I have found several books on my shelves which ought to have been inserted. These have their titles set out at the commencement of their articles, in leading paragraphs; the casuals are without this formality.[6]]

Before proceeding to open the Budget, I say something on my personal knowledge of the class of discoverers who square the circle, upset Newton, etc. I suspect I know more of the English class than any man in Britain. I never kept any reckoning; but I know that one year with another--and less of late years than in earlier time--I have talked to more than five in each year, giving more than a hundred and fifty specimens. Of this I am sure, that it is my own fault if they have not been a thousand. Nobody knows how they swarm, except those to whom they naturally resort. They are in all ranks and occupations, of all ages and characters. They are very earnest people, and their purpose is bona fide the dissemination of their paradoxes. A great many--the mass, indeed--are illiterate, and a great many waste their means, and are in or approaching penury. But I must say that never, in any one instance, has the quadrature of the circle, or the like, been made a pretext for begging; even to be asked to purchase a book is of the very rarest occurrence--it has happened, and that is all.

These discoverers despise one another: if there were the concert among them which there is among foreign mendicants, a man who admitted one to a conference would be plagued to death. I once gave something to a very genteel French applicant, who overtook me in the street, at my own door, saying he had picked up my handkerchief: whether he picked it up in my pocket for an introduction, I know not. {9} But that day week came another Frenchman to my house, and that day fortnight a French lady; both failed, and I had no more trouble. The same thing happened with Poles. It is not so with circle-squarers, etc.: they know nothing of each other. Some will read this list, and will say I am right enough, generally speaking, but that there is an exception, if I could but see it.

I do not mean, by my confession of the manner in which I have sinned against the twenty-four hours, to hold myself out as accessible to personal explanation of new plans. Quite the contrary: I consider myself as having made my report, and being discharged from further attendance on the subject. I will not, from henceforward, talk to any squarer of the circle, trisector of the angle, duplicator of the cube, constructor of perpetual motion, subverter of gravitation, stagnator of the earth, builder of the universe, etc. I will receive any writings or books which require no answer, and read them when I please: I will certainly preserve them--this list may be enlarged at some future time.

There are three subjects which I have hardly anything upon; astrology, mechanism, and the infallible way of winning at play. I have never cared to preserve astrology. The mechanists make models, and not books. The infallible winners--though I have seen a few--think their secret too valuable, and prefer mutare quadrata rotundis--to turn dice into coin--at the gaming-house: verily they have their reward.

I shall now select, to the mystic number seven, instances of my personal knowledge of those who think they have discovered, in illustration of as many misconceptions.

1. Attempt by help of the old philosophy, the discoverer not being in possession of modern knowledge. A poor schoolmaster, in rags, introduced himself to a scientific friend with whom I was talking, and announced that he had found out the composition of the sun. "How was that done?"--"By consideration of the four elements."--"What are {10} they?"--"Of course, fire, air, earth, and water."--"Did you not know that air, earth, and water, have long been known to be no elements at all, but compounds?"--"What do you mean, sir? Who ever heard of such a thing?"

2. The notion that difficulties are enigmas, to be overcome in a moment by a lucky thought. A nobleman of very high rank, now long dead, read an article by me on the quadrature, in an early number of the Penny Magazine. He had, I suppose, school recollections of geometry. He put pencil to paper, drew a circle, and constructed what seemed likely to answer, and, indeed, was--as he said--certain, if only this bit were equal to that; which of course it was not. He forwarded his diagram to the Secretary of the Diffusion Society, to be handed to the author of the article, in case the difficulty should happen to be therein overcome.

3. Discovery at all hazards, to get on in the world. Thirty years ago, an officer of rank, just come from foreign service, and trying for a decoration from the Crown, found that his claims were of doubtful amount, and was told by a friend that so and so, who had got the order, had the additional claim of scientific distinction. Now this officer, while abroad, had bethought himself one day, that there really could be no difficulty in finding the circumference of a circle: if a circle were rolled upon a straight line until the undermost point came undermost again, there would be the straight line equal to the circle. He came to me, saying that he did not feel equal to the statement of his claim in this respect, but that if some clever fellow would put the thing in a proper light, he thought his affair might be managed. I was clever enough to put the thing in a proper light to himself, to this extent at least, that, though perhaps they were wrong, the advisers of the Crown would never put the letters K.C.B. to such a circle as his.

4. The notion that mathematicians cannot find the circle for common purposes. A working man measured the altitude of a cylinder accurately, and--I think the process of {11} Archimedes was one of his proceedings--found its bulk. He then calculated the ratio of the circumference to the diameter, and found it answered very well on other modes of trial. His result was about 3.14. He came to London, and somebody sent him to me. Like many others of his pursuit, he seemed to have turned the whole force of his mind upon one of his points, on which alone he would be open to refutation. He had read some of Kater's experiments, and had got the Act of 1825 on weights and measures. Say what I would, he had for a long time but one answer--"Sir! I go upon Captain Kater and the Act of Parliament." But I fixed him at last. I happened to have on the table a proof-sheet of the Astronomical Memoirs, in which were a large number of observed places of the planets compared with prediction, and asked him whether it could be possible that persons who did not know the circle better than he had found it could make the calculations, of which I gave him a notion, so accurately? He was perfectly astonished, and took the titles of some books which he said he would read.

5. Application for the reward from abroad. Many years ago, about twenty-eight, I think, a Jesuit came from South America, with a quadrature, and a cutting from a newspaper announcing that a reward was ready for the discovery in England. On this evidence he came over. After satisfying him that nothing had ever been offered here, I discussed his quadrature, which was of no use. I succeeded better when I told him of Richard White, also a Jesuit, and author of a quadrature published before 1648, under the name of Chrysæspis, of which I can give no account, having never seen it. This White (Albius) is the only quadrator who was ever convinced of his error.

My Jesuit was struck by the instance, and promised to read more geometry--he was no Clavius--before he published his book. He relapsed, however, for I saw his book advertised in a few days. I may say, as sufficient proof of my being no collector, that I had not the curiosity to buy his book; and my friend the {12} Jesuit did not send me a copy, which he ought to have done, after the hour I had given him.

6. Application for the reward at home. An agricultural laborer squared the circle, and brought the proceeds to London. He left his papers with me, one of which was the copy of a letter to the Lord Chancellor, desiring his Lordship to hand over forthwith 100,000 pounds, the amount of the alleged offer of reward. He did not go quite so far as M. de Vausenville, who, I think in 1778, brought an action against the Academy of Sciences to recover a reward to which he held himself entitled. I returned the papers, with a note, stating that he had not the knowledge requisite to see in what the problem consisted. I got for answer a letter in which I was told that a person who could not see that he had done the thing should "change his business, and appropriate his time and attention to a Sunday-school, to learn what he could, and keep the litle children from durting their close." I also received a letter from a friend of the quadrator, informing me that I knew his friend had succeeded, and had been heard to say so. These letters were printed--without the names of the writers--for the amusement of the readers of Notes and Queries, First Series, xii. 57, and they will appear again in the sequel.

[There are many who have such a deep respect for any attempt at thought that they are shocked at ridicule even of those who have made themselves conspicuous by pretending to lead the world in matters which they have not studied. Among my anonyms is a gentleman who is angry at my treatment of the "poor but thoughtful" man who is described in my introduction as recommending me to go to a Sunday-school because I informed him that he did not know in what the difficulty of quadrature consisted. My impugner quite forgets that this man's "thoughtfulness" chiefly consisted in his demanding a hundred thousand pounds from the Lord Chancellor for his discovery; and I may add, that his greatest stretch of invention was finding out that "the clergy" {13} were the means of his modest request being unnoticed. I mention this letter because it affords occasion to note a very common error, namely, that men unread in their subjects have, by natural wisdom, been great benefactors of mankind. My critic says, "Shakspeare, whom the Pro^r (sic) may admit to be a wisish man, though an object of contempt as to learning ..." Shakespeare an object of contempt as to learning! Though not myself a thoroughgoing Shakespearean--and adopting the first half of the opinion given by George III, "What! is there not sad stuff? only one must not say so"--I am strongly of opinion that he throws out the masonic signs of learning in almost every scene, to all who know what they are. And this over and above every kind of direct evidence. First, foremost, and enough, the evidence of Ben Jonson that he had "little Latin and less Greek"; then Shakespeare had as much Greek as Jonson would call some, even when he was depreciating. To have any Greek at all was in those days exceptional. In Shakespeare's youth St. Paul's and Merchant Taylor's schools were to have masters learned in good and clean Latin literature, and also in Greek if such may be gotten. When Jonson spoke as above, he intended to put Shakespeare low among the learned, but not out of their pale; and he spoke as a rival dramatist, who was proud of his own learned sock; and it may be a subject of inquiry how much Latin he would call little. If Shakespeare's learning on certain points be very much less visible than Jonson's, it is partly because Shakespeare's writings hold it in chemical combination, Jonson's in mechanical aggregation.]

7. An elderly man came to me to show me how the universe was created. There was one molecule, which by vibration became--Heaven knows how!--the Sun. Further vibration produced Mercury, and so on. I suspect the nebular hypothesis had got into the poor man's head by reading, in some singular mixture with what it found there. Some modifications of vibration gave heat, electricity, etc. I {14} listened until my informant ceased to vibrate--which is always the shortest way--and then said, "Our knowledge of elastic fluids is imperfect." "Sir!" said he, "I see you perceive the truth of what I have said, and I will reward your attention by telling you what I seldom disclose, never, except to those who can receive my theory--the little molecule whose vibrations have given rise to our solar system is the Logos of St. John's Gospel!" He went away to Dr. Lardner, who would not go into the solar system at all--the first molecule settled the question. So hard upon poor discoverers are men of science who are not antiquaries in their subject! On leaving, he said,

"Sir, Mr. De Morgan received me in a very different way! he heard me attentively, and I left him perfectly satisfied of the truth of my system." I have had much reason to think that many discoverers, of all classes, believe they have convinced every one who is not peremptory to the verge of incivility.

My list is given in chronological order. My readers will understand that my general expressions, where slighting or contemptuous, refer to the ignorant, who teach before they have learned. In every instance, those of whom I am able to speak with respect, whether as right or wrong, have sought knowledge in the subject they were to handle before they completed their speculations. I shall further illustrate this at the conclusion of my list.

Before I begin the list, I give prominence to the following letter, addressed by me to the Correspondent of October 28, 1865. Some of my paradoxers attribute to me articles in this or that journal; and others may think--I know some do think--they know me as the writer of reviews of some of the very books noticed here. The following remarks will explain the way in which they may be right, and in which they may be wrong. {15}

* * * * *

THE EDITORIAL SYSTEM

"Sir,--I have reason to think that many persons have a very inaccurate notion of the Editorial System. What I call by this name has grown up in the last centenary--a word I may use to signify the hundred years now ending, and to avoid the ambiguity of century. It cannot conveniently be explained by editors themselves, and edited journals generally do not like to say much about it. In your paper perhaps, in which editorial duties differ somewhat from those of ordinary journals, the common system may be freely spoken of.

"When a reviewed author, as very often happens, writes to the editor of the reviewing journal to complain of what has been said of him, he frequently--even more often than not--complains of 'your reviewer.' He sometimes presumes that 'you' have, 'through inadvertence' in this instance, 'allowed some incompetent person to lower the character of your usually accurate pages.' Sometimes he talks of 'your scribe,' and, in extreme cases, even of 'your hack.' All this shows perfect ignorance of the journal system, except where it is done under the notion of letting the editor down easy. But the editor never accepts the mercy.

"All that is in a journal, except what is marked as from a correspondent, either by the editor himself or by the correspondent's real or fictitious signature, is published entirely on editorial responsibility, as much as if the editor had written it himself. The editor, therefore, may claim, and does claim and exercise, unlimited right of omission, addition, and alteration.

This is so well understood that the editor performs his last function on the last revise without the 'contributor' knowing what is done. The word contributor is the proper one; it implies that he furnishes materials without stating what he furnishes or how much of it is accepted, or whether he be the only contributor. All this applies both to political and literary journals. No editor acknowledges {16} the right of a contributor to withdraw an article, if he should find alterations in the proof sent to him for correction which would make him wish that the article should not appear. If the demand for suppression were made--I say nothing about what might be granted to request--the answer would be, 'It is not your article, but mine; I have all the responsibility; if it should contain a libel, I could not give you up, even at your own desire. You have furnished me with materials, on the known and common understanding that I was to use them at my discretion, and you have no right to impede my operations by making the appearance of the article depend on your approbation of my use of your materials.'

"There is something to be said for this system, and something against it--I mean simply on its own merits. But the all-conquering argument in its favor is, that the only practicable alternative is the modern French plan of no articles without the signature of the writers. I need not discuss this plan; there is no collective party in favor of it. Some may think it is not the only alternative; they have not produced any intermediate proposal in which any dozen of persons have concurred. Many will say, Is not all this, though perfectly correct, well known to be matter of form? Is it not practically the course of events that an engaged contributor writes the article, and sends it to the editor, who admits it as written--substantially, at least? And is it not often very well known, by style and in other ways, who it was wrote the article? This system is matter of form just as much as loaded pistols are matter of form so long as the wearer is not assailed; but matter of form takes the form of matter in the pulling of a trigger, so soon as the need arises. Editors and contributors who can work together find each other out by elective affinity, so that the common run of events settles down into most articles appearing much as they are written. And there are two safety-valves; that is, when judicious persons come together. In the first place, the editor himself, when he has selected his contributor, feels that {17} the contributor is likely to know his business better than an editor can teach him; in fact, it is on that principle that the selection is made. But he feels that he is more competent than the writer to judge questions of strength and of tone, especially when the general purpose of the journal is considered, of which the editor is the judge without appeal. An editor who meddles with substantive matter is likely to be wrong, even when he knows the subject; but one who prunes what he deems excess, is likely to be right, even when he does not know the subject. In the second place, a contributor knows that he is supplying an editor, and learns, without suppressing truth or suggesting falsehood, to make the tone of his communications suit the periodical in which they are to appear. Hence it very often arises that a reviewed author, who thinks he knows the name of his reviewer, and proclaims it with expressions of dissatisfaction, is only wrong in supposing that his critic has given all his mind. It has happened to myself more than once, to be announced as the author of articles which I could not have signed, because they did not go far enough to warrant my affixing my name to them as to a sufficient expression of my own opinion.

"There are two other ways in which a reviewed author may be wrong about his critic. An editor frequently makes slight insertions or omissions--I mean slight in quantity of type--as he goes over the last proof; this he does in a comparative hurry, and it may chance that he does not know the full sting of his little alteration. The very bit which the writer of the book most complains of may not have been seen by the person who is called the writer of the article until after the appearance of the journal; nay, if he be one of those--few, I daresay--who do not read their own articles, may never have been seen by him at all. Possibly, the insertion or omission would not have been made if the editor could have had one minute's conversation with his contributor. Sometimes it actually contradicts something which is {18} allowed to remain in another part of the article; and sometimes, especially in the case of omission, it renders other parts of the article unintelligible.

These are disadvantages of the system, and a judicious editor is not very free with his unus et alter pannus. Next, readers in general, when they see the pages of a journal with the articles so nicely fitting, and so many ending with the page or column, have very little notion of the cutting and carving which goes to the process. At the very last moment arises the necessity of some trimming of this kind; and the editor, who would gladly call the writer to counsel if he could, is obliged to strike out ten or twelve lines. He must do his best, but it may chance that the omission selected would take from the writer the power of owning the article. A few years ago, an able opponent of mine wrote to a journal some criticisms upon an article which he expressly attributed to me. I replied as if I were the writer, which, in a sense, I was. But if any one had required of me an unmodified 'Yes' or 'No' to the question whether I wrote the article, I must, of two falsehoods, have chosen 'No': for certain omissions, dictated by the necessities of space and time, would have amounted, had my signature been affixed, to a silent surrender of points which, in my own character, I must have strongly insisted on, unless I had chosen to admit certain inferences against what I had previously published in my own name. I may here add that the forms of journalism obliged me in this case to remind my opponent that it could not be permitted to me, in that journal, either to acknowledge or deny the authorship of the articles. The cautions derived from the above remarks are particularly wanted with reference to the editorial comments upon letters of complaint. There is often no time to send these letters to the contributor, and even when this can be done, an editor is--and very properly--never of so editorial a mind as when he is revising the comments of a contributor upon an assailant of the article. He is then in a better position as to information, and a more {19} critical position as to responsibility. Of course, an editor never meddles, except under notice, with the letter of a correspondent, whether of a complainant, of a casual informant, or of a contributor who sees reason to become a correspondent. Omissions must sometimes be made when a grievance is too highly spiced. It did once happen to me that a waggish editor made an insertion without notice in a letter signed by me with some fiction, which insertion contained the name of a friend of mine, with a satire which I did not believe, and should not have written if I had. To my strong rebuke, he replied--'I know it was very wrong; but human nature could not resist.' But this was the only occasion on which such a thing ever happened to me.

"I daresay what I have written may give some of your readers to understand some of the pericula et commoda of modern journalism. I have known men of deep learning and science as ignorant of the prevailing system as any uneducated reader of a newspaper in a country town. I may perhaps induce some writers not to be too sure about this, that, or the other person. They may detect their reviewer, and they may be safe in attributing to him the general matter and tone of the article. But about one and another point, especially if it be a short and stinging point, they may very easily chance to be wrong. It has happened to myself, and within a few weeks to publication, to be wrong in two ways in reading a past article--to attribute to editorial insertion what was really my own, and to attribute to myself what was really editorial insertion."

What is a man to do who is asked whether he wrote an article? He may, of course, refuse to answer; which is regarded as an admission. He may say, as Swift did to Serjeant Bettesworth, "Sir, when I was a young man, a friend of mine advised me, whenever I was asked whether I had written a certain paper, to deny it; and I accordingly tell that I did not write it." He may say, as I often do, {20} when charged with having invented a joke, story, or epigram, "I want all the credit I can get, and therefore I always acknowledge all that is attributed to me, truly or not; the story, etc. is mine." But for serious earnest, in the matter of imputed criticism, the answer may be, "The article was of my material, but the editor has not let it stand as I gave it; I cannot own it as a whole." He may then refuse to be particular as to the amount of the editor's interference. Of this there are two extreme cases. The editor may have expunged nothing but a qualifying adverb. Or he may have done as follows. We all remember the account of Adam which satirizes woman, but eulogizes her if every second and third line be transposed. As in:

"Adam could find no solid peace When Eve was given him for a mate, Till he beheld a woman's face, Adam was in a happy state."

If this had been the article, and a gallant editor had made the transpositions, the author could not with truth acknowledge. If the alteration were only an omitted adverb, or a few things of the sort, the author could not with truth deny. In all that comes between, every man must be his own casuist. I stared, when I was a boy, to hear grave persons approve of Sir Walter Scott's downright denial that he was the author of Waverley, in answer to the Prince Regent's downright question. If I remember rightly, Samuel Johnson would have approved of the same course.

It is known that, whatever the law gives, it also gives all that is necessary to full possession; thus a man whose land is environed by land of others has a right of way over the land of these others. By analogy, it is argued that when a man has a right to his secret, he has a right to all that is necessary to keep it, and that is not unlawful. If, then, he can only keep his secret by denial, he has a right to denial. This I admit to be an answer against all men except the denier himself; if conscience and self-respect will allow {21} it, no one can impeach it. But the question cannot be solved on a case. That question is, A lie, is it malum in se, without reference to meaning and circumstances? This is a question with two sides to it. Cases may be invented in which a lie is the only way of preventing a murder, or in which a lie may otherwise save a life. In these cases it is difficult to acquit, and almost impossible to blame; discretion introduced, the line becomes very hard to draw.

I know but one work which has precisely--as at first appears--the character and object of my Budget. It is the Review of the Works of the Royal Society of London, by Sir John Hill, M.D. (1751 and 1780, 4to.). This man offended many: the Royal Society, by his work, the medical profession, by inventing and selling extra-pharmacopoeian doses; Garrick, by resenting the rejection of a play. So Garrick wrote:

"For physic and farces his equal there scarce is; His farces are physic; his physic a farce is."

I have fired at the Royal Society and at the medical profession, but I have given a wide berth to the drama and its wits; so there is no epigram out against me, as yet. He was very able and very eccentric. Dr. Thomson (Hist. Roy. Soc.) says he has no humor, but Dr. Thomson was a man who never would have discovered humor.

Mr. Weld (Hist. Roy. Soc.) backs Dr. Thomson, but with a remarkable addition. Having followed his predecessor in observing that the Transactions in Martin Folkes's time have an unusual proportion of trifling and puerile papers, he says that Hill's book is a poor attempt at humor, and glaringly exhibits the feelings of a disappointed man. It is probable, he adds, that the points told with some effect on the Society; for shortly after its publication the Transactions possess a much higher scientific value.

I copy an account which I gave elsewhere.

When the Royal Society was founded, the Fellows set {22} to work to prove all things, that they might hold fast that which was good. They bent themselves to the question whether sprats were young herrings. They made a circle of the powder of a unicorn's horn, and set a spider in the middle of it; "but it immediately ran out." They tried several times, and the spider "once made some stay in the powder." They inquired into Kenelm Digby's sympathetic powder. "Magnetic cures being discoursed of, Sir Gilbert Talbot promised to communicate what he knew of sympathetical cures; and those members who had any of the powder of sympathy, were desired to bring some of it at the next meeting."

June 21, 1661, certain gentlemen were appointed "curators of the proposal of tormenting a man with the sympathetic powder"; I cannot find any record of the result. And so they went on until the time of Sir John Hill's satire, in 1751. This once well-known work is, in my judgment, the greatest compliment the Royal Society ever received. It brought forward a number of what are now feeble and childish researches in the Philosophical Transactions. It showed that the inquirers had actually been inquiring; and that they did not pronounce decision about "natural knowledge" by help of "natural knowledge." But for this, Hill would neither have known what to assail, nor how. Matters are now entirely changed. The scientific bodies are far too well established to risk themselves. Ibit qui zonam perdidit:

"Let him take castles who has ne'er a groat."

These great institutions are now without any collective purpose, except that of promoting individual energy; they print for their contributors, and guard themselves by a general declaration that they will not be answerable for the things they print. Of course they will not put forward anything for everybody; but a writer of a certain reputation, or matter of a certain look of plausibility and safety, {23} will find admission. This is as it should be; the pasturer of flocks and herds and the hunters of wild beasts are two very different bodies, with very different policies. The scientific academies are what a spiritualist might call "publishing mediums," and their spirits fall occasionally into writing which looks as if minds in the higher state were not always impervious to nonsense.

The following joke is attributed to Sir John Hill. I cannot honestly say I believe it; but it shows that his contemporaries did not believe he had no humor. Good stories are always in some sort of keeping with the characters on which they are fastened. Sir John Hill contrived a communication to the Royal Society from Portsmouth, to the effect that a sailor had broken his leg in a fall from the mast-head; that bandages and a plentiful application of tarwater had made him, in three days, able to use his leg as well as ever.

While this communication was under grave discussion--it must be remembered that many then thought tarwater had extraordinary remedial properties--the joker contrived that a second letter should be delivered, which stated that the writer had forgotten, in his previous communication, to mention that the leg was a wooden leg! Horace Walpole told this story, I suppose for the first time; he is good authority for the fact of circulation, but for nothing more.

Sir John Hill's book is droll and cutting satire. Dr. Maty, (Sec. Royal Society) wrote thus of it in the Journal Britannique (Feb. 1751), of which he was editor:

"Il est fâcheux que cet ingénieux Naturaliste, qui nous a déjà donné et qui nous prépare encore des ouvrages plus utiles, emploie à cette odieuse tâche une plume qu'il trempe dans le fiel et dans l'absinthe. Il est vrai que plusieurs de ses remarques sont fondées, et qu'à l'erreur qu'il indique, il joint en même tems la correction. Mais il n'est pas toujours équitable, et ne manque jamais d'insulter. Que peut {24} après tout prouver son livre, si ce n'est que la quarante-cinquième partie d'un très-ample et très-utile Recueil n'est pas exempte d'erreurs? Devoit-il confondre avec des Ecrivains superficiels, dont la Liberté du Corps ne permet pas de restreindre la fertilité, cette foule de savans du Premier ordre, dont les Ecrits ont orné et ornent encore les Transactions? A-t-il oublié qu'on y a vu fréquemment les noms des Boyle, des Newton, des Halley, des De Moivres, des Hans Sloane, etc.? Et qu'on y trouve encore ceux des Ward, des Bradley, des Graham, des Ellicot, des Watson, et d'un Auteur que Mr. Hill préfère à tous les autres, je veux dire de Mr. Hill lui-même?"[7]

This was the only answer; but it was no answer at all. Hill's object was to expose the absurdities; he therefore collected the absurdities. I feel sure that Hill was a benefactor of the Royal Society; and much more than he would have been if he had softened their errors and enhanced their praises. No reviewer will object to me that I have omitted Young, Laplace, etc. But then my book has a true title. Hill should not have called his a review of the "Works."

It was charged against Sir John Hill that he had tried to become a Fellow of the Royal Society and had failed. This he denied, and challenged the production of the certificate which a candidate always sends in, and which is preserved. {25} But perhaps he could not get so far as a certificate--that is, could not find any one to recommend him; he was a likely man to be in such a predicament. As I have myself run foul of the Society on some little points, I conceive it possible that I may fall under a like suspicion. Whether I could have been a Fellow, I cannot know; as the gentleman said who was asked if he could play the violin, I never tried. I have always had a high opinion of the Society upon its whole history. A person used to historical inquiry learns to look at wholes; the Universities of Oxford and Cambridge, the College of Physicians, etc. are taken in all their duration. But those who are not historians--I mean not possessed of the habit of history--hold a mass of opinions about current things which lead them into all kinds of confusion when they try to look back. Not to give an instance which will offend any set of existing men--this merely because I can do without it--let us take the country at large. Magna Charta for ever! glorious safeguard of our liberties! Nullus liber homo capiatur aut imprisonetur ... aut aliquo modo destruatur, nisi per judicium parium ....[8] Liber homo: frank home; a capital thing for him--but how about the villeins? Oh, there are none now! But there were.

Who cares for villains, or barbarians, or helots? And so England, and Athens, and Sparta, were free States; all the freemen in them were free. Long after Magna Charta, villains were sold with their "chattels and offspring," named in that order. Long after Magna Charta, it was law that "Le Seigniour poit rob, naufrer, et chastiser son villein a son volunt, salve que il ne poit luy maim."[9]

The Royal Society was founded as a co-operative body, and co-operation was its purpose. The early charters, etc. do not contain a trace of the intention to create a scientific distinction, a kind of Legion of Honor. It is clear that the {26} qualification was ability and willingness to do good work for the promotion of natural knowledge, no matter in how many persons, nor of what position in society. Charles II gave a smart rebuke for exclusiveness, as elsewhere mentioned. In time arose, almost of course, the idea of distinction attaching to the title; and when I first began to know the Society, it was in this state. Gentlemen of good social position were freely elected if they were really educated men; but the moment a claimant was announced as resting on his science, there was a disposition to inquire whether he was scientific enough. The maxim of the poet was adopted; and the Fellows were practically divided into Drink-deeps and Taste-nots.

I was, in early life, much repelled by the tone taken by the Fellows of the Society with respect to their very mixed body. A man high in science--some thirty-seven years ago (about 1830)--gave me some encouragement, as he thought. "We shall have you a Fellow of the Royal Society in time," said he. Umph! thought I: for I had that day heard of some recent elections, the united science of which would not have demonstrated I. 1, nor explained the action of a pump. Truly an elevation to look up at! It came, further, to my knowledge that the Royal Society--if I might judge by the claims made by very influential Fellows--considered itself as entitled to the best of everything: second-best being left for the newer bodies. A secretary, in returning thanks for the Royal at an anniversary of the Astronomical, gave rather a lecture to the company on the positive duty of all present to send the very best to the old body, and the absolute right of the old body to expect it. An old friend of mine, on a similar occasion, stated as a fact that the thing was always done, as well as that it ought to be done.

Of late years this pretension has been made by a President of the Society. In 1855, Lord Rosse presented a confidential memorandum to the Council on the expediency of enlarging their number. He says, "In a Council so small it {27} is impossible to secure a satisfactory representation of the leading scientific Societies, and it is scarcely to be expected that, under such circumstances, they will continue to publish inferior papers while they send the best to our Transactions."

And, again, with all the Societies represented on the Council, "even if every Science had its Society, and if they published everything, withholding their best papers [i.e., from the Royal Society], which they would not be likely to do, still there would remain to the Royal Society ...." Lord Rosse seems to imagine that the minor Societies themselves transfer their best papers to the Royal Society; that if, for instance, the Astronomical Society were to receive from A.B. a paper of unusual merit, the Society would transfer it to the Royal Society. This is quite wrong: any preference of the Royal to another Society is the work of the contributor himself. But it shows how well hafted is the Royal Society's claim, that a President should acquire the notion that it is acknowledged and acted upon by the other Societies, in their joint and corporate capacities. To the pretension thus made I never could give any sympathy. When I first heard Mr. Christie, Sec. R. S., set it forth at the anniversary dinner of the Astronomical Society, I remembered the Baron in Walter Scott:

"Of Gilbert the Galliard a heriot he sought, Saying, Give thy best steed as a vassal ought."

And I remembered the answer:

"Lord and Earl though thou be, I trow I can rein Buck's-foot better than thou."

Fully conceding that the Royal Society is entitled to preeminent rank and all the respect due to age and services, I could not, nor can I now, see any more obligation in a contributor to send his best to that Society than he can make out to be due to himself. This pretension, in my mind, was hooked on, by my historical mode of viewing things already mentioned, to my knowledge of the fact that the Royal {28} Society--the chief fault, perhaps, lying with its President, Sir Joseph Banks--had sternly set itself against the formation of other societies; the Geological and Astronomical, for instance, though it must be added that the chief rebels came out of the Society itself. And so a certain not very defined dislike was generated in my mind--an anti-aristocratic affair--to the body which seemed to me a little too uplifted. This would, I daresay, have worn off; but a more formidable objection arose. My views of physical science gradually arranged themselves into a form which would have rendered F.R.S., as attached to my name, a false representation symbol. The Royal Society is the great fortress of general physics: and in the philosophy of our day, as to general physics, there is something which makes the banner of the R.S. one under which I cannot march. Everybody who saw the three letters after my name would infer certain things as to my mode of thought which would not be true inference. It would take much space to explain this in full. I may hereafter, perhaps, write a budget of collected results of the a priori philosophy, the nibbling at the small end of omniscience, and the effect it has had on common life, from the family parlor to the jury-box, from the girls'-school to the vestry-meeting. There are in the Society those who would, were there no others, prevent my criticism, be its conclusions true or false, from having any basis; but they are in the minority.

There is no objection to be made to the principles of philosophy in vogue at the Society, when they are stated as principles; but there is an omniscience in daily practice which the principles repudiate. In like manner, the most retaliatory Christians have a perfect form of round words about behavior to those who injure them; none of them are as candid as a little boy I knew, who, to his mother's admonition, You should love your enemies, answered--Catch me at it!

Years ago, a change took place which would alone have {29} put a sufficient difficulty in the way. The co-operative body got tired of getting funds from and lending name to persons who had little or no science, and wanted F.R.S. to be in every case a Fellow Really Scientific. Accordingly, the number of yearly elections was limited to fifteen recommended by the Council, unless the general body should choose to elect more; which it does not do. The election is now a competitive examination: it is no longer--Are you able and willing to promote natural knowledge; it is--Are you one of the upper fifteen of those who make such claim. In the list of candidates--a list rapidly growing in number--each year shows from thirty to forty of those whom Newton and Boyle would have gladly welcomed as fellow-laborers. And though the rejected of one year may be the accepted of the next--or of the next but one, or but two, if self-respect will permit the candidate to hang on--yet the time is clearly coming when many of those who ought to be welcomed will be excluded for life, or else shelved at last, when past work, with a scientific peerage. Coupled with this attempt to create a kind of order of knighthood is an absurdity so glaring that it should always be kept before the general eye. This distinction, this mark set by science upon successful investigation, is of necessity a class-distinction.

Rowan Hamilton, one of the greatest names of our day in mathematical science, never could attach F.R.S. to his name--he could not afford it. There is a condition precedent--Four Red Sovereigns. It is four pounds a year, or--to those who have contributed to the Transactions--forty pounds down. This is as it should be: the Society must be supported. But it is not as it should be that a kind of title of honor should be forged, that a body should take upon itself to confer distinctions for science, when it is in the background--and kept there when the distinction is trumpeted--that the wearer is a man who can spare four pounds a year. I am well aware that in England a person who is not gifted either by nature or art, with this amount of money power, {30} is, with the mass, a very second-rate sort of Newton, whatever he may be in the field of investigation. Even men of science, so called, have this feeling. I know that the scientific advisers of the Admiralty, who, years ago, received 100 pounds a year each for his trouble, were sneered at by a wealthy pretender as "fellows to whom a hundred a year is an object." Dr. Thomas Young was one of them. To a bookish man--I mean a man who can manage to collect books--there is no tax. To myself, for example, 40 pounds worth of books deducted from my shelves, and the life-use of the Society's splendid library instead, would have been a capital exchange. But there may be, and are, men who want books, and cannot pay the Society's price. The Council would be very liberal in allowing books to be consulted. I have no doubt that if a known investigator were to call and ask to look at certain books, the Assistant-Secretary would forthwith seat him with the books before him, absence of F.R.S. not in any wise withstanding. But this is not like having the right to consult any book on any day, and to take it away, if farther wanted.

So much for the Royal Society as concerns myself. I must add that there is not a spark of party feeling against those who wilfully remain outside. The better minds of course know better; and the smaller savants look complacently on the idea of an outer world which makes élite of them. I have done such a thing as serve on a committee of the Society, and report on a paper: they had the sense to ask, and I had the sense to see that none of my opinions were compromised by compliance. And I will be of any use which does not involve the status of homo trium literarum; as I have elsewhere explained, I would gladly be Fautor Realis Scientiæ, but I would not be taken for Falsæ Rationis Sacerdos.

Nothing worse will ever happen to me than the smile which individuals bestow on a man who does not groove. Wisdom, like religion, belongs to majorities; who can {31} wonder that it should be so thought, when it is so clearly pictured in the New Testament from one end to the other?

The counterpart of paradox, the isolated opinion of one or of few, is the general opinion held by all the rest; and the counterpart of false and absurd paradox is what is called the "vulgar error," the pseudodox. There is one great work on this last subject, the Pseudodoxia Epidemica of Sir Thomas Browne, the famous author of the Religio Medici; it usually goes by the name of Browne "On Vulgar Errors" (1st ed. 1646; 6th, 1672). A careful analysis of this work would show that vulgar errors are frequently opposed by scientific errors; but good sense is always good sense, and Browne's book has a vast quantity of it.

As an example of bad philosophy brought against bad observation. The Amphisbæna serpent was supposed to have two heads, one at each end; partly from its shape, partly because it runs backwards as well as forwards. On this Sir Thomas Browne makes the following remarks:

"And were there any such species or natural kind of animal, it would be hard to make good those six positions of body which, according to the three dimensions, are ascribed unto every Animal; that is, infra, supra, ante, retro, dextrosum, sinistrosum: for if (as it is determined) that be the anterior and upper part wherein the senses are placed, and that the posterior and lower part which is opposite thereunto, there is no inferior or former part in this Animal; for the senses, being placed at both extreams, doth make both ends anterior, which is impossible; the terms being Relative, which mutually subsist, and are not without each other. And therefore this duplicity was ill contrived to place one head at both extreams, and had been more tolerable to have settled three or four at one. And therefore also Poets have been more reasonable than Philosophers, and Geryon or Cerberus less monstrous than Amphisbæna." {32}

There may be paradox upon paradox: and there is a good instance in the eighth century in the case of Virgil, an Irishman, Bishop of Salzburg and afterwards Saint, and his quarrels with Boniface, an Englishman, Archbishop of Mentz, also afterwards Saint. All we know about the matter is, that there exists a letter of 748 from Pope Zachary, citing Virgil--then, it seems, at most a simple priest, though the Pope was not sure even of that--to Rome to answer the charge of maintaining that there is another world (mundus) under our earth (terra), with another sun and another moon. Nothing more is known: the letter contains threats in the event of the charge being true; and there history drops the matter. Since Virgil was afterwards a Bishop and a Saint, we may fairly conclude that he died in the full flower of his orthodox reputation. It has been supposed--and it seems probable--that Virgil maintained that the earth is peopled all the way round, so that under some spots there are antipodes; that his contemporaries, with very dim ideas about the roundness of the earth, and most of them with none at all, interpreted him as putting another earth under ours--turned the other way, probably, like the second piece of bread-and-butter in a sandwich, with a sun and moon of its own. In the eighth century this would infallibly have led to an underground Gospel, an underground Pope, and an underground Avignon for him to live in. When, in later times, the idea of inhabitants for the planets was started, it was immediately asked whether they had sinned, whether Jesus Christ died for them, whether their wine and their water could be lawfully used in the sacraments, etc.

On so small a basis as the above has been constructed a companion case to the persecution of Galileo. On one side the positive assertion, with indignant comment, that Virgil was deposed for antipodal heresy, on the other, serious attempts at justification, palliation, or mystification. Some writers say that Virgil was found guilty; others that he gave satisfactory explanation, and became very good friends with {33} Boniface: for all which see Bayle. Some have maintained that the antipodist was a different person from the canonized bishop: there is a second Virgil, made to order. When your shoes pinch, and will not stretch, always throw them away and get another pair: the same with your facts. Baronius was not up to the plan of a substitute: his commentator Pagi (probably writing about 1690) argues for it in a manner which I think Baronius would not have approved. This Virgil was perhaps a slippery fellow. The Pope says he hears that Virgil pretended licence from him to claim one of some new bishoprics: this he declares is totally false. It is part of the argument that such a man as this could not have been created a Bishop and a Saint: on this point there will be opinions and opinions.[10]

Lactantius, four centuries before, had laughed at the antipodes in a manner which seems to be ridicule thrown on the idea of the earth's roundness.

Ptolemy, without reference to the antipodes, describes the extent of the inhabited part of the globe in a way which shows that he could have had no objection to men turned opposite ways. Probably, in the eighth century, the roundness of the earth was matter of thought only to astronomers. It should always be remembered, especially by those who affirm persecution of a true opinion, that but for our knowing from Lactantius that the antipodal notion had been matter of assertion and denial among theologians, we could never have had any great confidence in Virgil really having maintained the simple theory of the existence of antipodes. And even now we are not entitled to affirm it as having historical proof: the evidence {34} goes to Virgil having been charged with very absurd notions, which it seems more likely than not were the absurd constructions which ignorant contemporaries put upon sensible opinions of his.

One curious part of this discussion is that neither side has allowed Pope Zachary to produce evidence to character. He shall have been an Urban, say the astronomers; an Urban he ought to have been, say the theologians.

What sort of man was Zachary? He was eminently sensible and conciliatory; he contrived to make northern barbarians hear reason in a way which puts him high among that section of the early popes who had the knack of managing uneducated swordsmen. He kept the peace in Italy to an extent which historians mention with admiration. Even Bale, that Maharajah of pope-haters, allows himself to quote in favor of Zachary, that "multa Papalem dignitatem decentia, eademque præclara (scilicet) opera confecit."[11] And this, though so willing to find fault that, speaking of Zachary putting a little geographical description of the earth on the portico of the Lateran Church, he insinuates that it was intended to affirm that the Pope was lord of the whole. Nor can he say how long Zachary held the see, except by announcing his death in 752, "cum decem annis pestilentiæ sedi præfuisset."[12]

There was another quarrel between Virgil and Boniface which is an illustration. An ignorant priest had baptized "in nomine Patria, et Filia et Spiritua Sancta." Boniface declared the rite null and void: Virgil maintained the contrary; and Zachary decided in favor of Virgil, on the ground that the absurd form was only ignorance of Latin, and not heresy. It is hard to believe that this man deposed a priest for asserting the whole globe to be inhabited. To me the little information that we have seems {35} to indicate--but not with certainty--that Virgil maintained the antipodes: that his ignorant contemporaries travestied his theory into that of an underground cosmos; that the Pope cited him to Rome to explain his system, which, as reported, looked like what all would then have affirmed to be heresy; that he gave satisfactory explanations, and was dismissed with honor. It may be that the educated Greek monk, Zachary, knew his Ptolemy well enough to guess what the asserted heretic would say; we have seen that he seems to have patronized geography. The description of the earth, according to historians, was a map; this Pope may have been more ready than another to prick up his ears at any rumor of geographical heresy, from hope of information. And Virgil, who may have entered the sacred presence as frightened as Jacquard, when Napoleon I sent for him and said, with a stern voice and threatening gesture, "You are the man who can tie a knot in a stretched string," may have departed as well pleased as Jacquard with the riband and pension which the interview was worth to him.

A word more about Baronius. If he had been pope, as he would have been but for the opposition of the Spaniards, and if he had lived ten years longer than he did, and if Clavius, who would have been his astronomical adviser, had lived five years longer than he did, it is probable, nay almost certain, that the great exhibition, the proceeding against Galileo, would not have furnished a joke against theology in all time to come. For Baronius was sensible and witty enough to say that in the Scriptures the Holy Spirit intended to teach how to go to Heaven, not how Heaven goes; and Clavius, in his last years, confessed that the whole system of the heavens had broken down, and must be mended.

The manner in which the Galileo case, a reality, and the Virgil case, a fiction, have been hawked against the Roman see are enough to show that the Pope and his adherents have not cared much about physical philosophy. In truth, orthodoxy has always had other fish to fry. Physics, which {36} in modern times has almost usurped the name philosophy, in England at least, has felt a little disposed to clothe herself with all the honors of persecution which belong to the real owner of the name. But the bishops, etc. of the Middle Ages knew that the contest between nominalism and realism, for instance, had a hundred times more bearing upon orthodoxy than anything in astronomy, etc. A wrong notion about substance might play the mischief with transubstantiation.

The question of the earth's motion was the single point in which orthodoxy came into real contact with science. Many students of physics were suspected of magic, many of atheism: but, stupid as the mistake may have been, it was bona fide the magic or the atheism, not the physics, which was assailed. In the astronomical case it was the very doctrine, as a doctrine, independently of consequences, which was the corpus delicti: and this because it contradicted the Bible. And so it did; for the stability of the earth is as clearly assumed from one end of the Old Testament to the other as the solidity of iron. Those who take the Bible to be totidem verbis dictated by the God of Truth can refuse to believe it; and they make strange reasons. They undertake, a priori, to settle Divine intentions. The Holy Spirit did not mean to teach natural philosophy: this they know beforehand; or else they infer it from finding that the earth does move, and the Bible says it does not. Of course, ignorance apart, every word is truth, or the writer did not mean truth. But this puts the whole book on its trial: for we never can find out what the writer meant, until we otherwise find out what is true.

Those who like may, of course, declare for an inspiration over which they are to be viceroys; but common sense will either accept verbal meaning or deny verbal inspiration.

* * * * *

{37}

THE STORY OF BURIDAN'S ASS

Questiones Morales, folio, 1489 [Paris]. By T. Buridan.

This is the title from the Hartwell Catalogue of Law Books. I suppose it is what is elsewhere called the "Commentary on the Ethics of Aristotle," printed in 1489.[13] Buridan[14] (died about 1358) is the creator of the famous ass which, as Burdin's[15] ass, was current in Burgundy, perhaps is, as a vulgar proverb. Spinoza[16] says it was a jenny ass, and that a man would not have been so foolish; but whether the compliment is paid to human or to masculine character does not appear--perhaps to both in one.

The story told about the famous paradox is very curious. The Queen of France, Joanna or Jeanne, was in the habit of sewing her lovers up in sacks, and throwing them into the Seine; not for blabbing, but that they might not blab--certainly the safer plan. Buridan was exempted, and, in gratitude, invented the sophism. What it has to do with the matter {38} has never been explained. Assuredly qui facit per alium facit per se will convict Buridan of prating. The argument is as follows, and is seldom told in full. Buridan was for free-will--that is, will which determines conduct, let motives be ever so evenly balanced. An ass is equally pressed by hunger and by thirst; a bundle of hay is on one side, a pail of water on the other. Surely, you will say, he will not be ass enough to die for want of food or drink; he will then make a choice--that is, will choose between alternatives of equal force. The problem became famous in the schools; some allowed the poor donkey to die of indecision; some denied the possibility of the balance, which was no answer at all.

MICHAEL SCOTT'S DEVILS

The following question is more difficult, and involves free-will to all who answer--"Which you please." If the northern hemisphere were land, and all the southern hemisphere water, ought we to call the northern hemisphere an island, or the southern hemisphere a lake? Both the questions would be good exercises for paradoxers who must be kept employed, like Michael Scott's[17] devils. The wizard {39} knew nothing about squaring the circle, etc., so he set them to make ropes out of sea sand, which puzzled them.

Stupid devils; much of our glass is sea sand, and it makes beautiful thread. Had Michael set them to square the circle or to find a perpetual motion, he would have done his work much better. But all this is conjecture: who knows that I have not hit on the very plan he adopted? Perhaps the whole race of paradoxers on hopeless subjects are Michael's subordinates, condemned to transmigration after transmigration, until their task is done.

The above was not a bad guess. A little after the time when the famous Pascal papers[18] were produced, I came into possession of a correspondence which, but for these papers, I should have held too incredible to be put before the world. But when one sheep leaps the ditch, another will follow: so I gave the following account in the Athenæum of October 5, 1867:

"The recorded story is that Michael Scott, being bound by contract to produce perpetual employment for a number of young demons, was worried out of his life in inventing jobs for them, until at last he set them to make ropes out of sea sand, which they never could do. We have obtained a very curious correspondence between the wizard Michael and his demon-slaves; but we do not feel at liberty to say how it came into our hands. We much regret that we did not receive it in time for the British Association. It appears that the story, true as far as it goes, was never finished. The demons easily conquered the rope difficulty, by the simple process of making the sand into glass, and spinning the glass into thread, which they twisted. Michael, thoroughly disconcerted, hit upon the plan of setting some to {40} square the circle, others to find the perpetual motion, etc. He commanded each of them to transmigrate from one human body into another, until their tasks were done. This explains the whole succession of cyclometers, and all the heroes of the Budget. Some of this correspondence is very recent; it is much blotted, and we are not quite sure of its meaning: it is full of figurative allusions to driving something illegible down a steep into the sea. It looks like a humble petition to be allowed some diversion in the intervals of transmigration; and the answer is--Rumpat et serpens iter institutum,[19] --a line of Horace, which the demons interpret as a direction to come athwart the proceedings of the Institute by a sly trick. Until we saw this, we were suspicious of M. Libri,[20] the unvarying blunders of the correspondence look like knowledge. To be always out of the road requires a map: genuine ignorance occasionally lapses into truth. We thought it possible M. Libri might have played the trick to show how easily the French are deceived; but with our present information, our minds are at rest on the subject. We see M. Chasles does not like to avow the real source of information: he will not confess himself a spiritualist."

PHILO OF GADARA

Philo of Gadara[21] is asserted by Montucla,[22] on the {41} authority of Eutocius,[23] the commentator on Archimedes, to have squared the circle within the ten-thousandth part of a unit, that is, to four places of decimals. A modern classical dictionary represents it as done by Philo to ten thousand places of decimals. Lacroix comments on Montucla to the effect that myriad (in Greek ten thousand) is here used as we use it, vaguely, for an immense number. On looking into Eutocius, I find that not one definite word is said about the extent to which Philo carried the matter. I give a translation of the passage:

"We ought to know that Apollonius Pergæus, in his Ocytocium [this work is lost], demonstrated the same by other numbers, and came nearer, which seems more accurate, but has nothing to do with Archimedes; for, as before said, he aimed only at going near enough for the wants of life. Neither is Porus of Nicæa fair when he takes Archimedes to task for not giving a line accurately equal to the circumference. He says in his Cerii that his teacher, Philo of Gadara, had given a more accurate approximation ([Greek: eis akribesterous arithmous agagein]) than that of Archimedes, or than 7 to 22. But all these [the rest as well as Philo] miss the intention. They multiply and divide by tens of thousands, which no one can easily do, unless he be versed in the logistics [fractional computation] of Magnus [now unknown]."

Montucla, or his source, ought not to have made this mistake. He had been at the Greek to correct Philo Gadetanus, as he had often been called, and he had brought away {42} and quoted [Greek: apo Gadarôn]. Had he read two sentences further, he would have found the mistake.

We here detect a person quite unnoticed hitherto by the moderns, Magnus the arithmetician. The phrase is ironical; it is as if we should say, "To do this a man must be deep in Cocker."[24] Accordingly, Magnus, Baveme,[25] and Cocker, are three personifications of arithmetic; and there may be more.

ON SQUARING THE CIRCLE

Aristotle, treating of the category of relation, denies that the quadrature has been found, but appears to assume that it can be done. Boethius,[26] in his comment on the passage, says that it has been done since Aristotle, but that the demonstration is too long for him to give. Those who have no notion of the quadrature question may look at the English Cyclopædia, art. "Quadrature of the Circle."

Tetragonismus. Id est circuli quadratura per Campanum, Archimedem Syracusanum, atque Boetium mathematicæ perspicacissimos adinventa.--At the end, Impressum Venetiis per Ioan. Bapti. Sessa. Anno ab incarnatione Domini, 1503. Die 28 Augusti.

{43}

This book has never been noticed in the history of the subject, and I cannot find any mention of it. The quadrature of Campanus[27] takes the ratio of Archimedes,[28] 7 to 22 to be absolutely correct; the account given of Archimedes is not a translation of his book; and that of Boetius has more than is in Boethius. This book must stand, with the next, as the earliest in print on the subject, until further showing: Murhard[29] and Kastner[30] have nothing so early. It is edited by Lucas Gauricus,[31] who has given a short preface. Luca Gaurico, Bishop of Civita Ducale, an astrologer of astrologers, published this work at about thirty years of age, and lived to eighty-two. His works are collected in folios, but I do not know whether they contain this production. The poor fellow could never tell his own fortune, because his father neglected to note the hour and minute of his birth. But if there had been anything in astrology, he could have worked back, as

Adams[32] and Leverrier[33] did when they caught {44} Neptune: at sixty he could have examined every minute of his day of birth, by the events of his life, and so would have found the right minute. He could then have gone on, by rules of prophecy. Gauricus was the mathematical teacher of Joseph Scaliger,[34] who did him no credit, as we shall see.

BOVILLUS ON THE QUADRATURE PROBLEM

In hoc opere contenta Epitome.... Liber de quadratura Circuli.... Paris, 1503, folio.

The quadrator is Charles Bovillus,[35] who adopted the views of Cardinal Cusa,[36] presently mentioned. Montucla is hard on his compatriot, who, he says, was only saved from the laughter of geometers by his obscurity. Persons must guard against most historians of mathematics in one point: they frequently attribute to his own age the obscurity which a writer has in their own time. This tract was printed by Henry Stephens,[37] at the instigation of Faber Stapulensis,[38] {45} and is recorded by Dechales,[39] etc. It was also introduced into the Margarita Philosophica of 1815,[40] in the same appendix with the new perspective from Viator. This is not extreme obscurity, by any means. The quadrature deserved it; but that is another point.

It is stated by Montucla that Bovillus makes [pi] = [root]10. But Montucla cites a work of 1507, Introductorium Geometricum, which I have never seen.[41] He finds in it an account which Bovillus gives of the quadrature of the peasant laborer, and describes it as agreeing with his own. But the description makes [pi] = 3-1/8, which it thus appears Bovillus could not distinguish from [root]10. It seems also that this 3-1/8, about which we shall see so much in the sequel, takes its rise in the thoughtful head of a poor laborer. It does him great honor, being so near the truth, and he having no means of instruction. In our day, when an ignorant person chooses to bring his fancy forward in opposition to demonstration which he will not study, he is deservedly laughed at. {46}

THE STORY OF LACOMME'S ATTEMPT AT QUADRATURE

Mr. James Smith,[42] of Liverpool--hereinafter notorified--attributes the first announcement of 3-1/8 to M. Joseph Lacomme, a French well-sinker, of whom he gives the following account:

"In the year 1836, at which time Lacomme could neither read nor write, he had constructed a circular reservoir and wished to know the quantity of stone that would be required to pave the bottom, and for this purpose called on a professor of mathematics. On putting his question and giving the diameter, he was surprised at getting the following answer from the Professor: 'Qu'il lui était impossible de le lui dire au juste, attendu que personne n'avait encore pu trouver d'une manière exacte le rapport de la circonférence au diametre.'[43] From this he was led to attempt the solution of the problem. His first process was purely mechanical, and he was so far convinced he had made the discovery that he took to educating himself, and became an expert arithmetician, and then found that arithmetical results agreed with his mechanical experiments. He appears to have eked out a bare existence for many years by teaching arithmetic, all the time struggling to get a hearing from some of the learned societies, but without success. In the year 1855 he found his way to Paris, where, as if by accident, he made the acquaintance of a young gentleman, son of M. Winter, a commissioner of police, and taught him his peculiar methods of calculation. The young man was so enchanted that he strongly recommended Lacomme to his father, and {47} subsequently through M. Winter he obtained an introduction to the President of the Society of Arts and Sciences of Paris. A committee of the society was appointed to examine and report upon his discovery, and the society at its séance of March 17, 1856, awarded a silver medal of the first class to M. Joseph Lacomme for his discovery of the true ratio of diameter to circumference in a circle. He subsequently received three other medals from other societies. While writing this I have his likeness before me, with his medals on his breast, which stands as a frontispiece to a short biography of this extraordinary man, for which I am indebted to the gentleman who did me the honor to publish a French translation of the pamphlet I distributed at the meeting of the British Association for the Advancement of Science, at Oxford, in 1860."--Correspondent, May 3, 1866.

My inquiries show that the story of the medals is not incredible. There are at Paris little private societies which have not so much claim to be exponents of scientific opinion as our own Mechanics' Institutes. Some of them were intended to give a false lustre: as the "Institut Historique," the members of which are "Membre de l'Institut Historique."

That M. Lacomme should have got four medals from societies of this class is very possible: that he should have received one from any society at Paris which has the least claim to give one is as yet simply incredible.

NICOLAUS OF CUSA'S ATTEMPT

Nicolai de Cusa Opera Omnia. Venice, 1514. 3 vols. folio.

The real title is "Hæc accurata recognitio trium voluminum operum clariss.

P. Nicolai Cusæ ... proxime sequens pagina monstrat."[44] Cardinal Cusa, who died in 1464, is one of the earliest modern attempters. His quadrature is found in the second volume, and is now quite unreadable.

{48} In these early days every quadrator found a geometrical opponent, who finished him. Regimontanus[45] did this office for the Cardinal.

HENRY CORNELIUS AGRIPPA

De Occulta Philosophia libri III. By Henry Cornelius Agrippa. Lyons, 1550, 8vo.

De incertitudine et vanitate scientiarum. By the same. Cologne, 1531, 8vo.

The first editions of these works were of 1530, as well as I can make out; but the first was in progress in 1510.[46] In the second work Agrippa repents of having wasted time on the magic of the first; but all those who actually deal with demons are destined to eternal fire with Jamnes and Mambres and Simon Magus. This means, as is the fact, that his occult philosophy did not actually enter upon black magic, but confined itself to the power of the stars, of numbers, etc. The fourth book, which appeared after the death of Agrippa, and really concerns dealing with evil spirits, is undoubtedly spurious. It is very difficult to make out what Agrippa really believed on the subject. I have introduced his books as the most marked specimens of treatises on magic, a paradox of our day, though not far from orthodoxy in his; and here I should have ended my notice, if I had not casually found something more interesting to the reader of our day.

{49}

WHICH LEADS TO WALTER SCOTT

Walter Scott, it is well known, was curious on all matters connected with magic, and has used them very widely. But it is hardly known how much pains he has taken to be correct, and to give the real thing. The most decided detail of a magical process which is found in his writings is that of Dousterswivel in The Antiquary; and it is obvious, by his accuracy of process, that he does not intend the adept for a mere impostor, but for one who had a lurking belief in the efficacy of his own processes, coupled with intent to make a fraudulent use of them. The materials for the process are taken from Agrippa. I first quote Mr. Dousterswivel:

"... I take a silver plate when she [the moon] is in her fifteenth mansion, which mansion is in de head of Libra, and I engrave upon one side de worts Schedbarschemoth Schartachan [ch should be t]--dat is, de Intelligence of de Intelligence of de moon--and I make his picture like a flying serpent with a turkey-cock's head--vary well--Then upon this side I make de table of de moon, which is a square of nine, multiplied into itself, with eighty-one numbers [nine] on every side and diameter nine...."

In the De Occulta Philosophia, p. 290, we find that the fifteenth mansion of the moon incipit capite Libræ, and is good pro extrahendis thesauris, the object being to discover hidden treasure. In p. 246, we learn that a silver plate must be used with the moon. In p. 248, we have the words which denote the Intelligence, etc. But, owing to the falling of a number into a wrong line, or the misplacement of a line, one or other--which takes place in all the editions I have examined--Scott has, sad to say, got hold of the wrong words; he has written down the demon of the demons of the moon.

Instead of the gibberish above, it should have been Malcha betarsisim hed beruah schenhakim. In p. 253, we have the magic square of the moon, with eighty-one numbers, and the symbol for the Intelligence, which Scott likens to a flying {50} serpent with a turkey-cock's head. He was obliged to say something; but I will stake my character--and so save a woodcut--on the scratches being more like a pair of legs, one shorter than the other, without a body, jumping over a six-barred gate placed side uppermost. Those who thought that Scott forged his own nonsense, will henceforth stand corrected. As to the spirit Peolphan, etc., no doubt Scott got it from the authors he elsewhere mentions, Nicolaus Remigius[47] and Petrus Thyracus; but this last word should be Thyræus.

The tendency of Scott's mind towards prophecy is very marked, and it is always fulfilled. Hyder, in his disguise, calls out to Tippoo: "Cursed is the prince who barters justice for lust; he shall die in the gate by the sword of the stranger." Tippoo was killed in a gateway at Seringapatam.[48]

FINAEUS ON CIRCLE SQUARING

Orontii Finaei ... Quadratura Circuli. Paris, 1544, 4to.

Orontius[49] squared the circle out of all comprehension; but he was killed by a feather from his own wing. His {51} former pupil, John Buteo,[50] the same who--I believe for the first time--calculated the question of Noah's ark, as to its power to hold all the animals and stores, unsquared him completely. Orontius was the author of very many works, and died in 1555. Among the laudatory verses which, as was usual, precede this work, there is one of a rare character: a congratulatory ode to the wife of the author.

The French now call this writer Oronce Finée; but there is much difficulty about delatinization. Is this more correct than Oronce Fine, which the translator of De Thou uses? Or than Horonce Phine, which older writers give? I cannot understand why M. de Viette[51] should be called Viète, because his Latin name is Vieta. It is difficult to restore Buteo; for not only now is butor a blockhead as well as a bird, but we really cannot know what kind of bird Buteo stood for. We may be sure that Madame Fine was Denise Blanche; for Dionysia Candida can mean nothing else. Let her shade rejoice in the fame which Hubertus Sussannæus has given her.

I ought to add that the quadrature of Orontius, and solutions of all the other difficulties, were first published in De Rebus Mathematicis Hactenus Desideratis,[52] of which I have not the date.

{52}

DUCHESNE, AND A DISQUISITION ON ETYMOLOGY

Nicolai Raymari Ursi Dithmarsi Fundamentum Astronomicum, id est, nova doctrina sinuum et triangulorum.... Strasburg, 1588, 4to.[53]

People choose the name of this astronomer for themselves: I take Ursus, because he was a bear. This book gave the quadrature of Simon Duchesne,[54] or à Quercu, which excited Peter Metius,[55] as presently noticed. It also gave that unintelligible reference to Justus Byrgius which has been used in the discussion about the invention of logarithms.[56]

The real name of Duchesne is Van der Eycke. I have met with a tract in Dutch, Letterkundige Aanteekeningen, upon Van Eycke, Van Ceulen,[57] etc., by J. J. Dodt van Flensburg,[58] which I make out to be since 1841 in date. I should {53} much like a translation of this tract to be printed, say in the Phil. Mag. Dutch would be clear English if it were properly spelt. For example, learn-master would be seen at once to be teacher; but they will spell it leermeester. Of these they write as van deze; widow they make weduwe. All this is plain to me, who never saw a Dutch dictionary in my life; but many of their misspellings are quite unconquerable.

FALCO'S RARE TRACT

Jacobus Falco Valentinus, miles Ordinis Montesiani, hanc circuli quadraturam invenit. Antwerp, 1589, 4to.[59]

The attempt is more than commonly worthless; but as Montucla and others have referred to the verses at the end, and as the tract is of the rarest, I will quote them:

Circulus loquitur. Vocabar ante circulus Eramque curvus undique Ut alta solis orbita Et arcus ille nubium. Eram figura nobilis Carensque sola origine Carensque sola termino. Modo indecora prodeo Novisque foedor angulis. Nec hoc peregit Archytas[60] Neque Icari pater neque Tuus, Iapete, filius. Quis ergo casus aut Deus Meam quadravit aream?

Respondet auctor. Ad alta Turiæ ostia Lacumque limpidissimum Sita est beata civitas {54} Parum Saguntus abfuit Abestque Sucro plusculum. Hic est poeta quispiam Libenter astra consulens Sibique semper arrogans Negata doctioribus, Senex ubique cogitans Sui frequenter immemor Nec explicare circinum Nec exarare lineas Sciens ut ipse prædicat. Hic ergo bellus artifex Tuam quadravit aream.[61]

Falco's verses are pretty, if the U-mysteries be correct; but of these things I have forgotten--what I knew. [One mistake has been pointed out to me: it is Arch[=y]tas].

As a specimen of the way in which history is written, I copy the account which Montucla--who is accurate when he writes about what he has seen--gives of these verses. He gives the date 1587; he places the verses at the beginning instead of the end; he says the circle thanks its quadrator affectionately; and he says the good and modest chevalier gives all the glory to the patron saint of his order. All of little consequence, as it happens; but writing at second-hand makes as complete mistakes about more important matters.
{55}

BUNGUS ON THE MYSTERY OF NUMBER

Petri Bungi Bergomatis Numerorum mysteria. Bergomi [Bergamo], 1591, 4to. Second Edition.

The first edition is said to be of 1585;[62] the third, Paris, 1618. Bungus is not for my purpose on his own score, but those who gave the numbers their mysterious characters: he is but a collector. He quotes or uses 402 authors, as we are informed by his list; this just beats Warburton,[63] whom some eulogist or satirist, I forget which, holds up as having used 400 authors in some one work. Bungus goes through 1, 2, 3, etc., and gives the account of everything remarkable in which each number occurs; his accounts not being always mysterious. The numbers which have nothing to say for themselves are omitted: thus there is a gap between 50 and 60. In treating 666, Bungus, a good Catholic, could not compliment the Pope with it, but he fixes it on Martin Luther with a little forcing. If from A to I represent 1-10, from K to S 10-90, and from T to Z 100-500, we see:

M A R T I N L U T E R A 30 1 80 100 9 40 20 200 100 5 80 1 which gives 666. Again, in Hebrew, Lulter does the same: [Hebrew: R T L W L] 200 400 30 6 30 And thus two can play at any game. The second is better than the first: to Latinize the surname and not the Christian {56} name is very unscholarlike. The last number mentioned is a thousand millions; all greater numbers are dismissed in half a page. Then follows an accurate distinction between number and multitude--a thing much wanted both in arithmetic and logic.

WHICH LEADS TO A STORY ABOUT THE ROYAL SOCIETY

What may be the use of such a book as this? The last occasion on which it was used was the following. Fifteen or sixteen years ago the Royal Society determined to restrict the number of yearly admissions to fifteen men of science, and noblemen ad libitum; the men of science being selected and recommended by the Council, with a power, since practically surrendered, to the Society to elect more. This plan appears to me to be directly against the spirit of their charter, the true intent of which is, that all who are fit should be allowed to promote natural knowledge in association, from and after the time at which they are both fit and willing. It is also working more absurdly from year to year; the tariff of fifteen per annum will soon amount to the practical exclusion of many who would be very useful. This begins to be felt already, I suspect. But, as appears above, the body of the Society has the remedy in its own hands. When the alteration was discussed by the Council, my friend the late Mr. Galloway,[64] then one of the body, opposed it strongly, and inquired particularly into the reason why fifteen, of all numbers, was the one to be selected. Was it because fifteen is seven and eight, typifying the Old Testament Sabbath, and the New Testament day of the resurrection following? Was it because Paul strove fifteen days against Peter, proving that he was a doctor both of the Old and New Testament?

Was it because the prophet Hosea bought a lady {57} for fifteen pieces of silver? Was it because, according to Micah, seven shepherds and eight chiefs should waste the Assyrians? Was it because Ecclesiastes commands equal reverence to be given to both Testaments--such was the interpretation--in the words "Give a portion to seven, and also to eight"?

Was it because the waters of the Deluge rose fifteen cubits above the mountains?--or because they lasted fifteen decades of days? Was it because Ezekiel's temple had fifteen steps? Was it because Jacob's ladder has been supposed to have had fifteen steps? Was it because fifteen years were added to the life of Hezekiah? Was it because the feast of unleavened bread was on the fifteenth day of the month? Was it because the scene of the Ascension was fifteen stadia from Jerusalem? Was it because the stone-masons and porters employed in Solomon's temple amounted to fifteen myriads? etc. The Council were amused and astounded by the volley of fifteens which was fired at them; they knowing nothing about Bungus, of which Mr. Galloway--who did not, as the French say, indicate his sources--possessed the copy now before me. In giving this anecdote I give a specimen of the book, which is exceedingly rare. Should another edition ever appear, which is not very probable, he would be but a bungling Bungus who should forget the fifteen of the Royal Society.

AND ALSO TO A QUESTION OF EVIDENCE

[I make a remark on the different colors which the same person gives to one story, according to the bias under which he tells it. My friend Galloway told me how he had quizzed the Council of the Royal Society, to my great amusement. Whenever I am struck by the words of any one, I carry away a vivid recollection of position, gestures, tones, etc. I do not know whether this be common or uncommon. I never recall this joke without seeing before me my friend, leaning against his bookcase, with Bungus open in his hand, and a certain half-depreciatory tone which he often used {58} when speaking of himself. Long after his death, an F.R.S. who was present at the discussion, told me the story. I did not say I had heard it, but I watched him, with Galloway at the bookcase before me. I wanted to see whether the two would agree as to the fact of an enormous budget of fifteens having been fired at the Council, and they did agree perfectly. But when the paragraph of the Budget appeared in the Athenæum, my friend, who seemed rather to object to the showing-up, assured me that the thing was grossly exaggerated; there was indeed a fifteen or two, but nothing like the number I had given. I had, however, taken sharp note of the previous narration.

AND TO ANOTHER QUESTION OF EVIDENCE

I will give another instance. An Indian officer gave me an account of an elephant, as follows. A detachment was on the march, and one of the gun-carriages got a wheel off the track, so that it was also off the ground, and hanging over a precipice. If the bullocks had moved a step, carriages, bullocks, and all must have been precipitated. No one knew what could be done until some one proposed to bring up an elephant, and let him manage it his own way. The elephant took a moment's survey of the fix, put his trunk under the axle of the free wheel, and waited. The surrounders, who saw what he meant, moved the bullocks gently forward, the elephant followed, supporting the axle, until there was ground under the wheel, when he let it quietly down. From all I had heard of the elephant, this was not too much to believe. But when, years afterwards, I reminded my friend of his story, he assured me that I had misunderstood him, that the elephant was directed to put his trunk under the wheel, and saw in a moment why.

This is reasonable sagacity, and very likely the correct account; but I am quite sure that, in the fit of elephant-worship under which the story was first told, it was told as I have first stated it.] {59}

GIORDANO BRUNO AND HIS PARADOXES

[Jordani Bruni Nolani de Monade, Numero et Figura ... item de Innumerabilibus, Immenso, et Infigurabili ... Frankfort, 1591, 8vo.[65]

I cannot imagine how I came to omit a writer whom I have known so many years, unless the following story will explain it. The officer reproved the boatswain for perpetual swearing; the boatswain answered that he heard the officers swear. "Only in an emergency," said the officer. "That's just it," replied the other; "a boatswain's life is a life of 'mergency." Giordano Bruno was all paradox; and my mind was not alive to his paradoxes, just as my ears might have become dead to the boatswain's oaths. He was, as has been said, a vorticist before Descartes,[66] an optimist before Leibnitz, a Copernican before Galileo. It would be easy to collect a hundred strange opinions of his. He was born about 1550, and was roasted alive at Rome, February 17, 1600, for the maintenance and defence of the holy Church, and the rights and liberties of the same. These last words are from the writ of our own good James I, under which Leggatt[67] was roasted at Smithfield, in March 1612; and if I had a copy of the instrument under which Wightman[68] was roasted at Lichfield, a month afterwards, I daresay I should {60} find something quite as edifying. I extract an account which I gave of Bruno in the Comp. Alm. for 1855:

"He was first a Dominican priest, then a Calvinist; and was roasted alive at Rome, in 1600, for as many heresies of opinion, religious and philosophical, as ever lit one fire. Some defenders of the papal cause have at least worded their accusations so to be understood as imputing to him villainous actions. But it is positively certain that his death was due to opinions alone, and that retractation, even after sentence, would have saved him. There exists a remarkable letter, written from Rome on the very day of the murder, by Scioppius[69] (the celebrated scholar, a waspish convert from Lutheranism, known by his hatred to Protestants and Jesuits) to Rittershusius,[70] a well-known Lutheran writer on civil and canon law, whose works are in the index of prohibited books. This letter has been reprinted by Libri (vol. iv. p. 407). The writer informs his friend (whom he wished to convince that even a Lutheran would have burnt Bruno) that all Rome would tell him that Bruno died for Lutheranism; but this is because the Italians do not know the difference between one heresy and another, in which simplicity (says the writer) may God preserve them. That is to say, they knew the difference between a live heretic and a roasted one by actual inspection, but had no idea of the difference between a Lutheran and a Calvinist. The countrymen of Boccaccio would have smiled at the idea which the German scholar entertained of them. They said Bruno was burnt for Lutheranism, a name under which they classed all Protestants: and they are better witnesses than Schopp, or Scioppius. He then proceeds to describe to his Protestant friend (to whom he would certainly not have omitted any act which both their churches would have condemned) the mass of opinions with which Bruno was charged; as that there {61} are innumerable worlds, that souls migrate, that Moses was a magician, that the Scriptures are a dream, that only the Hebrews descended from Adam and Eve, that the devils would be saved, that Christ was a magician and deservedly put to death, etc. In fact, says he, Bruno has advanced all that was ever brought forward by all heathen philosophers, and by all heretics, ancient and modern. A time for retractation was given, both before sentence and after, which should be noted, as well for the wretched palliation which it may afford, as for the additional proof it gives that opinions, and opinions only, brought him to the stake. In this medley of charges the Scriptures are a dream, while Adam, Eve, devils, and salvation are truths, and the Saviour a deceiver. We have examined no work of Bruno except the De Monade, etc., mentioned in the text. A strong though strange theism runs through the whole, and Moses, Christ, the Fathers, etc., are cited in a manner which excites no remark either way. Among the versions of the cause of Bruno's death is atheism: but this word was very often used to denote rejection of revelation, not merely in the common course of dispute, but by such writers, for instance, as Brucker[71] and Morhof.[72] Thus Morhof says of the De Monade, etc., that it exhibits no manifest signs of atheism. What he means by the word is clear enough, when he thus speaks of a work which acknowledges God in hundreds of places, and rejects opinions as blasphemous in several. The work of Bruno in which his astronomical opinions are contained is De Monade, etc. (Frankfort, 1591, 8vo). He is the most thorough-going Copernican possible, and throws out almost every opinion, true or false, which has ever been discussed by astronomers, from the theory of innumerable inhabited worlds and systems to that {62} of the planetary nature of comets. Libri (vol. iv)[73] has reprinted the most striking part of his expressions of Copernican opinion."

THIS LEADS TO THE CHURCH QUESTION

The Satanic doctrine that a church may employ force in aid of its dogma is supposed to be obsolete in England, except as an individual paradox; but this is difficult to settle. Opinions are much divided as to what the Roman Church would do in England, if she could: any one who doubts that she claims the right does not deserve an answer. When the hopes of the Tractarian section of the High Church were in bloom, before the most conspicuous intellects among them had transgressed their ministry, that they might go to their own place, I had the curiosity to see how far it could be ascertained whether they held the only doctrine which makes me the personal enemy of a sect. I found in one of their tracts the assumption of a right to persecute, modified by an asserted conviction that force was not efficient. I cannot now say that this tract was one of the celebrated ninety; and on looking at the collection I find it so poorly furnished with contents, etc., that nothing but searching through three thick volumes would decide. In these volumes I find, augmenting as we go on, declarations about the character and power of "the Church" which have a suspicious appearance. The suspicion is increased by that curious piece of sophistry, No. 87, on religious reserve. The queer paradoxes of that tract leave us in doubt as to everything but this, that the church(man) is not bound to give his whole counsel in all things, and not bound to say what the things are in which he does not give it. It is likely enough that some of the "rights and liberties" are but scantily described. There is now no fear; but the time was when, if not fear, there might be a looking for of fear to come; nobody could then be so {63} sure as we now are that the lion was only asleep. There was every appearance of a harder fight at hand than was really found needful.

Among other exquisite quirks of interpretation in the No. 87 above mentioned is the following. God himself employs reserve; he is said to be decked with light as with a garment (the old or prayer-book version of Psalm civ. 2). To an ordinary apprehension this would be a strong image of display, manifestation, revelation; but there is something more. "Does not a garment veil in some measure that which it clothes? Is not that very light concealment?"

This No. 87, admitted into a series, fixes upon the managers of the series, who permitted its introduction, a strong presumption of that underhand intent with which they were charged. At the same time it is honorable to our liberty that this series could be published: though its promoters were greatly shocked when the Essayists and Bishop Colenso[74] took a swing on the other side. When No. 90 was under discussion, Dr. Maitland,[75] the librarian at Lambeth, asked Archbishop Howley[76] a question about No. 89. "I did not so much as know there was a No. 89," was the answer. I am almost sure I have seen this in print, and quite sure that Dr. Maitland told it to me. It is creditable that there was so much freedom; but No. 90 was too bad, and was stopped.

The Tractarian mania has now (October 1866) settled down into a chronic vestment disease, complicated with fits of transubstantiation, which has taken the name of {64} Ritualism. The common sense of our national character will not put up with a continuance of this grotesque folly; millinery in all its branches will at last be advertised only over the proper shops. I am told that the Ritualists give short and practical sermons; if so, they may do good in the end. The English Establishment has always contained those who want an excitement; the New Testament, in its plain meaning, can do little for them. Since the Revolution, Jacobitism, Wesleyanism, Evangelicism, Puseyism,[77] and Ritualism, have come on in turn, and have furnished hot water for those who could not wash without it. If the Ritualists should succeed in substituting short and practical teaching for the high-spiced lectures of the doctrinalists, they will be remembered with praise. John the Baptist would perhaps not have brought all Jerusalem out into the wilderness by his plain and good sermons: it was the camel's hair and the locusts which got him a congregation, and which, perhaps, added force to his precepts. When at school I heard a dialogue, between an usher and the man who cleaned the shoes, about Mr. ----, a minister, a very corporate body with due area of waistcoat. "He is a man of great erudition," said the first. "Ah, yes sir," said Joe; "any one can see that who looks at that silk waistcoat."]

OF THOMAS GEPHYRANDER SALICETUS

[When I said at the outset that I had only taken books from my own store, I should have added that I did not make any search for information given as part of a work. Had I looked through all my books, I might have made some curious additions. For instance, in Schott's Magia Naturalis[78] {65} (vol. iii. pp. 756-778) is an account of the quadrature of Gephyrauder, as he is misprinted in Montucla. He was Thomas Gephyrander Salicetus; and he published two editions, in 1608 and 1609.[79] I never even heard of a copy of either. His work is of the extreme of absurdity: he makes a distinction between geometrical and arithmetical fractions, and evolves theorems from it. More curious than his quadrature is his name; what are we to make of it? If a German, he is probably a German form of Bridgeman. and Salicetus refers him to Weiden. But Thomas was hardly a German Christian name of his time; of 526 German philosophers, physicians, lawyers, and theologians who were biographed by Melchior Adam,[80] only two are of this name.

Of these one is Thomas Erastus,[81] the physician whose theological writings against the Church as a separate power have given the name of Erastians to those who follow his doctrine, whether they have heard of him or not. Erastus is little known; accordingly, some have supposed that he must be Erastus, the friend of St. Paul and Timothy (Acts xix. 22; 2 Tim. iv. 20; Rom. xvi. 23), but what this gentleman did to earn the character is not hinted at. Few words would have done: Gaius (Rom. xvi. 23) has an immortality which many more noted men have missed, given by John Bunyan, out of seven words of St. Paul. I was once told that the Erastians got their name from Blastus, and I could not solve bl = er: at last I remembered that Blastus was a chamberlain[82] as well as Erastus; hence the association which {66} caused the mistake. The real heresiarch was a physician who died in 1583; his heresy was promulgated in a work, published immediately after his death by his widow, De Excommunicatione Ecclesiastica. He denied the power of excommunication on the principle above stated; and was answered by Besa.[83] The work was translated by Dr. R. Lee[84] (Edinb. 1844, 8vo). The other is Thomas Grynæus,[85] a theologian, nephew of Simon, who first printed Euclid in Greek; of him Adam says that of works he published none, of learned sons four. If Gephyrander were a Frenchman, his name is not so easily guessed at; but he must have been of La Saussaye. The account given by Schott is taken from a certain Father Philip Colbinus, who wrote against him.

In some manuscripts lately given to the Royal Society, David Gregory,[86] who seems to have seen Gephyrander's work, calls him Salicetus Westphalus, which is probably on the title-page. But the only Weiden I can find is in Bavaria. Murhard has both editions in his Catalogue, but had plainly never seen the books: he gives the author as Thomas Gep.

Hyandrus, Salicettus Westphalus. Murhard is a very old referee of mine; but who the non nominandus was to see Montucla's Gephyrander in Murhard's Gep. Hyandrus, both writers being usually accurate?]

NAPIER ON REVELATIONS

A plain discoverie of the whole Revelation of St. John ... whereunto are annexed certain oracles of Sibylla.... Set Foorth by John Napeir L. of Marchiston. London, 1611, 4to.[87]

{67}

The first edition was Edinburgh, 1593,[88] 4to. Napier[89] always believed that his great mission was to upset the Pope, and that logarithms, and such things, were merely episodes and relaxations. It is a pity that so many books have been written about this matter, while Napier, as good as any, is forgotten and unread. He is one of the first who gave us the six thousand years. "There is a sentence of the house of Elias reserved in all ages, bearing these words: The world shall stand six thousand years, and then it shall be consumed by fire: two thousand yeares voide or without lawe, two thousand yeares under the law, and two thousand yeares shall be the daies of the Messias...."

I give Napier's parting salute: it is a killing dilemma:

"In summar conclusion, if thou o Rome aledges thyselfe reformed, and to beleeue true Christianisme, then beleeue Saint John the Disciple, whome Christ loued, publikely here in this Reuelation proclaiming thy wracke, but if thou remain Ethnick in thy priuate thoghts, beleeuing[90] the old Oracles of the Sibyls reuerently keeped somtime in thy Capitol: then doth here this Sibyll proclame also thy wracke. Repent therefore alwayes, in this thy latter breath, as thou louest thine Eternall salvation. Amen."

--Strange that Napier should not have seen that this appeal could not succeed, unless the prophecies of the Apocalypse were no true prophecies at all.

{68}

OF GILBERT'S DE MAGNETE

De Magnete magneticisque corporibus, et de magno magnete tellure. By William Gilbert. London, 1600, folio.--There is a second edition; and a third, according to Watt.[91]

Of the great work on the magnet there is no need to speak, though it was a paradox in its day. The posthumous work of Gilbert, "De Mundo nostro sublunari philosophia nova" (Amsterdam, 1651, 4to)[92] is, as the title indicates, confined to the physics of the globe and its atmosphere. It has never excited attention: I should hope it would be examined with our present lights.

OF GIOVANNI BATISTA PORTA

Elementorum Curvilineorium Libri tres. By John Baptista Porta. Rome, 1610, 4to.[93]

This is a ridiculous attempt, which defies description, except that it is all about lunules. Porta was a voluminous writer. His printer announces fourteen works printed, and four to come, besides thirteen plays printed, and eleven waiting. His name is, and will be, current in treatises on physics for more reasons than one.

{69}

CATALDI ON THE QUADRATURE

Trattato della quadratura del cerchio. Di Pietro Antonio Cataldi. Bologna, 1612, folio.[94]

Rheticus,[95] Vieta, and Cataldi are the three untiring computers of Germany, France, and Italy; Napier in Scotland, and Briggs[96] in England, come just after them. This work claims a place as beginning with the quadrature of Pellegrino Borello[97] of Reggio, who will have the circle to be exactly 3 diameters and 69/484 of a diameter. Cataldi, taking Van Ceulen's approximation, works hard at the finding of integers which nearly represent the ratio. He had not then the continued fraction, a mode of representation which he gave the next year in his work on the square root. He has but twenty of Van Ceulen's thirty places, which he takes from Clavius[98]: and any one might be puzzled to know whence the Italians got the result; Van Ceulen, in 1612, not having been translated from Dutch. But Clavius names his comrade Gruenberger, and attributes the approximation to them {70} jointly; "Lud. a Collen et Chr. Gruenbergerus[99] invenerunt," which he had no right to do, unless, to his private knowledge, Gruenberger had verified Van Ceulen. And Gruenberger only handed over twenty of the places. But here is one instance, out of many, of the polyglot character of the Jesuit body, and its advantages in literature.

OF LANSBERGIUS

Philippi Lausbergii Cyclometriæ Novæ Libri Duo. Middleburg, 1616, 4to.[100]

This is one of the legitimate quadratures, on which I shall here only remark that by candlelight it is quadrature under difficulties, for all the diagrams are in red ink.

A TEXT LEADING TO REMARKS ON PRESTER JOHN

Recherches Curieuses des Mesures du Monde. By S. C. de V. Paris, 1626, 8vo (pp. 48).[101]

It is written by some Count for his son; and if all the French nobility would have given their sons the same kind of instruction about rank, the old French aristocracy would have been as prosperous at this moment as the English peerage and squireage. I sent the tract to Capt. Speke,[102] shortly after his arrival in England, thinking he might like {71} to see the old names of the Ethiopian provinces. But I first made a copy of all that relates to Prester John,[103] himself a paradox. The tract contains, inter alia, an account of the four empires; of the great Turk, the great Tartar, the great Sophy, and the great Prester John. This word great (grand), which was long used in the phrase "the great Turk," is a generic adjunct to an emperor. Of the Tartars it is said that "c'est vne nation prophane et barbaresque, sale et vilaine, qui mangent la chair demie cruë, qui boiuent du laict de jument, et qui n'vsent de nappes et seruiettes que pour essuyer leurs bouches et leurs mains."[104] Many persons have heard of Prester John, and have a very indistinct idea of him. I give all that is said about him, since the recent discussions about the Nile may give an interest to the old notions of geography.

"Le grand Prestre Jean qui est le quatriesme en rang, est Empereur d'Ethiopie, et des Abyssins, et se vante d'estre issu de la race de Dauid, comme estant descendu de la Royne de Saba, Royne d'Ethiopie, laquelle estant venuë en Hierusalem pour voir la sagesse de Salomon, enuiron l'an du monde 2952, s'en retourna grosse d'vn fils qu'ils nomment Moylech, duquel ils disent estre descendus en ligne directe. Et ainsi il se glorifie d'estre le plus ancien Monarque de la terre, disant que son Empire a duré plus de trois mil ans, ce que nul autre Empire ne peut dire. Aussi met-il en ses tiltres ce qui s'ensuit: Nous, N. Souuerain en mes Royaumes, vniquement aymé de Dieu, colomne de la foy, sorty de la race de Inda, etc. Les limites de cet Empire touchent à la mer Rouge, et aux montagnes d'Azuma vers {72} l'Orient, et du costé de l'Occident, il est borné du fleuue du Nil, qui le separe de la Nubie, vers le Septentrion il a l'Ægypte, et au Midy les Royaumes de Congo, et de Mozambique, sa longueur contenant quarante degré, qui font mille vingt cinq lieuës, et ce depuis Congo ou Mozambique qui sont au Midy, iusqu'en Ægypte qui est au Septentrion, et sa largeur contenant depuis le Nil qui est à l'Occident, iusqu'aux montagnes d'Azuma, qui sont à l'Orient, sept cens vingt cinq lieues, qui font vingt neuf degrez. Cét empire a sous soy trente grandes Prouinces, sçavoir, Medra, Gaga, Alchy, Cedalon, Mantro, Finazam, Barnaquez, Ambiam, Fungy, Angoté, Cigremaon, Gorga, Cafatez, Zastanla, Zeth, Barly, Belangana, Tygra, Gorgany, Barganaza, d'Ancut, Dargaly, Ambiacatina, Caracogly, Amara, Maon (sic), Guegiera, Bally, Dobora et Macheda. Toutes ces Prouinces cy dessus sont situées iustement sous la ligne equinoxiale, entres les Tropiques de Capricorne, et de Cancer. Mais elles s'approchent de nostre Tropique, de deux cens cinquante lieuës plus qu'elles ne font de l'autre Tropique. Ce mot de Prestre Jean signifie grand Seigneur, et n'est pas Prestre comme plusieurs pense, il a esté tousiours Chrestien, mais souuent Schismatique: maintenant il est Catholique, et reconnaist le Pape pour Souuerain Pontife. I'ay veu quelqu'vn des ses Euesques, estant en Hierusalem, auec lequel i'ay conferé souuent par le moyen de nostre trucheman: il estoit d'vn port graue et serieux, succiur (sic) en son parler, mais subtil à merueilles en tout ce qu'il disoit. Il prenoit grand plaisir au recit que je luy faisais de nos belles ceremonies, et de la grauité de nos Prelats en leurs habits Pontificaux, et autres choses que je laisse pour dire, que l'Ethiopien est ioyoux et gaillard, ne ressemblant en rien a la saleté du Tartare, ny à l'affreux regard du miserable Arabe, mais ils sont fins et cauteleux, et ne se fient en personne, soupçonneux à merueilles, et fort devotieux, ils ne sont du tout noirs comme l'on croit, i'entens parler de ceux qui ne sont pas sous la ligne Equinoxiale, ny trop proches {73} d'icelle, car ceux qui sont dessous sont les Mores que nous voyons."[105]

It will be observed that the author speaks of his conversation with an Ethiopian bishop, about that bishop's sovereign. Something must have passed between the two which satisfied the writer that the bishop acknowledged his own sovereign under some title answering to Prester John.

{74}

CONCERNING A TRACT BY FIENUS

De Cometa anni 1618 dissertationes Thomæ Fieni[106] et Liberti Fromondi[107] ... Equidem Thomæ Fieni epistolica quæstio, An verum sit Coelum moveri et Terram quiescere? London, 1670, 8vo.

This tract of Fienus against the motion of the earth is a reprint of one published in 1619.[108] I have given an account of it as a good summary of arguments of the time, in the Companion to the Almanac for 1836.

{75}

ON SNELL'S WORK

Willebrordi Snellii. R. F. Cyclometricus. Leyden, 1621, 4to.

This is a celebrated work on the approximative quadrature, which, having the suspicious word cyclometricus, must be noticed here for distinction.[109]

ON BACON'S NOVUM ORGANUM

1620. In this year, Francis Bacon[110] published his Novum Organum,[111] which was long held in England--but not until the last century--to be the work which taught Newton and all his successors how to philosophize. That Newton never mentions Bacon, nor alludes in any way to his works, passed for nothing. Here and there a paradoxer ventured not to find all this teaching in Bacon, but he was pronounced blind. In our day it begins to be seen that, great as Bacon was, and great as his book really is, he is not the philosophical father of modern discovery.

But old prepossession will find reason for anything. A learned friend of mine wrote to me that he had discovered proof that Newton owned Bacon for his master: the proof was that Newton, in some of his earlier writings, used the {76} phrase experimentum crucis, which is Bacon's. Newton may have read some of Bacon, though no proof of it appears. I have a dim idea that I once saw the two words attributed to the alchemists: if so, there is another explanation; for Newton was deeply read in the alchemists.

I subjoin a review which I wrote of the splendid edition of Bacon by Spedding,[112] Ellis,[113] and Heath.[114] All the opinions therein expressed had been formed by me long before: most of the materials were collected for another purpose.

The Works of Francis Bacon. Edited by James Spedding, R. Leslie Ellis, and Douglas D. Heath. 5 vols.[115]

No knowledge of nature without experiment and observation: so said Aristotle, so said Bacon, so acted Copernicus, Tycho Brahé,[116] Gilbert, Kepler, Galileo, Harvey, etc., before Bacon wrote.[117] No derived knowledge until experiment and observation are concluded: so said Bacon, and no one else. We do not mean to say that he laid down his principle in these words, or that he carried it to the utmost extreme: we mean that Bacon's ruling idea was the {77} collection of enormous masses of facts, and then digested processes of arrangement and elimination, so artistically contrived, that a man of common intelligence, without any unusual sagacity, should be able to announce the truth sought for. Let Bacon speak for himself, in his editor's English:

"But the course I propose for the discovery of sciences is such as leaves but little to the acuteness and strength of wits, but places all wits and understandings nearly on a level. For, as in the drawing of a straight line or a perfect circle, much depends on the steadiness and practice of the hand, if it be done by aim of hand only, but if with the aid of rule or compass little or nothing, so it is exactly with my plan.... For my way of discovering sciences goes far to level men's wits, and leaves but little to individual excellence; because it performs everything by the surest rules and demonstrations."

To show that we do not strain Bacon's meaning, we add what is said by Hooke,[118] whom we have already mentioned as his professed disciple, and, we believe, his only disciple of the day of Newton. We must, however, remind the reader that Hooke was very little of a mathematician, and spoke of algebra from his own idea of what others had told him:

"The intellect is not to be suffered to act without its helps, but is continually to be assisted by some method or engine, which shall be as a guide to regulate its actions, so as that it shall not be able to act amiss. Of this engine, no man except the incomparable Verulam hath had any thoughts and he indeed hath promoted it to a very good pitch; but there is yet somewhat more to be added, which he seemed to want time to complete.

By this, as by that {78} art of algebra in geometry, 'twill be very easy to proceed in any natural inquiry, regularly and certainly.... For as 'tis very hard for the most acute wit to find out any difficult problem in geometry without the help of algebra ... and altogether as easy for the meanest capacity acting by that method to complete and perfect it, so will it be in the inquiry after natural knowledge."

Bacon did not live to mature the whole of this plan. Are we really to believe that if he had completed the Instauratio we who write this--and who feel ourselves growing bigger as we write it--should have been on a level with Newton in physical discovery? Bacon asks this belief of us, and does not get it. But it may be said, Your business is with what he did leave, and with its consequences. Be it so. Mr. Ellis says: "That his method is impracticable cannot, I think, be denied, if we reflect not only that it never has produced any result, but also that the process by which scientific truths have been established cannot be so presented as even to appear to be in accordance with it." That this is very true is well known to all who have studied the history of discovery: those who deny it are bound to establish either that some great discovery has been made by Bacon's method--we mean by the part peculiar to Bacon--or, better still, to show that some new discovery can be made, by actually making it. No general talk about induction: no reliance upon the mere fact that certain experiments or observations have been made; let us see where Bacon's induction has been actually used or can be used. Mere induction, enumeratio simplex, is spoken of by himself with contempt, as utterly incompetent. For Bacon knew well that a thousand instances may be contradicted by the thousand and first: so that no enumeration of instances, however large, is "sure demonstration," so long any are left.

The immortal Harvey, who was inventing--we use the word in its old sense--the circulation of the blood, while {79} Bacon was in the full flow of thought upon his system, may be trusted to say whether, when the system appeared, he found any likeness in it to his own processes, or what would have been any help to him, if he had waited for the Novum Organum. He said of Bacon, "He writes philosophy like a Lord Chancellor." This has been generally supposed to be only a sneer at the sutor ultra crepidam; but we cannot help suspecting that there was more intended by it. To us, Bacon is eminently the philosopher of error prevented, not of progress facilitated. When we throw off the idea of being led right, and betake ourselves to that of being kept from going wrong, we read his writings with a sense of their usefulness, his genius, and their probable effect upon purely experimental science, which we can be conscious of upon no other supposition. It amuses us to have to add that the part of Aristotle's logic of which he saw the value was the book on refutation of fallacies. Now is this not the notion of things to which the bias of a practised lawyer might lead him? In the case which is before the Court, generally speaking, truth lurks somewhere about the facts, and the elimination of all error will show it in the residuum. The two senses of the word law come in so as to look almost like a play upon words. The judge can apply the law so soon as the facts are settled: the physical philosopher has to deduce the law from the facts. Wait, says the judge, until the facts are determined: did the prisoner take the goods with felonious intent? did the defendant give what amounts to a warranty? or the like. Wait, says Bacon, until all the facts, or all the obtainable facts, are brought in: apply my rules of separation to the facts, and the result shall come out as easily as by ruler and compasses. We think it possible that Harvey might allude to the legal character of Bacon's notions: we can hardly conceive so acute a man, after seeing what manner of writer Bacon was, meaning only that he was a lawyer and had better stick to his business. We do ourselves believe that Bacon's philosophy {80} more resembles the action of mind of a common-law judge--not a Chancellor--than that of the physical inquirers who have been supposed to follow in his steps. It seems to us that Bacon's argument is, there can be nothing of law but what must be either perceptible, or mechanically deducible, when all the results of law, as exhibited in phenomena, are before us. Now the truth is, that the physical philosopher has frequently to conceive law which never was in his previous thought--to educe the unknown, not to choose among the known. Physical discovery would be very easy work if the inquirer could lay down his this, his that, and his t'other, and say, "Now, one of these it must be; let us proceed to try which." Often has he done this, and failed; often has the truth turned out to be neither this, that, nor t'other. Bacon seems to us to think that the philosopher is a judge who has to choose, upon ascertained facts, which of known statutes is to rule the decision: he appears to us more like a person who is to write the statute-book, with no guide except the cases and decisions presented in all their confusion and all their conflict.

Let us take the well-known first aphorism of the Novum Organum:

"Man being the servant and interpreter of nature, can do and understand so much, and so much only, as he has observed in fact or in thought of the course of nature: beyond this he neither knows anything nor can do anything."

This aphorism is placed by Sir John Herschel[119] at the head of his Discourse on the Study of Natural Philosophy: a book containing notions of discovery far beyond any of which Bacon ever dreamed; and this because it was written {81} after discovery, instead of before. Sir John Herschel, in his version, has avoided the translation of re vel mente observaverit, and gives us only "by his observation of the order of nature." In making this the opening of an excellent sermon, he has imitated the theologians, who often employ the whole time of the discourse in stuffing matter into the text, instead of drawing matter out of it. By observation he (Herschel) means the whole course of discovery, observation, hypothesis, deduction, comparison, etc. The type of the Baconian philosopher as it stood in his mind, had been derived from a noble example, his own father, William Herschel,[120] an inquirer whose processes would have been held by Bacon to have been vague, insufficient, compounded of chance work and sagacity, and too meagre of facts to deserve the name of induction. In another work, his treatise on Astronomy,[121] Sir John Herschel, after noting that a popular account can only place the reader on the threshold, proceeds to speak as follows of all the higher departments of science. The italics are his own:

"Admission to its sanctuary, and to the privileges and feelings of a votary, is only to be gained by one means--sound and sufficient knowledge of mathematics, the great instrument of all exact inquiry, without which no man can ever make such advances in this or any other of the higher departments of science as can entitle him to form an independent opinion on any subject of discussion within their range."

How is this? Man can know no more than he gets from observation, and yet mathematics is the great instrument of all exact inquiry. Are the results of mathematical deduction results of observation? We think it likely that {82} Sir John Herschel would reply that Bacon, in coupling together observare re and observare mente, has done what some wags said Newton afterwards did in his study-door--cut a large hole of exit for the large cat, and a little hole for the little cat.[122] But Bacon did no such thing: he never included any deduction under observation. To mathematics he had a dislike. He averred that logic and mathematics should be the handmaids, not the mistresses, of philosophy. He meant that they should play a subordinate and subsequent part in the dressing of the vast mass of facts by which discovery was to be rendered equally accessible to Newton and to us. Bacon himself was very ignorant of all that had been done by mathematics; and, strange to say, he especially objected to astronomy being handed over to the mathematicians. Leverrier and Adams, calculating an unknown planet into visible existence by enormous heaps of algebra, furnish the last comment of note on this specimen of the goodness of Bacon's views. The following account of his knowledge of what had been done in his own day or before it, is Mr. Spedding's collection of casual remarks in Mr. Ellis's several prefaces:

"Though he paid great attention to astronomy, discussed carefully the methods in which it ought to be studied, constructed for the satisfaction of his own mind an elaborate theory of the heavens, and listened eagerly for the news from the stars brought by Galileo's telescope, he appears to have been utterly ignorant of the discoveries which had just been made by Kepler's calculations. Though he complained in 1623 of the want of compendious methods for facilitating arithmetical computations, especially with regard to the doctrine of Series, and fully recognized the importance of them as an aid to physical inquiries--he does not say a word about Napier's Logarithms, which had been published only nine years before and reprinted more than once in the {83} interval. He complained that no considerable advance had made in geometry beyond Euclid, without taking any notice of what had been done by Archimedes and Apollonius. He saw the importance of determining accurately the specific gravity of different substances, and himself attempted to form a table of them by a rude process of his own, without knowing of the more scientific though still imperfect methods previously employed by Archimedes, Ghetaldus,[123] and Porta. He speaks of the [Greek: heurêka] of Archimedes in a manner which implies that he did not clearly apprehend either the nature of the problem to be solved or the principles upon which the solution depended. In reviewing the progress of mechanics, he makes no mention of Archimedes himself, or of Stevinus,[124] Galileo, Guldinus,[125] or Ghetaldus. He makes no allusion to the theory of equilibrium. He observes that a ball of one pound weight will fall nearly as fast through the air as a ball of two, without alluding to the theory of the acceleration of falling bodies, which had been made known by Galileo more than thirty years before. He proposes an inquiry with regard to the lever--namely, whether in a balance with arms of different length but equal weight the distance from the fulcrum has any effect upon the inclination,--though the theory of the lever was as well understood in his own time as it is now. In making an experiment {84} of his own to ascertain the cause of the motion of a windmill, he overlooks an obvious circumstance which makes the experiment inconclusive, and an equally obvious variation of the same experiment which would have shown him that his theory was false. He speaks of the poles of the earth as fixed, in a manner which seems to imply that he was not acquainted with the precession of the equinoxes; and in another place, of the north pole being above and the south pole below, as a reason why in our hemisphere the north winds predominate over the south."

Much of this was known before, but such a summary of Bacon's want of knowledge of the science of his own time was never yet collected in one place. We may add, that Bacon seems to have been as ignorant of Wright's[126] memorable addition to the resources of navigation as of Napier's addition to the means of calculation. Mathematics was beginning to be the great instrument of exact inquiry: Bacon threw the science aside, from ignorance, just at the time when his enormous sagacity, applied to knowledge, would have made him see the part it was to play. If Newton had taken Bacon for his master, not he, but somebody else, would have been Newton.[127]

ON METEOROLOGICAL OBSERVATORIES

There is an attempt at induction going on, which has yielded little or no fruit, the observations made in the meteorological observatories. This attempt is carried on in a manner which would have caused Bacon to dance for joy; for he lived in times when Chancellors did dance. {85} Russia, says M. Biot,[128] is covered by an army of meteorographs, with generals, high officers, subalterns, and privates with fixed and defined duties of observation. Other countries have also their systematic observations. And what has come of it? Nothing, says M. Biot, and nothing will ever come of it; the veteran mathematician and experimental philosopher declares, as does Mr. Ellis, that no single branch of science has ever been fruitfully explored in this way. There is no special object, he says. Any one would suppose that M. Biot's opinion, given to the French Government upon the proposal to construct meteorological observatories in Algeria (Comptes Rendus, vol. xli, Dec. 31, 1855), was written to support the mythical Bacon, modern physics, against the real Bacon of the Novum Organum. There is no special object. In these words lies the difference between the two methods.

[In the report to the Greenwich Board of Visitors for 1867 Mr. Airy,[129] speaking of the increase of meteorological observatories, remarks, "Whether the effect of this movement will be that millions of useless observations will be added to the millions that already exist, or whether something may be expected to result which will lead to a meteorological theory, I cannot hazard a conjecture." This is a conjecture, and a very obvious one: if Mr. Airy would have given 2-3/4d. for the chance of a meteorological theory formed by masses of observations, he would never have said what I have quoted.]

BASIS OF MODERN DISCOVERY

Modern discoveries have not been made by large collections of facts, with subsequent discussion, separation, and {86} resulting deduction of a truth thus rendered perceptible. A few facts have suggested an hypothesis, which means a supposition, proper to explain them. The necessary results of this supposition are worked out, and then, and not till then, other facts are examined to see if these ulterior results are found in nature. The trial of the hypothesis is the special object: prior to which, hypothesis must have been started, not by rule, but by that sagacity of which no description can be given, precisely because the very owners of it do not act under laws perceptible to themselves.[130] The inventor of hypothesis, if pressed to explain his method, must answer as did Zerah Colburn,[131] when asked for his mode of instantaneous calculation. When the poor boy had been bothered for some time in this manner, he cried out in a huff, "God put it into my head, and I can't put it into yours."[132] {87} Wrong hypotheses, rightly worked from, have produced more useful results than unguided observation. But this is not the Baconian plan. Charles the Second, when informed of the state of navigation, founded a Baconian observatory at Greenwich, to observe, observe, observe away at the moon, until her motions were known sufficiently well to render her useful in guiding the seaman. And no doubt Flamsteed's[133] observations, twenty or thirty of them at least, were of signal use. But how? A somewhat fanciful thinker, one Kepler, had hit upon the approximate orbits of the planets by trying one hypothesis after another: he found the ellipse, which the Platonists, well despised of Bacon, and who would have despised him as heartily if they had known him, had investigated and put ready to hand nearly 2000 years before.[134] The sun in the focus, the motions of the planet more and more rapid as they approach the sun, led Kepler--and Bacon would have reproved him for his rashness--to imagine that a force residing in the sun might move the planets, a force inversely as the distance. Bouillaud,[135] upon a fanciful analogy, rejected the inverse distance, {88} and, rejecting the force altogether, declared that if such a thing there were, it would be as the inverse square of the distance. Newton, ready prepared with the mathematics of the subject, tried the fall of the moon towards the earth, away from her tangent, and found that, as compared with the fall of a stone, the law of the inverse square did hold for the moon. He deduced the ellipse, he proceeded to deduce the effect of the disturbance of the sun upon the moon, upon the assumed theory of universal gravitation. He found result after result of his theory in conformity with observed fact: and, by aid of Flamsteed's observations, which amended what mathematicians call his constants, he constructed his lunar theory. Had it not been for Newton, the whole dynasty of Greenwich astronomers, from Flamsteed of happy memory, to Airy whom Heaven preserve,[136] might have worked away at nightly observation and daily reduction, without any remarkable result: looking forward, as to a millennium, to the time when any man of moderate intelligence was to see the whole explanation. What are large collections of facts for? To make theories from, says Bacon: to try ready-made theories by, says the history of discovery: it's all the same, says the idolater: nonsense, say we!

Time and space run short: how odd it is that of the three leading ideas of mechanics, time, space, and matter, the first two should always fail a reviewer before the third. We might dwell upon many points, especially if we attempted a more descriptive account of the valuable edition before us. No one need imagine that the editors, by their uncompromising attack upon the notion of Bacon's influence common even among mathematicians and experimental philosophers, have lowered the glory of the great man whom it was, many will think, their business to defend through thick and thin.

They have given a clearer notion of his {89} excellencies, and a better idea of the power of his mind, than ever we saw given before. Such a correction as theirs must have come, and soon, for as Hallam says--after noting that the Novum Organum was never published separately in England, Bacon has probably been more read in the last thirty years--now forty--than in the two hundred years which preceded. He will now be more read than ever he was. The history of the intellectual world is the history of the worship of one idol after another. No sooner is it clear that a Hercules has appeared among men, than all that imagination can conceive of strength is attributed to him, and his labors are recorded in the heavens. The time arrives when, as in the case of Aristotle, a new deity is found, and the old one is consigned to shame and reproach. A reaction may afterwards take place, and this is now happening in the case of the Greek philosopher. The end of the process is, that the opposing deities take their places, side by side, in a Pantheon dedicated not to gods, but to heroes.

THE REAL VALUE OF BACON'S WORKS

Passing over the success of Bacon's own endeavors to improve the details of physical science, which was next to nothing, and of his method as a whole, which has never been practised, we might say much of the good influence of his writings. Sound wisdom, set in sparkling wit, must instruct and amuse to the end of time: and, as against error, we repeat that Bacon is soundly wise, so far as he goes. There is hardly a form of human error within his scope which he did not detect, expose, and attach to a satirical metaphor which never ceases to sting. He is largely indebted to a very extensive reading; but the thoughts of others fall into his text with such a close-fitting compactness that he can make even the words of the Sacred Writers pass for his own. A saying of the prophet Daniel, rather a hackneyed quotation in our day, Multi pertransibunt, et augebitur scientia, stands in the title-page of the first edition {90} of Montucla's History of Mathematics as a quotation from Bacon--and it is not the only place in which this mistake occurs. When the truth of the matter, as to Bacon's system, is fully recognized, we have little fear that there will be a reaction against the man. First, because Bacon will always live to speak for himself, for he will not cease to be read: secondly, because those who seek the truth will find it in the best edition of his works, and will be most ably led to know what Bacon was, in the very books which first showed at large what he was not.

THE CONGREGATION OF THE INDEX, ON COPERNICUS

In this year (1620) appeared the corrections under which the Congregation of the Index--i.e., the Committee of Cardinals which superintended the Index of forbidden books--proposed to allow the work of Copernicus to be read. I insert these conditions in full, because they are often alluded to, and I know of no source of reference accessible to a twentieth part of those who take interest in the question.

By a decree of the Congregation of the Index, dated March 5, 1616, the work of Copernicus, and another of Didacus Astunica,[137] are suspended donec corrigantur, as teaching:

"Falsam illam doctrinam Pythagoricam, divinæ que Scripturæ omnino adversantem, de mobilitate Terræ et immobilitate Solis."[138]

But a work of the Carmelite Foscarini[139] is:

{91}

"Omnino prohibendum atque damnandum," because "ostendere conatur præfatam doctrinam ... consonam esse veritati et non adversari Sacræ Scripturæ."[140]

Works which teach the false doctrine of the earth's motion are to be corrected; those which declare the doctrine conformable to Scripture are to be utterly prohibited.

In a "Monitum ad Nicolai Copernici lectorem, ejusque emendatio, permissio, et correctio," dated 1620 without the month or day, permission is given to reprint the work of Copernicus with certain alterations; and, by implication, to read existing copies after correction in writing. In the preamble the author is called nobilis astrologus; not a compliment to his birth, which was humble, but to his fame. The suspension was because:

"Sacræ Scripturæ, ejusque veræ et Catholicæ interpretationi repugnantia (quod in homine Christiano minime tolerandum) non per hypothesin tractare, sed ut verissima adstruere non dubitat!"[141]

And the corrections relate:

"Locis in quibus non ex hypothesi, sed asserendo de situ et motu Terræ disputat."[142]

That is, the earth's motion may be an hypothesis for elucidation of the heavenly motions, but must not be asserted as a fact.

(In Pref. circa finem.) "Copernicus. Si fortasse erunt [Greek: mataiologoi], qui cum omnium Mathematum ignari sint, tamen de illis judicium sibi summunt, propter aliquem locum scripturæ, male ad suum propositum detortum, ausi fuerint meum {92} hoc institutum reprehendere ac insectari: illos nihil moror adeo ut etiam illorum judicium tanquam temerarium contemnam. Non enim obscurum est Lactantium, celebrem alioqui scriptorem, sed Mathematicum parum, admodum pueriliter de forma terræ loqui, cum deridet eos, qui terram globi formam habere prodiderunt. Itaque non debet mirum videri studiosis, si qui tales nos etiam videbunt.
Mathemata Mathematicis scribuntur, quibus et hi nostri labores, si me non fallit opinio, videbuntur etiam Reipub. ecclesiasticæ conducere aliquid.... Emend. Ibi si fortasse dele omnia, usque ad verbum hi nostri labores et sic accommoda--Coeterum hi nostri labores."[143]

All the allusion to Lactantius, who laughed at the notion of the earth being round, which was afterwards found true, is to be struck out.

(Cap. 5. lib. i. p. 3) "Copernicus. Si tamen attentius rem consideremus, videbitur hæc quæstio nondum absoluta, et ideireo minime contemnenda. Emend. Si tamen attentius rem consideremus, nihil refert an Terram in medio Mundi, an extra Medium existere, quoad solvendas coelestium motuum apparentias existimemus."[144]
{93}

We must not say the question is not yet settled, but only that it may be settled either way, so far as mere explanation of the celestial motions is concerned.

(Cap. 8. lib. i.) "Totum hoc caput potest expungi, quia ex professo tractat de veritate motus Terræ, dum solvit veterum rationes probantes ejus quietem.

Cum tamen problematice videatur loqui; ut studiosis satisfiat, seriesque et ordo libri integer maneat; emendetur ut infra."[145]

A chapter which seems to assert the motion should perhaps be expunged; but it may perhaps be problematical; and, not to break up the book, must be amended as below.

(p. 6.) "Copernicus. Cur ergo hesitamus adhuc, mobilitatem illi formæ suæ a natura congruentem concedere, magisquam quod totus labatur mundus, cujus finis ignoratur, scirique nequit, neque fateamur ipsius cotidianæ revolutionis in coelo apparentiam esse, et in terra veritatem? Et hæc perinde se habere, ac si diceret Virgilianus Æneas: Provehimur portu ... Emend. Cur ergo non possum mobilitatem illi formæ suæ concedere, magisque quod totus labatur mundus, cujus finis ignoratur scirique nequit, et quæ apparent in coelo, perinde se habere ac si ..."[146]

{94}

"Why should we hesitate to allow the earth's motion," must be altered into "I cannot concede the earth's motion."

(p. 7.) "Copernicus. Addo etiam, quod satis absurdum videretur, continenti sive locanti motum adscribi, et non potius contento et locato, quod est terra. Emend. Addo etiam difficilius non esse contento et locato, quod est Terra, motum adscribere, quam continenti."[147]

We must not say it is absurd to refuse motion to the contained and located, and to give it to the containing and locating; say that neither is more difficult than the other.

(p. 7.) "Copernicus. Vides ergo quod ex his omnibus probabilior sit mobilitas Terræ, quam ejus quies, præsertim in cotidiana revolutione, tanquam terræ maxime propria. Emend. Vides ... delendus est usque ad finem capitis."[148]

Strike out the whole of the chapter from this to the end; it says that the motion of the earth is the most probable hypothesis.

(Cap. 9. lib. i. p. 7.) "Copernicus. Cum igitur nihil prohibeat mobilitatem Terræ, videndum nunc arbitror, an etiam plures illi motus conveniant, ut possit una errantium syderum existimari. Emend. Cum igitur Terram moveri assumpserim, videndum nunc arbitror, an etiam illi plures possint convenire motus."[149]

{95}

We must not say that nothing prohibits the motion of the earth, only that having assumed it, we may inquire whether our explanations require several motions.

(Cap. 10. lib. i. p. 9.) "Copernicus. Non pudet nos fateri ... hoc potius in mobilitate terræ verificari. Emend. Non pudet nos assumere ... hoc consequenter in mobilitate verificari."[150]

(Cap. 10. lib. i. p. 10.) "Copernicus. Tanta nimirum est divina hæc. Opt. Max. fabrica. Emend. Dele illa verba postrema."[151]

(Cap. ii. lib. i.[152]) "Copernicus. De triplici motu telluris demonstratio. Emend. De hypothesi triplicis motus Terræ, ejusque demonstratione."[153]

(Cap. 10. lib. iv. p. 122.[154]) "Copernicus. De magnitudine horum trium siderum, Solis, Lunæ, et Terræ. Emend. Dele verba horum trium siderum, quia terra non est sidus, ut facit eam Copernicus."[155]

We must not say we are not ashamed to acknowledge; assume is the word. We must not call this assumption a Divine work. A chapter must not be headed demonstration, but hypothesis. The earth must not be called a star; the word implies motion.

It will be seen that it does not take much to reduce Copernicus to pure hypothesis. No personal injury being done to the author--who indeed had been 17 years out of {96} reach--the treatment of his book is now an excellent joke. It is obvious that the Cardinals of the Index were a little ashamed of their position, and made a mere excuse of a few corrections. Their mode of dealing with chap. 8, this problematice videtur loqui, ut studiosis satisfiat,[156] is an excuse to avoid corrections. But they struck out the stinging allusion to Lactantius[157] in the preface, little thinking, honest men, for they really believed what they said--that the light of Lactantius would grow dark before the brightness of their own.

THE CONVOCATION AT OXFORD EQUALLY AT FAULT

1622. I make no reference to the case of Galileo, except this. I have pointed out (Penny Cycl. Suppl. "Galileo"; Engl. Cycl. "Motion of the Earth") that it is clear the absurdity was the act of the Italian Inquisition--for the private and personal pleasure of the Pope, who knew that the course he took would not commit him as Pope--and not of the body which calls itself the Church. Let the dirty proceeding have its right name. The Jesuit Riccioli,[158] the stoutest and most learned Anti-Copernican in Europe, and the Puritan Wilkins, a strong Copernican and Pope-hater, are equally positive that the Roman Church never pronounced any decision: and this in the time immediately following the ridiculous proceeding of the Inquisition. In like manner a decision of the Convocation of Oxford is not a law of the English Church; which is fortunate, for that Convocation, in 1622, came to a decision quite as absurd, and a great deal {97} more wicked than the declaration against the motion of the earth. The second was a foolish mistake; the first was a disgusting surrender of right feeling. The story is told without disapprobation by Anthony Wood, who never exaggerated anything against the university of which he is writing eulogistic history.

In 1622, one William Knight[159] put forward in a sermon preached before the University certain theses which, looking at the state of the times, may have been improper and possibly of seditious intent. One of them was that the bishop might excommunicate the civil magistrate: this proposition the clerical body could not approve, and designated it by the term erronea,[160] the mildest going. But Knight also declared as follows:

"Subditis mere privatis, si Tyrannus tanquam latro aut stuprator in ipsos faciat impetum, et ipsi nec potestatem ordinariam implorare, nec alia ratione effugere periculum possint, in presenti periculo se et suos contra tyrannum, sicut contra privatum grassatorem, defendere licet."[161]

That is, a man may defend his purse or a woman her honor, against the personal attack of a king, as against that of a private person, if no other means of safety can be found. The Convocation sent Knight to prison, declared the proposition "falsa, periculosa, et impia," and enacted that all applicants for degrees should subscribe this censure, and make oath that they would neither hold, teach, nor defend Knight's opinions.

The thesis, in the form given, was unnecessary and improper. Though strong opinions of the king's rights were advanced at the time, yet no one ventured to say that, {98} ministers and advisers apart, the king might personally break the law; and we know that the first and only attempt which his successor made brought on the crisis which cost him his throne and his head. But the declaration that the proposition was false far exceeds in all that is disreputable the decision of the Inquisition against the earth's motion. We do not mention this little matter in England. Knight was a Puritan, and Neal[162] gives a short account of his sermon. From comparison with Wood,[163] I judge that the theses, as given, were not Knight's words, but the digest which it was customary to make in criminal proceedings against opinion. This heightens the joke, for it appears that the qualifiers of the Convocation took pains to present their condemnation of Knight in the terms which would most unequivocally make their censure condemn themselves. This proceeding took place in the interval between the two proceedings against Galileo: it is left undetermined whether we must say pot-kettle-pot or kettle-pot-kettle.

Liberti Fromondi.... Ant-Aristarchus, sive orbis terræ immobilis. Antwerp, 1631, 8vo.[164]

This book contains the evidence of an ardent opponent of Galileo to the fact, that Roman Catholics of the day did not consider the decree of the Index or of the Inquisition as a declaration of their Church. Fromond would have been glad to say as much, and tries to come near it, but confesses he must abstain. See Penny Cyclop. Suppl. "Galileo," and Eng. Cycl. "Motion of the Earth." The author of a celebrated article in the Dublin Review, in defence of the {99} Church of Rome, seeing that Drinkwater Bethune[165] makes use of the authority of Fromondus, but for another purpose, sneers at him for bringing up a "musty old Professor." If he had known Fromondus, and used him he would have helped his own case, which is very meagre for want of knowledge.[166]

Advis à Monseigneur l'eminentissime Cardinal Duc de Richelieu, sur la Proposition faicte par le Sieur Morin pour l'invention des longitudes. Paris, 1634, 8vo.[167]

This is the Official Report of the Commissioners appointed by the Cardinal, of whom Pascal is the one now best known, to consider Morin's plan. See the full account in Delambre, Hist. Astr. Mod. ii. 236, etc.

THE METIUS APPROXIMATION

Arithmetica et Geometria practica. By Adrian Metius. Leyden, 1640, 4to.[168]

This book contains the celebrated approximation guessed at by his father, Peter Metius,[169] namely that the diameter is {100} to the circumference as 113 to 355. The error is at the rate of about a foot in 2,000 miles. Peter Metius, having his attention called to the subject by the false quadrature of Duchesne, found that the ratio lay between 333/106 and 377/120. He then took the liberty of taking the mean of both numerators and denominators, giving 355/113. He had no right to presume that this mean was better than either of the extremes; nor does it appear positively that he did so. He published nothing; but his son Adrian,[170] when Van Ceulen's work showed how near his father's result came to the truth, first made it known in the work above. (See Eng. Cyclop., art. "Quadrature.")

ON INHABITABLE PLANETS

A discourse concerning a new world and another planet, in two books. London, 1640, 8vo.[171]

Cosmotheoros: or conjectures concerning the planetary worlds and their inhabitants. Written in Latin, by Christianus Huyghens. This translation was first published in 1698. Glasgow, 1757, 8vo. [The original is also of 1698.][172]

The first work is by Bishop Wilkins, being the third edition, [first in 1638] of the first book, "That the Moon may be a Planet"; and the first edition of the second work, {101} "That the Earth may be a Planet." [See more under the reprint of 1802.] Whether other planets be inhabited or not, that is, crowded with organisations some of them having consciousness, is not for me to decide; but I should be much surprised if, on going to one of them, I should find it otherwise. The whole dispute tacitly assumes that, if the stars and planets be inhabited, it must be by things of which we can form some idea. But for aught we know, what number of such bodies there are, so many organisms may there be, of which we have no way of thinking nor of speaking. This is seldom remembered. In like manner it is usually forgotten that the matter of other planets may be of different chemistry from ours.

There may be no oxygen and hydrogen in Jupiter, which may have gens of its own.[173] But this must not be said: it would limit the omniscience of the a priori school of physical inquirers, the larger half of the whole, and would be very unphilosophical. Nine-tenths of my best paradoxers come out from among this larger half, because they are just a little more than of it at their entrance.

There was a discussion on the subject some years ago, which began with The plurality of worlds: an Essay. London, 1853, 8vo. [By Dr. Wm. Whewell, Master of Trinity College, Cambridge]. A dialogue on the plurality of worlds, being a supplement to the Essay on that subject. [First found in the second edition, 1854; removed to the end in subsequent editions, and separate copies issued.][174]

A work of skeptical character, insisting on analogies which prohibit the positive conclusion that the planets, stars, etc., are what we should call inhabited worlds. It produced {102} several works and a large amount of controversy in reviews. The last predecessor of whom I know was Plurality of Worlds.... By Alexander Maxwell. Second Edition. London, 1820, 8vo.

This work is directed against the plurality by an author who does not admit modern astronomy. It was occasioned by Dr. Chalmers's[175] celebrated discourses on religion in connection with astronomy. The notes contain many citations on the gravity controversy, from authors now very little read: and this is its present value. I find no mention of Maxwell, not even in Watt.[176] He communicated with mankind without the medium of a publisher; and, from Vieta till now, this method has always been favorable to loss of books.

A correspondent informs me that Alex. Maxwell, who wrote on the plurality of worlds, in 1820, was a law-bookseller and publisher (probably his own publisher) in Bell Yard. He had peculiar notions, which he was fond of discussing with his customers. He was a bit of a Swedenborgian.

INHABITED PLANETS IN FICTION

There is a class of hypothetical creations which do not belong to my subject, because they are acknowledged to be fictions, as those of Lucian,[177] Rabelais,[178] Swift, Francis {103} Godwin,[179] Voltaire, etc. All who have more positive notions as to either the composition or organization of other worlds, than the reasonable conclusion that our Architect must be quite able to construct millions of other buildings on millions of other plans, ought to rank with the writers just mentioned, in all but self-knowledge. Of every one of their systems I say, as the Irish Bishop said of Gulliver's book,--I don't believe half of it. Huyghens had been preceded by Fontenelle,[180] who attracted more attention. Huyghens is very fanciful and very positive; but he gives a true account of his method. "But since there's no hopes of a Mercury to carry us such a journey, we shall e'en be contented with what's in our power: we shall suppose ourselves there...." And yet he says, "We have proved that they live in societies, have hands and feet...." Kircher[181] had gone to the stars before him, but would not find any life in them, either animal or vegetable.

The question of the inhabitants of a particular planet is one which has truth on one side or the other: either there are some inhabitants, or there are none. Fortunately, it is of no consequence which is true. But there are many cases where the balance is equally one of truth and falsehood, in which the choice is a matter of importance. My work selects, for the most part, sins against demonstration: but the world is full of questions of fact or opinion, in which a struggling minority will become a majority, or else will {104} be gradually annihilated: and each of the cases subdivides into results of good, and results of evil. What is to be done?

"Periculosum est credere et non credere; Hippolitus obiit quia novercæ creditum est; Cassandræ quia non creditum ruit Ilium: Ergo exploranda est veritas multum prius Quam stulta prove judicet sententia."[182]

Nova Demonstratio immobilitatis terræ petita ex virtute magnetica. By Jacobus Grandamicus. Flexiae (La Flèche), 1645, 4to.[183]

No magnetic body can move about its poles: the earth is a magnetic body, therefore, etc. The iron and its magnetism are typical of two natures in one person; so it is said, "Si exaltatus fuero à terra, omnia traham ad me ipsum."[184]

A VENETIAN BUDGET OF PARADOXES

Le glorie degli incogniti, o vero gli huomini illustri dell' accademia de' signori incogniti di Venetia. Venice, 1647, 4to.

This work is somewhat like a part of my own: it is a budget of Venetian nobodies who wished to be somebodies; but paradox is not the only means employed. It is of a serio-comic character, gives genuine portraits in copperplate, and grave lists of works; but satirical accounts. The astrologer Andrew Argoli[185] is there, and his son; both of whom, with some of the others, have place in modern works {105} on biography. Argoli's discovery that logarithms facilitate easy processes, but increase the labor of difficult ones, is worth recording.

Controversiæ de vera circuli mensura ... inter ... C. S. Longomontanum et Jo. Pellium.[186] Amsterdam, 1647, 4to.

Longomontanus,[187] a Danish astronomer of merit, squared the circle in 1644: he found out that the diameter 43 gives the square root of 18252 for the circumference; which gives 3.14185... for the ratio. Pell answered him, and being a kind of circulating medium, managed to engage in the controversy names known and unknown, as Roberval, Hobbes, Carcavi, Lord Charles Cavendish, Pallieur, Mersenne, Tassius, Baron Wolzogen, Descartes, Cavalieri and Golius.[188] Among them, of course, Longomontanus was made {106} mincemeat: but he is said to have insisted on the discovery of his epitaph.[189]

{107}

THE CIRCULATING MEDIA OF MATHEMATICS

The great circulating mediums, who wrote to everybody, heard from everybody, and sent extracts to everybody else, have been Father Mersenne, John Collins, and the late Professor Schumacher: all "late" no doubt, but only the last recent enough to be so styled. If M.C.S. should ever again stand for "Member of the Corresponding Society," it should raise an acrostic thought of the three. There is an allusion to Mersenne's occupation in Hobbes's reply to him. He wanted to give Hobbes, who was very ill at Paris, the Roman Eucharist: but Hobbes said, "I have settled all that long ago; when did you hear from Gassendi?" We are reminded of William's answer to Burnet. John Collins disseminated Newton, among others.

Schumacher ought to have been called the postmaster-general of astronomy, as Collins was called the attorney-general of mathematics.[190]

{108}

THE SYMPATHETIC POWDER

A late discourse ... by Sir Kenelme Digby.... Rendered into English by R. White. London, 1658, 12mo.

On this work see Notes and Queries, 2d series, vii. 231, 299, 445, viii. 190. It contains the celebrated sympathetic powder. I am still in much doubt as to the connection of Digby with this tract.[191] Without entering on the subject here, I observe that in Birch's History of the Royal Society,[192] to which both Digby and White belonged, Digby, though he brought many things before the Society, never mentioned the powder, which is connected only with the names of Evelyn[193] and Sir Gilbert Talbot.[194] The sympathetic powder was that which cured by anointing the weapon with its salve instead of the wound. I have long been convinced that it was efficacious. The directions were to keep the {109} wound clean and cool, and to take care of diet, rubbing the salve on the knife or sword.[195] If we remember the dreadful notions upon drugs which prevailed, both as to quantity and quality, we shall readily see that any way of not dressing the wound would have been useful. If the physicians had taken the hint, had been careful of diet etc., and had poured the little barrels of medicine down the throat of a practicable doll, they would have had their magical cures as well as the surgeons.[196] Matters are much improved now; the quantity of medicine given, even by orthodox physicians, would have been called infinitesimal by their professional ancestors. Accordingly, the College of Physicians has a right to abandon its motto, which is Ars longa, vita brevis, meaning Practice is long, so life is short.

HOBBES AS A MATHEMATICIAN

Examinatio et emendatio Mathematicæ Hodiernæ. By Thomas Hobbes. London, 1666, 4to.

In six dialogues: the sixth contains a quadrature of the circle.[197] But there is another edition of this work, without place or date on the title-page, in which the quadrature is omitted. This seems to be connected with the publication {110} of another quadrature, without date, but about 1670, as may be judged from its professing to answer a tract of Wallis, printed in 1669.[198] The title is "Quadratura circuli, cubatio sphæræ, duplicatio cubi," 4to.[199] Hobbes, who began in 1655, was very wrong in his quadrature; but, though not a Gregory St. Vincent,[200] he was not the ignoramus in geometry that he is sometimes supposed. His writings, erroneous as they are in many things, contain acute remarks on points of principle. He is wronged by being coupled with Joseph Scaliger, as the two great instances of men of letters who have come into geometry to help the mathematicians out of their difficulty. I have never seen Scaliger's quadrature,[201] except in the answers of Adrianus Romanus,[202] Vieta and Clavius, and in the extracts of Kastner.[203] Scaliger had no right to such strong opponents: Erasmus or Bentley might just as well have tried the problem, and either would have done much better in any twenty minutes of his life.[204]

AN ESTIMATE OF SCALIGER

Scaliger inspired some mathematicians with great respect for his geometrical knowledge. Vieta, the first man of his time, who answered him, had such regard for his opponent {111} as made him conceal Scaliger's name. Not that he is very respectful in his manner of proceeding: the following dry quiz on his opponent's logic must have been very cutting, being true. "In grammaticis, dare navibus Austros, et dare naves Austris, sunt æque significantia. Sed in Geometricis, aliud est adsumpsisse circulum BCD non esse majorem triginta sex segmentis BCDF, aliud circulo BCD non esse majora triginta sex segmenta BCDF. Illa adsumptiuncula vera est, hæc falsa."[205] Isaac Casaubon,[206] in one of his letters to De Thou,[207] relates that, he and another paying a visit to Vieta, the conversation fell upon Scaliger, of whom the host said that he believed Scaliger was the only man who perfectly understood mathematical writers, especially the Greek ones: and that he thought more of Scaliger when wrong than of many others when right; "pluris se Scaligerum vel errantem facere quam multos [Greek: katorthountas]."[208] This must have been before Scaliger's quadrature (1594). There is an old story of some one saying, "Mallem cum Scaligero errare, quam cum Clavio recte sapere."[209] This I cannot help suspecting to have been a version of Vieta's speech with Clavius satirically inserted, on account of the great hostility which Vieta showed towards Clavius in the latter years of his life.

Montucla could not have read with care either Scaliger's quadrature or Clavius's refutation. He gives the first a wrong date: he assures the world that there is no question about Scaliger's quadrature being wrong, in the eyes of geometers at least: and he states that Clavius mortified him {112} extremely by showing that it made the circle less than its inscribed dodecagon, which is, of course, equivalent to asserting that a straight line is not always the shortest distance between two points. Did Clavius show this? No, it was Scaliger himself who showed it, boasted of it, and declared it to be a "noble paradox" that a theorem false in geometry is true in arithmetic; a thing, he says with great triumph, not noticed by Archimedes himself! He says in so many words that the periphery of the dodecagon is greater than that of the circle; and that the more sides there are to the inscribed figure, the more does it exceed the circle in which it is. And here are the words, on the independent testimonies of Clavius and Kastner:

"Ambitus dodecagoni circulo inscribendi plus potest quam circuli ambitus. Et quanto deinceps plurium laterum fuerit polygonum circulo inscribendum, tanto plus poterit ambitus polygoni quam ambitus circuli."[210]

There is much resemblance between Joseph Scaliger and William Hamilton,[211] in a certain impetuousity of character, and inaptitude to think of quantity. Scaliger maintained that the arc of a circle is less than its chord in arithmetic, though greater in geometry; Hamilton arrived at two quantities which are identical, but the greater the one the less the other. But, on the whole, I liken Hamilton rather to Julius than to Joseph. On this last hero of literature I repeat Thomas Edwards,[212] who says that a man is unlearned who, be his other knowledge what it may, does not {113} understand the subject he writes about. And now one of many instances in which literature gives to literature character in science. Anthony Teissier,[213] the learned annotator of De Thou's biographies, says of Finæus, "Il se vanta sans raison avoir trouvé la quadrature du cercle; la gloire de cette admirable découverte était réservée à Joseph Scalinger, comme l'a écrit Scévole de St. Marthe."[214]

JOHN GRAUNT AS A PARADOXER

Natural and Political Observations ... upon the Bills of Mortality. By John Graunt, citizen of London. London, 1662, 4to.[215]

This is a celebrated book, the first great work upon mortality. But the author, going ultra crepidam, has attributed to the motion of the moon in her orbit all the tremors which she gets from a shaky telescope.[216] But there is another paradox about this book: the above absurd opinion is attributed to that excellent mechanist, Sir William Petty, who passed his days among the astronomers. Graunt did not write his own book! Anthony Wood[217] hints that Petty "assisted, or put into a way" his old benefactor: no doubt the two friends talked the matter over many a time. Burnet and Pepys[218] state that Petty wrote the book. It is enough for me that {114} Graunt, whose honesty was never impeached, uses the plainest incidental professions of authorship throughout; that he was elected into the Royal Society because he was the author; that Petty refers to him as author in scores of places, and published an edition, as editor, after Graunt's death, with Graunt's name of course. The note on Graunt in the Biographia Britannica may be consulted; it seems to me decisive. Mr. C. B. Hodge, an able actuary, has done the best that can be done on the other side in the Assurance Magazine, viii. 234. If I may say what is in my mind, without imputation of disrespect, I suspect some actuaries have a bias: they would rather have Petty the greater for their Coryphæus than Graunt the less.[219]

Pepys is an ordinary gossip: but Burnet's account has an animus which is of a worse kind. He talks of "one Graunt, a Papist, under whose name Sir William Petty[220] published his observations on the bills of mortality." He then gives the cock without a bull story of Graunt being a trustee of the New River Company, and shutting up the cocks and carrying off their keys, just before the fire of London, by which a supply of water was delayed.[221] It was one of the first objections made to Burnet's work, that Graunt was not a trustee at the time; and Maitland, the historian of London, ascertained from the books of the Company that he was not admitted until twenty-three days after the breaking out of the fire. Graunt's first admission {115} to the Company took place on the very day on which a committee was appointed to inquire into the cause of the fire. So much for Burnet. I incline to the view that Graunt's setting London on fire strongly corroborates his having written on the bills of mortality: every practical man takes stock before he commences a grand operation in business.

MANKIND A GULLIBLE LOT

De Cometis: or a discourse of the natures and effects of Comets, as they are philosophically, historically, and astrologically considered. With a brief (yet full) account of the III late Comets, or blazing stars, visible to all Europe. And what (in a natural way of judicature) they portend. Together with some observations on the nativity of the Grand Seignior. By John Gadbury, [Greek: Philomathêmatikos]. London, 1665, 4to.

Gadbury, though his name descends only in astrology, was a well-informed astronomer.[222] D'Israeli[223] sets down Gadbury, Lilly, Wharton, Booker, etc., as rank rogues: I think him quite wrong. The easy belief in roguery and intentional imposture which prevails in educated society is, to my mind, a greater presumption against the honesty of mankind than all the roguery and imposture itself. Putting aside mere swindling for the sake of gain, and looking at speculation and paradox, I find very little reason to suspect wilful deceit.[224] My opinion of mankind is founded upon the {116} mournful fact that, so far as I can see, they find within themselves the means of believing in a thousand times as much as there is to believe in, judging by experience. I do not say anything against Isaac D'Israeli for talking his time. We are all in the team, and we all go the road, but we do not all draw.

A FORERUNNER OF A WRITTEN ESPERANTO

An essay towards a real character and a philosophical language. By John Wilkins [Dean of Ripon, afterwards Bishop of Chester].[225] London, 1668, folio.

This work is celebrated, but little known. Its object gives it a right to a place among paradoxes. It proposes a language--if that be the proper name--in which things and their relations shall be denoted by signs, not words: so that any person, whatever may be his mother tongue, may read it in his own words. This is an obvious possibility, and, I am afraid, an obvious impracticability. One man may construct such a system--Bishop Wilkins has done it--but where is the man who will learn it? The second tongue makes a language, as the second blow makes a fray. There has been very little curiosity about his performance, the work is scarce; and I do not know where to refer the reader for any account of its details, except, to the partial reprint of Wilkins presently mentioned under 1802, in which there is an unsatisfactory abstract. There is nothing in the Biographia Britannica, except discussion of Anthony Wood's statement that the hint was derived from Dalgarno's book, {117} De Signis, 1661.[226] Hamilton (Discussions, Art. 5, "Dalgarno") does not say a word on this point, beyond quoting Wood; and Hamilton, though he did now and then write about his countrymen with a rough-nibbed pen, knew perfectly well how to protect their priorities.

GREGOIRE DE ST. VINCENT

Problema Austriacum. Plus ultra Quadratura Circuli. Auctore P. Gregorio a Sancto Vincentio Soc. Jesu., Antwerp, 1647, folio.--Opus Geometricum posthumum ad Mesolabium. By the same. Gandavi [Ghent], 1668, folio.[227]

The first book has more than 1200 pages, on all kinds of geometry. Gregory St. Vincent is the greatest of circle-squarers, and his investigations led him into many truths: he found the property of the area of the hyperbola[228] which led to Napier's logarithms being called hyperbolic. Montucla says of him, with sly truth, that no one has ever squared the circle with so much genius, or, excepting his principal object, with so much success.[229] His reputation, and the many merits of his work, led to a sharp controversy on his quadrature, which ended in its complete exposure by Huyghens and others. He had a small school of followers, who defended him in print.

{118}

RENE DE SLUSE

Renati Francisci Slusii Mesolabum. Leodii Eburonum [Liège], 1668, 4to.[230]

The Mesolabum is the solution of the problem of finding two mean proportionals, which Euclid's geometry does not attain. Slusius is a true geometer, and uses the ellipse, etc.: but he is sometimes ranked with the trisecters, for which reason I place him here, with this explanation.

The finding of two mean proportionals is the preliminary to the famous old problem of the duplication of the cube, proposed by Apollo (not Apollonius) himself. D'Israeli speaks of the "six follies of science,"--the quadrature, the duplication, the perpetual motion, the philosopher's stone, magic, and astrology. He might as well have added the trisection, to make the mystic number seven: but had he done so, he would still have been very lenient; only seven follies in all science, from mathematics to chemistry!

Science might have said to such a judge--as convicts used to say who got seven years, expecting it for life, "Thank you, my Lord, and may you sit there till they are over,"--may the Curiosities of Literature outlive the Follies of Science!

JAMES GREGORY

1668. In this year James Gregory, in his Vera Circuli et Hyperbolæ Quadratura,[231] held himself to have proved that {119} the geometrical quadrature of the circle is impossible. Few mathematicians read this very abstruse speculation, and opinion is somewhat divided. The regular circle-squarers attempt the arithmetical quadrature, which has long been proved to be impossible. Very few attempt the geometrical quadrature. One of the last is Malacarne, an Italian, who published his Solution Géométrique, at Paris, in 1825. His method would make the circumference less than three times the diameter.

BEAULIEU'S QUADRATURE

La Géométrie Françoise, ou la Pratique aisée.... La quadracture du cercle. Par le Sieur de Beaulieu, Ingénieur, Géographe du Roi ... Paris, 1676, 8vo. [not Pontault de Beaulieu, the celebrated topographer; he died in 1674].[232]

If this book had been a fair specimen, I might have pointed to it in connection with contemporary English works, and made a scornful comparison. But it is not a fair specimen. Beaulieu was attached to the Royal Household, and throughout the century it may be suspected that the household forced a royal road to geometry. Fifty years before, Beaugrand, the king's secretary, made a fool of himself, and [so?] contrived to pass for a geometer. He had interest enough to get Desargues, the most powerful geometer of his time,[233] the teacher and friend of Pascal, prohibited from {120} lecturing. See some letters on the History of Perspective, which I wrote in the Athenæum, in October and November, 1861. Montucla, who does not seem to know the true secret of Beaugrand's greatness, describes him as "un certain M. de Beaugrand, mathématicien, fort mal traité par Descartes, et à ce qu'il paroit avec justice."[234]

Beaulieu's quadrature amounts to a geometrical construction[235] which gives [pi] = [root]10. His depth may be ascertained from the following extracts. First on Copernicus:

"Copernic, Allemand, ne s'est pas moins rendu illustre par ses doctes écrits; et nous pourrions dire de luy, qu'il seroit le seul et unique en la force de ses Problèmes, si sa trop grande présomption ne l'avoit porté à avancer en cette Science une proposition aussi absurde, qu'elle est contre la Foy et raison, en faisant la circonférence d'un Cercle fixe, immobile, et le centre mobile, sur lequel principe Géométrique, il a avancé en son Traitté Astrologique le Soleil fixe, et la Terre mobile."[236]

I digress here to point out that though our quadrators, etc., very often, and our historians sometimes, assert that men of the character of Copernicus, etc., were treated with contempt and abuse until their day of ascendancy came, nothing can be more incorrect. From Tycho Brahé[237] to Beaulieu, there is but one expression of admiration for the genius of Copernicus.

There is an exception, which, I {121} believe, has been quite misunderstood. Maurolycus,[238] in his De Sphæra, written many years before its posthumous publication in 1575, and which it is not certain he would have published, speaking of the safety with which various authors may be read after his cautions, says, "Toleratur et Nicolaus Copernicus qui Solem fixum et Terram in girum circumverti posuit: et scutica potius, aut flagello, quam reprehensione dignus est."[239] Maurolycus was a mild and somewhat contemptuous satirist, when expressing disapproval: as we should now say, he pooh-poohed his opponents; but, unless the above be an instance, he was never savage nor impetuous. I am fully satisfied that the meaning of the sentence is, that Copernicus, who turned the earth like a boy's top, ought rather to have a whip given him wherewith to keep up his plaything than a serious refutation. To speak of tolerating a person as being more worthy of a flogging than an argument, is almost a contradiction. I will now extract Beaulieu's treatise on algebra, entire.

"L'Algebre est la science curieuse des Sçavans et specialement d'un General d'Armée ou Capitaine, pour promptement ranger une Armée en bataille, et nombre de Mousquetaires et Piquiers qui composent les bataillons d'icelle, outre les figures de l'Arithmetique. Cette science a 5 figures particulieres en cette sorte. P signifie plus au commerce, et à l'Armée Piquiers. M signifie moins, et Mousquetaire en l'Art des bataillons. [It is quite true that P and M were used for plus and minus in a great many old works.] R signifie racine en la mesure du Cube, et en l'Armée rang. Q signifie quaré en l'un et l'autre usage. C signifie cube en la mesure, et Cavallerie en la composition des bataillons et escadrons. Quant à l'operation de cette science, c'est {122} d'additionner un plus d'avec plus, la somme sera plus, et moins d'avec plus, on soustrait le moindre du plus, et la reste est la somme requise ou nombre trouvé. Je dis seulement cecy en passant pour ceux qui n'en sçavent rien du tout."[240]

This is the algebra of the Royal Household, seventy-three years after the death of Vieta. Quære, is it possible that the fame of Vieta, who himself held very high stations in the household all his life, could have given people the notion that when such an officer chose to declare himself an algebraist, he must be one indeed? This would explain Beaugrand, Beaulieu, and all the beaux. Beaugrand--not only secretary to the king, but "mathematician" to the Duke of Orleans--I wonder what his "fool" could have been like, if indeed he kept the offices separate,--would have been in my list if I had possessed his Geostatique, published about 1638.[241] He makes bodies diminish in weight as they approach the earth, because the effect of a weight on a lever is less as it approaches the fulcrum.

{123}

SIR MATTHEW HALE.

Remarks upon two late ingenious discourses.... By Dr. Henry More.[242] London, 1676, 8vo.

In 1673 and 1675, Matthew Hale,[243] then Chief Justice, published two tracts, an "Essay touching Gravitation," and "Difficiles Nugæ" on the Torricellian experiment. Here are the answers by the learned and voluminous Henry More. The whole would be useful to any one engaged in research about ante-Newtonian notions of gravitation.

Observations touching the principles of natural motions; and especially touching rarefaction and condensation.... By the author of Difficiles Nugæ. London, 1677, 8vo.

This is another tract of Chief Justice Hale, published the year after his death. The reader will remember that motion, in old philosophy, meant any change from state to state: what we now describe as motion was local motion. This is a very philosophical book, about flux and materia prima, virtus activa and essentialis, and other fundamentals. I think Stephen Hales, the author of the "Vegetable Statics," has the writings of the Chief Justice sometimes attributed to him, which is very puny justice indeed.[244] Matthew Hale died in 1676, and from his devotion to science it probably arose that his famous Pleas of the Crown[245] and other law works did not appear until after his death. One of his {124} contemporaries was the astronomer Thomas Street, whose Caroline Tables[246] were several times printed: another contemporary was his brother judge, Sir Thomas Street.[247] But of the astronomer absolutely nothing is known: it is very unlikely that he and the judge were the same person, but there is not a bit of positive evidence either for or against, so far as can be ascertained.

Halley[248]--no less a person--published two editions of the Caroline Tables, no doubt after the death of the author: strange indeed that neither Halley nor any one else should leave evidence that Street was born or died.

Matthew Hale gave rise to an instance of the lengths a lawyer will go when before a jury who cannot detect him. Sir Samuel Shepherd,[249] the Attorney General, in opening Hone's[250] first trial, calls him "one who was the most learned man that ever adorned the Bench, the most even man that ever blessed domestic life, the most eminent man that ever advanced the progress of science, and one of the [very moderate] best and most purely religious men that ever lived."

{125}

ON THE DISCOVERY OF ANTIMONY

Basil Valentine his triumphant Chariot of Antimony, with annotations of Theodore Kirkringius, M.D. With the true book of the learned Synesius, a Greek abbot, taken out of the Emperour's library, concerning the Philosopher's Stone. London, 1678, 8vo.[251]

There are said to be three Hamburg editions of the collected works of Valentine, who discovered the common antimony, and is said to have given the name antimoine, in a curious way. Finding that the pigs of his convent throve upon it, he gave it to his brethren, who died of it.[252] The impulse given to chemistry by R. Boyle[253] seems to have brought out a vast number of translations, as in the following tract:

ON ALCHEMY

Collectanea Chymica: A collection of ten several treatises in chymistry, concerning the liquor Alkehest, the Mercury of Philosophers, and other curiosities worthy the perusal. Written by Eir. Philaletha,[254] Anonymus, J. B. Van-Helmont,[255] Dr. Fr. {126} Antonie,[256] Bernhard Earl of Trevisan,[257] Sir Geo. Ripley,[258] Rog. Bacon,[259] Geo. Starkie,[260] Sir Hugh Platt,[261] and the Tomb of Semiramis. See more in the contents. London, 1684, 8vo.

In the advertisements at the ends of these tracts there are upwards of a hundred English tracts, nearly all of the period, and most of them translations. Alchemy looks up since the chemists have found perfectly different substances composed of the same elements and proportions. It is true the chemists cannot yet transmute; but they may in time: they poke about most assiduously. It seems, then, that the conviction that alchemy must be impossible was a delusion: but we do not mention it.

{127}

The astrologers and the alchemists caught it in company in the following, of which I have an unreferenced note.

"Mendacem et futilem hominem nominare qui volunt, calendariographum dicunt; at qui sceleratum simul ac impostorem, chimicum.[262]

"Crede ratem ventis corpus ne crede chimistis; Est quævis chimica tutior aura fide."[263]

Among the smaller paradoxes of the day is that of the Times newspaper, which always spells it chymistry: but so, I believe, do Johnson, Walker, and others. The Arabic work is very likely formed from the Greek: but it may be connected either with [Greek: chêmeia] or with [Greek: chumeia].

Lettre d'un gentil-homme de province à une dame de qualité, sur le sujet de la Comète. Paris, 1681, 4to.

An opponent of astrology, whom I strongly suspect to have been one of the members of the Academy of Sciences under the name of a country gentleman,[264] writes very good sense on the tremors excited by comets.

The Petitioning-Comet: or a brief Chronology of all the famous Comets and their events, that have happened from the birth of Christ to this very day.

Together with a modest enquiry into this present comet, London, 1681, 4to. A satirical tract against the cometic prophecy:

"This present comet (it's true) is of a menacing aspect, but if the new parliament (for whose convention so many good men pray) continue long to sit, I fear not but the star will lose its virulence and malignancy, or at least its portent be averted from this our nation; which being the humble request to God of all good men, makes me thus entitle it, a

Petitioning-Comet."

{128}

The following anecdote is new to me:

"Queen Elizabeth (1558) being then at Richmond, and being disswaded from looking on a comet which did then appear, made answer, jacta est alea, the dice are thrown; thereby intimating that the pre-order'd providence of God was above the influence of any star or comet."

The argument was worth nothing: for the comet might have been on the dice with the event; the astrologers said no more, at least the more rational ones, who were about half of the whole.

An astrological and theological discourse upon this present great conjunction (the like whereof hath not (likely) been in some ages) ushered in by a great comet. London, 1682, 4to. By C. N.[265]

The author foretells the approaching "sabbatical jubilee," but will not fix the date: he recounts the failures of his predecessors.

A judgment of the comet which became first generally visible to us in Dublin, December 13, about 15 minutes before 5 in the evening, A.D. 1680. By a person of quality. Dublin, 1682, 4to.

The author argues against cometic astrology with great ability.

A prophecy on the conjunction of Saturn and Jupiter in this present year 1682. With some prophetical predictions of what is likely to ensue therefrom in the year 1684. By John Case, Student in physic and astrology.[266] London, 1682, 4to.

{129}

According to this writer, great conjunctions of Jupiter and Saturn occur "in the fiery trigon," about once in 800 years. Of these there are to be seven: six happened in the several times of Enoch, Noah, Moses, Solomon, Christ,

Charlemagne. The seventh, which is to happen at "the lamb's marriage with the bride," seems to be that of 1682; but this is only vaguely hinted.

De Quadrature van de Circkel. By Jacob Marcelis. Amsterdam, 1698, 4to. Ampliatie en demonstratie wegens de Quadrature ... By Jacob Marcelis.

Amsterdam, 1699, 4to.

Eenvoudig vertoog briev-wys geschrevem am J. Marcelis ... Amsterdam, 1702, 4to.

De sleutel en openinge van de quadrature ... Amsterdam, 1704, 4to.

Who shall contradict Jacob Marcelis?[267] He says the circumference contains the diameter exactly times

1008449087377541679894282184894 3 -------------------------------- 6997183637540819440035239271702

But he does not come very near, as the young arithmetician will find. MATHEMATICAL THEOLOGY. Theologiæ Christianæ Principia Mathematica. Auctore Johanne Craig.[268] London, 1699, 4to.

This is a celebrated speculation, and has been reprinted abroad, and seriously answered. Craig is known in the early history of fluxions, and was a good mathematician. {130} He professed to calculate, on the hypothesis that the suspicions against historical evidence increase with the square of the time, how long it will take the evidence of Christianity to die out. He finds, by formulæ, that had it been oral only, it would have gone out A.D. 800; but, by aid of the written evidence, it will last till A.D. 3150. At this period he places the second coming, which is deferred until the extinction of evidence, on the authority of the question "When the Son of Man cometh, shall he find faith on the earth?" It is a pity that Craig's theory was not adopted: it would have spared a hundred treatises on the end of the world, founded on no better knowledge than his, and many of them falsified by the event. The most recent (October, 1863) is a tract in proof of Louis Napoleon being Antichrist, the Beast, the eighth Head, etc.; and the present dispensation is to close soon after 1864.

In order rightly to judge Craig, who added speculations on the variations of pleasure and pain treated as functions of time, it is necessary to remember that in Newton's day the idea of force, as a quantity to be measured, and as following a law of variation, was very new: so likewise was that of probability, or belief, as an object of measurement.[269] The success of the Principia of Newton put it into many heads to speculate about applying notions of quantity to other things not then brought under measurement.

Craig imitated Newton's title, and evidently thought he was making a step in advance: but it is not every one who can plough with Samson's heifer.

It is likely enough that Craig took a hint, directly or indirectly, from Mohammedan writers, who make a reply to the argument that the Koran has not the evidence derived {131} from miracles. They say that, as evidence of Christian miracles is daily becoming weaker, a time must at last arrive when it will fail of affording assurance that they were miracles at all: whence would arise the necessity of another prophet and other miracles. Lee,[270] the Cambridge Orientalist, from whom the above words are taken, almost certainly never heard of Craig or his theory.

THE ARISTOCRAT AS A SCIENTIST

Copernicans of all sorts convicted ... to which is added a Treatise of the Magnet. By the Hon. Edw. Howard, of Berks. London, 1705, 8vo.

Not all the blood of all the Howards will gain respect for a writer who maintains that eclipses admit no possible explanation under the Copernican hypothesis, and who asks how a man can "go 200 yards to any place if the moving superficies of the earth does carry it from him?" Horace Walpole, at the beginning of his Royal and Noble Authors, has mottoed his book with the Cardinal's address to Ariosto, "Dove diavolo, Messer Ludovico, avete pigliato tante coglionerie?"[271] Walter Scott says you could hardly pick out, on any principle of selection--except badness itself, he means of course--the same number of plebeian authors whose works are so bad. But his implied satire on aristocratic writing forgets two points. First, during a large period of our history, when persons of rank condescended to write, they veiled themselves under "a person of honor," "a person of quality," and the like, when not wholly undescribed. Not one of these has Walpole got; he omits, {132} for instance, Lord Brounker's[272] translation of Descartes on Music. Secondly, Walpole only takes the heads of houses: this cuts both ways; he equally eliminates the Hon. Robert Boyle and the precious Edward Howard. The last writer is hardly out of the time in which aristocracy suppressed its names; the avowal was then usually meant to make the author's greatness useful to the book. In our day, literary peers and honorables are very favorably known, and contain an eminent class.[273] They rough it like others, and if such a specimen as Edw.

Howard were now to appear, he would be greeted with "Hereditary noodle! knowest thou not Who would be wise, himself must make him so?"

THE LONGITUDE PROBLEM

A new and easy method to find the longitude at land or sea. London, 1710, 4to.

This tract is a little earlier than the great epoch of such publications (1714), and professes to find the longitude by the observed altitudes of the moon and two stars.[274] {133}

A new method for discovering the longitude both at sea and land, humbly proposed to the consideration of the public.[275] By Wm. Whiston[276] and Humphry Ditton.[277] London, 1714, 8vo.

This is the celebrated tract, written by the two Arian heretics. Swift, whose orthodoxy was as undoubted as his meekness, wrote upon it the epigram--if, indeed, that be epigram of which the point is pious wish--which has been so often recited for the purity of its style, a purity which transcends modern printing. Perhaps some readers may think that Swift cared little for Whiston and Ditton, except as a chance hearing of their plan pointed them out as good marks. But it was not so: the clique had their eye on the guilty pair before the publication of the tract. The preface is dated July 7; and ten days afterwards Arbuthnot[278] writes as follows to Swift:

"Whiston has at last published his project of the longitude; the most ridiculous thing that ever was thought on. But a pox on him! he has spoiled one of my papers of Scriblerus, which was a proposition for the longitude not very unlike his, to this purpose; that since there was no pole for east and west, that all the princes of Europe should join and build two prodigious poles, upon high mountains, {134} with a vast lighthouse to serve for a polestar. I was thinking of a calculation of the time, charges, and dimensions. Now you must understand his project is by lighthouses, and explosion of bombs at a certain hour."

The plan was certainly impracticable; but Whiston and Ditton might have retorted that they were nearer to the longitude than their satirist to the kingdom of heaven, or even to a bishopric. Arbuthnot, I think, here and elsewhere, reveals himself as the calculator who kept Swift right in his proportions in the matter of the Lilliputians, Brobdingnagians, etc. Swift was very ignorant about things connected with number. He writes to Stella that he has discovered that leap-year comes every four years, and that all his life he had thought it came every three years. Did he begin with the mistake of Cæsar's priests? Whether or no, when I find the person who did not understand leap-year inventing satellites of Mars in correct accordance with Kepler's third law, I feel sure he must have had help.

THE AURORA BOREALIS

An essay concerning the late apparition in the heavens on the 6th of March. Proving by mathematical, logical, and moral arguments, that it cou'd not have been produced meerly by the ordinary course of nature, but must of necessity be a prodigy. Humbly offered to the consideration of the Royal Society. London, 1716, 8vo.

The prodigy, as described, was what we should call a very decided and unusual aurora borealis. The inference was, that men's sins were bringing on the end of the world. The author thinks that if one of the old "threatening prophets" were then alive, he would give "something like the following." I quote a few sentences of the notion which the author had of the way in which Ezekiel, for instance, would have addressed his Maker in the reign of George the First:

"Begin! Begin! O Sovereign, for once, with an {135} effectual clap of thunder.... O Deity! either thunder to us no more, or when you thunder, do it home, and strike with vengeance to the mark.... 'Tis not enough to raise a storm, unless you follow it with a blow, and the thunder without the bolt, signifies just nothing at all.... Are then your lightnings of so short a sight, that they don't know how to hit, unless a mountain stands like a barrier in their way? Or perhaps so many eyes open in the firmament make you lose your aim when you shoot the arrow? Is it this? No! but, my dear Lord, it is your custom never to take hold of your arms till you have first bound round your majestic countenance with gathered mists and clouds."

The principles of the Philosophy of the Expansive and Contractive Forces ... By Robert Greene,[279] M.A., Fellow of Clare Hall. Cambridge, 1727, folio.

Sanderson[280] writes to Jones,[281] "The gentleman has been reputed mad for these two years last past, but never gave the world such ample testimony of it before." This was said of a former work of Greene's, on solid geometry, published in 1712, in which he gives a quadrature.[282] He gives the same or another, I do not know which, in the present work, in which the circle is 3-1/5 diameters. This volume is of 981 good folio pages, and treats of all things, mental and material. The author is not at all mad, only wrong on {136} many points. It is the weakness of the orthodox follower of any received system to impute insanity to the solitary dissentient: which is voted (in due time) a very wrong opinion about Copernicus, Columbus, or Galileo, but quite right about Robert Greene. If misconceptions, acted on by too much self-opinion, be sufficient evidence of madness, it would be a curious inquiry what is the least per-centage of the reigning school which has been insane at any one time. Greene is one of the sources for Newton being led to think of gravitation by the fall of an apple: his authority is the gossip of Martin Folkes.[283] Probably Folkes had it from Newton's niece, Mrs. Conduitt, whom Voltaire acknowledges as his authority.[284] It is in the draft found among Conduitt's papers of memoranda to be sent to Fontenelle. But Fontenelle, though a great retailer of anecdote, does not mention it in his éloge of Newton; whence it may be suspected that it was left out in the copy forwarded to France. D'Israeli has got an improvement on the story: the apple "struck him a smart blow on the head": no doubt taking him just on the organ of causality. He was "surprised at the force of the stroke" from so small an apple: but then the apple had a mission; Homer would have said {137} it was Minerva in the form of an apple. "This led him to consider the accelerating motion of falling bodies," which Galileo had settled long before: "from whence he deduced the principle of gravity," which many had considered before him, but no one had deduced anything from it. I cannot imagine whence D'Israeli got the rap on the head, I mean got it for Newton: this is very unlike his usual accounts of things. The story is pleasant and possible: its only defect is that various writings, well known to Newton, a very learned mathematician, had given more suggestion than a whole sack of apples could have done, if they had tumbled on that mighty head all at once. And Pemberton, speaking from Newton himself, says nothing more than that the idea of the moon being retained by the same force which causes the fall of bodies struck him for the first time while meditating in a garden. One particular tree at Woolsthorpe has been selected as the gallows of the appleshaped goddess: it died in 1820, and Mr. Turnor[285] kept the wood; but Sir D. Brewster[286] brought away a bit of root in 1814, and must have had it on his conscience for 43 years that he may have killed the tree.

Kepler's suggestion of gravitation with the inverse distance, and Bouillaud's proposed substitution of the inverse square of the distance, are things which Newton knew better than his modern readers. I discovered two anagrams on his name, which are quite conclusive; the notion of gravitation was not new; but Newton went on. Some wandering spirit, probably whose business it was to resent any liberty taken with Newton's name, put into the head of a friend of mine eighty-one anagrams on my own pair, some of which hit harder than any apple.

{138}

DE MORGAN ANAGRAMS

This friend, whom I must not name, has since made it up to about 800 anagrams on my name, of which I have seen about 650. Two of them I have joined in the title-page: the reader may find the sense. A few of the others are personal remarks.

"Great gun! do us a sum!"

is a sneer at my pursuits: but,

"Go! great sum! [Integral]a u^{n} du" is more dignified.
"Sunt agro! gaudemus,"[287]

is happy as applied to one of whom it may be said:

"Ne'er out of town; 'tis such a horrid life; But duly sends his family and wife."

"Adsum, nugator, suge!"[288] is addressed to a student who continues talking after the lecture has commenced: oh! the rascal!

"Graduatus sum! nego"[289] applies to one who declined to subscribe for an M.A. degree. "Usage mounts guard" symbolizes a person of very fixed habits.

"Gus! Gus! a mature don! August man! sure, god! And Gus must argue, O! Snug as mud to argue, Must argue on gauds. A mad rogue stung us. Gag a numerous stud Go! turn us! damage us! Tug us! O drag us! Amen. Grudge us! moan at us! {139} Daunt us! gag us more! Dog-ear us, man! gut us! D---- us! a rogue tugs!" are addressed to me by the circle-squarers; and, "O! Gus! tug a mean surd!" is smart upon my preference of an incommensurable value of [pi] to 3-1/5, or some such simple substitute. While, "Gus! Gus! at 'em a' round!" ought to be the backing of the scientific world to the author of the Budget of Paradoxes.

The whole collection commenced existence in the head of a powerful mathematician during some sleepless nights. Seeing how large a number was practicable, he amused himself by inventing a digested plan of finding more.

Is there any one whose name cannot be twisted into either praise or satire? I have had given to me,

"Thomas Babington Macaulay Mouths big: a Cantab anomaly."

NEWTON'S DE MUNDI SYSTEMATE LIBER

A treatise of the system of the world. By Sir Isaac Newton. Translated into English. London, 1728, 8vo.

I think I have a right to one little paradox of my own: I greatly doubt that Newton wrote this book. Castiglione,[290] in his Newtoni Opuscula,[291] gives it in the Latin which appeared in 1731,[292] not for the first time; he says Angli omnes Newtono tribuunt.[293] It appeared just after Newton's death, without the name of any editor, or any allusion to Newton's {140} recent departure, purporting to be that popular treatise which Newton, at the beginning of the third book of the Principia, says he wrote, intending it to be the third book. It is very possible that some observant turnpenny might construct such a treatise as this from the third book, that it might be ready for publication the moment Newton could not disown it. It has been treated with singular silence: the name of the editor has never been given.

Rigaud[294] mentions it without a word: I cannot find it in Brewster's Newton, nor in the Biographia Britannica. There is no copy in the Catalogue of the Royal Society's Library, either in English or Latin, except in Castiglione. I am open to correction; but I think nothing from Newton's acknowledged works will prove--as laid down in the suspected work--that he took Numa's temple of Vesta, with a central fire, to be intended to symbolize the sun as the center of our system, in the Copernican sense.[295]

Mr. Edleston[296] gives an account of the lectures "de motu corporum," and gives the corresponding pages of the Latin "De Systemate Mundi" of 1731. But no one mentions the English of 1728. This English seems to agree with the Latin; but there is a mystery about it. The preface says, "That this work as here published is genuine will so clearly appear by the intrinsic marks it bears, that it will be but losing words and the reader's time to take pains in giving him any other satisfaction." Surely fewer words would have been lost if the prefator had said at once that the work was from the manuscript preserved at Cambridge. Perhaps it was a mangled copy clandestinely taken and interpreted. {141}

A BACONIAN CONTROVERSY

Lord Bacon not the author of "The Christian Paradoxes," being a reprint of "Memorials of Godliness and Christianity," by Herbert Palmer, B.D.[297] With Introduction, Memoir, and Notes, by the Rev. Alexander B. Grosart,[298] Kenross. (Private circulation, 1864).

I insert the above in this place on account of a slight connection with the last. Bacon's Paradoxes,--so attributed--were first published as his in some asserted "Remains," 1648.[299] They were admitted into his works in 1730, and remain there to this day. The title is "The Character of a believing Christian, set forth in paradoxes and seeming contradictions." The following is a specimen:

"He believes three to be one and one to be three; a father not to be older than his son; a son to be equal with his father; and one proceeding from both to be equal with both: he believes three persons in one nature, and two natures in one person.... He believes the God of all grace to have been angry with one that never offended Him; and that God that hates sin to be reconciled to himself though sinning continually, and never making or being able to make Him any satisfaction. He believes a most just God to have punished a most just person, and to have justified himself, though a most ungodly sinner. He believes himself freely pardoned, and yet a sufficient satisfaction was made for him."

Who can doubt that if Bacon had written this it must have been wrong? Many writers, especially on the {142} Continent, have taken him as sneering at (Athanasian) Christianity right and left. Many Englishmen have taken him to be quite in earnest, and to have produced a body of edifying doctrine. More than a century ago the Paradoxes were published as a penny tract; and, again, at the same price, in the Penny Sunday Reader, vol. vi, No. 148, a few passages were omitted, as too strong. But all did not agree: in my copy of Peter Shaw's [300] edition (vol. ii, p. 283) the Paradoxes have been cut out by the binder, who has left the backs of the leaves. I never had the curiosity to see whether other copies of the edition have been served in the same way. The Religious Tract Society republished them recently in Selections from the Writings of Lord Bacon, (no date; bad plan; about 1863, I suppose). No omissions were made, so far as I find.

I never believed that Bacon wrote this paper; it has neither his sparkle nor his idiom. I stated my doubts even before I heard that Mr. Spedding, one of Bacon's editors, was of the same mind. (Athenæum, July 16, 1864). I was little moved by the wide consent of orthodox men: for I knew how Bacon, Milton, Newton, Locke, etc., were always claimed as orthodox until almost the present day. Of this there is a remarkable instance.

LOCKE AND SOCINIANISM

Among the books which in my younger day were in some orthodox publication lists--I think in the list of the Christian Knowledge Society, but I am not sure--was Locke's [301] "Reasonableness of Christianity." It seems to have come down from the eighteenth century, when the battle was belief in Christ against unbelief, simpliciter, as the {143} logicians say.

Now, if ever there was a Socinian[302] book in the world, it is this work of Locke. "These two," says Locke, "faith and repentance, i.e., believing Jesus to be the Messiah, and a good life, are the indispensable conditions of the new covenant, to be performed by all those who would obtain eternal life." All the book is amplification of this doctrine. Locke, in this and many other things, followed Hobbes, whose doctrine, in the Leviathan, is fidem, quanta ad salutem necessaria est, contineri in hoc articulo, Jesus est Christus.[303] For this Hobbes was called an atheist, which {144} many still believe him to have been: some of his contemporaries called him, rightly, a Socinian. Locke was known for a Socinian as soon as his work appeared: Dr. John Edwards,[304] his assailant, says he is "Socinianized all over." Locke, in his reply, says "there is not one word of Socinianism in it:" and he was right: the positive Socinian doctrine has not one word of Socinianism in it; Socinianism consists in omissions. Locke and Hobbes did not dare deny the Trinity: for such a thing Hobbes might have been roasted, and Locke might have been strangled. Accordingly, the well-known way of teaching Unitarian doctrine was the collection of the asserted essentials of Christianity, without naming the Trinity, etc. This is the plan Newton followed, in the papers which have at last been published.[305]

So I, for one, thought little about the general tendency of orthodox writers to claim Bacon by means of the Paradoxes. I knew that, in his "Confession of Faith"[306] he is a Trinitarian of a heterodox stamp. His second Person takes human nature before he took flesh, not for redemption, but as a condition precedent of creation. "God is so holy, pure, and jealous, that it is impossible for him to be pleased in any creature, though the work of his own hands.... [Gen. i. 10, 12, 18, 21, 25, 31, freely rendered].

But--purposing to become a Creator, and to communicate to his creatures, he ordained in his eternal counsel that one person of the Godhead should be united to one nature, and to one particular of his creatures; that so, in the person of the Mediator, the true ladder might be fixed, whereby God might {145} descend to his creatures and his creatures might ascend to God...."

This is republished by the Religious Tract Society, and seems to suit their theology, for they confess to having omitted some things of which they disapprove.

In 1864, Mr. Grosart published his discovery that the Paradoxes are by Herbert Palmer; that they were first published surreptitiously, and immediately afterwards by himself, both in 1645; that the "Remains" of Bacon did not appear until 1648; that from 1645 to 1708, thirteen editions of the "Memorials" were published, all containing the Paradoxes. In spite of this, the Paradoxes were introduced into Bacon's works in 1730, where they have remained.

Herbert Palmer was of good descent, and educated as a Puritan. He was an accomplished man, one of the few of his day who could speak French as well as English. He went into the Church, and was beneficed by Laud,[307] in spite of his puritanism; he sat in the Assembly of Divines, and was finally President of Queens' College, Cambridge, in which post he died, August 13, 1647, in the 46th year of his age.

Mr. Grosart says, speaking of Bacon's "Remains," "All who have had occasion to examine our early literature are aware that it was a common trick to issue imperfect, false, and unauthorized writings under any recently deceased name that might be expected to take. The Puritans, down to John Bunyan, were perpetually expostulating and protesting against such procedure." I have met with instances of all this; but I did not know that there was so much of it: a good collection would be very useful. The work of 1728, attributed to Newton, is likely enough to be one of the class.

{146}

Demonstration de l'immobilitez de la Terre.... Par M. de la Jonchere,[308] Ingénieur Français. Londres, 1728, 8vo.

A synopsis which is of a line of argument belonging to the beginning of the preceding century.

TWO FORGOTTEN CIRCLE SQUARERS

The Circle squared; together with the Ellipsis and several reflections on it. The finding two geometrical mean proportionals, or doubling the cube geometrically. By Richard Locke[309].... London, no date, probably about 1730, 8vo.

According to Mr. Locke, the circumference is three diameters, three-fourths the difference of the diameter and the side of the inscribed equilateral triangle, and three-fourths the difference between seven-eighths of the diameter and the side of the same triangle. This gives, he says, 3.18897.

There is an addition to this tract, being an appendix to a book on the longitude.

The Circle squar'd. By Thos. Baxter, Crathorn, Cleaveland, Yorkshire. London, 1732, 8vo.

Here [pi] = 3.0625. No proof is offered.[310]

The longitude discovered by the Eclipses, Occultations, and Conjunctions of Jupiter's planets. By William Whiston. London, 1738.

This tract has, in some copies, the celebrated preface containing the account of Newton's appearance before the Parliamentary Committee on the longitude question, in 1714 {147} (Brewster, ii. 257-266). This "historical preface," is an insertion and is dated April 28, 1741, with four additional pages dated August 10, 1741. The short "preface" is by the publisher, John Whiston,[311] the author's son.

THE STEAMSHIP SUGGESTED

A description and draught of a new-invented machine for carrying vessels or ships out of, or into any harbour, port, or river, against wind and tide, or in a calm. For which, His Majesty has granted letters patent, for the sole benefit of the author, for the space of fourteen years. By Jonathan Hulls.[312] London: printed for the author, 1737. Price sixpence (folding plate and pp. 48, beginning from title).

(I ought to have entered this tract in its place. It is so rare that its existence was once doubted. It is the earliest description of steam-power applied to navigation. The plate shows a barge, with smoking funnel, and paddles at the stem, towing a ship of war. The engine, as described, is Newcomen's.[313]

In 1855, John Sheepshanks,[314] so well known as a friend of Art and a public donor, reprinted this tract, in fac-simile, from his own copy; twenty-seven copies of the original 12mo size, and twelve on old paper, small 4to. I have an original copy, wanting the plate, and with "Price sixpence" carefully erased, to the honor of the book.[315]

{148}

It is not known whether Hulls actually constructed a boat.[316] In all probability his tract suggested to Symington, as Symington[317] did to Fulton.)

THE NEWTONIANS ATTACKED

Le vrai système de physique générale de M. Isaac Newton exposé et analysé en parallèle avec celui de Descartes. By Louis Castel[318] [Jesuit and F.R.S.] Paris, 1743, 4to.

This is an elaborate correction of Newton's followers, and of Newton himself, who it seems did not give his own views with perfect fidelity. Father Castel, for instance, assures us that Newton placed the sun at rest in the center of the system. Newton left the sun to arrange that matter with the planets and the rest of the universe. In this volume of 500 pages there is right and wrong, both clever.

A dissertation on the Æther of Sir Isaac Newton. By Bryan Robinson,[319] M.D. Dublin, 1743, 8vo.[320]

{149}

A mathematical work professing to prove that the assumed ether causes gravitation.

MATHEMATICAL THEOLOGY

Mathematical principles of theology, or the existence of God geometrically demonstrated. By Richard Jack, teacher of Mathematics. London, 1747, 8vo.[321]

Propositions arranged after the manner of Euclid, with beings represented by circles and squares. But these circles and squares are logical symbols, not geometrical ones. I brought this book forward to the Royal Commission on the British Museum as an instance of the absurdity of attempting a classed catalogue from the titles of books. The title of this book sends it either to theology or geometry: when, in fact, it is a logical vagary. Some of the houses which Jack built were destroyed by the fortune of war in 1745, at Edinburgh: who will say the rebels did no good whatever? I suspect that Jack copied the ideas of J.B. Morinus, "Quod Deus sit," Paris, 1636,[322] 4to, containing an attempt of the same kind, but not stultified with diagrams.

TWO MODEL INDORSEMENTS

Dissertation, découverte, et démonstrations de la quadrature mathématique du cercle. Par M. de Fauré, géomètre. [s. l., probably Geneva] 1747, 8vo.

Analyse de la Quadrature du Cercle. Par M. de Fauré, Gentilhomme Suisse. Hague, 1749,[323] 4to.

According to this octavo geometer and quarto gentleman, a diameter of 81 gives a circumference of 256. There is an amusing circumstance about the quarto which has been overlooked, if indeed the book has ever been {150} examined. John Bernoulli (the one of the day)[324] and Koenig[325] have both given an attestation: my mathematical readers may stare as they please, such is the fact. But, on examination, there will be reason to think the two sly Swiss played their countryman the same trick as the medical man played Miss Pickle, in the novel of that name. The lady only wanted to get his authority against sousing her little nephew, and said, "Pray, doctor, is it not both dangerous and cruel to be the means of letting a poor tender infant perish by sousing it in water as cold as ice?"--"Downright murder, I affirm," said the doctor; and certified accordingly. De Fauré had built a tremendous scaffolding of equations, quite out of place, and feeling cock-sure that his solutions, if correct, would square the circle, applied to Bernoulli and Koenig--who after his tract of two years before, must have known what he was at--for their approbation of the solutions. And he got it, as follows, well guarded:

"Suivant les suppositions posées dans ce Mémoire, il est si évident que t doit être = 34, y = 1, et z = 1, que cela n'a besoin ni de preuve ni d'autorité pour être reconnu par tout le monde.[326]

"à Basle le 7e Mai 1749.

JEAN BERNOULLI."

"Je souscris au jugement de Mr. Bernoulli, en conséquence de ces suppositions.[327] "à la Haye le 21 Juin 1749. S. KOENIG."

On which de Fauré remarks with triumph--as I have no doubt it was intended he should do--"il conste clairement par ma présente Analyse et Démonstration, qu'ils y ont déja {151} reconnu et approuvé parfaitement que la quadrature du cercle est mathématiquement démontrée."[328] It should seem that it is easier to square the circle than to get round a mathematician.

An attempt to demonstrate that all the Phenomena in Nature may be explained by two simple active principles, Attraction and Repulsion, wherein the attraction of Cohesion, Gravity and Magnetism are shown to be one the same. By Gowin Knight. London, 1748, 4to.

Dr. Knight[329] was Mr. Panizzi's[330] archetype, the first Principal Librarian of the British Museum. He was celebrated for his magnetical experiments. This work was long neglected; but is now recognized as of remarkable resemblance to modern speculations.

THOMAS WRIGHT OF DURHAM

An original theory or Hypothesis of the Universe. By Thomas Wright[331] of Durham. London, 4to, 1750.

Wright is a speculator whose thoughts are now part of our current astronomy. He took that view--or most of it--of the milky way which afterwards suggested itself to William Herschel. I have given an account of him and his work in the Philosophical Magazine for April, 1848.

Wright was mathematical instrument maker to the King, {152} and kept a shop in Fleet Street. Is the celebrated business of Troughton & Simms, also in Fleet Street, a lineal descendant of that of Wright? It is likely enough, more likely that that--as I find him reported to have affirmed--Prester John was the descendant of Solomon and the Queen of Sheba. Having settled it thus, it struck me that I might apply to Mr. Simms, and he informs me that it is as I thought, the line of descent being Wright, Cole, John Troughton, Edward Troughton,[332] Troughton & Simms.[333]

BISHOP HORNE ON NEWTON

The theology and philosophy in Cicero's Somnium Scipionis explained. Or, a brief attempt to demonstrate, that the Newtonian system is perfectly agreeable to the notions of the wisest ancients: and that mathematical principles are the only sure ones. [By Bishop Horne,[334] at the age of nineteen.] London, 1751, 8vo.

This tract, which was not printed in the collected works, and is now excessively rare, is mentioned in Notes and Queries, 1st S., v, 490, 573; 2d S., ix, 15. The boyish satire on Newton is amusing. Speaking of old Benjamin Martin,[335] he goes on as follows:

{153}

"But the most elegant account of the matter [attraction] is by that hominiform animal, Mr. Benjamin Martin, who having attended Dr. Desaguliers'[336] fine, raree, gallanty shew for some years [Desaguliers was one of the first who gave public experimental lectures, before the saucy boy was born] in the capacity of a turnspit, has, it seems, taken it into his head to set up for a philosopher."

Thus is preserved the fact, unknown to his biographers, that Benj. Martin was an assistant to Desaguliers in his lectures. Hutton[337] says of him, that "he was well skilled in the whole circle of the mathematical and philosophical sciences, and wrote useful books on every one of them": this is quite true; and even at this day he is read by twenty where Horne is read by one; see the stalls, passim. All that I say of him, indeed my knowledge of the tract, is due to this contemptuous mention of a more durable man than himself. My assistant secretary at the Astronomical Society, the late Mr. Epps,[338] bought the copy at a stall because his eye was caught by the notice of "Old Ben Martin," of whom he was a great reader. Old Ben could not be a Fellow of the Royal Society, because he kept a shop: even though the shop sold nothing but philosophical instruments. Thomas Wright, similarly situated as to shop and goods, never was a Fellow. The Society of our day has greatly degenerated: those of the old time would be pleased, no doubt, that the glories of their day {154} should be commemorated. In the early days of the Society, there was a similar difficulty about Graunt, the author of the celebrated work on mortality. But their royal patron, "who never said a foolish thing," sent them a sharp message, and charged them if they found any more such tradesmen, they should "elect them without more ado."

Horne's first pamphlet was published when he was but twenty-one years old. Two years afterwards, being then a Fellow of his college, and having seen more of the world, he seems to have felt that his manner was a little too pert. He endeavored, it is said, to suppress his first tract: and copies are certainly of extreme rarity. He published the following as his maturer view:

A fair, candid, and impartial state of the case between Sir Isaac Newton and Mr. Hutchinson.[339] In which is shown how far a system of physics is capable of mathematical demonstration; how far Sir Isaac's, as such a system, has that demonstration; and consequently, what regard Mr. Hutchinson's claim may deserve to have paid to it. By George Horne, M.A. Oxford, 1753, 8vo.

It must be remembered that the successors of Newton were very apt to declare that Newton had demonstrated attraction as a physical cause: he had taken reasonable pains to show that he did not pretend to this. If any one had said to Newton, I hold that every particle of matter is a responsible being of vast intellect, ordered by the Creator to move as it would do if every other particle attracted it, and gifted with power to make its way in true accordance with that law, as easily as a lady picks her way across the street; what have you to say against it?--Newton must have replied, Sir! if you really undertake to maintain this as demonstrable, your soul had better borrow a little power {155} from the particles of which your body is made: if you merely ask me to refute it, I tell you that I neither can nor need do it; for whether attraction comes in this way or in any other, it comes, and that is all I have to do with it.

The reader should remember that the word attraction, as used by Newton and the best of his followers, only meant a drawing towards, without any implication as to the cause. Thus whether they said that matter attracts matter, or that young lady attracts young gentleman, they were using one word in one sense. Newton found that the law of the first is the inverse square of the distance: I am not aware that the law of the second has been discovered; if there be any chance, we shall see it at the year 1856 in this list.

In this point young Horne made a hit. He justly censures those who fixed upon Newton a more positive knowledge of what attraction is than he pretended to have. "He has owned over and over he did not know what he meant by it--it might be this, or it might be that, or it might be anything, or it might be nothing." With the exception of the nothing clause, this is true, though Newton might have answered Horne by "Thou hast said it."

(I thought everybody knew the meaning of "Thou hast said it": but I was mistaken. In three of the evangelists [Greek: Su legeis] is the answer to "Art thou a king?" The force of this answer, as always understood, is "That is your way of putting it." The Puritans, who lived in Bible phrases, so understood it: and Walter Scott, who caught all peculiarities of language with great effect, makes a marked instance, "Were you armed?--I was not--I went in my calling, as a preacher of God's word, to encourage them that drew the sword in His cause. In other words, to aid and abet the rebels, said the Duke. Thou hast spoken it, replied the prisoner.")

Again, Horne quotes Rowning[340] as follows:

{156}

"Mr. Rowning, pt. 2, p. 5 in a note, has a very pretty conceit upon this same subject of attraction, about every particle of a fluid being intrenched in three spheres of attraction and repulsion, one within another, 'the innermost of which (he says) is a sphere of repulsion, which keeps them from approaching into contact; the next, a sphere of attraction, diffused around this of repulsion, by which the particles are disposed to run together into drops; and the outermost of all, a sphere of repulsion, whereby they repel each other, when removed out of the attraction.' So that between the urgings, and solicitations, of one and t'other, a poor unhappy particle must ever be at his wit's end, not knowing which way to turn, or whom to obey first."

Rowning has here started the notion which Boscovich[341] afterwards developed.

I may add to what precedes that it cannot be settled that, as Granger[342] says, Desaguliers was the first who gave experimental lectures in London. William Whiston gave some, and Francis Hauksbee[343] made the experiments. The prospectus, as we should now call it, is extant, a quarto tract of plates and descriptions, without date. Whiston, in his life, {157} gives 1714 as the first date of publication, and therefore, no doubt, of the lectures. Desaguliers removed to London soon after 1712, and commenced his lectures soon after that. It will be rather a nice point to settle which lectured first; probabilities seem to go in favor of Whiston.

FALLACIES IN A THEORY OF ANNUITIES

An Essay to ascertain the value of leases, and annuities for years and lives. By W[eyman] L[ee]. London, 1737, 8vo.

A valuation of Annuities and Leases certain, for a single life. By Weyman Lee, Esq. of the Inner Temple. London, 1751, 8vo. Third edition, 1773.

Every branch of exact science has its paradoxer. The world at large cannot tell with certainty who is right in such questions as squaring the circle, etc. Mr. Weyman Lee[344] was the assailant of what all who had studied called demonstration in the question of annuities. He can be exposed to the world: for his error arose out of his not being able to see that the whole is the sum of all its parts.

By an annuity, say of £100, now bought, is meant that the buyer is to have for his money £100 in a year, if he be then alive, £100 at the end of two years, if then alive, and so on. It is clear that he would buy a life annuity if he should buy the first £100 in one office, the second in another, and so on. All the difference between buying the whole from one office and buying all the separate contingent payments at different offices, is immaterial to calculation. Mr. Lee would have agreed with the rest of the world about the payments to be made to the several different offices, in consideration of their several contracts: but he differed from every one else about the sum to be paid to one office. He contended that the way to value an annuity is to find out the term of years which the individual has an even chance of surviving, and to charge for the life annuity the value of an annuity certain for that term.

{158}

It is very common to say that Lee took the average life, or expectation, as it is wrongly called, for his term: and this I have done myself, taking the common story. Having exposed the absurdity of this second supposition, taking it for Lee's, in my Formal Logic,[345] I will now do the same with the first.

A mathematical truth is true in its extreme cases. Lee's principle is that an annuity on a life is the annuity made certain for the term within which it is an even chance the life drops. If, then, of a thousand persons, 500 be sure to die within a year, and the other 500 be immortal, Lee's price of an annuity to any one of these persons is the present value of one payment: for one year is the term which each one has an even chance of surviving and not surviving. But the true value is obviously half that of a perpetual annuity: so that at 5 percent Lee's rule would give less than the tenth of the true value. It must be said for the poor circle-squarers, that they never err so much as this.

Lee would have said, if alive, that I have put an extreme case: but any universal truth is true in its extreme cases. It is not fair to bring forward an extreme case against a person who is speaking as of usual occurrences: but it is quite fair when, as frequently happens, the proposer insists upon a perfectly general acceptance of his assertion. And yet many who go the whole hog protest against being tickled with the tail. Counsel in court are good instances: they are paradoxers by trade. June 13, 1849, at Hertford, there was an action about a ship, insured against a total loss: some planks were saved, and the underwriters refused to pay. Mr. Z. (for deft.) "There can be no degrees of totality; and some timbers were saved."--L. C. B. "Then if the vessel were burned to the water's edge, and some rope saved in the boat, there would be no total loss."--Mr. Z. "This is putting a very extreme case."--L. C. B. "The argument {159} would go that length." What would Judge Z.--as he now is--say to the extreme case beginning somewhere between six planks and a bit of rope?

MONTUCLA'S WORK ON THE QUADRATURE

Histoire des recherches sur la quadrature du cercle ... avec une addition concernant les problèmes de la duplication du cube et de la trisection de l'angle. Paris, 1754, 12mo. [By Montucla.]

This is the history of the subject.[346] It was a little episode to the great history of mathematics by Montucla, of which the first edition appeared in 1758. There was much addition at the end of the fourth volume of the second edition;

this is clearly by Montucla, though the bulk of the volume is put together, with help from Montucla's papers, by Lalande.[347] There is also a second edition of the history of the quadrature, Paris, 1831, 8vo, edited, I think, by Lacroix; of which it is the great fault that it makes hardly any use of the additional matter just mentioned.

Montucla is an admirable historian when he is writing from his own direct knowledge: it is a sad pity that he did not tell us when he was depending on others. We are not to trust a quarter of his book, and we must read many other books to know which quarter. The fault is common enough, but Montucla's good three-quarters is so good that the fault is greater in him than in most others: I mean the fault of not acknowledging; for an historian cannot read everything. But it must be said that mankind give little encouragement to candor on this point. Hallam, in his {160} History of Literature, states with his own usual instinct of honesty every case in which he depends upon others: Montucla does not. And what is the consequence?--Montucla is trusted, and believed in, and cried up in the bulk; while the smallest talker can lament that Hallam should be so unequal and apt to depend on others, without remembering to mention that Hallam himself gives the information. As to a universal history of any great subject being written entirely upon primary knowledge, it is a thing of which the possibility is not yet proved by an example. Delambre attempted it with astronomy, and was removed by death before it was finished,[348] to say nothing of the gaps he left.

Montucla was nothing of a bibliographer, and his descriptions of books in the first edition were insufficient. The Abbé Rive[349] fell foul of him, and as the phrase is, gave it him. Montucla took it with great good humor, tried to mend, and, in his second edition, wished his critic had lived to see the vernis de bibliographe which he had given himself.

I have seen Montucla set down as an esprit fort, more than once: wrongly, I think. When he mentions Barrow's[350] address to the Almighty, he adds, "On voit, au reste, par là, que Barrow étoit un pauvre philosophe; car il croyait en l'immortalité de l'âme, et en une Divinité autre que la nature {161} universelle."[351] This is irony, not an expression of opinion. In the book of mathematical recreations which Montucla constructed upon that of Ozanam,[352] and Ozanam upon that of Van Etten,[353] now best known in England by Hutton's similar treatment of Montucla, there is an amusing chapter on the quadrators. Montucla refers to his own anonymous book of 1754 as a curious book published by Jombert.[354] He seems to have been a little ashamed of writing about circle-squarers: what a slap on the face for an unborn Budgeteer!

Montucla says, speaking of France, that he finds three notions prevalent among the cyclometers: (1) that there is a large reward offered for success; (2) that the longitude problem depends on that success; (3) that the solution is the great end and object of geometry. The same three {162} notions are equally prevalent among the same class in England. No reward has ever been offered by the government of either country. The longitude problem in no way depends upon perfect solution; existing approximations are sufficient to a point of accuracy far beyond what can be wanted.[355] And geometry, content with what exists, has long passed on to other matters. Sometimes a cyclometer persuades a skipper who has made land in the wrong place that the astronomers are in fault, for using a wrong measure of the circle; and the skipper thinks it a very comfortable solution! And this is the utmost that the problem ever has to do with longitude.

ANTINEWTONIANISMUS

Antinewtonianismus.[356] By Cælestino Cominale,[357] M.D. Naples, 1754 and 1756, 2 vols. 4to.

The first volume upsets the theory of light; the second vacuum, vis inertiæ, gravitation, and attraction. I confess I never attempted these big Latin volumes, numbering 450 closely-printed quarto pages. The man who slays Newton in a pamphlet is the man for me. But I will lend them to anybody who will give security, himself in £500, and two sureties in £250 each, that he will read them through, and give a full abstract; and I will not exact security for their return. I have never seen any mention of this book: it has a printer, but not a publisher, as happens with so many unrecorded books.

{163}

OFFICIAL BLOW TO CIRCLE SQUARERS

1755. The French Academy of Sciences came to the determination not to examine any more quadratures or kindred problems. This was the consequence, no doubt, of the publication of Montucla's book: the time was well chosen; for that book was a full justification of the resolution. The Royal Society followed the same course, I believe, a few years afterwards. When our Board of Longitude was in existence, most of its time was consumed in listening to schemes, many of which included the quadrature of the circle. It is certain that many quadrators have imagined the longitude problem to be connected with theirs: and no doubt the notion of a reward offered by Government for a true quadrature is a result of the reward offered for the longitude. Let it also be noted that this longitude reward was not a premium upon excogitation of a mysterious difficulty. The legislature was made to know that the rational hopes of the problem were centered in the improvement of the lunar tables and the improvement of chronometers. To these objects alone, and by name, the offer was directed: several persons gained rewards for both; and the offer was finally repealed.

AN INTERESTING HOAX

Fundamentalis Figura Geometrica, primas tantum lineas circuli quadraturæ possibilitatis ostendens. By Niels Erichsen (Nicolaus Ericius), shipbuilder, of Copenhagen. Copenhagen, 1755, 12mo.

This was a gift from my oldest friend who was not a relative, Dr. Samuel Maitland of the "Dark Ages."[358] He found it among his books, and could not imagine how he came by it: I could have told him. He once collected interpretations of the Apocalypse: and auction lots of such {164} books often contain quadratures. The wonder is he never found more than one.

The quadrature is not worth notice. Erichsen is the only squarer I have met with who has distinctly asserted the particulars of that reward which has been so frequently thought to have been offered in England. He says that in 1747 the Royal Society on the 2d of June, offered to give a large reward for the quadrature of the circle and a true explanation of magnetism, in addition to £30,000 previously promised for the same. I need hardly say that the Royal Society had not £30,000 at that time, and would not, if it had had such a sum, have spent it on the circle, nor on magnetic theory; nor would it have coupled the two things. On this book, see Notes and Queries, 1st S., xii, 306. Perhaps Erichsen meant that the £30,000 had been promised by the Government, and the addition by the Royal Society.

October 8, 1866. I receive a letter from a cyclometer who understands that a reward is offered to any one who will square the circle, and that all competitors are to send their plans to me. The hoaxers have not yet failed out of the land.

TWO JESUIT CONTRIBUTIONS

Theoria Philosophiæ Naturalis redacta ad unicam legem virium in natura existentium. Editio Veneta prima. By Roger Joseph Boscovich. Venice, 1763, 4to.

The first edition is said to be of Vienna, 1758.[359] This is a celebrated work on the molecular theory of matter, grounded on the hypothesis of spheres of alternate attraction and repulsion. Boscovich was a Jesuit of varied pursuit. During his measurement of a degree of the meridian, while on horseback or waiting for his observations, he composed a Latin poem of about five thousand verses on eclipses, {165} with notes, which he dedicated to the Royal Society: De Solis et Lunæ defectibus,[360] London, Millar and Dodsley, 1760, 4to.

Traité de paix entre Des Cartes et Newton, précédé des vies littéraires de ces deux chefs de la physique moderne.... By Aimé Henri Paulian.[361] Avignon, 1763, 12mo.

I have had these books for many years without feeling the least desire to see how a lettered Jesuit would atone Descartes and Newton. On looking at my two volumes, I find that one contains nothing but the literary life of Descartes; the other nothing but the literary life of Newton. The preface indicates more: and Watt mentions three volumes.[362] I dare say the first two contain all that is valuable. On looking more attentively at the two volumes, I find them both readable and instructive; the account of Newton is far above that of Voltaire, but not so popular. But he should not have said that Newton's family came from Newton in Ireland. Sir Rowland Hill gives fourteen Newtons in Ireland;[363] twice the number of the cities that contended for the birth of Homer may now contend for the origin of Newton, on the word of Father Paulian.

Philosophical Essays, in three parts. By R. Lovett, Lay Clerk of the Cathedral Church of Worcester. Worcester, 1766, 8vo.

The Electrical Philosopher: containing a new system of physics {166} founded upon the principle of an universal Plenum of elementary fire.... By R. Lovett, Worcester, 1774, 8vo.

Mr. Lovett[364] was one of those ether philosophers who bring in elastic fluid as an explanation by imposition of words, without deducing any one phenomenon from what we know of it. And yet he says that attraction has received no support from geometry; though geometry, applied to a particular law of attraction, had shown how to predict the motions of the bodies of the solar system. He, and many of his stamp, have not the least idea of the confirmation of a theory by accordance of deduced results with observation posterior to the theory.

BAILLY'S EXAGGERATED VIEW OF ASTRONOMY

Lettres sur l'Atlantide de Platon, et sur l'ancien Histoire de l'Asie, pour servir de suite aux lettres sur l'origine des Sciences, adressées à M. de Voltaire, par M. Bailly.[365] London and Paris, 1779, 8vo.

I might enter here all Bailly's histories of astronomy.[366] The paradox which runs through them all more or less, is the doctrine that astronomy is of immense antiquity, coming from some forgotten source, probably the drowned island of Plato, peopled by a race whom Bailly makes, as has {167} been said, to teach us everything except their existence and their name. These books, the first scientific histories which belong to readable literature, made a great impression by power of style: Delambre created a strong reaction, of injurious amount, in favor of history founded on contemporary documents, which early astronomy cannot furnish. These letters are addressed to Voltaire, and continue the discussion. There is one letter of Voltaire, being the fourth, dated Feb. 27, 1777, and signed "le vieux malade de Ferney, V. puer centum annorum."[367] Then begin Bailly's letters, from January 16 to May 12, 1778. From some ambiguous expressions in the Preface, it would seem that these are fictitious letters, supposed to be addressed to Voltaire at their dates. Voltaire went to Paris February 10, 1778, and died there May 30. Nearly all this interval was his closing scene, and it is very unlikely that Bailly would have troubled him with these letters.[368]

An inquiry into the cause of motion, or a general theory of physics. By S. Miller. London, 1781, 4to

Newton all wrong: matter consists of two kinds of particles, one inert, the other elastic and capable of expanding themselves ad infinitum.

SAINT-MARTIN ON ERRORS AND TRUTH

Des Erreurs et de la Vérité, ou les hommes rappelés au principe universel de la science; ouvrage dans lequel, en faisant remarquer aux observateurs l'incertitude de leurs recherches, et leurs méprises continuelles, on leur indique la route qu'ils auroient dû suivre, pour acquérir l'évidence physique sur l'origine du bien et du mal, sur l'homme, sur la nature matérielle, et la nature sacrée; sur la base des gouvernements {168} politiques, sur l'autorité des souverains, sur la justice civile et criminelle, sur les sciences, les langues, et les arts. Par un Ph.... Inc.... A Edimbourg. 1782.[369] Two vols. 8vo.

This is the famous work of Louis Claude de Saint-Martin[370] (1743-1803), for whose other works, vagaries included, the reader must look elsewhere: among other things, he was a translator of Jacob Behmen.[371] The title promises much, and the writer has smart thoughts now and then; but the whole is the wearisome omniscience of the author's day and country, which no reader of our time can tolerate. Not that we dislike omniscience; but we have it of our own country, both home-made and imported; and fashions vary. But surely there can be but one omniscience? Must a man have but one wife? Nay, may not a man have a new wife while the old one is living? There was a famous instrumental professor forty years ago, who presented a friend to Madame ----. The friend started, and looked surprised; for, not many weeks before, he had been presented to another lady, with the same title, at Paris. The musician observed his surprise, and quietly said, "Celle-ci est Madame ---- de Londres." In like manner we have a London omniscience now current, which would make any one start who only knew the old French article.

The book was printed at Lyons, but it was a trick of French authors to pretend to be afraid of prosecution: it {169} made a book look wicked-like to have a feigned place of printing, and stimulated readers. A Government which had undergone Voltaire would never have drawn its sword upon quiet Saint-Martin. To make himself look still worse, he was only ph[ilosophe] Inc...., which is generally read Inconnu[372] but sometimes Incrédule; [373] most likely the ambiguity was intended. There is an awful paradox about the book, which explains, in part, its leaden sameness. It is all about l'homme, l'homme, l'homme,[374] except as much as treats of les hommes, les hommes, les hommes;[375] but not one single man is mentioned by name in its 500 pages. It reminds one of "Water, water everywhere, And not a drop to drink."

Not one opinion of any other man is referred to, in the way of agreement or of opposition. Not even a town is mentioned: there is nothing which brings a capital letter into the middle of a sentence, except, by the rarest accident, such a personification as Justice. A likely book to want an Edimbourg godfather!

Saint-Martin is great in mathematics. The number four essentially belongs to straight lines, and nine to curves. The object of a straight line is to perpetuate ad infinitum the production of a point from which it emanates. A circle [circle] bounds the production of all its radii, tends to destroy them, and is in some sort their enemy. How is it possible that things so distinct should not be distinguished in their number as well as in their action? If this important observation had been made earlier, immense trouble would have been saved to the mathematicians, who would have been prevented from searching for a common measure to lines which have nothing in common.

But, though all straight lines have the number four, it must not be supposed that they are all equal, for a line is the result of its law and {170} its number; but though both are the same for all lines of a sort, they act differently, as to force, energy, and duration, in different individuals; which explains all differences of length, etc. I congratulate the reader who understands this; and I do not pity the one who does not.

Saint-Martin and his works are now as completely forgotten as if they had never been born, except so far as this, that some one may take up one of the works as of heretical character, and lay it down in disappointment, with the reflection that it is as dull as orthodoxy. For a person who was once in some vogue, it would be difficult to pick out a more fossil writer, from Aa to Zypoeus, except,--though it is unusual for (,--) to represent an interval of more than a year--his unknown opponent. This opponent, in the very year of the Des Erreurs ... published a book in two parts with the same fictitious place of printing;

Tableau Naturel des Rapports qui existent entre Dieu, l'Homme, et l'Univers. A Edimbourg, 1782, 8vo.[376]

There is a motto from the Des Erreurs itself, "Expliquer les choses par l'homme, et non l'homme par les choses. Des Erreurs et de la Vérité, par un PH.... INC...., p. 9."[377] This work is set down in various catalogues and biographies as written by the PH.... INC.... himself. But it is not usual for a writer to publish two works in the same year, one of which takes a motto from the other. And the second work is profuse in capitals and italics, and uses Hebrew learning: its style differs much from the first work. The first work sets out from man, and has nothing to do with God: the second is religious and raps the knuckles of the first as follows: "Si nous voulons nous préserver de toutes {171} les illusions, et surtout des amorces de l'orgueil par lesquelles l'homme est si souvent séduit, ne prenons jamais les hommes, mais toujours Dieu pour notre terme de comparaison."[378] The first uses four and nine in various ways, of which I have quoted one: the second says, "Et ici se trouve déjà une explication des nombres quatre et neuf, qui ont peu embarrassé dans l'ouvrage déjà cité. L'homme s'est égaré en allant de quatre à neuf...."[379] The work cited is the Erreurs, etc., and the citation is in the motto, which is the text of the opposition sermon.

A FORERUNNER OF THE METRIC SYSTEM.

Method to discover the difference of the earth's diameters; proving its true ratio to be not less variable than as 45 is to 46, and shortest in its pole's axis 174 miles.... likewise a method for fixing an universal standard for weights and measures. By Thomas Williams.[380] London, 1788, 8vo.

Mr. Williams was a paradoxer in his day, and proposed what was, no doubt, laughed at by some. He proposed the sort of plan which the French--independently of course--carried into effect a few years after. He would have the 52d degree of latitude divided into 100,000 parts and each part a geographical yard. The geographical ton was to be the cube of a geographical yard filled with sea-water taken some leagues from land. All multiples and sub-divisions were to be decimal.

I was beginning to look up those who had made similar proposals, when a learned article on the proposal of a {172} metrical system came under my eye in the Times of Sept. 15, 1863. The author cites Mouton,[381] who would have the minute of a degree divided into 10,000 virgulæ; James Cassini,[382] whose foot was to be six thousandths of a minute; and Paucton,[383] whose foot was the 400,000th of a degree. I have verified the first and third statements; surely the second ought to be the six-thousandth.

An inquiry into the Copernican system ... wherein it is proved, in the clearest manner, that the earth has only her diurnal motion ... with an attempt to point out the only true way whereby mankind can receive any real benefit from the study of the heavenly bodies. By John Cunningham.[384] London, 1789, 8vo.

The "true way" appears to be the treatment of heaven and earth as emblematical of the Trinity.

Cosmology. An inquiry into the cause of what is called gravitation or attraction, in which the motions of the heavenly bodies, and the preservation and operations of all nature, are deduced from an universal principle of efflux and reflux. By T. Vivian,[385] vicar of Cornwood, Devon. Bath, 1792, 12mo.

{173}

Attraction, an influx of matter to the sun; centrifugal force, the solar rays; cohesion, the pressure of the atmosphere. The confusion about centrifugal force, so called, as demanding an external agent, is very common.

THOMAS PAINE'S RIGHTS OF MAN

The rights of MAN, being an answer to Mr. Burke's attack on the French Revolution.[386] By Thomas Paine.[387] In two parts. 1791-1792. 8vo. (Various editions.)[388]

A vindication of the rights of WOMAN, with strictures on political and moral subjects. By Mary Wollstonecraft.[389] 1792. 8vo.

A sketch of the rights of BOYS and GIRLS. By Launcelot Light, of Westminster School; and Lætitia Lookabout, of Queen's Square, Bloomsbury. [By the Rev. Samuel Parr,[390] LL.D.] 1792. 8vo. (pp.64).

When did we three meet before? The first work has sunk into oblivion: had it merited its title, it might have {174} lived. It is what the French call a pièce de circonstance; it belongs in time to the French Revolution, and in matter to Burke's opinion of that movement. Those who only know its name think it was really an attempt to write a philosophical treatise on what we now call socialism. Silly government prosecutions gave it what it never could have got for itself.

Mary Wollstonecraft seldom has her name spelled right. I suppose the O! O! character she got made her Woolstonecraft. Watt gives double insinuation, for his cross-reference sends us to Goodwin.[391] No doubt the title of the book was an act of discipleship to Paine's Rights of Man; but this title is very badly chosen. The book was marred by it, especially when the authoress and her husband assumed the right of dispensing with legal sanction until the approach of offspring brought them to a sense of their child's interest.[392] Not a hint of such a claim is found in the book, which is mostly about female education. The right claimed for woman is to have the education of a rational human being, and not to be considered as nothing but woman throughout youthful training. The maxims of Mary Wollstonecraft are now, though not derived from her, largely followed in the education of girls, especially in home education: just as many of the political principles of Tom Paine, again not derived from him, are the guides of our actual legislation. I remember, forty years ago, an old lady used to declare that she disliked girls from the age of sixteen to five-and-twenty. "They are full," said she, "of femalities." She spoke of their behavior to women as well as to men. She {175} would have been shocked to know that she was a follower of Mary Wollstonecraft, and had packed half her book into one sentence.

The third work is a satirical attack on Mary Wollstonecraft and Tom Paine. The details of the attack would convince any one that neither has anything which would now excite reprobation. It is utterly unworthy of Dr. Parr, and has quite disappeared from lists of his works, if it were ever there. That it was written by him I take to be evident, as follows. Nichols,[393] who could not fail to know, says (Anecd., vol. ix, p. 120): "This is a playful essay by a first-rate scholar, who is elsewhere noticed in this volume, but whose name I shall not bring forward on so trifling an occasion." Who the scholar was is made obvious by Master Launcelot being made to talk of Bellendenus.[394] Further, the same boy is made to say, "Let Dr. Parr lay his hand upon his heart, if his conscience will let him, and ask himself how many thousands of wagon-loads of this article [birch] he has cruelly misapplied." How could this apply to Parr, with his handful of private pupils,[395] and no reputation for severity? Any one except himself would have called on the head-master of Westminster or Eton. I doubt whether the name of Parr could be connected with the rod by anything in print, except the above and an anecdote of his pupil, Tom Sheridan.[396] The Doctor had dressed for a dinner visit, and {176} was ready a quarter of an hour too soon to set off. "Tom," said he, "I think I had better whip you now; you are sure to do something while I am out."--"I wish you would, sir!" said the boy; "it would be a letter of licence for the whole evening." The Doctor saw the force of the retort: my two tutelaries will see it by this time. They paid in advance; and I have given liberal interpretation to the order.

The following story of Dr. Parr was told me and others, about 1829, by the late Leonard Horner,[397] who knew him intimately. Parr was staying in a house full of company, I think in the north of England. Some gentlemen from America were among the guests, and after dinner they disputed some of Parr's assertions or arguments. So the Doctor broke out with "Do you know what country you come from? You come from the place to which we used to send our thieves!" This made the host angry, and he gave Parr such a severe rebuke as sent him from the room in ill-humor. The rest walked on the lawn, amusing the Americans with sketches of the Doctor. There was a dark cloud overhead, and from that cloud presently came a voice which called Tham (Parr-lisp for Sam). The company were astonished for a moment, but thought the Doctor was calling his servant in the house, and that the apparent direction was an illusion arising out of inattention. But presently the sound was repeated, certainly from the cloud, "And nearer, clearer, deadlier than before."

There was now a little alarm: where could the Doctor have got to? They ran to his bedroom, and there they discovered a sufficient rather than satisfactory explanation. The Doctor had taken his pipe into his bedroom, and had seated himself, in sulky mood, upon the higher bar of a large and deep old-fashioned grate with a high mantelshelf. Here he had {177} tumbled backwards, and doubled himself up between the bars and the back of the grate. He was fixed tight, and when he called for help, he could only throw his voice up the chimney. The echo from the cloud was the warning which brought his friends to the rescue.

ATTACKS ON RELIGIOUS CUSTOMS

Days of political paradox were coming, at which we now stare. Cobbett[398] said, about 1830, in earnest, that in the country every man who did not take off his hat to the clergyman was suspected, and ran a fair chance of having something brought against him. I heard this assertion canvassed, when it was made, in a party of elderly persons. The Radicals backed it, the old Tories rather denied it, but in a way which satisfied me they ought to have denied it less if they could not deny it more. But it must be said that the Governments stopped far short of what their partisans would have had them do. All who know Robert Robinson's[399] very quiet assault on church-made festivals in his History and Mystery of Good Friday (1777)[400] will hear or remember with surprise that the British Critic pronounced it a direct, unprovoked, and malicious libel on the most {178} sacred institutions of the national Church. It was reprinted again and again: in 1811 it was in a cheap form at 6s. 6d. a hundred. When the Jacobin day came, the State was really in a fright: people thought twice before they published what would now be quite disregarded. I examined a quantity of letters addressed to George Dyer[401] (Charles Lamb's G.D.) and what between the autographs of Thelwall, Hardy, Horne Tooke, and all the rebels,[402] put together a packet which produced five guineas, or thereabouts, for the widow. Among them were the following verses, sent by the author--who would not put his name, even in a private letter, for fear of accidents--for consultation whether they could safely be sent to an editor: and they were not sent. The occasion was the public thanksgiving at St. Paul's for the naval victories, December 19, 1797.

"God bless me! what a thing! Have you heard that the King Goes to St. Paul's? {179} Good Lord! and when he's there, He'll roll his eyes in prayer, To make poor Johnny stare At this fine thing.

"No doubt the plan is wise To blind poor Johnny's eyes By this grand show; For should he once suppose That he's led by the nose, Down the whole fabric goes, Church, lords, and king.

"As he shouts Duncan's[403] praise, Mind how supplies they'll raise In wondrous haste. For while upon the sea We gain one victory, John still a dupe will be And taxes pay.

"Till from his little store Three-fourths or even more Goes to the Crown. Ah, John! you little think How fast we downward sink And touch the fatal brink At which we're slaves."

I would have indicted the author for not making his thirds and sevenths rhyme. As to the rhythm, it is not much better than what the French sang in the Calais theater when the Duke of Clarence[404] took over Louis XVIII in 1814.

"God save noble Clarence, Who brings our king to France; God save Clarence! He maintains the glory Of the British navy, etc., etc."

{180} Perhaps had this been published, the Government would have assailed it as a libel on the church service. They got into the way of defending themselves by making libels on the Church, of what were libels, if on anything, on the rulers of the State; until the celebrated trials of Hone settled the point for ever, and established that juries will not convict for one offence, even though it have been committed, when they know the prosecution is directed at another offence and another intent.

HONE'S FAMOUS TRIALS

The results of Hone's trials (William Hone, 1779-1842) are among the important constitutional victories of our century. He published parodies on the Creeds, the Lord's Prayer, the Catechism, etc., with intent to bring the Ministry into contempt: everybody knew that was his purpose. The Government indicted him for impious, profane, blasphemous intent, but not for seditious intent. They hoped to wear him out by proceeding day by day. December 18, 1817, they hid themselves under the Lord's Prayer, the Creed, and the Commandments; December 19, under the Litany; December 20, under the Athanasian Creed, an odd place for shelter when they could not find it in the previous places. Hone defended himself for six, seven, and eight hours on the several days: and the jury acquitted him in 15, 105, and 20 minutes. In the second trial the offense was laid both as profanity and as sedition, which seems to have made the jury hesitate. And they probably came to think that the second count was false pretence: but the length of their deliberation is a satisfactory addition to the value of the whole. In the first trial the Attorney-General (Shepherd) had the impudence to say that the libel had nothing of a political tendency about it, but was avowedly set off against the religion and worship of the Church of England. The whole {181} is political in every sentence; neither more nor less political than the following, which is part of the parody on the Catechism: "What is thy duty towards the Minister? My duty towards the Minister is, to trust him as much as I can; to honor him with all my words, with all my bows, with all my scrapes, and with all my cringes; to flatter him; to give him thanks; to give up my whole soul to him; to idolize his name, and obey his word, and serve him blindly all the days of his political life." And the parody on the Creed begins, "I believe in George, the Regent almighty, maker of new streets and Knights of the Bath." This is what the Attorney-General said had nothing of a political tendency about it. But this was on the first trial:

Hone was not known. The first day's trial was under Justice Abbott (afterwards C. J. Tenterden).[405] It was perfectly understood, when Chief Justice Ellenborough[406] appeared in Court on the second day, that he was very angry at the first result, and put his junior aside to try his own rougher dealing. But Hone tamed the lion. An eye-witness told me that when he implored of Hone not to detail his own father Bishop Law's[407] views on the Athanasian Creed, which humble petition Hone kindly granted, he held by the desk for support. And the same when--which is not reported--the Attorney-General appealed to the Court for protection against a {182} stinging attack which Hone made on the Bar: he held on, and said, "Mr. Attorney, what can I do!" I was a boy of twelve years old, but so strong was the feeling of exultation at the verdicts that boys at school were not prohibited from seeing the parodies, which would have been held at any other time quite unfit to meet their eyes. I was not able to comprehend all about the Lord Chief Justice until I read and heard again in after years. In the meantime, Joe Miller had given me the story of the leopard which was sent home on board a ship of war, and was in two days made as docile as a cat by the sailors.[408] "You have got that fellow well under," said an officer. "Lord bless your Honor!" said Jack, "if the Emperor of Marocky would send us a cock rhinoceros, we'd bring him to his bearings in no time!" When I came to the subject again, it pleased me to entertain the question whether, if the Emperor had sent a cock rhinoceros to preside on the third day in the King's Bench, Hone would have mastered him: I forget how I settled it. There grew up a story that Hone caused Lord Ellenborough's death, but this could not have been true. Lord Ellenborough resigned his seat in a few months, and died just a year after the trials; but sixty-eight years may have had more to do with it than his defeat.

A large subscription was raised for Hone, headed by the Duke of Bedford[409] for £105. Many of the leading anti-ministerialists joined: but there were many of the other side who avowed their disapprobation of the false pretense. Many could not venture their names. In the list I find: {183} A member of the House of Lords, an enemy to persecution, and especially to religious persecution employed for political purposes--No parodist, but an enemy to persecution--A juryman on the third day's trial--Ellen Borough--My name would ruin me--Oh! minions of Pitt--Oil for the Hone--The Ghosts of Jeffries[410] and Sir William Roy [Ghosts of Jeffries in abundance]--A conscientious Jury and a conscientious Attorney, £1 6s. 8d.--To Mr. Hone, for defending in his own person the freedom of the press, attacked for a political object, under the old pretense of supporting Religion--A cut at corruption--An Earldom for myself and a translation for my brother--One who disapproves of parodies, but abhors persecution--From a schoolboy who wishes Mr. Hone to have a very grand subscription--"For delicacy's sake forbear," and "Felix trembled"--"I will go myself to-morrow"--Judge Jeffries' works rebound in calf by Law--Keep us from Law, and from the Shepherd's paw--I must not give you my name, but God bless you!--As much like Judge Jeffries as the present times will permit--May Jeffries' fame and Jeffries' fate on every modern Jeffries wait--No parodist, but an admirer of the man who has proved the fallacy of the Lawyer's Law, that when a man is his own advocate he has a fool for his client--A Mussulman who thinks it would not be an impious libel to parody the Koran--May the suspenders of the Habeas Corpus Act be speedily suspended--Three times twelve for thrice-tried Hone, who cleared the cases himself alone, and won three heats by twelve to one, £1 16s.--A conscientious attorney, £1 6s. 8d.--Rev. T. B. Morris, rector of Shelfanger, who disapproves of the parodies, but abhors the making an affected zeal for religion the pretext for political persecution--A Lawyer opposed in principle to {184} Law--For the Hone that set the razor that shaved the rats--Rev. Dr. Samuel Parr, who most seriously disapproves of all parodies upon the hallowed language of Scripture and the contents of the Prayer-book, but acquits Mr. Hone of intentional impiety, admires his talents and fortitude, and applauds the good sense and integrity of his juries--Religion without hypocrisy, and Law without impartiality--O Law! O Law! O Law!

These are specimens of a great many allusive mottoes. The subscription was very large, and would have bought a handsome annuity, but Hone employed it in the bookselling trade, and did not thrive. His Everyday Book[411] and his Apocryphal New Testament,[412] are useful books. On an annuity he would have thriven as an antiquarian writer and collector. It is well that the attack upon the right to ridicule Ministers roused a dormant power which was equal to the occasion. Hone declared, on his honor, that he had never addressed a meeting in his life, nor spoken a word before more than twelve persons. Had he--which however could not then be done--employed counsel and had a guilty defense made for him, he would very likely have been convicted, and the work would have been left to be done by another. No question that the parodies disgusted all who reverenced Christianity, and who could not separate the serious and the ludicrous, and prevent their existence in combination.

My extracts, etc., are from the nineteenth, seventeenth, and sixteenth editions of the three trials, which seem to have been contemporaneous (all in 1818) as they are made up into one book, with additional title over all, and the motto "Thrice the brindled cat hath mew'd." They are published by Hone himself, who I should have said was a publisher {185} as well as was to be. And though the trials only ended Dec. 20, 1817, the preface attached to this common title is dated Jan. 23, 1818.[413]

The spirit which was roused against the false dealing of the Government, i.e., the pretense of prosecuting for impiety when all the world knew the real offense was, if anything, sedition--was not got up at the moment: there had been previous exhibitions of it. For example, in the spring of 1818 Mr. Russell, a little printer in Birmingham, was indicted for publishing the Political Litany[414] on which Hone was afterwards tried. He took his witnesses to the summer Warwick assizes, and was told that the indictment had been removed by certiorari into the King's Bench. He had notice of trial for the spring assizes at Warwick: he took his witnesses there, and the trial was postponed by the Crown. He then had notice for the summer assizes at Warwick; and so on. The policy seems to have been to wear out the obnoxious parties, either by delays or by heaping on trials. The Government was odious, and knew it could not get verdicts against ridicule, and could get verdicts against impiety. No difficulty was found in convicting the sellers of Paine's works, and the like. When Hone was held to bail it was seen that a crisis was at hand. All parties in politics furnished him with parodies in proof of religious persons having made instruments of them. The parodies by Addison and Luther were contributed by a Tory lawyer, who was afterwards a judge.

Hone had published, in 1817, tracts of purely political ridicule: Official Account of the Noble Lord's Bite,[415] Trial of the Dog for Biting the Noble Lord, etc. These were not touched. After the trials, it is manifest that Hone was {186} to be unassailed, do what he might. The Political House that Jack built, in 1819; The Man in the Moon, 1820; The Queen's Matrimonial Ladder, Non mi ricordo, The R--l Fowls, 1820; The Political Showman at Home, with plates by G. Cruickshank,[416] 1821 [he did all the plates]; The Spirit of Despotism, 1821--would have been legitimate marks for prosecution in previous years. The biting caricature of several of these works are remembered to this day. The Spirit of Despotism was a tract of 1795, of which a few copies had been privately circulated with great secrecy. Hone reprinted it, and prefixed the following address to "Robert Stewart, alias Lord Castlereagh"[417]: "It appears to me that if, unhappily, your counsels are allowed much longer to prevail in the Brunswick Cabinet, they will bring on a crisis, in which the king may be dethroned or the people enslaved. Experience has shown that the people will not be enslaved--the alternative is the affair of your employers." Hone might say this without notice.

In 1819 Mr. Murray[418] published Lord Byron's Don Juan,[419] and Hone followed it with Don John, or Don Juan Unmasked, a little account of what the publisher to the Admiralty was allowed to issue without prosecution. The parody on the Commandments was a case very much in point: and Hone makes a stinging allusion to the use of the "unutterable Name, with a profane levity unsurpassed by {187} any other two lines in the English language." The lines are "'Tis strange--the Hebrew noun which means 'I am,' The English always use to govern d----n."

Hone ends with: "Lord Byron's dedication of 'Don Juan' to Lord Castlereagh was suppressed by Mr. Murray from delicacy to Ministers. Q. Why did not Mr. Murray suppress Lord Byron's parody on the Ten Commandments? A. Because it contains nothing in ridicule of Ministers, and therefore nothing that they could suppose would lead to the displeasure of Almighty God."

The little matters on which I have dwelt will never appear in history from their political importance, except in a few words of result. As a mode of thought, silly evasions of all kinds belong to such a work as the present.

Ignorance, which seats itself in the chair of knowledge, is a mother of revolutions in politics, and of unread pamphlets in circle-squaring. From 1815 to 1830 the question of revolution or no revolution lurked in all our English discussions. The high classes must govern; the high classes shall not govern; and thereupon issue was to be joined. In 1828-33 the question came to issue; and it was, Revolution with or without civil war; choose.

The choice was wisely made; and the Reform Bill started a new system so well dovetailed into the old that the joinings are hardly visible. And now, in 1867, the thing is repeated with a marked subsidence of symptoms; and the party which has taken the place of the extinct Tories is carrying through Parliament a wider extension of the franchise than their opponents would have ventured. Napoleon used to say that a decided nose was a sign of power: on which it has been remarked that he had good reason to say so before the play was done. And so had our country; it was saved from a religious war, and from a civil war, by the power of that nose over its colleagues. {188}

THOMAS TAYLOR, THE PLATONIST

The Commentaries of Proclus.[420] Translated by Thomas Taylor.[421] London, 1792, 2 vols. 4to.[422]

The reputation of "the Platonist" begins to grow, and will continue to grow. The most authentic account is in the Penny Cyclopædia, written by one of the few persons who knew him well, and one of the fewer who possess all his works. At page lvi of the Introduction is Taylor's notion of the way to find the circumference. It is not geometrical, for it proceeds on the motion of a point: the words "on account of the simplicity of the impulsive motion, such a line must be either straight or circular" will suffice to show how Platonic it is. Taylor certainly professed a kind of heathenism. D'Israeli said, "Mr. T. Taylor, the Platonic philosopher and the modern Plethon,[423] consonant to that philosophy, professes polytheism." Taylor printed this in large type, in a page by itself after the dedication, without any disavowal. I have seen the following, Greek and translation both, in his handwriting: "[Greek: Pas agathos hêi agathos ethnikos; kai pas christianos hêi christianos kakos.] Every good man, so far as he is a good man, is a heathen; and every Christian, so far as he is a Christian, is a bad man." Whether Taylor had in his head the Christian of the New Testament, or whether he drew from those members of the "religious world" who make manifest the religious flesh and the religious devil, {189} cannot be decided by us, and perhaps was not known to himself. If a heathen, he was a virtuous one.

A NEW ERA IN FICTION

(1795.) This is the date of a very remarkable paradox. The religious world--to use a name claimed by a doctrinal sect--had long set its face against amusing literature, and all works of imagination. Bunyan, Milton, and a few others were irresistible; but a long face was pulled at every attempt to produce something readable for poor people and poor children. In 1795, a benevolent association began to circulate the works of a lady who had been herself a dramatist, and had nourished a pleasant vein of satire in the society of Garrick and his friends; all which is carefully suppressed in some biographies. Hannah More's[424] Cheap Repository Tracts,[425] which were bought by millions of copies, destroyed the vicious publications with which the hawkers deluged the country, by the simple process of furnishing the hawkers with something more saleable.

Dramatic fiction, in which the characters are drawn by themselves, was, at the middle of the last century, the monopoly of writers who required indecorum, such as Fielding and Smollett. All, or nearly all, which could be permitted to the young, was dry narrative, written by people who could not make their personages talk character; they all spoke {190} alike. The author of the Rambler[426] is ridiculed, because his young ladies talk Johnsonese; but the satirists forget that all the presentable novel-writers were equally incompetent; even the author of Zeluco (1789)[427] is the strongest possible case in point.

Dr. Moore,[428] the father of the hero of Corunna,[429] with good narrative power, some sly humor, and much observation of character, would have been, in our day, a writer of the Peacock[430] family.

Nevertheless, to one who is accustomed to our style of things, it is comic to read the dialogue of a jealous husband, a suspected wife, a faithless maid-servant, a tool of a nurse, a wrong-headed pomposity of a priest, and a sensible physician, all talking Dr. Moore through their masks. Certainly an Irish soldier does say "by Jasus," and a cockney footman "this here" and "that there"; and this and the like is all the painting of characters which is effected out of the mouths of the bearers by a narrator of great power. I suspect that some novelists repressed their power under a rule that a narrative should narrate, and that the dramatic should be confined to the drama.

I make no exception in favor of Miss Burney;[431] though she was the forerunner of a new era. Suppose a country {191} in which dress is always of one color; suppose an importer who brings in cargoes of blue stuff, red stuff, green stuff, etc., and exhibits dresses of these several colors, that person is the similitude of Miss Burney. It would be a delightful change from a universal dull brown, to see one person all red, another all blue, etc.; but the real inventor of pleasant dress would be the one who could mix his colors and keep down the bright and gaudy. Miss Burney's introduction was so charming, by contrast, that she nailed such men as Johnson, Burke, Garrick, etc., to her books. But when a person who has read them with keen pleasure in boyhood, as I did, comes back to them after a long period, during which he has made acquaintance with the great novelists of our century, three-quarters of the pleasure is replaced by wonder that he had not seen he was at a puppet-show, not at a drama. Take some labeled characters out of our humorists, let them be put together into one piece, to speak only as labeled: let there be a Dominie with nothing but "Prodigious!" a Dick Swiveller with nothing but adapted quotations; a Dr. Folliott with nothing but sneers at Lord Brougham;[432] and the whole will pack up into one of Miss Burney's novels.

Maria Edgeworth,[433] Sydney Owenson (Lady Morgan),[434] Jane Austen,[435] Walter Scott,[436] etc., are all of our century; as {192} are, I believe, all the Minerva Press novels, as they were called, which show some of the power in question. Perhaps dramatic talent found its best encouragement in the drama itself. But I cannot ascertain that any such power was directed at the multitude, whether educated or uneducated, with natural mixture of character, under the restraints of decorum, until the use of it by two religious writers of the school called "evangelical," Hannah More and Rowland Hill.[437] The Village Dialogues, though not equal to the Repository Tracts, are in many parts an approach, and perhaps a copy; there is frequently humorous satire, in that most effective form, self-display. They were published in 1800, and, partly at least, by the Religious Tract Society, the lineal successor of the Repository association, though knowing nothing about its predecessor. I think it right to add that Rowland Hill here mentioned is not the regenerator of the Post Office.[438] Some do not distinguish accurately; I have heard of more than one who took me to have had a logical controversy with a diplomatist who died some years before I was born.

THE RELIGIOUS TRACT SOCIETY

A few years ago, an attempt was made by myself and others to collect some information about the Cheap Repository (see Notes and Queries, 3d Series, vi. 241, 290, 353; Christian Observer, Dec. 1864, pp. 944-49). It appeared that after the Religious Tract Society had existed more than fifty years, a friend presented it with a copy of the original prospectus of the Repository, a thing the existence of which was not known. In this prospectus it is announced that from the plan "will be carefully excluded whatever is enthusiastic, absurd, or superstitious." The "evangelical" {193} party had, from the foundation of the Religious Tract Society, regretted that the Repository Tracts "did not contain a fuller statement of the great evangelical principles"; while in the prospectus it is also stated that "no cause of any particular party is intended to be served by it, but general Christianity will be promoted upon practical principles." This explains what has often been noticed, that the tracts contain a mild form of "evangelical" doctrine, free from that more fervid dogmatism which appears in the Village Dialogues; and such as H. More's friend, Bishop Porteus[439]--a great promoter of the scheme--might approve. The Religious Tract Society (in 1863) republished some of H. More's tracts, with alterations, additions, and omissions ad libitum. This is an improper way of dealing with the works of the dead; especially when the reprints are of popular works. A small type addition to the preface contains: "Some alterations and abridgements have been made to adapt them to the present times and the aim of the Religious Tract Society." I think every publicity ought to be given to the existence of such a practice; and I reprint what I said on the subject in Notes and Queries.

Alterations in works which the Society republishes are a necessary part of their plan, though such notes as they should judge to be corrective would be the best way of proceeding. But the fact of alteration should be very distinctly announced on the title of the work itself, not left to a little bit of small type at the end of the preface, in the place where trade advertisements, or directions to the binder, are often found. And the places in which alteration has been made should be pointed out, either by marks of omission, when omission is the alteration, or by putting the altered sentences in brackets, when change has been made. May any one alter the works of the dead at his own discretion? {194} We all know that readers in general will take each sentence to be that of the author whose name is on the title; so that a correcting republisher makes use of his author's name to teach his own variation. The tortuous logic of "the trade," which is content when "the world" is satisfied, is not easily answered, any more than an eel is easily caught; but the Religious Tract Society may be convinced [in the old sense] in a sentence. On which course would they feel most safe in giving their account to the God of truth? "In your own conscience, now?"

I have tracked out a good many of the variations made by the Religious Tract Society in the recently published volume of Repository Tracts. Most of them are doctrinal insertions or amplifications, to the matter of which Hannah More would not have objected--all that can be brought against them is the want of notice. But I have found two which the respect I have for the Religious Tract Society, in spite of much difference on various points, must not prevent my designating as paltry. In the story of Mary Wood, a kind-hearted clergyman converses with the poor girl who has ruined herself by lying. In the original, he "assisted her in the great work of repentance;" in the reprint it is to be shown in some detail how he did this. He is to begin by pointing out that "the heart is deceitful above all things and desperately wicked."

Now the clergyman's name is Heartwell: so to prevent his name from contradicting his doctrine, he is actually cut down to Harwell. Hannah Moore meant this good man for one of those described in Acts xv. 8, 9, and his name was appropriate.

Again, Mr. Flatterwell, in persuasion of Parley the porter to let him into the castle, declares that the worst he will do is to "play an innocent game of cards just to keep you awake, or sing a cheerful song with the maids." Oh fie! Miss Hannah More! and you a single lady too, and a contemporary of the virtuous Bowdler![440] Though Flatterwell be an {195} allegory of the devil, this is really too indecorous, even for him. Out with the three last words! and out it is.

The Society cuts a poor figure before a literary tribunal. Nothing was wanted except an admission that the remarks made by me were unanswerable, and this was immediately furnished by the Secretary (N. and Q., 3d S., vi. 290). In a reply of which six parts out of seven are a very amplified statement that the Society did not intend to reprint all Hannah More's tracts, the remaining seventh is as follows:

"I am not careful [perhaps this should be careful not] to notice Professor De Morgan's objections to the changes in 'Mary Wood' or 'Parley the Porter,' but would merely reiterate that the tracts were neither designed nor announced to be 'reprints' of the originals [design is only known to the designers; as to announcement, the title is "Tis all for the best, The Shepherd of Salisbury Plain, and other narratives by Hannah More']; and much less [this must be careful not; further removed from answer than not careful] can I occupy your space by a treatise on the Professor's question: 'May any one alter the works of the dead at his own discretion?'"

To which I say: Thanks for help!

I predict that Hannah More's Cheap Repository Tracts will somewhat resemble the Pilgrim's Progress in their fate. Written for the cottage, and long remaining in their original position, they will become classical works of their kind. Most assuredly this will happen if my assertion cannot be upset, namely, that they contain the first specimens of fiction addressed to the world at large, and widely circulated, in which dramatic--as distinguished from puppet--power is shown, and without indecorum.

{196}

According to some statements I have seen, but which I have not verified, other publishing bodies, such as the Christian Knowledge Society, have taken the same liberty with the names of the dead as the Religious Tract Society. If it be so, the impropriety is the work of the smaller spirits who have not been sufficiently overlooked. There must be an overwhelming majority in the higher councils to feel that, whenever altered works are published, the fact of alteration should be made as prominent as the name of the author. Everything short of this is suppression of truth, and will ultimately destroy the credit of the Society. Equally necessary is it that the alterations should be noted. When it comes to be known that the author before him is altered, he knows not where nor how nor by whom, the lowest reader will lose his interest.

A TRIBUTE TO WILLIAM FREND

The principles of Algebra. By William Frend.[441] London, 1796, 8vo. Second Part, 1799.

This Algebra, says Dr. Peacock,[442] shows "great distrust {197} of the results of algebraical science which were in existence at the time when it was written." Truly it does; for, as Dr. Peacock had shown by full citation, it makes war of extermination upon all that distinguishes algebra from arithmetic. Robert Simson[443] and Baron Maseres[444] were Mr. Frend's predecessors in this opinion.

The genuine respect which I entertained for my father-in-law did not prevent my canvassing with perfect freedom his anti-algebraical and anti-Newtonian opinions, in a long obituary memoir read at the Astronomical Society in February 1842, which was written by me. It was copied into the Athenæum of March 19. It must be said that if the manner in which algebra was presented to the learner had been true algebra, he would have been right: and if he had confined himself to protesting against the imposition of attraction as a fundamental part of the existence of matter, he would have been in unity with a great many, including Newton himself. I wish he had preferred amendment to rejection when he was a college tutor: he wrote and spoke English with a clearness which is seldom equaled.

His anti-Newtonian discussions are confined to the preliminary chapters of his Evening Amusements,[445] a series of astronomical lessons in nineteen volumes, following the moon through a period of the golden numbers.

There is a mistake about him which can never be destroyed. It is constantly said that, at his celebrated trial in 1792, for sedition and opposition to the Liturgy, etc., he was expelled from the University. He was banished.

People cannot see the difference; but it made all the difference to {198} Mr. Frend. He held his fellowship and its profits till his marriage in 1808, and was a member of the University and of its Senate till his death in 1841, as any Cambridge Calendar up to 1841 will show. That they would have expelled him if they could, is perfectly true; and there is a funny story--also perfectly true--about their first proceedings being under a statute which would have given the power, had it not been discovered during the proceedings that the statute did not exist. It had come so near to existence as to be entered into the Vice-Chancellor's book for his signature, which it wanted, as was not seen till Mr. Frend exposed it: in fact, the statute had never actually passed.

There is an absurd mistake in Gunning's[446] Reminiscences of Cambridge. In quoting a passage of Mr. Frend's pamphlet, which was very obnoxious to the existing Government, it is printed that the poor market-women complained that they were to be scotched a quarter of their wages by taxation; and attention is called to the word by its being three times printed in italics. In the pamphlet it is "sconced"; that very common old word for fined or mulcted.

Lord Lyndhurst,[447] who has [1863] just passed away under a load of years and honors, was Mr. Frend's private pupil at Cambridge. At the time of the celebrated trial, he and two others amused themselves, and vented the feeling which was very strong among the undergraduates, by chalking the walls of Cambridge with "Frend for ever!" While thus engaged in what, using the term legally, we are probably to call his first publication, he and his friends were surprised by the proctors. Flight and chase followed of course: Copley and one of the others, Serjeant Rough,[448] escaped: the {199} third, whose name I forget, but who afterwards, I have been told was a bishop,[449] being lame, was captured and impositioned. Looking at the Cambridge Calendar to verify the fact that Copley was an undergraduate at the time, I find that there are but two other men in the list of honors of his year whose names are now widely remembered. And they were both celebrated schoolmasters; Butler[450] of Harrow, and Tate[451] of Richmond.

But Mr. Frend had another noted pupil. I once had a conversation with a very remarkable man, who was generally called "Place,[452] the tailor," but who was politician, political economist, etc., etc. He sat in the room above his shop--he was then a thriving master tailor at Charing Cross--surrounded by books enough for nine, to shame a proverb. The blue books alone, cut up into strips, would have measured Great Britain for oh-no-we-never-mention-'ems, the Highlands included. I cannot find a biography of this worthy and able man. I happened to mention William Frend, and he said, "Ah! my old master, as I always call him. Many and many a time, and year after year, did he come in every {200} now and then to give me instruction, while I was sitting on the board, working for my living, you know."

Place, who really was a sound economist, is joined with Cobbett, because they were together at one time, and because he was, in 1800, etc., a great Radical. But for Cobbett he had a great contempt. He told me the following story. He and others were advising with Cobbett about the defense he was to make on a trial for seditious libel which was coming on. Said Place, "You must put in the letters you have received from Ministers, members of the Commons from the Speaker downwards, etc., about your Register, and their wish to have subjects noted. You must then ask the jury whether a person so addressed must be considered as a common sower of sedition, etc. You will be acquitted; nay, if your intention should get about, very likely they will manage to stop proceedings." Cobbett was too much disturbed to listen; he walked about the room ejaculating "D---- the prison!" and the like. He had not the sense to follow the advice, and was convicted.

Cobbett, to go on with the chain, was a political acrobat, ready for any kind of posture. A friend of mine gave me several times an account of a mission to him. A Tory member--those who know the old Tory world may look for his initials in initials of two consecutive words of "Pay his money with interest"--who was, of course, a political opponent, thought Cobbett had been hardly used, and determined to subscribe handsomely towards the expenses he was incurring as a candidate. My friend was commissioned to hand over the money--a bag of sovereigns, that notes might not be traced.

He went into Cobbett's committee-room, told the patriot his errand, and put the money on the table. "And to whom, sir, am I indebted?" said Cobbett. "The donor," was the answer, "is Mr. Andrew Theophilus Smith," or some such unlikely pair of baptismals. "Ah!" said Cobbett, "I have known Mr. A. T. S. a long time! he was always a true friend of his country!" {201}

To return to Place. He is a noted instance of the advantage of our jury system, which never asks a man's politics, etc. The late King of Hanover, when Duke of Cumberland, being unpopular, was brought under unjust suspicions by the suicide of his valet: he must have seduced the wife and murdered the husband. The charges were as absurd as those brought against the Englishman in the Frenchman's attempt at satirical verses upon him:

"The Englishman is a very bad man; He drink the beer and he steal the can: He kiss the wife and he beat the man; And the Englishman is a very G---- d----."

The charges were revived in a much later day, and the defense might have given some trouble. But Place, who had been the foreman at the inquest, came forward, and settled the question in a few lines. Every one knew that the old Radical was quite free of all disposition to suppress truth from wish to curry favor with royalty.

John Speed,[453] the author of the English History,[454] (1632) which Bishop Nicolson[455] calls the best chronicle extant, was a man, like Place, of no education, but what he gave himself. The bishop says he would have done better if he had a better training: but what, he adds, could have been expected from a tailor! This Speed was, as well as Place. But he was {202} released from manual labor by Sir Fulk Grevil,[456] who enabled him to study.

A STORY ON SIMSON.

I have elsewhere noticed that those who oppose the mysteries of algebra do not ridicule them; this I want the cyclometers to do. Of the three who wrote against the great point, the negative quantity, and the uses of 0 which are connected with it, only one could fire a squib. That Robert Simson[457] should do such a thing will be judged impossible by all who admit tradition. I do not vouch for the following; I give it as a proof of the impression which prevailed about him:

He used to sit at his open window on the ground floor, as deep in geometry as a Robert Simson ought to be. Here he would be accosted by beggars, to whom he generally gave a trifle, he roused himself to hear a few words of the story, made his donation, and instantly dropped down into his depths.

Some wags one day stopped a mendicant who was on his way to the window with "Now, my man, do as we tell you, and you will get something from that gentleman, and a shilling from us besides. You will go and say you are in distress, he will ask you who you are, and you will say you are Robert Simson, son of John Simson of Kirktonhill." The man did as he was told; Simson quietly gave him a coin, and dropped off. The wags watched a little, and saw him rouse himself again, and exclaim "Robert Simson, son of John Simson of Kirktonhill! why, that is myself. That man must be an impostor." Lord Brougham tells the same story, with some difference of details.

{203}

BARON MASERES.

Baron Maseres[458] was, as a writer, dry; those who knew his writings will feel that he seldom could have taken in a joke or issued a pun. Maseres was the fourth wrangler of 1752, and first Chancellor's medallist (or highest in classics); his second was Porteus[459] (afterward Bishop of London).

Waring[460] came five years after him: he could not get Maseres through the second page of his first book on algebra; a negative quantity stood like a lion in the way. In 1758 he published his Dissertation on the Use of the Negative Sign,[461] 4to. There are some who care little about + and -, who would give it house-room for the sake of the four words "Printed by Samuel Richardson."

Maseres speaks as follows: "A single quantity can never be marked with either of those signs, or considered as either affirmative or negative; for if any single quantity, as b, is marked either with the sign + or with the sign - without assigning some other quantity, as a, to which it is to be added, or from which it is to be subtracted, the mark will have no meaning or signification: thus if it be said that the square of -5, or the product of -5 into -5, is equal to +25, such an assertion must either signify no more than that 5 times 5 is equal to 25 without any regard to the signs, or it must be mere nonsense and unintelligible jargon. I speak according to the foregoing definition, by which the affirmativeness or negativeness of any quantity implies a relation to another quantity of the same kind to which it {204} is added, or from which it is subtracted; for it may perhaps be very clear and intelligible to those who have formed to themselves some other idea of affirmative and negative quantities different from that above defined."

Nothing can be more correct, or more identically logical: +5 and -5, standing alone, are jargon if +5 and -5 are to be understood as without reference to another quantity. But those who have "formed to themselves some other idea" see meaning enough. The great difficulty of the opponents of algebra lay in want of power or will to see extension of terms. Maseres is right when he implies that extension, accompanied by its refusal, makes jargon. One of my paradoxers was present at a meeting of the Royal Society (in 1864, I think) and asked permission to make some remarks upon a paper. He rambled into other things, and, naming me, said that I had written a book in which two sides of a triangle are pronounced equal to the third.[462] So they are, in the sense in which the word is used in complete algebra; in which A + B = C makes A, B, C, three sides of a triangle, and declares that going over A and B, one after the other, is equivalent, in change of place, to going over C at once. My critic, who might, if he pleased, have objected to extension, insisted upon reading me in unextended meaning.

On the other hand, it must be said that those who wrote on the other idea wrote very obscurely about it and justified Des Cartes (De Methodo)[463] when he said: "Algebram vero, ut solet doceri, animadverti certis regulis et numerandi formulis ita esse contentam, ut videatur potius ars quædam confusa, cujus usu ingenium quodam modo turbatur et obscuratur, quam scientia qua excolatur et perspicacius {205} reddatur."[464] Maseres wrote this sentence on the title of his own work, now before me; he would have made it his motto if he had found it earlier.

There is, I believe, in Cobbett's Annual Register,[465] an account of an interview between Maseres and Cobbett when in prison.

The conversation of Maseres was lively, and full of serious anecdote: but only one attempt at humorous satire is recorded of him; it is an instructive one. He was born in 1731 (Dec. 15), and his father was a refugee. French was the language of the house, with the pronunciation of the time of Louis XIV. He lived until 1824 (May 19), and saw the race of refugees who were driven out by the first Revolution. Their pronunciation differed greatly from his own; and he used to amuse himself by mimicking them. Those who heard him and them had the two schools of pronunciation before them at once; a thing which seldom happens. It might even yet be worth while to examine the Canadian pronunciation.

Maseres went as Attorney-General to Quebec; and was appointed Cursitor Baron of our Exchequer in 1773. There is a curious story about his mission to Canada, which I have heard as good tradition, but have never seen in print. The reader shall have it as cheap as I; and I confess I rather believe it. Maseres was inveterately honest; he could not, at the bar, bear to see his own client victorious, when he knew his cause was a bad one. On a certain occasion he was in a cause which he knew would go against him if a certain case were quoted. Neither the judge nor the opposite counsel seemed to remember this case, and Maseres could not help dropping an allusion which brought it out. {206} His business as a barrister fell off, of course. Some time after, Mr. Pitt (Chatham) wanted a lawyer to send to Canada on a private mission, and wanted a very honest man. Some one mentioned Maseres, and told the above story: Pitt saw that he had got the man he wanted. The mission was satisfactorily performed, and Maseres remained as Attorney-General.

The Doctrine of Life Annuities[466] (4to, 726 pages, 1783) is a strange paradox. Its size, the heavy dissertations on the national debt, and the depth of algebra supposed known, put it out of the question as an elementary work, and it is unfitted for the higher student by its elaborate attempt at elementary character, shown in its rejection of forms derived from chances in favor of the average, and its exhibition of the separate values of the years of an annuity, as arithmetical illustrations. It is a climax of unsaleability, unreadability, and inutility. For intrinsic nullity of interest, and dilution of little matter with much ink, I can compare this book to nothing but that of Claude de St. Martin, elsewhere mentioned, or the lectures On the Nature and Properties of Logarithms, by James Little,[467] Dublin, 1830, 8vo. (254 heavy pages of many words and few symbols), a wonderful weight of weariness.

The stock of this work on annuities, very little diminished, was given by the author to William Frend, who paid warehouse room for it until about 1835, when he consulted me as to its disposal. As no publisher could be found who would take it as a gift, for any purpose of sale, it was consigned, all but a few copies, to a buyer of waste paper.

Baron Maseres's republications are well known: the Scriptores Logarithmici[468] is a set of valuable reprints, mixed {207} with much which might better have entered into another collection. It is not so well known that there is a volume of optical reprints, Scriptores Optici, London, 1823, 4to, edited for the veteran of ninety-two by Mr. Babbage[469] at twenty-nine. This excellent volume contains James Gregory, Des Cartes, Halley, Barrow, and the optical writings of Huyghens, the Principia of the undulatory theory. It also contains, by the sort of whim in which such men as Maseres, myself, and some others are apt to indulge, a reprint of "The great new Art of weighing Vanity,"[470] by M. Patrick Mathers, Arch-Bedel to the University of St. Andrews, Glasgow, 1672. Professor Sinclair,[471] of Glasgow, a good man at clearing mines of the water which they did not want, and furnishing cities with water which they did want, seems to have written absurdly about hydrostatics, and to have attacked a certain Sanders,[472] M.A. So Sanders, assisted by James Gregory, published a heavy bit of jocosity about him. This story of the authorship rested on a note made in his {208} copy by Robert Gray, M.D.; but it has since been fully confirmed by a letter of James Gregory to Collins, in the Macclesfield Correspondence. "There is one Master Sinclair, who did write the Ars Magna et Nova,[473] a pitiful ignorant fellow, who hath lately written horrid nonsense in the hydrostatics, and hath abused a master in the University, one Mr. Sanders, in print. This Mr. Sanders ... is resolved to cause the Bedel of the University to write against him.... We resolve to make excellent sport with him."

On this I make two remarks: First, I have learned from experience that old notes, made in books by their possessors, are statements of high authority: they are almost always confirmed. I do not receive them without hesitation; but I believe that of all the statements about books which rest on one authority, there is a larger percentage of truth in the written word than in the printed word. Secondly, I mourn to think that when the New Zealander picks up his old copy of this book, and reads it by the associations of his own day, he may, in spite of the many assurances I have received that my Athenæum Budget was amusing, feel me to be as heavy as I feel James Gregory and Sanders. But he will see that I knew what was coming, which Gregory did not.

MR. FREND'S BURLESQUE.

It was left for Mr. Frend to prove that an impugner of algebra could attempt ridicule. He was, in 1803, editor of a periodical The Gentleman's Monthly Miscellany, which lasted a few months.[474] To this, among other things, he contributed the following, in burlesque of the use made of 0, to which he objected.[475] The imitation of Rabelais, a writer {209} in whom he delighted, is good: to those who have never dipped, it may give such a notion as they would not easily get elsewhere. The point of the satire is not so good. But in truth it is not easy to make pungent scoffs upon what is common sense to all mankind. Who can laugh with effect at six times nothing is nothing, as false or unintelligible? In an article intended for that undistinguishing know-0 the "general reader," there would have been no force of satire, if division by 0 had been separated from multiplication by the same.

I have followed the above by another squib, by the same author, on the English language. The satire is covertly aimed at theological phraseology; and any one who watches this subject will see that it is a very just observation that the Greek words are not boiled enough.

PANTAGRUEL'S DECISION of the QUESTION about NOTHING.

"Pantagruel determined to have a snug afternoon with Epistemon and Panurge. Dinner was ordered to be set in a small parlor, and a particular batch of Hermitage with some choice Burgundy to be drawn from a remote corner of the cellar upon the occasion. By way of lunch, about an hour before dinner, Pantagruel was composing his stomach with German sausages, reindeer's tongues, oysters, brawn, and half a dozen different sorts of English beer just come into fashion, when a most thundering knocking was heard at the great gate, and from the noise they expected it to announce the arrival at least of the First Consul, or king Gargantua.

Panurge was sent to reconnoiter, and after a quarter of an hour's absence, returned with the news that the University of Pontemaca was waiting his highness's leisure in the great hall, to propound a question which {210} had turned the brains of thirty-nine students, and had flung twenty-seven more into a high fever. With all my heart, says Pantagruel, and swallowed down three quarts of Burton ale; but remember, it wants but an hour of dinner time, and the question must be asked in as few words as possible; for I cannot deprive myself of the pleasure I expected to enjoy in the company of my good friends for a set of mad-headed masters. I wish brother John was here to settle these matters with the black gentry.

"Having said or rather growled this, he proceeded to the hall of ceremony, and mounted his throne; Epistemon and Panurge standing on each side, but two steps below him. Then advanced to the throne the three beadles of the University of Pontemaca with their silver staves on their shoulders, and velvet caps on their heads, and they were followed by three times three doctors, and thrice three times three masters of art; for everything was done in Pontemaca by the number three, and on this account the address was written on parchment, one foot in breadth, and thrice three times thrice three feet in length. The beadles struck the ground with their heads and their staves three times in approaching the throne; the doctors struck the ground with their heads thrice three times, and the masters did the same thrice each time, beating the ground with their heads thrice three times.

This was the accustomed form of approaching the throne, time out of mind, and it was said to be emblematic of the usual prostration of science to the throne of greatness.

"The mathematical professor, after having spit, and hawked, and cleared his throat, and blown his nose on a handkerchief lent to him, for he had forgotten to bring his own, began to read the address. In this he was assisted by three masters of arts, one of whom, with a silver pen, pointed out the stops; the second with a small stick rapped his knuckles when he was to raise or lower his voice; and a third pulled his hair behind when he was to look Pantagruel in the face. Pantagruel began to chafe like a lion:

{211} he turned first on one side, then on the other: he listened and groaned, and groaned and listened, and was in the utmost cogitabundity of cogitation. His countenance began to brighten, when, at the end of an hour, the reader stammered out these words:

"'It has therefore been most clearly proved that as all matter may be divided into parts infinitely smaller than the infinitely smallest part of the infinitesimal of nothing, so nothing has all the properties of something, and may become, by just and lawful right, susceptible of addition, subtraction, multiplication, division, squaring, and cubing: that it is to all intents and purposes as good as anything that has been, is, or can be taught in the nine universities of the land, and to deprive it of its rights is a most cruel innovation and usurpation, tending to destroy all just subordination in the world, making all universities superfluous, leveling vice-chancellors, doctors, and proctors, masters, bachelors, and scholars, to the mean and contemptible state of butchers and tallow-chandlers, bricklayers and chimney-sweepers, who, if it were not for these learned mysteries, might think that they knew as much as their betters. Every one then, who has the good of science at heart, must pray for the interference of his highness to put a stop to all the disputes about nothing, and by his decision to convince all gainsayers that the science of nothing is taught in the best manner in the universities, to the great edification and improvement of all the youth in the land.'

"Here Pantagruel whispered in the ear of Panurge, who nodded to Epistemon, and they two left the assembly, and did not return for an hour, till the orator had finished his task. The three beadles had thrice struck the ground with their heads and staves, the doctors had finished their compliments, and the masters were making their twenty-seven prostrations. Epistemon and Panurge went up to Pantagruel, whom they found fast asleep and snoring; nor could he be roused but by as many tugs as there had been {212} bowings from the corps of learning. At last he opened his eyes, gave a good stretch, made half a dozen yawns, and called for a stoup of wine. I thank you, my masters, says he; so sound a nap I have not had since I came from the island of Priestfolly. Have you dined, my masters? They answered the question by as many bows as at entrance; but his highness left them to the care of Panurge, and retired to the little parlor with Epistemon, where they burst into a fit of laughter, declaring that this learned Baragouin about nothing was just as intelligible as the lawyer's Galimathias. Panurge conducted the learned body into a large saloon, and each in his way hearing a clattering of plates and glasses, congratulated himself on his approaching good cheer. There they were left by Panurge, who took his chair by Pantagruel just as the soup was removed, but he made up for the want of that part of his dinner by a pint of champagne. The learning of the university had whetted their appetites; what they each ate it is needless to recite; good wine, good stories, and hearty laughs went round, and three hours elapsed before one soul of them recollected the hungry students of Pontemaca.

"Epistemon reminded them of the business in hand, and orders were given for a fresh dozen of hermitage to be put upon table, and the royal attendants to get ready. As soon as the dozen bottles were emptied, Pantagruel rose from table, the royal trumpets sounded, and he was accompanied by the great officers of his court into the large dining hall, where was a table with forty-two covers. Pantagruel sat at the head, Epistemon at the bottom, and Panurge in the middle, opposite an immense silver tureen, which would hold fifty gallons of soup. The wise men of Pontemaca then took their seats according to seniority. Every countenance glistened with delight; the music struck up; the dishes were uncovered. Panurge had enough to do to handle the immense silver ladle: Pantagruel and Epistemon had no time for eating, they were fully employed in carving. The bill {213} of fare announced the names of a hundred different dishes. From Panurge's ladle came into the soup plate as much as he took every time out of the tureen; and as it was the rule of the court that every one should appear to eat, as long as he sat at table, there was the clattering of nine and thirty spoons against the silver soup-plates for a quarter of an hour. They were then removed, and knives and forks were in motion for half an hour. Glasses were continually handed round in the mean time, and then everything was removed, except the great tureen of soup. The second course was now served up, in dispatching which half an hour was consumed; and at the conclusion the wise men of Pontemaca had just as much in their stomachs as Pantagruel in his head from their address: for nothing was cooked up for them in every possible shape that Panurge could devise.

"Wine-glasses, large decanters, fruit dishes, and plates were now set on. Pantagruel and Epistemon alternately gave bumper toasts: the University of Pontemaca, the eye of the world, the mother of taste and good sense and universal learning, the patroness of utility, and the second only to Pantagruel in wisdom and virtue (for these were her titles), was drank standing with thrice three times three, and huzzas and clattering of glasses; but to such wine the wise men of Pontemaca had not been accustomed; and though Pantagruel did not suffer one to rise from table till the eighty-first glass had been emptied, not even the weakest headed master of arts felt his head in the least indisposed. The decanters indeed were often removed, but they were brought back replenished, filled always with nothing.

"Silence was now proclaimed, and in a trice Panurge leaped into the large silver tureen. Thence he made his bows to Pantagruel and the whole company, and commenced an oration of signs, which lasted an hour and a half, and in which he went over all the matter contained in the Pontemaca address; and though the wise men looked very serious during the whole time, Pantagruel himself and his whole {214} court could not help indulging in repeated bursts of laughter. It was universally acknowledged that he excelled himself, and that the arguments by which he beat the English masters of arts at Paris were nothing to the exquisite selection of attitudes which he this day assumed. The greatest shouts of applause were excited when he was running thrice round the tureen on its rim, with his left hand holding his nose, and the other exercising itself nine and thirty times on his back. In this attitude he concluded with his back to the professor of mathematics; and at the instant he gave his last flap, by a sudden jump, and turning heels over head in the air, he presented himself face to face to the professor, and standing on his left leg, with his left hand holding his nose, he presented to him, in a white satin bag, Pantagruel's royal decree. Then advancing his right leg, he fixed it on the professor's head, and after three turns, in which he clapped his sides with both hands thrice three times, down he leaped, and Pantagruel, Epistemon, and himself took their leaves of the wise men of Pontemaca.

"The wise men now retired, and by royal orders were accompanied by a guard, and according to the etiquette of the court, no one having a royal order could stop at any public house till it was delivered. The procession arrived at Pontemaca at nine o'clock the next morning, and the sound of bells from every church and college announced their arrival. The congregation was assembled; the royal decree was saluted in the same manner as if his highness had been there in person; and after the proper ceremonies had been performed, the satin bag was opened exactly at twelve o'clock. A finely emblazoned roll was drawn forth, and the public orator read to the gaping assembly the following words:

"'They who can make something out of nothing shall have nothing to eat at the court of--PANTAGRUEL.'" {215}

ORIGIN of the ENGLISH LANGUAGE, related by a SWEDE.

"Some months ago in a party in Holland, consisting of natives of various countries, the merit of their respective languages became a topic of conversation. A Swede, who had been a great traveler, and could converse in most of the modern languages of Europe, laughed very heartily at an Englishman, who had ventured to speak in praise of the tongue of his dear country. I never had any trouble, says he, in learning English. To my very great surprise, the moment I sat foot on shore at Gravesend, I found out, that I could understand, with very little trouble, every word that was said. It was a mere jargon, made up of German, French, and Italian, with now and then a word from the Spanish, Latin or Greek. I had only to bring my mouth to their mode of speaking, which was done with ease in less than a week, and I was everywhere taken for a true-born Englishman; a privilege by the way of no small importance in a country, where each man, God knows why, thinks his foggy island superior to any other part of the world: and though his door is never free from some dun or other coming for a tax, and if he steps out of it he is sure to be knocked down or to have his pocket picked, yet he has the insolence to think every foreigner a miserable slave, and his country the seat of everything wretched. They may talk of liberty as they please, but Spain or Turkey for my money: barring the bowstring and the inquisition, they are the most comfortable countries under heaven, and you need not be afraid of either, if you do not talk of religion and politics. I do not see much difference too in this respect in England, for when I was there, one of their most eminent men for learning was put in prison for a couple of years, and got his death for translating one of Æsop's fables into English, which every child in Spain and Turkey is taught, as soon as he comes out of his leading strings. Here all the company unanimously cried out against the Swede, that it was {216} impossible: for in England, the land of liberty, the only thing its worst enemies could say against it, was, that they paid for their liberty a much greater price than it was worth.--Every man there had a fair trial according to laws, which everybody could understand; and the judges were cool, patient, discerning men, who never took the part of the crown against the prisoner, but gave him every assistance possible for his defense.

"The Swede was borne down, but not convinced; and he seemed determined to spit out all his venom. Well, says he, at any rate you will not deny that the English have not got a language of their own, and that they came by it in a very odd way. Of this at least I am certain, for the whole history was related to me by a witch in Lapland, whilst I was bargaining for a wind. Here the company were all in unison again for the story.

"In ancient times, said the old hag, the English occupied a spot in Tartary, where they lived sulkily by themselves, unknowing and unknown. By a great convulsion that took place in China, the inhabitants of that and the adjoining parts of Tartary were driven from their seats, and after various wanderings took up their abode in Germany. During this time nobody could understand the English, for they did not talk, but hissed like so many snakes. The poor people felt uneasy under this circumstance, and in one of their parliaments, or rather hissing meetings, it was determined to seek a remedy: and an embassy was sent to some of our sisterhood then living on Mount Hecla. They were put to a nonplus, and summoned the Devil to their relief. To him the English presented their petitions, and explained their sad case; and he, upon certain conditions, promised to befriend them, and to give them a language. The poor Devil was little aware of what he had promised; but he is, as all the world knows, a man of too much honor to break his word. Up and down the world then he went in quest of this new language: visited all the universities, and all {217} the schools, and all the courts of law, and all the play-houses, and all the prisons; never was poor devil so fagged. It would have made your heart bleed to see him. Thrice did he go round the earth in every parallel of latitude; and at last, wearied and jaded out, back came he to Hecla in despair, and would have thrown himself into the volcano, if he had been made of combustible materials.

Luckily at that time our sisters were engaged in settling the balance of Europe; and whilst they were looking over projects, and counter-projects, and ultimatums, and post ultimatums, the poor Devil, unable to assist them was groaning in a corner and ruminating over his sad condition.

"On a sudden, a hellish joy overspread his countenance; up he jumped, and, like Archimedes of old, ran like a madman amongst the throng, turning over tables, and papers, and witches, roaring out for a full hour together nothing else but 'tis found, 'tis found! Away were sent the sisterhood in every direction, some to traverse all the corners of the earth, and others to prepare a larger caldron than had ever yet been set upon Hecla. The affairs of Europe were at a stand: its balance was thrown aside; prime ministers and ambassadors were everywhere in the utmost confusion; and, by the way, they have never been able to find the balance since that time, and all the fine speeches upon the subject, with which your newspapers are every now and then filled, are all mere hocus-pocus and rhodomontade. However, the caldron was soon set on, and the air was darkened by witches riding on broomsticks, bringing a couple of folios under each arm, and across each shoulder. I remember the time exactly: it was just as the council of Nice had broken up, so that they got books and papers there dog cheap; but it was a bad thing for the poor English, as these were the worst materials that entered into the caldron. Besides, as the Devil wanted some amusement, and had not seen an account of the transactions of this famous council, he had all the books brought from it laid before him, and split his sides almost {218} with laughing, whilst he was reading the speeches and decrees of so many of his old friends and acquaintances. All this while the witches were depositing their loads in the great caldron. There were books from the Dalai Lama, and from China: there were books from the Hindoos, and tallies from the Caffres: there were paintings from Mexico, and rocks of hieroglyphics from Egypt: the last country supplied besides the swathings of two thousand mummies, and four-fifths of the famed library of Alexandria. Bubble! bubble! toil and trouble! never was a day of more labor and anxiety; and if our good master had but flung in the Greek books at the proper time, they would have made a complete job of it. He was a little too impatient: as the caldron frothed up, he skimmed it off with a great ladle, and filled some thousands of our wind-bags with the froth, which the English with great joy carried back to their own country. These bags were sent to every district: the chiefs first took their fill, and then the common people; hence they now speak a language which no foreigner can understand, unless he has learned half a dozen other languages; and the poor people, not one in ten, understand a third part of what is said to them. The hissing, however, they have not entirely got rid of, and every seven years, when the Devil, according to agreement, pays them a visit, they entertain him at their common halls and county meetings with their original language.

"The good-natured old hag told me several other circumstances, relative to this curious transaction, which, as there is an Englishman in company, it will be prudent to pass over in silence: but I cannot help mentioning one thing which she told me as a very great secret. You know, says she to me, that the English have more religions among them than any other nation in Europe, and that there is more teaching and sermonizing with them than in any other country. The fact is this; it matters not who gets up to teach them, the hard words of the Greek were not sufficiently {219} boiled, and whenever they get into a sentence, the poor people's brains are turned, and they know no more what the preacher is talking about, than if he harangued them in Arabic. Take my word for it if you please; but if not, when you get to England, desire the bettermost sort of people that you are acquainted with to read to you an act of parliament, which of course is written in the clearest and plainest style in which anything can be written, and you will find that not one in ten will be able to make tolerable sense of it. The language would have been an excellent language, if it had not been for the council of Nice, and the words had been well boiled.

"Here the company burst out into a fit of laughter. The Englishman got up and shook hands with the Swede: si non è vero, said he, è ben trovato.[476] But, however I may laugh at it here, I would not advise you to tell this story on the other side of the water. So here's a bumper to Old England for ever, and God save the king."

ON YOUTHFUL PRODIGIES

The accounts given of extraordinary children and adolescents frequently defy credence.[477] I will give two well-attested instances.

The celebrated mathematician Alexis Claude Clairault (now Clairaut)[478] was certainly born in May, 1713. His treatise on curves of double curvature (printed in 1731)[479] received {220} the approbation of the Academy of Sciences, August 23, 1729. Fontenelle, in his certificate of this, calls the author sixteen years of age, and does not strive to exaggerate the wonder, as he might have done, by reminding his readers that this work, of original and sustained mathematical investigation, must have been coming from the pen at the ages of fourteen and fifteen. The truth was, as attested by De Molières,[480] Clairaut had given public proofs of his power at twelve years old. His age being thus publicly certified, all doubt is removed: say he had been--though great wonder would still have been left--twenty-one instead of sixteen, his appearance, and the remembrances of his friends, schoolfellows, etc., would have made it utterly hopeless to knock off five years of that age while he was on view in Paris as a young lion. De Molières, who examined the work officially for the Garde des Sceaux, is transported beyond the bounds of official gravity, and says that it "ne mérite pas seulement d'être imprimé, mais d'être admiré comme un prodige d'imagination, de conception, et de capacité."[481]

That Blaise Pascal was born in June, 1623, is perfectly well established and uncontested.[482] That he wrote his conic sections at the age of sixteen might be difficult to establish, though tolerably well attested, if it were not for {221} one circumstance, for the book was not published. The celebrated theorem, "Pascal's hexagram,"[483] makes all the rest come very easy.

Now Curabelle,[484] in a work published in 1644, sneers at Desargues,[485] whom he quotes, for having, in 1642, deferred a discussion until "cette grande proposition nommée le Pascale verra le jour."[486] That is, by the time Pascal was nineteen, the hexagram was circulating under a name derived from the author. The common story about Pascal, given by his sister,[487] is an absurdity which no doubt has prejudiced many against tales of early proficiency. He is made, when quite a boy, to invent geometry in the order of Euclid's propositions: as if that order were natural sequence of investigation. The hexagram at ten years old would be a hundred times less unlikely.

The instances named are painfully astonishing: I give one which has fallen out of sight, because it will preserve an imperfect biography. John Wilson[488] is Wilson of that {222} Ilk, that is, of "Wilson's Theorem." It is this: if p be a prime number, the product of all the numbers up to p-1, increased by 1, is divisible without remainder by p. All mathematicians know this as Wilson's theorem, but few know who Wilson was. He was born August 6, 1741, at the Howe in Applethwaite, and he was heir to a small estate at Troutbeck in Westmoreland. He was sent to Peterhouse, at Cambridge, and while an undergraduate was considered stronger in algebra than any one in the University, except Professor Waring, one of the most powerful algebraists of the century.[489] He was the senior wrangler of 1761, and was then for some time a private tutor. When Paley,[490] then in his third year, determined to make a push for the senior wranglership, which he got, Wilson was recommended to him as a tutor. Both were ardent in their work, except that sometimes Paley, when he came for his lesson, would find "Gone a fishing" written on his tutor's outer door: which was insult added to injury, for Paley was very fond of fishing. Wilson soon left Cambridge, and went to the bar. He practised on the northern circuit with great success; and, one day, while passing his vacation on his little property at Troutbeck, he received information, to his great surprise, that Lord Thurlow,[491] with whom he had {223} no acquaintance, had recommended him to be a Judge of the Court of Common Pleas. He died, Oct. 18, 1793, with a very high reputation as a lawyer and a Judge. These facts are partly from Meadley's Life of Paley,[492] no doubt from Paley himself, partly from the Gentleman's Magazine, and from an epitaph written by Bishop Watson.[493] Wilson did not publish anything: the theorem by which he has cut his name in the theory of numbers was communicated to Waring, by whom it was published. He married, in 1788, a daughter of Serjeant Adair,[494] and left issue. Had a family, many will say: but a man and his wife are a family, even without children. An actuary may be allowed to be accurate in this matter, of which I was reminded by what an actuary wrote of another actuary. William Morgan,[495] in the life of his uncle Dr. Richard Price,[496] says that the Doctor and his {224} wife were "never blessed with an addition to their family." I never met with such accuracy elsewhere. Of William Morgan I add that my surname and pursuits have sometimes, to my credit be it said, made a confusion between him and me. Dates are nothing to the mistaken; the last three years of Morgan's life were the first three years of my actuary-life (1830-33). The mistake was to my advantage as well as to my credit. I owe to it the acquaintance of one of the noblest of the human race, I mean Elizabeth Fry,[497] who came to me for advice about a philanthropic design, which involved life questions, under a general impression that some Morgan had attended to such things.[498]

{225}

NEWTON AGAIN OVERTHROWN

A treatise on the sublime science of heliography, satisfactorily demonstrating our great orb of light, the sun, to be absolutely no other than a body of ice! Overturning all the received systems of the universe hitherto extant; proving the celebrated and indefatigable Sir Isaac Newton, in his theory of the solar system, to be as far distant from the truth, as many of the heathen authors of Greece and Rome. By Charles Palmer,[499] Gent. London, 1798, 8vo.

Mr. Palmer burned some tobacco with a burning glass, saw that a lens of ice would do as well, and then says:

"If we admit that the sun could be removed, and a terrestrial body of ice placed in its stead, it would produce the same effect. The sun is a crystaline body receiving the radiance of God, and operates on this earth in a similar manner as the light of the sun does when applied to a convex mirror or glass."

Nov. 10, 1801. The Rev. Thomas Cormouls,[500] minister of Tettenhall, addressed a letter to Sir Wm. Herschel, from which I extract the following:

"Here it may be asked, then, how came the doctrines of Newton to solve all astronomic Phenomina, and all problems concerning the same, both a parte ante and a parte post.[501] It is answered that he certainly wrought the principles he made use of into strickt analogy with the real Phenomina of the heavens, and that the rules and results arizing from them {226} agree with them and resolve accurately all questions concerning them. Though they are not fact and true, or nature, but analogous to it, in the manner of the artificial numbers of logarithms, sines, &c. A very important question arises here, Did Newton mean to impose upon the world? By no means: he received and used the doctrines reddy formed; he did a little extend and contract his principles when wanted, and commit a few oversights of consequences. But when he was very much advanced in life, he suspected the fundamental nullity of them: but I have from a certain anecdote strong ground to believe that he knew it before his decease and intended to have retracted his error. But, however, somebody did deceive, if not wilfully, negligently at least. That was a man to whom the world has great obligations too. It was no less a philosopher than Galileo."

That Newton wanted to retract before his death, is a notion not uncommon among paradoxers. Nevertheless, there is no retraction in the third edition of the Principia, published when Newton was eighty-four years old! The moral of the above is, that a gentleman who prefers instructing William Herschel to learning how to spell, may find a proper niche in a proper place, for warning to others. It seems that gravitation is not truth, but only the logarithm of it.

BISHOPS AS PARADOXERS

The mathematical and philosophical works of the Right Rev. John Wilkins[502].... In two volumes. London, 1802, 8vo.

This work, or at least part of the edition--all for aught I know--is printed on wood; that is, on paper made from wood-pulp. It has a rough surface; and when held before a candle is of very unequal transparency. There is in it a reprint of the works on the earth and moon. The discourse on the possibility of going to the moon, in this and the edition of 1640, is incorporated: but from the account in the {227} life prefixed, and a mention by D'Israeli, I should suppose that it had originally a separate title-page, and some circulation as a separate tract. Wilkins treats this subject half seriously, half jocosely; he has evidently not quite made up his mind. He is clear that "arts are not yet come to their solstice," and that posterity will bring hidden things to light. As to the difficulty of carrying food, he thinks, scoffing Puritan that he is, the Papists may be trained to fast the voyage, or may find the bread of their Eucharist "serve well enough for their viaticum."[503] He also puts the case that the story of Domingo Gonsales may be realized, namely, that wild geese find their way to the moon. It will be remembered--to use the usual substitute for, It has been forgotten--that the posthumous work of Bishop Francis Godwin[504] of Llandaff was published in 1638, the very year of Wilkins's first edition, in time for him to mention it at the end. Godwin makes Domingo Gonsales get to the moon in a chariot drawn by wild geese, and, as old books would say, discourses fully on that head. It is not a little amusing that Wilkins should have been seriously accused of plagiarizing Godwin, Wilkins writing in earnest, or nearly so, and Godwin writing fiction. It may serve to show philosophers how very near pure speculation comes to fable. From the sublime to the ridiculous is but a step: which is the sublime, and which the ridiculous, every one must settle for himself. With me, good fiction is the sublime, and bad speculation the ridiculous. The number of bishops in my list is small. I might, had I possessed the book, have opened the list of quadrators with an Archbishop of Canterbury, or at least with a divine who was not wholly not archbishop. Thomas Bradwardine[505] (Bragvardinus, Bragadinus) was elected in {228} 1348; the Pope put in another, who died unconsecrated; and Bradwardine was again elected in 1349, and lived five weeks longer, dying, I suppose, unconfirmed and unconsecrated.[506] Leland says he held the see a year, unus tantum annulus,[507] which seems to be a confusion: the whole business, from the first election, took about a year. He squared the circle, and his performance was printed at Paris in 1494. I have never seen it, nor any work of the author, except a tract on proportion.

As Bradwardine's works are very scarce indeed, I give two titles from one of the Libri catalogues.

"ARITHMETIC. BRAUARDINI (Thomæ) Arithmetica speculativa revisa et correcta a Petro Sanchez Ciruelo Aragonesi, black letter, elegant woodcut title-page, VERY RARE, folio. Parisiis, per Thomam Anguelast (pro Olivier Senant), s. a. circa 1510.[508]

"This book, by Thomas Bradwardine, Archbishop of Canterbury must be exceedingly scarce as it has escaped the notice of Professor De Morgan, who, in his Arithmetical Books, speaks of a treatise of the same author on proportions,[509] printed at Vienna in 1515, but does not mention the present work.

{229}

"Bradwardine (Archbp. T.). Brauardini (Thomæ) Geometria speculativa, com Tractato de Quadratura Circuli bene revisa a Petro Sanchez Ciruelo, SCARCE, folio. Parisiis, J. Petit, 1511.[510]

"In this work we find the polygones étoilés,[511] see Chasles (Aperçu, pp. 480, 487, 521, 523, &c.) on the merit of the discoveries of this English mathematician, who was Archbishop of Canterbury in the XIVth Century (tempore Edward III. A.D. 1349); and who applied geometry to theology.

M. Chasles says that the present work of Bradwardine contains 'Une théorie nouvelle qui doit faire honneur au XIVe Siècle.'"[512]

The titles do not make it quite sure that Bradwardine is the quadrator; it may be Peter Sanchez after all.[513]

THE QUESTION OF PARALLELS.

Nouvelle théorie des parallèles. Par Adolphe Kircher[514] [so signed at the end of the appendix]. Paris, 1803, 8vo.

An alleged emendation of Legendre.[515] The author refers {230} to attempts by Hoffman,[516] 1801, by Hauff,[517] 1799, and to a work of Karsten,[518] or at least a theory of Karsten, contained in "Tentamen novæ parallelarum theoriæ notione situs fundatæ; auctore G. C. Schwal,[519] Stuttgardæ, 1801, en 8 volumes." Surely this is a misprint; eight volumes on the theory of parallels? If there be such a work, I trust I and it may never meet, though ever so far produced.

{231}

Soluzione ... della quadratura del Circolo. By Gaetano Rossi.[520] London, 1804, 8vo.

The three remarkable points of this book are, that the household of the Prince of Wales took ten copies, Signora Grassini[521] sixteen, and that the circumference is 3-1/5 diameters. That is, the appetite of Grassini for quadrature exceeded that of the whole household (loggia) of the Prince of Wales in the ratio in which the semi-circumference exceeds the diameter.

And these are the first two in the list of subscribers. Did the author see this theorem?

A PATRIOTIC PARADOX

Britain independent of commerce; or proofs, deduced from an investigation into the true cause of the wealth of nations, that our riches, prosperity, and power are derived from sources inherent in ourselves, and would not be affected, even though our commerce were annihilated. By Wm. Spence.[522] 4th edition, 1808, 8vo.

A patriotic paradox, being in alleviation of the Commerce panic which the measures of Napoleon I.--who felt our Commerce, while Mr. Spence only saw it--had awakened. In this very month (August, 1866), the Pres. Brit.

Assoc. has applied a similar salve to the coal panic; it is fit that science, which rubbed the sore, should find a plaster. We ought to have an iron panic and a timber panic; and {232} a solemn embassy to the Americans, to beg them not to whittle, would be desirable. There was a gold panic beginning, before the new fields were discovered. For myself, I am the unknown and unpitied victim of a chronic gutta-percha panic: I never could get on without it; to me, gutta percha and Rowland Hill are the great discoveries of our day; and not unconnected either, gutta percha being to the submarine post what Rowland Hill is to the superterrene. I should be sorry to lose cow-choke--I gave up trying to spell it many years ago--but if gutta percha go, I go too. I think, that perhaps when, five hundred years hence, the people say to the Brit.

Assoc. (if it then exist) "Pray gentlemen, is it not time for the coal to be exhausted?" they will be answered out of Molière (who will certainly then exist): "Cela était autrefois ainsi, mais nous avons changé tout cela."[523] A great many people think that if the coal be used up, it will be announced some unexpected morning by all the yards being shut up and written notice outside, "Coal all gone!" just like the "Please, ma'am, there ain't no more sugar," with which the maid servant damps her mistress just at breakfast-time. But these persons should be informed that there is every reason to think that there will be time, as the city gentleman said, to venienti the occurrite morbo.[524]

SOME SCIENTIFIC PARADOXES.

An appeal to the republic of letters in behalf of injured science, from the opinions and proceedings of some modern authors of elements of geometry. By George Douglas.[525] Edinburgh, 1810, 8vo.

Mr. Douglas was the author of a very good set of {233} mathematical tables, and of other works. He criticizes Simson,[526] Playfair,[527] and others,--sometimes, I think, very justly. There is a curious phrase which occurs more than once. When he wants to say that something or other was done before Simson or another was born, he says "before he existed, at least as an author." He seems to reserve the possibility of Simson's pre-existence, but at the same time to assume that he never wrote anything in his previous state. Tell me that Simson pre-existed in any other way than as editor of some pre-existent Euclid? Tell Apella![528]

1810. In this year Jean Wood, Professor of Mathematics in the University of Virginia (Richmond),[529] addressed a printed circular to "Dr. Herschel, Astronomer, Greenwich Observatory." No mistake was more common than the natural one of imagining that the Private Astronomer of the king was the Astronomer Royal. The letter was on the {234} difference of velocities of the two sides of the earth, arising from the composition of the rotation and the orbital motion. The paradox is a fair one, and deserving of investigation; but, perhaps it would not be easy to deduce from it tides, trade-winds, aerolithes, &c., as Mr. Wood thought he had done in a work from which he gives an extract, and which he describes as published. The composition of rotations, &c., is not for the world at large: the paradox of the non-rotation of the moon about her axis is an instance. How many persons know that when a wheel rolls on the ground, the lowest point is moving upwards, the highest point forwards, and the intermediate points in all degrees of betwixt and between? This is too short an explanation, with some good difficulties.

The Elements of Geometry. In 2 vols. [By the Rev. J. Dobson,[530] B.D.] Cambridge, 1815. 4to.

Of this unpunctuating paradoxer I shall give an account in his own way: he would not stop for any one; why should I stop for him? It is worth while to try how unpunctuated sentences will read.

The reverend J Dobson BD late fellow of saint Johns college Cambridge was rector of Brandesburton in Yorkshire he was seventh wrangler in 1798 and died in 1847 he was of that sort of eccentricity which permits account of his private life if we may not rather say that in such cases private life becomes public there is a tradition that he was called Death Dobson on account of his head and aspect of countenance being not very unlike the ordinary pictures of a human skull his mode of life is reported to have been very singular whenever he visited Cambridge he was never known to go twice to the same inn he never would sleep at the rectory with another person in the house some ancient charwoman used to attend to the house but never slept in it he has been known in the time of coach travelling to have {235} deferred his return to Yorkshire on account of his disinclination to travel with a lady in the coach he continued his mathematical studies until his death and till his executors sold the type all his tracts to the number of five were kept in type at the university press none of these tracts had any stops except full stops at the end of paragraphs only neither had they capitals except one at the beginning of a paragraph so that a full stop was generally followed by some white as there is not a single proper name in the whole of the book I have I am not able to say whether he would have used capitals before proper names I have inserted them as usual for which I hope his spirit will forgive me if I be wrong he also published the elements of geometry in two volumes quarto Cambridge 1815 this book had also no stops except when a comma was wanted between letters as in the straight lines AB, BC I should also say that though the title is unpunctuated in the author's part it seems the publishers would not stand it in their imprint this imprint is punctuated as usual and Deighton and Sons to prove the completeness of their allegiance have managed that comma semicolon and period shall all appear in it why could they not have contrived interrogation and exclamation this is a good precedent to establish the separate right of the publisher over the imprint it is said that only twenty of the tracts were printed and very few indeed of the book on geometry it is doubtful whether any were sold there is a copy of the geometry in the university library at Cambridge and I have one myself the matter of the geometry differs entirely from Euclid and is so fearfully prolix that I am sure no mortal except the author ever read it the man went on without stops and without stop save for a period at the end of a paragraph this is the unpunctuated account of the unpunctuating geometer suum cuique tribuito[531] Mrs Thrale[532] would have been amused {236} at a Dobson who managed to come to a full stop without either of the three warnings.

I do not find any difficulty in reading Dobson's geometry; and I have read more of it to try reading without stops than I should have done had it been printed in the usual way. Those who dip into the middle of my paragraph may be surprised for a moment to see "on account of his disinclination to travel with a lady in the coach he continued his mathematical studies until his death and [further, of course] until his executors sold the type." But a person reading straight through would hardly take it so. I should add that, in order to give a fair trial, I did not compose as I wrote, but copied the words of the correspondent who gave me the facts, so far as they went.

A RELIGIOUS PARADOX

Philosophia Sacra, or the principles of natural Philosophy. Extracted from Divine Revelation. By the Rev. Samuel Pike.[533] Edited by the Rev. Samuel Kittle.[534] Edinburgh, 1815, 8vo.

This is a work of modified Hutchinsonianism, which I have seen cited by several. Though rather dark on the subject, it seems not to contradict the motion of the earth, or the doctrine of gravitation. Mr. Kittle gives a list of some Hutchinsonians,--as Bishop Horne;[535] Dr. Stukeley;[536] the Rev. {237} W. Jones,[537] author of Physiological Disquisitions; Mr. Spearman,[538] author of Letters on the Septuagint and editor of Hutchinson; Mr. Barker,[539] author of Reflexions on Learning; Dr. Catcott,[540] author of a work on the creation, &c.; Dr. Robertson,[541] author of a Treatise on the Hebrew Language; Dr. Holloway,[542] author of Originals, Physical and Theological; Dr. Walter Hodges,[543] author of a work on Elohim; Lord President Forbes (ob. 1747).[544]

The Rev. William Jones, above mentioned (1726-1800), the friend and biographer of Bishop Horne and his stout {238} defender, is best known as William Jones of Nayland, who (1757)[545] published the Catholic Doctrine of the Trinity; he was also strong for the Hutchinsonian physical trinity of fire, light, and spirit. This well-known work was generally recommended, as the defence of the orthodox system, to those who could not go into the learning of the subject. There is now a work more suited to our time: The Rock of Ages, by the Rev. E. H. Bickersteth,[546] now published by the Religious Tract Society, without date, answered by the Rev. Dr. Sadler,[547] in a work (1859) entitled Gloria Patri, in which, says Mr. Bickersteth, "the author has not even attempted to grapple with my main propositions." I have read largely on the controversy, and I think I know what this means. Moreover, when I see the note "There are two other passages to which Unitarians sometimes refer, but the deduction they draw from them is, in each case, refuted by the context"--I think I see why the two texts are not named. Nevertheless, the author is a little more disposed to yield to criticism than his foregoers; he does not insist on texts and readings which the greatest editors have rejected. And he writes with courtesy, both direct and oblique, towards his antagonists; which, on his side of this subject, is like letting in fresh air. So that I suspect the two books will together make a tolerably good introduction to the subject for those who cannot go deep. Mr. Bickersteth's book is well arranged and indexed, which is a point of superiority to Jones of Nayland. There is a point which I should gravely recommend to writers on the orthodox side.

The Unitarians in {239} England have frequently contended that the method of proving the divinity of Jesus Christ from the New Testament would equally prove the divinity of Moses. I have not fallen in the way of any orthodox answers specially directed at the repeated tracts written by Unitarians in proof of their assertion. If there be any, they should be more known; if there be none, some should be written. Which ever side may be right, the treatment of this point would be indeed coming to close quarters. The heterodox assertion was first supported, it is said, by John Bidle or Biddle (1615-1662) of Magdalen College, Oxford, the earliest of the English Unitarian writers, previously known by a translation of part of Virgil and part of Juvenal.[548] But I cannot find that he wrote on it.[549] It is the subject of "[Greek: haireseôn anastasis], or a new way of deciding old controversies. By Basanistes. Third edition, enlarged," London, 1815, 8vo.[550] It is the appendix to the amusing, "Six more letters to Granville Sharp, Esq., ... By Gregory Blunt, Esq." London, 8vo., 1803.[551] This much I can confidently say, that the study of these tracts would prevent orthodox writers from some curious slips, which are slips obvious to all sides of opinion. The lower defenders of orthodoxy frequently vex the spirits of the higher ones.

Since writing the above I have procured Dr. Sadler's answer. I thought I knew what the challenger meant when he said the respondent had not grappled with his main {240} propositions. I should say that he is clung on to from beginning to end. But perhaps Mr. B. has his own meaning of logical terms, such as "proposition": he certainly has his own meaning of "cumulative." He says his evidence is cumulative; not a catena, the strength of which is in its weakest part, but distinct and independent lines, each of which corroborates the other. This is the very opposite of cumulative: it is distributive. When different arguments are each necessary to a conclusion, the evidence is cumulative; when any one will do, even though they strengthen each other, it is distributive. The word "cumulative" is a synonym of the law word "constructive"; a whole which will do made out of parts which separately will not. Lord Strafford [552] opens his defence with the use of both words: "They have invented a kind of accumulated or constructive evidence; by which many actions, either totally innocent in themselves, or criminal in a much inferior degree, shall, when united, amount to treason." The conclusion is, that Mr. B. is a Cambridge man; the Oxford men do not confuse the elementary terms of logic. O dear old Cambridge! when the New Zealander comes let him find among the relics of your later sons some proof of attention to the elementary laws of thought. A little-go of logic, please!

Mr. B., though apparently not a Hutchinsonian, has a nibble at a physical Trinity. "If, as we gaze on the sun shining in the firmament, we see any faint adumbration of the doctrine of the Trinity in the fontal orb, the light ever generated, and the heat proceeding from the sun and its beams--threefold and yet one, the sun, its light, and its {241} heat,--that luminous globe, and the radiance ever flowing from it, are both evident to the eye; but the vital warmth is felt, not seen, and is only manifested in the life it transfuses through creation. The proof of its real existence is self-demonstrating."

We shall see how Revilo[553] illustrates orthodoxy by mathematics. It was my duty to have found one of the many illustrations from physics; but perhaps I should have forgotten it if this instance had not come in my way. It is very bad physics. The sun, apart from its light, evident to the eye! Heat more self-demonstrating than light, because felt! Heat only manifested by the life it diffuses! Light implied not necessary to life! But the theology is worse than Sabellianism[554]. To adumbrate--i.e., make a picture of--the orthodox doctrine, the sun must be heavenly body, the light heavenly body, the heat heavenly body; and yet, not three heavenly bodies, but one heavenly body. The truth is, that this illustration and many others most strikingly illustrate the Trinity of fundamental doctrine held by the Unitarians, in all its differences from the Trinity of persons held by the Orthodox. Be right which may, the right or wrong of the Unitarians shines out in the comparison. Dr. Sadler confirms me--by which I mean that I wrote the above before I saw what he says--in the following words: "The sun is one object with two properties, and these properties have a parallel not in the second and third persons of the Trinity, but in the attributes of Deity."

The letting light alone, as self-evident, and making heat self-demonstrating, because felt--i.e., perceptible now and then--has the character of the Irishman's astronomy:

{242}

"Long life to the moon, for a dear noble cratur, Which serves us for lamplight all night in the dark, While the sun only shines in the day, which by natur, Wants no light at all, as ye all may remark."

SIR RICHARD PHILLIPS

Sir Richard Phillips[555] (born 1768) was conspicuous in 1793, when he was sentenced to a year's imprisonment[556] for selling Paine's Rights of Man; and again when, in 1807[557], he was knighted as Sheriff of London. As a bookseller, he was able to enforce his opinions in more ways than others. For instance, in James Mitchell's[558] Dictionary of the Mathematical and Physical Sciences, 1823, 12mo, which, though he was not technically a publisher, was printed for him--a book I should recommend to the collector of works of reference--there is a temperate description of his doctrines, which one may almost swear was one of his conditions previous to undertaking the work. Phillips himself was not only an anti-Newtonian, but carried to a fearful excess the notion that statesmen and Newtonians were in league to deceive the world. He saw this plot in Mrs. Airy's[559] pension, and in Mrs. Somerville's[560]. In 1836, he {243} did me the honor to attempt my conversion. In his first letter he says:

"Sir Richard Phillips has an inveterate abhorrence of all the pretended wisdom of philosophy derived from the monks and doctors of the middle ages, and not less of those of higher name who merely sought to make the monkish philosophy more plausible, or so to disguise it as to mystify the mob of small thinkers."

So little did his writings show any knowledge of antiquity, that I strongly suspect, if required to name one of the monkish doctors, he would have answered--Aristotle. These schoolmen, and the "philosophical trinity of gravitating force, projectile force, and void space," were the bogies of his life.

I think he began to publish speculations in the Monthly Magazine (of which he was editor) in July 1817: these he republished separately in 1818. In the Preface, perhaps judging the feelings of others by his own, he says that he "fully expects to be vilified, reviled, and anathematized, for many years to come." Poor man! he was let alone. He appeals with confidence to the "impartial decision of posterity"; but posterity does not appoint a hearing for one per cent. of the appeals which are made; and it is much to be feared that an article in such a work of reference as this will furnish nearly all her materials fifty years hence. The following, addressed to M. Arago,[561] in 1835, will give posterity as good a notion as she will probably need:

"Even the present year has afforded EVER-MEMORABLE examples, paralleled only by that of the Romish Conclave which persecuted Galileo. Policy has adopted that maxim of Machiavel which teaches that it is more prudent to reward {244} partisans than to persecute opponents. Hence, a bigotted party had influence enough with the late short-lived administration [I think he is wrong as to the administration] of Wellington, Peel, &c., to confer munificent royal pensions on three writers whose sole distinction was their advocacy of the Newtonian philosophy. A Cambridge professor last year published an elaborate volume in illustration of Gravitation, and on him has been conferred a pension of 300l. per annum. A lady has written a light popular view of the Newtonian Dogmas, and she has been complimented by a pension of 200l. per annum. And another writer, who has recently published a volume to prove that the only true philosophy is that of Moses, has been endowed with a pension of 200l. per annum.

Neither of them were needy persons, and the political and ecclesiastical bearing of the whole was indicated by another pension of 300l. bestowed on a political writer, the advocate of all abuses and prejudices. Whether the conduct of the Romish Conclave was more base for visiting with legal penalties the promulgation of the doctrines that the Earth turns on its axis and revolves around the Sun; or that of the British Court, for its craft in conferring pensions on the opponents of the plain corollary, that all the motions of the Earth are 'part and parcel' of these great motions, and those again and all like them consecutive displays of still greater motions in equality of action and reaction, is A QUESTION which must be reserved for the casuists of other generations.... I cannot expect that on a sudden you and your friends will come to my conclusion, that the present philosophy of the Schools and Universities of Europe, based on faith in witchcraft, magic, &c., is a system of execrable nonsense, by which quacks live on the faith of fools; but I desire a free and fair examination of my Aphorisms, and if a few are admitted to be true, merely as courteous concessions to arithmetic, my purpose will be effected, for men will thus be led to think; and if they think, then the fabric {245} of false assumptions, and degrading superstitions will soon tumble in ruins."

This for posterity. For the present time I ground the fame of Sir R. Phillips on his having squared the circle without knowing it, or intending to do it. In the Protest presently noted he discovered that "the force taken as 1 is equal to the sum of all its fractions ... thus 1 = 1/4 + 1/9 + 1/16 + 1/25, &c., carried to infinity." This the mathematician instantly sees is equivalent to the theorem that the circumference of any circle is double of the diagonal of the cube on its diameter.[562]

I have examined the following works of Sir R. Phillips, and heard of many others:

Essays on the proximate mechanical causes of the general phenomena of the Universe, 1818, 12mo.[563]

Protest against the prevailing principles of natural philosophy, with the development of a common sense system (no date, 8vo, pp. 16).[564]

Four dialogues between an Oxford Tutor and a disciple of the common-sense philosophy, relative to the proximate causes of material phenomena. 8vo, 1824.

A century of original aphorisms on the proximate causes of the phenomena of nature, 1835, 12mo.

Sir Richard Phillips had four valuable qualities; honesty, zeal, ability, and courage. He applied them all to teaching {246} matters about which he knew nothing; and gained himself an uncomfortable life and a ridiculous memory.

Astronomy made plain; or only way the true perpendicular distance of the Sun, Moon, or Stars, from this earth, can be obtained. By Wm. Wood.[565] Chatham, 1819, 12mo.

If this theory be true, it will follow, of course, that this earth is the only one God made, and that it does not whirl round the sun, but vice versa, the sun round it.

WHATELY'S FAMOUS PARADOX

Historic doubts relative to Napoleon Buonaparte. London, 1819, 8vo.

This tract has since been acknowledged by Archbishop Whately[566] and reprinted. It is certainly a paradox: but differs from most of those in my list as being a joke, and a satire upon the reasoning of those who cannot receive narrative, no matter what the evidence, which is to them utterly improbable a priori. But had it been serious earnest, it would not have been so absurd as many of those which I have brought forward. The next on the list is not a joke.

The idea of the satire is not new. Dr. King,[567] in the dispute on the genuineness of Phalaris, proved with humor that Bentley did not write his own dissertation. An attempt has lately been made, for the honor of Moses, to prove, {247} without humor, that Bishop Colenso did not write his own book. This is intolerable: anybody who tries to use such a weapon without banter, plenty and good, and of form suited to the subject, should get the drubbing which the poor man got in the Oriental tale for striking the dervishes with the wrong hand.

The excellent and distinguished author of this tract has ceased to live. I call him the Paley of our day: with more learning and more purpose than his predecessor; but perhaps they might have changed places if they had changed centuries. The clever satire above named is not the only work which he published without his name. The following was attributed to him, I believe rightly: "Considerations on the Law of Libel, as relating to Publications on the subject of Religion, by John Search." London, 1833, 8vo. This tract excited little attention: for those who should have answered, could not. Moreover, it wanted a prosecution to call attention to it: the fear of calling such attention may have prevented prosecutions. Those who have read it will have seen why.

The theological review elsewhere mentioned attributes the pamphlet of John Search on blasphemous libel to Lord Brougham. This is quite absurd: the writer states points of law on credence where the judge must have spoken with authority. Besides which, a hundred points of style are decisive between the two. I think any one who knows Whately's writing will soon arrive at my conclusion. Lord Brougham himself informs me that he has no knowledge whatever of the pamphlet.

It is stated in Notes and Queries (3 S. xi. 511) that Search was answered by the Bishop of Ferns[568] as S. N., with {248} a rejoinder by Blanco White.[569] These circumstances increase the probability that Whately was written against and for.

VOLTAIRE A CHRISTIAN

Voltaire Chrétien; preuves tirées de ses ouvrages. Paris, 1820, 12mo.

If Voltaire have not succeeded in proving himself a strong theist and a strong anti-revelationist, who is to succeed in proving himself one thing or the other in any matter whatsoever? By occasional confusion between theism and Christianity; by taking advantage of the formal phrases of adhesion to the Roman Church, which very often occur, and are often the happiest bits of irony in an ironical production; by citations of his morality, which is decidedly Christian, though often attributed to Brahmins; and so on--the author makes a fair case for his paradox, in the eyes of those who know no more than he tells them. If he had said that Voltaire was a better Christian than himself knew of, towards all mankind except men of letters, I for one should have agreed with him.

Christian! the word has degenerated into a synonym of man, in what are called Christian countries. So we have the parrot who "swore for all the world like a Christian," and the two dogs who "hated each other just like Christians." When the Irish duellist of the last century, whose name may be spared in consideration of its historic fame {249} and the worthy people who bear it, was (June 12, 1786) about to take the consequence of his last brutal murder, the rope broke, and the criminal got up, and exclaimed, "By ---- Mr. Sheriff, you ought to be ashamed of yourself! this rope is not strong enough to hang a dog, far less a Christian!" But such things as this are far from the worst depravations. As to a word so defiled by usage, it is well to know that there is a way of escape from it, without renouncing the New Testament. I suppose any one may assume for himself what I have sometimes heard contended for, that no New Testament word is to be used in religion in any sense except that of the New Testament. This granted, the question is settled. The word Christian, which occurs three times, is never recognized as anything but a term of contempt from those without the pale to those within. Thus, Herod Agrippa, who was deep in Jewish literature, and a correspondent of Josephus, says to Paul (Acts xxvi. 28), "Almost thou persuadest me to be (what I and other followers of the state religion despise under the name) a Christian." Again (Acts xi. 26), "The disciples (as they called themselves) were called (by the surrounding heathens) Christians first in Antioch." Thirdly (1 Peter iv. 16), "Let none of you suffer as a murderer.... But if as a Christian (as the heathen call it by whom the suffering comes), let him not be ashamed." That is to say, no disciple ever called himself a Christian, or applied the name, as from himself, to another disciple, from one end of the New Testament to the other; and no disciple need apply that name to himself in our day, if he dislike the associations with which the conduct of Christians has clothed it.

WRONSKI ON THE LONGITUDE PROBLEM

Address of M. Hoene Wronski to the British Board of Longitude, upon the actual state of the mathematics, their reform, {250} and upon the new celestial mechanics, giving the definitive solution of the problem of longitude.[570] London, 1820, 8vo.

M. Wronski[571] was the author of seven quartos on mathematics, showing very great power of generalization. He was also deep in the transcendental philosophy,[572] and had the Absolute at his fingers' ends. All this knowledge was rendered useless by a persuasion that he had greatly advanced beyond the whole world, with many hints that the Absolute would not be forthcoming, unless prepaid. He was a man of the widest extremes. At one time he desired people to see all possible mathematics in Fx = A{0}[Omega]{0} + A{1}[Omega]{1} + A{2}[Omega]{2} + A{3}[Omega]{3} + &c.

Which he did not explain, though there is meaning to it in the quartos. At another time he was proposing the general solution of the[573] fifth degree by help of 625 independent equations of one form and 125 of another. The first separate memoir from any Transactions that I ever possessed was given to me when at Cambridge; the refutation (1819) of this asserted solution, presented to the Academy of Lisbon by Evangelista Torriano. I cannot say I read it. The tract above is an attack on modern mathematicians in general, and on the Board of Longitude, and Dr. Young.[574]

{251}

DR. MILNER'S PARADOXES

1820. In this year died Dr. Isaac Milner,[575] President of Queens' College, Cambridge, one of the class of rational paradoxers. Under this name I include all who, in private life, and in matters which concern themselves, take their own course, and suit their own notions, no matter what other people may think of them. These men will put things to uses they were never intended for, to the great distress and disgust of their gregarious friends. I am one of the class, and I could write a little book of cases in which I have incurred absolute reproach for not "doing as other people do." I will name two of my atrocities: I took one of those butter-dishes which have for a top a dome with holes in it, which is turned inward, out of reach of accident, when not in use. Turning the dome inwards, I filled the dish with water, and put a sponge in the dome: the holes let it fill with water, and I had a penwiper, always moist, and worth its price five times over. "Why! what do you mean? It was made to hold butter. You are always at some queer thing or other!" I bought a leaden comb, intended to dye the hair, it being supposed that the application of lead will have this effect. I did not try: but I divided the comb into two, separated the part of closed prongs from the other; and thus I had two ruling machines. The lead marks paper, and by drawing the end of one of the machines along a ruler, I could rule twenty lines at a time, quite fit to write on. I thought I should have killed a friend to whom I explained it: he could not for the life of him understand how leaden lines on paper would dye the hair.

But Dr. Milner went beyond me. He wanted a seat suited to his shape, and he defied opinion to a fearful point. {252} He spread a thick block of putty over a wooden chair and sat in it until it had taken a ceroplast copy of the proper seat. This he gave to a carpenter to be imitated in wood. One of the few now living who knew him--my friend, General Perronet Thompson[576]--answers for the wood, which was shown him by Milner himself; but he does not vouch for the material being putty, which was in the story told me at Cambridge; William Frend[577] also remembered it.

Perhaps the Doctor took off his great seal in green wax, like the Crown; but some soft material he certainly adopted; and very comfortable he found the wooden copy.

[Illustration]

The same gentleman vouches for Milner's lamp: but this had visible science in it; the vulgar see no science in the construction of the chair. A hollow semi-cylinder, but not with a circular curve, revolved on pivots. The curve was calculated on the law that, whatever quantity of oil might be in the lamp, the position of equilibrium just brought the oil up to the edge of the cylinder, at which a bit of wick was placed. As the wick exhausted the oil, the cylinder slowly revolved about the pivots so as to keep the oil always touching the wick.

Great discoveries are always laughed at; but it is very often not the laugh of incredulity; it is a mode of distorting the sense of inferiority into a sense of superiority, or a mimicry of superiority interposed between the laugher and his feeling of inferiority. Two persons in conversation {253} agreed that it was often a nuisance not to be able to lay hands on a bit of paper to mark the place in a book, every bit of paper on the table was sure to contain something not to be spared. I very quietly said that I always had a stock of bookmarkers ready cut, with a proper place for them: my readers owe many of my anecdotes to this absurd practice. My two colloquials burst into a fit of laughter; about what? Incredulity was out of the question; and there could be nothing foolish in my taking measures to avoid what they knew was an inconvenience. I was in this matter obviously their superior, and so they laughed at me. Much more candid was the Royal Duke of the last century, who was noted for slow ideas. "The rain comes into my mouth," said he, while riding. "Had not your Royal Highness better shut your mouth?" said the equerry. The Prince did so, and ought, by rule, to have laughed heartily at his adviser; instead of this, he said quietly, "It doesn't come in now."

HERBART'S MATHEMATICAL PSYCHOLOGY

De Attentionis mensura causisque primariis. By J. F. Herbart.[578] Koenigsberg, 1822, 4to.

{254}

This celebrated philosopher maintained that mathematics ought to be applied to psychology, in a separate tract, published also in 1822: the one above seems, therefore, to be his challenge on the subject. It is on attention, and I think it will hardly support Herbart's thesis. As a specimen of his formula, let t be the time elapsed since the consideration began, [beta] the whole perceptive intensity of the individual, [phi] the whole of his mental force, and z the force given to a notion by attention during the time t. Then, z = [phi] (1 - [epsilon]^{-[beta]t})

Now for a test. There is a jactura, v, the meaning of which I do not comprehend. If there be anything in it, my mathematical readers ought to interpret it from the formula v = [pi][phi][beta]/(1 - [beta])[epsilon]^{-[beta]t} + C[epsilon]^{-t} and to this task I leave them, wishing them better luck than mine. The time may come when other manifestations of mind, besides belief, shall be submitted to calculation: at that time, should it arrive, a final decision may be passed upon Herbart.

ON THE WHIZGIG

The theory of the Whizgig considered; in as much as it mechanically exemplifies the three working properties of nature; which are now set forth under the guise of this toy, for children of all ages. London, 1822, 12mo (pp. 24, B. McMillan, Bow Street, Covent Garden).

The toy called the whizgig will be remembered by many. The writer is a follower of Jacob Behmen,[579] William Law,[580] {255} Richard Clarke,[581] and Eugenius Philalethes.[582] Jacob Behmen first announced the three working properties of nature, which Newton stole, as described in the Gentleman's Magazine, July, 1782, p. 329. These laws are illustrated in the whizgig. There is the harsh astringent, attractive compression; the bitter compunction, repulsive expansion; and the stinging anguish, duplex motion. The author hints that he has written other works, to which he gives no clue. I have heard that Behmen was pillaged by Newton, and Swedenborg[583] by Laplace,[584] and Pythagoras by Copernicus,[585] and Epicurus by Dalton,[586] &c. I do not think this mention will revive Behmen; but it may the whizgig, a very pretty toy, and philosophical withal, for few of those who used it could explain it.

{256}

SOME MYTHOLOGICAL PARADOXES

A Grammar of infinite forms; or the mathematical elements of ancient philosophy and mythology. By Wm. Howison.[587] Edinburgh, 1823, 8vo.

A curius combination of geometry and mythology. Perseus, for instance, is treated under the head, "the evolution of diminishing hyperbolic branches."

The Mythological Astronomy of the Ancients; part the second: or the key of Urania, the words of which will unlock all the mysteries of antiquity. Norwich, 1823, 12mo.

A Companion to the Mythological Astronomy, &c., containing remarks on recent publications.... Norwich, 1824, 12mo.

A new Theory of the Earth and of planetary motion; in which it is demonstrated that the Sun is vicegerent of his own system. Norwich, 1825, 12mo.

The analyzation of the writings of the Jews, so far as they are found to have any connection with the sublime science of astronomy. [This is pp. 97-180 of some other work, being all I have seen.]

These works are all by Sampson Arnold Mackey,[588] for whom see Notes and Queries, 1st S. viii. 468, 565, ix. 89, 179. Had it not been for actual quotations given by one correspondent only (1st S. viii. 565), that journal would have handed him down as a man of some real learning. An extraordinary man he certainly was: it is not one illiterate shoemaker in a thousand who could work upon such a singular mass of Sanskrit and Greek words, without showing {257} evidence of being able to read a line in any language but his own, or to spell that correctly. He was an uneducated Godfrey Higgins.[589] A few extracts will put this in a strong light: one for history of science, one for astronomy, and one for philology:

"Sir Isaac Newton was of opinion that 'the atmosphere of the earth was the sensory of God; by which he was enabled to see quite round the earth:' which proves that Sir Isaac had no idea that God could see through the earth.

"Sir Richard [Phillips] has given the most rational explanation of the cause of the earth's elliptical orbit that I have ever seen in print. It is because the earth presents its watery hemisphere to the sun at one time and that of solid land the other; but why has he made his Oxonian astonished at the coincidence? It is what I taught in my attic twelve years before.

"Again, admitting that the Eloim were powerful and intelligent beings that managed these things, we would accuse them of being the authors of all the sufferings of Chrisna. And as they and the constellation of Leo were below the horizon, and consequently cut off from the end of the zodiac, there were but eleven constellations of the zodiac to be seen; the three at the end were wanted, but those three would be accused of bringing Chrisna into the troubles which at last ended in his death. All this would be expressed in the Eastern language by saying that Chrisna was persecuted by those Judoth Ishcarioth!!!!! [the five notes of exclamation are the author's]. But the astronomy of those distant ages, when the sun was at the south pole in winter, would leave five of those Decans cut off from our view, in the latitude of twenty-eight degrees; hence Chrisna died of {258} wounds from five Decans, but the whole five may be included in Judoth Ishcarioth! for the phrase means 'the men that are wanted at the extreme parts.' Ishcarioth is a compound of ish, a man, and carat wanted or taken away, and oth the plural termination, more ancient than im...."

I might show at length how Michael is the sun, and the D'-ev-'l in French Di-ob-al, also 'L-evi-ath-an--the evi being the radical part both of devil and leviathan--is the Nile, which the sun dried up for Moses to pass: a battle celebrated by Jude. Also how Moses, the same name as Muses, is from mesha, drawn out of the water, "and hence we called our land which is saved from the water by the name of marsh." But it will be of more use to collect the character of S. A. M. from such correspondents of Notes and Queries as have written after superficial examination. Great astronomical and philological attainments, much ability and learning; had evidently read and studied deeply; remarkable for the originality of his views upon the very abstruse subject of mythological astronomy, in which he exhibited great sagacity. Certainly his views were original; but their sagacity, if it be allowable to copy his own mode of etymologizing, is of an ori-gin-ale cast, resembling that of a person who puts to his mouth liquors both distilled and fermented.

A KANTESIAN JEWELER

Principles of the Kantesian, or transcendental philosophy. By Thomas Wirgman.[590] London, 1824, 8vo.

Mr. Wirgman's mind was somewhat attuned to psychology; but he was cracky and vagarious. He had been a fashionable jeweler in St. James's Street, no doubt the son or grandson of Wirgman at "the well-known toy-shop in {259} St. James's Street," where Sam Johnson smartened himself with silver buckles. (Boswell, æt. 69). He would not have the ridiculous large ones in fashion; and he would give no more than a guinea a pair; such, says Boswell, in Italics, were the principles of the business: and I think this may be the first place in which the philosophical word was brought down from heaven to mix with men. However this may be, my Wirgman sold snuff-boxes, among other things, and fifty years ago a fashionable snuff-boxer would be under inducement, if not positively obliged, to have a stock with very objectionable pictures. So it happened that Wirgman--by reason of a trifle too much candor--came under the notice of the Suppression Society, and ran considerable risk. Mr. Brougham was his counsel; and managed to get him acquitted. Years and years after this, when Mr. Brougham was deep in the formation of the London University (now University College), Mr. Wirgman called on him. "What now?" said Mr. B. with his most sarcastic look--a very perfect thing of its kind--"you're in a scrape again, I suppose!" "No! indeed!" said W., "my present object is to ask your interest for the chair of Moral Philosophy in the new University!" He had taken up Kant!

Mr. Wirgman, an itinerant paradoxer, called on me in 1831: he came to convert me. "I assure you," said he, "I am nothing but an old brute of a jeweler;" and his eye and manner were of the extreme of jocosity, as good in their way, as the satire of his former counsel. I mention him as one of that class who go away quite satisfied that they have wrought conviction. "Now," said he, "I'll make it clear to you! Suppose a number of gold-fishes in a glass bowl,--you understand? Well! I come with my cigar and go puff, puff, puff, over the bowl, until there is a little cloud of smoke: now, tell me, what will the gold-fishes say to that?" "I should imagine," said I, "That they would not know what to make of it." "By Jove! you're a Kantian;" said he, and with this and the like, he left me, vowing that {260} it was delightful to talk to so intelligent a person. The greatest compliment Wirgman ever received was from James Mill, who used to say he did not understand Kant. That such a man as Mill should think this worth saying is a feather in the cap of the jocose jeweler.

Some of my readers will stare at my supposing that Boswell may have been the first down-bringer of the word principles into common life; the best answer will be a prior instance of the word as true vernacular; it has never happened to me to notice one. Many words have very common uses which are not old. Take the following from Nichols (Anecd. ix. 263): "Lord Thurlow presents his best respects to Mr. and Mrs. Thicknesse, and assures them that he knows of no cause to complain of any part of Mr. Thicknesse's carriage; least of all the circumstance of sending the head to Ormond Street."

Surely Mr. T. had lent Lord T. a satisfactory carriage with a movable head, and the above is a polite answer to inquiries. Not a bit of it! carriage is here conduct, and the head is a bust. The vehicles of the rich, at the time, were coaches, chariots, chaises, etc., never carriages, which were rather carts. Gibbon has the word for baggage-wagons. In Jane Austen's novels the word carriage is established.

WALSH'S DELUSIONS.

John Walsh,[591] of Cork (1786-1847). This discoverer has had the honor of a biography from Professor Boole, who, at my request, collected information about him on the scene of his labors. It is in the Philosophical Magazine for November, 1851, and will, I hope, be transferred to some biographical collection where it may find a larger class of readers. It is the best biography of a single hero of the kind that I know. Mr. Walsh introduced himself to me, {261} as he did to many others, in the anterowlandian days of the Post-office; his unpaid letters were double, treble, &c. They contained his pamphlets, and cost their weight in silver: all have the name of the author, and all are in octavo or in quarto letter-form: most are in four pages, and all dated from Cork. I have the following by me:

The Geometric Base, 1825.--The theory of plane angles. 1827.--Three Letters to Dr. Francis Sadleir. 1838.--The invention of polar geometry. By Irelandus. 1839.--The theory of partial functions. Letter to Lord Brougham. 1839.--On the invention of polar geometry. 1839.--Letter to the Editor of the Edinburgh Review. 1840.--Irish Manufacture. A new method of tangents. 1841.--The normal diameter in curves. 1843.--Letter to Sir R. Peel. 1845.--[Hints that Government should compel the introduction of Walsh's Geometry into Universities.]--Solution of Equations of the higher orders. 1845.

Besides these, there is a Metalogia, and I know not how many others.

Mr. Boole,[592] who has taken the moral and social features of Walsh's delusions from the commiserating point of view, which makes ridicule out of place, has been obliged to treat Walsh as Scott's Alan Fairford treated his client Peter Peebles; namely, keep the scarecrow out of court while the case was argued. My plan requires me to bring him in: and when he comes in at the door, pity and sympathy fly out at the window. Let the reader remember that he was not an ignoramus in mathematics: he might have won his spurs if he could have first served as an esquire. Though so illiterate that even in Ireland he never picked up anything more Latin than Irelandus, he was a very pretty mathematician spoiled in the making by intense self-opinion.

This is part of a private letter to me at the back of a page of print: I had never addressed a word to him:

{262}

"There are no limits in mathematics, and those that assert there are, are infinite ruffians, ignorant, lying blackguards. There is no differential calculus, no Taylor's theorem, no calculus of variations, &c. in mathematics. There is no quackery whatever in mathematics; no % equal to anything. What sheer ignorant blackguardism that!

"In mechanics the parallelogram of forces is quackery, and is dangerous; for nothing is at rest, or in uniform, or in rectilinear motion, in the universe. Variable motion is an essential property of matter. Laplace's demonstration of the parallelogram of forces is a begging of the question; and the attempts of them all to show that the difference of twenty minutes between the sidereal and actual revolution of the earth round the sun arises from the tugging of the Sun and Moon at the pot-belly of the earth, without being sure even that the earth has a pot-belly at all, is perfect quackery. The said difference arising from and demonstrating the revolution of the Sun itself round some distant center."

In the letter to Lord Brougham we read as follows:

"I ask the Royal Society of London, I ask the Saxon crew of that crazy hulk, where is the dogma of their philosophic god now?... When the Royal Society of London, and the Academy of Sciences of Paris, shall have read this memorandum, how will they appear? Like two cur dogs in the paws of the noblest beast of the forest.... Just as this note was going to press, a volume lately published by you was put into my hands, wherein you attempt to defend the fluxions and Principia of Newton. Man! what are you about? You come forward now with your special pleading, and fraught with national prejudice, to defend, like the philosopher Grassi,[593] the persecutor of Galileo, principles {263} and reasoning which, unless you are actually insane, or an ignorant quack in mathematics, you know are mathematically false. What a moral lesson this for the students of the University of London from its head! Man! demonstrate corollary 3, in this note, by the lying dogma of Newton, or turn your thoughts to something you understand.

"WALSH IRELANDUS."

Mr. Walsh--honor to his memory--once had the consideration to save me postage by addressing a pamphlet under cover to a Member of Parliament, with an explanatory letter. In that letter he gives a candid opinion of himself:

(1838.) "Mr. Walsh takes leave to send the enclosed corrected copy to Mr. Hutton as one of the Council of the University of London, and to save postage for the Professor of Mathematics there. He will find in it geometry more deep and subtle, and at the same time more simple and elegant, than it was ever contemplated human genius could invent."

He then proceeds to set forth that a certain "tomfoolery lemma," with its "tomfoolery" superstructure, "never had existence outside the shallow brains of its inventor," Euclid. He then proceeds thus:

"The same spirit that animated those philosophers who sent Galileo to the Inquisition animates all the philosophers of the present day without exception. If anything can free them from the yoke of error, it is the [Walsh] problem of double tangence. But free them it will, how deeply soever they may be sunk into mental slavery--and God knows that is deeply enough; and they bear it with an admirable grace; for none bear slavery with a better grace than tyrants. The lads must adopt my theory.... It will be a sad reverse for all our great professors to be compelled to become schoolboys in their gray years. But the sore scratch is to be compelled, as they had before been compelled one thousand years ago, to have recourse to Ireland for instruction." {264}

The following "Impromptu" is no doubt by Walsh himself: he was more of a poet than of an astronomer:

"Through ages unfriended, With sophistry blended, Deep science in Chaos had slept; Its limits were fettered, Its voters unlettered, Its students in movements but crept. Till, despite of great foes, Great WALSH first arose, And with logical might did unravel Those mazes of knowledge, Ne'er known in a college, Though sought for with unceasing travail. With cheers we now hail him, May success never fail him, In Polar Geometrical mining; Till his foes be as tamed As his works are far-famed For true philosophic refining."

Walsh's system is, that all mathematics and physics are wrong: there is hardly one proposition in Euclid which is demonstrated. His example ought to warn all who rely on their own evidence to their own success. He was not, properly speaking, insane; he only spoke his mind more freely than many others of his class. The poor fellow died in the Cork union, during the famine. He had lived a happy life, contemplating his own perfections, like Brahma on the lotus-leaf.[594]

{265}

GROWTH OF FREEDOM OF OPINION.

The year 1825 brings me to about the middle of my Athenæum list: that is, so far as mere number of names mentioned is concerned. Freedom of opinion, beyond a doubt, is gaining ground, for good or for evil, according to what the speaker happens to think: admission of authority is no longer made in the old way. If we take soul-cure and body-cure, divinity and medicine, it is manifest that a change has come over us. Time was when it was enough that dose or dogma should be certified by "Il a été ordonné, Monsieur, il a été ordonné,"[595] as the apothecary said when he wanted to operate upon poor de Porceaugnac. Very much changed: but whether for good or for evil does not now matter; the question is, whether contempt of demonstration such as our paradoxers show has augmented with the rejection of dogmatic authority. It ought to be just the other way: for the worship of reason is the system on which, if we trust them, the deniers of guidance ground their plan of life. The following attempt at an experiment on this point is the best which I can make; and, so far as I know, the first that ever was made.

Say that my list of paradoxers divides in 1825: this of itself proves nothing, because so many of the earlier books are lost, or not likely to be come at. It would be a fearful rate of increase which would make the number of paradoxes since 1825 equal to the whole number before that date. Let us turn now to another collection of mine, arithmetical books, of which I have published a list. The two collections are similarly circumstanced as to new and old books; the paradoxes had no care given to the collection of either; the arithmetical books equal care to both. The list of arithmetical books, published in 1847, divides at 1735; the paradoxes, up to 1863, divide at 1825. If we take the process which is most against the distinction, and allow every year {266} from 1847 to 1863 to add a year to 1735, we should say that the arithmetical writers divide at 1751. This rough process may serve, with sufficient certainty, to show that the proportion of paradoxes to books of sober demonstration is on the increase; and probably, quite as much as the proportion of heterodoxes to books of orthodox adherence. So that divinity and medicine may say to geometry, Don't you sneer: if rationalism, homoeopathy, and their congeners are on the rise among us, your enemies are increasing quite as fast. But geometry replies--Dear friends, content yourselves with the rational inference that the rise of heterodoxy within your pales is not conclusive against you, taken alone; for it rises at the same time within mine. Store within your garners the precious argument that you are not proved wrong by increase of dissent; because there is increase of dissent against exact science. But do not therefore even yourselves to me: remember that you, Dame Divinity, have inflicted every kind of penalty, from the stake to the stocks, in aid of your reasoning; remember that you, Mother Medicine, have not many years ago applied to Parliament for increase of forcible hindrance of antipharmacopoeal drenches, pills, and powders. Who ever heard of my asking the legislature to fine blundering circle-squarers? Remember that the D in dogma is the D in decay; but the D in demonstration is the D in durability.

THE STATUS OF MEDICINE

I have known a medical man--a young one--who was seriously of the opinion that the country ought to be divided into medical parishes, with a practitioner appointed to each, and a penalty for calling in any but the incumbent curer. How should people know how to choose? The hair-dressers once petitioned Parliament for an act to compel people to wear wigs. My own opinion is of the opposite extreme, as in the following letter (Examiner, April 5, 1856); which, to my surprise, I saw reprinted in a medical journal, as a {267} plan not absolutely to be rejected. I am perfectly satisfied that it would greatly promote true medical orthodoxy, the predominance of well educated thinkers, and the development of their desirable differences.

"SIR. The Medical Bill and the medical question generally is one on which experience would teach, if people would be taught.

"The great soul question took three hundred years to settle: the little body question might be settled in thirty years, if the decisions in the former question were studied.

"Time was when the State believed, as honestly as ever it believed anything, that it might, could, and should find out the true doctrine for the poor ignorant community; to which, like a worthy honest state, it added would. Accordingly, by the assistance of the Church, which undertook the physic, the surgery, and the pharmacy of sound doctrine all by itself, it sent forth its legally qualified teachers into every parish, and woe to the man who called in any other. They burnt that man, they whipped him, they imprisoned him, they did everything but what was Christian to him, all for his soul's health and the amendment of his excesses.

"But men would not submit. To the argument that the State was a father to the ignorant, they replied that it was at best the ignorant father of an ignorant son, and that a blind man could find his way into a ditch without another blind man to help him. And when the State said--But here we have the Church, which knows all about it, the ignorant community declared that it had a right to judge that question, and that it would judge it. It also said that the Church was never one thing long, and that it progressed, on the whole, rather more slowly than the ignorant community.

"The end of it was, in this country, that every one who chose taught all who chose to let him teach, on condition only of an open and true registration.

The State was {268} allowed to patronize one particular Church, so that no one need trouble himself to choose a pastor from the mere necessity of choosing. But every church is allowed its colleges, its studies, its diplomas; and every man is allowed his choice. There is no proof that our souls are worse off than in the sixteenth century; and, judging by fruits, there is much reason to hope they are better off.

"Now the little body question is a perfect parallel to the great soul question in all its circumstances. The only things in which the parallel fails are the following: Every one who believes in a future state sees that the soul question is incomparably more important than the body question, and every one can try the body question by experiment to a larger extent than the soul question. The proverb, which always has a spark of truth at the bottom, says that every man of forty is either a fool or a physician; but did even the proverb maker ever dare to say that every man is at any age either a fool or a fit teacher of religion?

"Common sense points out the following settlement of the medical question: and to this it will come sooner or later.

"Let every man who chooses--subject to one common law of manslaughter for all the crass cases--doctor the bodies of all who choose to trust him, and recover payment according to agreement in the courts of law. Provided always that every person practising should be registered at a moderate fee in a register to be republished every six months.

"Let the register give the name, address, and asserted qualification of each candidate--as licentiate, or doctor, or what not, of this or that college, hall, university, &c., home or foreign. Let it be competent to any man to describe himself as qualified by study in public schools without a diploma, or by private study, or even by intuition or divine inspiration, if he please. But whatever he holds his qualification to be, that let him declare. Let all qualification {269} which of its own nature admits of proof be proved, as by the diploma or certificate, &c., leaving things which cannot be proved, as asserted private study, intuition, inspiration, &c., to work their own way.

"Let it be highly penal to assert to the patient any qualification which is not in the register, and let the register be sold very cheap. Let the registrar give each registered practitioner a copy of the register in his own case; let any patient have the power to demand a sight of this copy; and let no money for attendance be recoverable in any case in which there has been false representation.

"Let any party in any suit have a right to produce what medical testimony he pleases. Let the medical witness produce his register, and let his evidence be for the jury, as is that of an engineer or a practitioner of any art which is not attested by diplomas.

"Let any man who practises without venturing to put his name on the register be liable to fine and imprisonment.

"The consequence would be that, as now, anybody who pleases might practise; for the medical world is well aware that there is no power of preventing what they call quacks from practising. But very different from what is now, every man who practises would be obliged to tell the whole world what his claim is, and would run a great risk if he dared to tell his patient in private anything different from what he had told the whole world.

"The consequence would be that a real education in anatomy, physiology, chemistry, surgery, and what is known of the thing called medicine, would acquire more importance than it now has.

"It is curious to see how completely the medical man of the nineteenth century squares with the priest of the sixteenth century. The clergy of all sects are now better divines and better men than they ever were. They have lost Bacon's reproach that they took a smaller measure of things than any other educated men; and the physicians are now {270} in this particular the rearguard of the learned world; though it may be true that the rear in our day is further on in the march than the van of Bacon's day. Nor will they ever recover the lost position until medicine is as free as religion.

"To this it must come. To this the public, which will decide for itself, has determined it shall come. To this the public has, in fact, brought it, but on a plan which it is not desirable to make permanent. We will be as free to take care of our bodies as of our souls and of our goods. This is the profession of all who sign as I do, and the practice of most of those who would not like the name

"HETEROPATH."

The motion of the Sun in the Ecliptic, proved to be uniform in a circular orbit ... with preliminary observations on the fallacy of the Solar System. By Bartholomew Prescott,[596] 1825, 8vo.

The author had published, in 1803, a Defence of the Divine System, which I never saw; also, On the inverted scheme of Copernicus. The above work is clever in its satire.

THE CHRISTIAN EVIDENCE SOCIETY.

Manifesto of the Christian Evidence Society, established Nov. 12, 1824. Twenty-four plain questions to honest men.

These are two broadsides of August and November, 1826, signed by Robert Taylor,[597] A.B., Orator of the Christian Evidence Society. This gentleman was a clergyman, {271} and was convicted of blasphemy in 1827, for which he suffered imprisonment, and got the name of the Devil's Chaplain. The following are quotations:

"For the book of Revelation, there was no original Greek at all, but Erasmus wrote it himself in Switzerland, in the year 1516. Bishop Marsh,[598] vol. i. p. 320."--"Is not God the author of your reason? Can he then be the author of anything which is contrary to your reason? If reason be a sufficient guide, why should God give you any other? if it be not a sufficient guide, why has he given you that?"

I remember a votary of the Society being asked to substitute for reason "the right leg," and for guide "support," and to answer the two last questions: he said there must be a quibble, but he did not see what. It is pleasant to reflect that the argumentum à carcere[599] is obsolete. One great defect of it was that it did not go far enough: there should have been laws against subscriptions for blasphemers, against dealing at their shops, and against rich widows marrying them.

Had I taken in theology, I must have entered books against Christianity. I mention the above, and Paine's Age of Reason, simply because they are the only English modern works that ever came in my way without my asking for them. The three parts of the Age of Reason were published in Paris 1793, Paris 1795, and New York 1807. Carlile's[600] edition is of London, 1818, 8vo. It must be republished when the time comes, to show what stuff governments and clergy were afraid of at the beginning of this century. I should never have seen the book, if it {272} had not been prohibited: a bookseller put it under my nose with a fearful look round him; and I could do no less, in common curiosity, than buy a work which had been so complimented by church and state. And when I had read it, I said in my mind to church and state,--Confound you! you have taken me in worse than any reviewer I ever met with. I forget what I gave for the book, but I ought to have been able to claim compensation somewhere.

THE CABBALA.

Cabbala Algebraica. Auctore Gul. Lud. Christmann.[601] Stuttgard, 1827, 4to.

Eighty closely printed pages of an attempt to solve equations of every degree, which has a process called by the author cabbala. An anonymous correspondent spells cabbala as follows, [Greek: chabball], and makes 666 out of its letters. This gentleman has sent me since my Budget commenced, a little heap of satirical communications, each having a 666 or two; for instance, alluding to my remarks on the spelling of chemistry, he finds the fated number in [Greek: chimeia]. With these are challenges to explain them, and hints about the end of the world. All these letters have different fantastic seals; one of them with the legend "keep your temper,"--another bearing "bank token five pence." The only signature is a triangle with a little circle in it, which I interpret to mean that the writer confesses himself to be the round man stuck in the three-cornered hole, to be explained as in Sydney Smith's joke.

{273}

There is a kind of Cabbala Alphabetica which the investigators of the numerals in words would do well to take up: it is the formation of sentences which contain all the letters of the alphabet, and each only once. No one has done it with v and j treated as consonants; but you and I can do it. Dr. Whewell[602] and I amused ourselves, some years ago, with attempts. He could not make sense, though he joined words: he gave me Phiz, styx, wrong, buck, flame, quid.

I gave him the following, which he agreed was "admirable sense": I certainly think the words would never have come together except in this way:

I, quartz pyx, who fling muck beds.

I long thought that no human being could say this under any circumstances.
At last I happened to be reading a religious writer--as he thought himself--who threw aspersions on his opponents thick and threefold.

Heyday! came into my head, this fellow flings muck beds; he must be a quartz pyx. And then I remembered that a pyx is a sacred vessel, and quartz is a hard stone, as hard as the heart of a religious foe-curser. So that the line is the motto of the ferocious sectarian, who turns his religious vessels into mudholders, for the benefit of those who will not see what he sees.

I can find no circumstances for the following, which I received from another:

Fritz! quick! land! hew gypsum box. From other quarters I have the following: Dumpy quiz! whirl back fogs next.
This might be said in time of haze to the queer little figure in the Dutch weather-toy, which comes out or goes in with the change in the atmosphere. Again, {274} Export my fund! Quiz black whigs.

This Squire Western might have said, who was always afraid of the whigs sending the sinking-fund over to Hanover. But the following is the best: it is good advice to a young man, very well expressed under the circumstances:

Get nymph; quiz sad brow; fix luck.

Which in more sober English would be, Marry; be cheerful; watch your business. There is more edification, more religion in this than in all the 666-interpretations put together.

Such things would make excellent writing copies, for they secure attention to every letter; v and j might be placed at the end.

ON GODFREY HIGGINS.

The Celtic Druids. By Godfrey Higgins,[603] Esq. of Skellow Grange, near Doncaster. London, 1827, 4to.

Anacalypsis, or an attempt to draw aside the veil of the Saitic Isis: or an inquiry into the origin of languages, nations, and religions. By Godfrey Higgins, &c..., London, 1836, 2 vols. 4to.

The first work had an additional preface and a new index in 1829. Possibly, in future time, will be found bound up with copies of the second work two sheets which Mr. Higgins circulated among his friends in 1831: the first a "Recapitulation," the second "Book vi. ch. 1."

The system of these works is that--

"The Buddhists of Upper India (of whom the Phenician Canaanite, Melchizedek, was a priest), who built the Pyramids, Stonehenge, Carnac, &c. will be shown to have founded all the ancient mythologies of the world, which, however varied and corrupted in recent times, were originally one, and that one founded on principles sublime, beautiful, and true."

{275}

These works contain an immense quantity of learning, very honestly put together. I presume the enormous number of facts, and the goodness of the index, to be the reasons why the Anacalypsis found a permanent place in the old reading-room of the British Museum, even before the change which greatly increased the number of books left free to the reader in that room.

Mr. Higgins, whom I knew well in the last six years of his life, and respected as a good, learned, and (in his own way) pious man, was thoroughly and completely the man of a system. He had that sort of mental connection with his theory that made his statements of his authorities trustworthy: for, besides perfect integrity, he had no bias towards alteration of facts: he saw his system in the way the fact was presented to him by his authority, be that what it might.

He was very sure of a fact which he got from any of his authorities: nothing could shake him. Imagine a conversation between him and an Indian officer who had paid long attention to Hindoo antiquities and their remains: a third person was present, ego qui scribo. G. H. "You know that in the temples of I-forget-who the Ceres is always sculptured precisely as in Greece." Col.

----, "I really do not remember it, and I have seen most of these temples."

G. H. "It is so, I assure you, especially at I-forget-where." Col. ----, "Well, I am sure! I was encamped for six weeks at the gate of that very temple, and, except a little shooting, had nothing to do but to examine its details, which I did, day after day, and I found nothing of the kind." It was of no use at all.

Godfrey Higgins began life by exposing and conquering, at the expense of two years of his studies, some shocking abuses which existed in the York Lunatic Asylum. This was a proceeding which called much attention to the treatment of the insane, and produced much good effect. He was very resolute and energetic. The magistracy of his {276} time had such scruples about using the severity of law to people of such station as well-to-do farmers, &c.: they would allow a great deal of resistance, and endeavor to mollify the rebels into obedience. A young farmer flatly refused to pay under an order of affiliation made upon him by Godfrey Higgins. He was duly warned; and persisted: he shortly found himself in gaol. He went there sure to conquer the Justice, and the first thing he did was to demand to see his lawyer. He was told, to his horror, that as soon as he had been cropped and prison-dressed, he might see as many lawyers as he pleased, to be looked at, laughed at, and advised that there was but one way out of the scrape. Higgins was, in his speculations, a regular counterpart of Bailly; but the celebrated Mayor of Paris had not his nerve. It was impossible to say, if their characters had been changed, whether the unfortunate crisis in which Bailly was not equal to the occasion would have led to very different results if Higgins had been in his place: but assuredly constitutional liberty would have had one chance more. There are two works of his by which he was known, apart from his paradoxes. First, An apology for the life and character of the celebrated prophet of Arabia, called Mohamed, or the Illustrious. London, 8vo. 1829. The reader will look at this writing of our English Buddhist with suspicious eye, but he will not be able to avoid confessing that the Arabian prophet has some reparation to demand at the hands of Christians. Next, Horæ Sabaticæ; or an attempt to correct certain superstitions and vulgar errors respecting the Sabbath. Second edition, with a large appendix. London, 12mo. 1833. This book was very heterodox at the time, but it has furnished material for some of the clergy of our day.

I never could quite make out whether Godfrey Higgins took that system which he traced to the Buddhists to have a Divine origin, or to be the result of good men's meditations. Himself a strong theist, and believer in a future

{277} state, one would suppose that he would refer a universal religion, spread in different forms over the whole earth from one source, directly to the universal Parent. And this I suspect he did, whether he knew it or not. The external evidence is balanced. In his preface he says:

"I cannot help smiling when I consider that the priests have objected to admit my former book, The Celtic Druids, into libraries, because it was antichristian; and it has been attacked by Deists, because it was superfluously religious. The learned Deist, the Rev. R. Taylor [already mentioned], has designated me as the religious Mr. Higgins."

The time will come when some profound historian of literature will make himself much clearer on the point than I am.

ON POPE'S DIPPING NEEDLE

The triumphal Chariot of Friction: or a familiar elucidation of the origin of magnetic attraction, &c. &c. By William Pope.[604] London, 1829, 4to.

Part of this work is on a dipping-needle of the author's construction. It must have been under the impression that a book of naval magnetism was proposed, that a great many officers, the Royal Naval Club, etc. lent their names to the subscription list. How must they have been surprised to find, right opposite to the list of subscribers, the plate presenting "the three emphatic letters, J. A. O." And how much more when they saw it set forth that if a square be inscribed in a circle, a circle within that, then a square again, &c., it is impossible to have more than fourteen circles, let the first circle be as large as you please. From this the seven attributes of God are unfolded; and further, that all matter was moral, until Lucifer churned it into physical "as far as the third circle in Deity": this Lucifer, called Leviathan in Job, being thus the moving cause of {278} chaos. I shall say no more, except that the friction of the air is the cause of magnetism.

Remarks on the Architecture, Sculpture, and Zodiac of Palmyra; with a Key to the Inscriptions. By B. Prescot.[605] London, 1830, 8vo.

Mr. Prescot gives the signs of the zodiac a Hebrew origin.

THE JACOTOT METHOD

Epitomé de mathématiques. Par F. Jacotot,[606] Avocat. 3ième edition, Paris, 1830, 8vo. (pp. 18).

Méthode Jacotot. Choix de propositions mathématiques. Par P. Y. Séprés.[607] 2nde édition. Paris, 1830, 8vo. (pp. 82).

Of Jacotot's method, which had some vogue in Paris, the principle was Tout est dans tout,[608] and the process Apprendre quelque chose, et à y rapporter tout le reste.[609] The first tract has a proposition in conic sections and its preliminaries: the second has twenty exercises, of which the first is finding the greatest common measure of two numbers, and the last is the motion of a point on a surface, acted on by given forces. This is topped up with the problem of sound in a tube, and a slice of Laplace's theory of the tides. All to be studied until known by heart, and all the rest will come, or at least join on easily when it comes. There is much truth in the assertion that new knowledge {279} hooks on easily to a little of the old, thoroughly mastered. The day is coming when it will be found out that crammed erudition, got up for examinations, does not cast out any hooks for more.

Lettre à MM. les Membres de l'Académie Royale des Sciences, contenant un développement de la réfutation du système de la gravitation universelle, qui leur a été présentée le 30 août, 1830. Par Félix Passot.[610] Paris, 1830, 8vo.

Works of this sort are less common in France than in England. In France there is only the Academy of Sciences to go to: in England there is a reading public out of the Royal Society, &c.

A DISCOURSE ON PROBABILITY

About 1830 was published, in the Library of Useful Knowledge, the tract on Probability, the joint work of the late Sir John Lubbock[611] and Mr. Drinkwater (Bethune).[612] It is one of the best elementary openings of the subject. A binder put my name on the outside (the work was anonymous) and the consequence was that nothing could drive out of people's heads that it was written by me. I do not know how many denials I have made, from a passage in one of my own works to a letter in the Times: and I am not sure that I have succeeded in establishing the truth, even now. I accordingly note the fact once more. But as a book has no right here unless it contain a paradox--or thing counter to general opinion or practice--I will produce two small ones. Sir John Lubbock, with whom lay the executive arrangement, had a strong objection to the last word in "Theory of Probabilities," he maintained that the singular probability, should be used; and I hold him quite right.

{280}

The second case was this: My friend Sir J. L., with a large cluster of intellectual qualities, and another of social qualities, had one point of character which I will not call bad and cannot call good; he never used a slang expression. To such a length did he carry his dislike, that he could not bear head and tail, even in a work on games of chance: so he used obverse and reverse. I stared when I first saw this: but, to my delight, I found that the force of circumstances beat him at last. He was obliged to take an example from the race-course, and the name of one of the horses was Bessy Bedlam! And he did not put her down as Elizabeth Bethlehem, but forced himself to follow the jockeys.

[Almanach Romain sur la Loterie Royale de France, ou les Etrennes nécessaires aux Actionnaires et Receveurs de la dite Loterie. Par M. Menut de St.-Mesmin. Paris, 1830. 12mo.

This book contains all the drawings of the French lottery (two or three, each month) from 1758 to 1830. It is intended for those who thought they could predict the future drawings from the past: and various sets of sympathetic numbers are given to help them. The principle is, that anything which has not happened for a long time must be soon to come. At rouge et noir, for example, when the red has won five times running, sagacious gamblers stake on the black, for they think the turn which must come at last is nearer than it was. So it is: but observation would have shown that if a large number of those cases had been registered which show a run of five for the red, the next game would just as often have made the run into six as have turned in favor of the black. But the gambling reasoner is incorrigible: if he would but take to squaring the circle, what a load of misery would be saved. A writer of 1823, who appeared to be thoroughly acquainted with the gambling of Paris and London, says that the gamesters by {281} profession are haunted by a secret foreboding of their future destruction, and seem as if they said to the banker at the table, as the gladiators said to the emperor, Morituri te salutant.[613]

In the French lottery, five numbers out of ninety were drawn at a time. Any person, in any part of the country, might stake any sum upon any event he pleased, as that 27 should be drawn; that 42 and 81 should be drawn; that 42 and 81 should be drawn, and 42 first; and so on up to a quine déterminé, if he chose, which is betting on five given numbers in a given order. Thus, in July, 1821, one of the drawings was 8 46 16 64 13.

A gambler had actually predicted the five numbers (but not their order), and won 131,350 francs on a trifling stake. M. Menut seems to insinuate that the hint what numbers to choose was given at his own office. Another won 20,852 francs on the quaterne, 8, 16, 46, 64, in this very drawing. These gains, of course, were widely advertised: of the multitudes who lost nothing was said. The enormous number of those who played is proved to all who have studied chances arithmetically by the numbers of simple quaternes which were gained: in 1822, fourteen; in 1823, six; in 1824, sixteen; in 1825, nine, &c.

The paradoxes of what is called chance, or hazard, might themselves make a small volume. All the world understands that there is a long run, a general average; but great part of the world is surprised that this general average should be computed and predicted. There are many remarkable cases of verification; and one of them relates to the quadrature of the circle. I give some account of this and another. Throw a penny time after time until head arrives, which it will do before long: let this be called a set. Accordingly, H is the smallest set, TH the next smallest, then TTH, &c. For abbreviation, let a set in which seven tails {282} occur before head turns up be T^{7}H. In an immense number of trials of sets, about half will be H; about a quarter TH; about an eighth, T^{2}H. Buffon[614] tried 2,048 sets; and several have followed him. It will tend to illustrate the principle if I give all the results; namely, that many trials will with moral certainty show an approach--and the greater the greater the number of trials--to that average which sober reasoning predicts. In the first column is the most likely number of the theory: the next column gives Buffon's result; the three next are results obtained from trial by correspondents of mine. In each case the number of trials is 2,048.

H 1,024 1,061 1,048 1,017 1,039 TH 512 494 507 547 480 T^{2}H 256 232 248 235 267 T^{3}H 128 137 99 118 126 T^{4}H 64 56 71 72 67

T^{5}H 32 29 38 32 33 T^{6}H 16 25 17 10 19 T^{7}H 8 8 9 9 10 T^{8}H 4 6 5 3 3 T^{9}H 2 3 2 4 T^{10}H 1 1 1 T^{11}H 0 1 T^{12}H 0 0 T^{13}H 1 1 0 T^{14}H 0 0 T^{15}H 1 1 &c. 0 0 ----- ----- ----- ----- ----- 2,048 2,048 2,048 2,048 2,048

{283}

In very many trials, then, we may depend upon something like the predicted average. Conversely, from many trials we may form a guess at what the average will be. Thus, in Buffon's experiment the 2,048 first throws of the sets gave head in 1,061 cases: we have a right to infer that in the long run something like 1,061 out of 2,048 is the proportion of heads, even before we know the reasons for the equality of chance, which tell us that 1,024 out of 2,048 is the real truth. I now come to the way in which such considerations have led to a mode in which mere pitch-and-toss has given a more accurate approach to the quadrature of the circle than has been reached by some of my paradoxers. What would my friend[615] in No. 14 have said to this? The method is as follows: Suppose a planked floor of the usual kind, with thin visible seams between the planks. Let there be a thin straight rod, or wire, not so long as the breadth of the plank. This rod, being tossed up at hazard, will either fall quite clear of the seams, or will lay across one seam. Now Buffon, and after him Laplace, proved the following: That in the long run the fraction of the whole number of trials in which a seam is intersected will be the fraction which twice the length of the rod is of the circumference of the circle having the breadth of a plank for its diameter. In 1855 Mr. Ambrose Smith, of Aberdeen, made 3,204 trials with a rod three-fifths of the distance between the planks: there were 1,213 clear intersections, and 11 contacts on which it was difficult to decide. Divide these contacts equally, and we have 1,218½ to 3,204 for the ratio of 6 to 5[pi], presuming that the greatness of the number of trials gives something near to the final average, or result in the long run: this gives [pi] = 3.1553. If all the 11 contacts had been treated as intersections, the result would have been {284} [pi] = 3.1412, exceedingly near. A pupil of mine made 600 trials with a rod of the length between the seams, and got [pi] = 3.137.

This method will hardly be believed until it has been repeated so often that "there never could have been any doubt about it."

The first experiment strongly illustrates a truth of the theory, well confirmed by practice: whatever can happen will happen if we make trials enough. Who would undertake to throw tail eight times running?

Nevertheless, in the 8,192 sets tail 8 times running occurred 17 times; 9 times running, 9 times; 10 times running, twice; 11 times and 13 times, each once; and 15 times twice.]

ON CURIOSITIES OF [pi].

1830. The celebrated interminable fraction 3.14159..., which the mathematician calls [pi], is the ratio of the circumference to the diameter. But it is thousands of things besides. It is constantly turning up in mathematics: and if arithmetic and algebra had been studied without geometry, [pi] must have come in somehow, though at what stage or under what name must have depended upon the casualties of algebraical invention. This will readily be seen when it is stated that [pi] is nothing but four times the series 1 - 1/3 + 1/5 - 1/7 + 1/9 - 1/11 + ... ad infinitum.[616] It would be wonderful if so simple a series {285} had but one kind of occurrence. As it is, our trigonometry being founded on the circle, [pi] first appears as the ratio stated. If, for instance, a deep study of probable fluctuation from average had preceded, [pi] might have emerged as a number perfectly indispensable in such problems as: What is the chance of the number of aces lying between a million + x and a million - x, when six million of throws are made with a die? I have not gone into any detail of all those cases in which the paradoxer finds out, by his unassisted acumen, that results of mathematical investigation cannot be: in fact, this discovery is only an accompaniment, though a necessary one, of his paradoxical statement of that which must be. Logicians are beginning to see that the notion of horse is inseparably connected with that of non-horse: that the first without the second would be no notion at all. And it is clear that the positive affirmation of that which contradicts mathematical demonstration cannot but be accompanied by a declaration, mostly overtly made, that demonstration is false. If the mathematician were interested in punishing this indiscretion, he could make his denier ridiculous by inventing asserted results which would completely take him in.

More than thirty years ago I had a friend, now long gone, who was a mathematician, but not of the higher branches: he was, inter alia, thoroughly up in all that relates to mortality, life assurance, &c. One day, explaining to him how it should be ascertained what the chance is of the survivors of a large number of persons now alive lying between given limits of number at the end of a certain time, I came, of course upon the introduction of [pi], which I could only describe as the ratio of the circumference of a circle to its diameter. "Oh, my dear friend! that must be a delusion; what can the circle have to do with the numbers alive at the end of a given time?"--"I cannot demonstrate it to you; but it is demonstrated."--"Oh! stuff! I think you can prove anything with your differential calculus: figment, {286} depend upon it." I said no more; but, a few days afterwards, I went to him and very gravely told him that I had discovered the law of human mortality in the Carlisle Table, of which he thought very highly. I told him that the law was involved in this circumstance. Take the table of expectation of life, choose any age, take its expectation and make the nearest integer a new age, do the same with that, and so on; begin at what age you like, you are sure to end at the place where the age past is equal, or most nearly equal, to the expectation to come. "You don't mean that this always happens?"--"Try it." He did try, again and again; and found it as I said. "This is, indeed, a curious thing; this is a discovery." I might have sent him about trumpeting the law of life: but I contented myself with informing him that the same thing would happen with any table whatsoever in which the first column goes up and the second goes down; and that if a proficient in the higher mathematics chose to palm a figment upon him, he could do without the circle: à corsaire, corsaire et demi,[617] the French proverb says. "Oh!" it was remarked, "I see, this was Milne!"[618] It was not Milne: I remember well showing the formula to him some time afterwards. He raised no difficulty about [pi]; he knew the forms of Laplace's results, and he was much interested. Besides, Milne never said stuff! and figment! And he would not have been taken in: he would have quietly tried it with the Northampton and all the other tables, and would have got at the truth.

{287}

EUCLID WITHOUT AXIOMS

The first book of Euclid's Elements. With alterations and familiar notes. Being an attempt to get rid of axioms altogether; and to establish the theory of parallel lines, without the introduction of any principle not common to other parts of the elements. By a member of the University of Cambridge.

Third edition. In usum serenissimæ filiolæ. London, 1830.

The author was Lieut. Col. (now General) Perronet Thompson,[619] the author of the "Catechism on the Corn Laws." I reviewed the fourth edition--which had the name of "Geometry without Axioms," 1833--in the quarterly Journal of Education for January, 1834. Col. Thompson, who then was a contributor to--if not editor of--the Westminster Review, replied in an article the authorship of which could not be mistaken.

Some more attempts upon the problem, by the same author, will be found in the sequel. They are all of acute and legitimate speculation; but they do not conquer the difficulty in the manner demanded by the conditions of the problem. The paradox of parallels does not contribute much to my pages: its cases are to be found for the most part in geometrical systems, or in notes to them. Most of them consist in the proposal of additional postulates; some are attempts to do without any new postulate. Gen. Perronet Thompson, whose paradoxes are always constructed on much study of previous writers, has collected in the work above named, a budget of attempts, the heads of which are in the Penny and English Cyclopædias, at "Parallels." He has given thirty instances, selected from what he had found.[620]

{288}

Lagrange,[621] in one of the later years of his life, imagined that he had overcome the difficulty. He went so far as to write a paper, which he took with him to the Institute, and began to read it. But in the first paragraph something struck him which he had not observed: he muttered Il faut que j'y songe encore,[622] and put the paper in his pocket.

THE LUNAR CAUSTIC JOKE

The following paragraph appeared in the Morning Post, May 4, 1831:

"We understand that although, owing to circumstances with which the public are not concerned, Mr. Goulburn[623] declined becoming a candidate for University honors, that his scientific attainments are far from inconsiderable. He is well known to be the author of an essay in the Philosophical Transactions on the accurate rectification of a circular arc, and of an investigation of the equation of a lunar caustic--a problem likely to become of great use in nautical astronomy."

{289}

This hoax--which would probably have succeeded with any journal--was palmed upon the Morning Post, which supported Mr. Goulburn, by some Cambridge wags who supported Mr. Lubbock, the other candidate for the University of Cambridge. Putting on the usual concealment, I may say that I always suspected Dr-nkw-t-r B-th-n-[624] of having a share in the matter. The skill of the hoax lies in avoiding the words "quadrature of the circle," which all know, and speaking of "the accurate rectification of a circular arc," which all do not know for its synonyme. The Morning Post next day gave a reproof to hoaxers in general, without referring to any particular case. It must be added, that although there are caustics in mathematics, there is no lunar caustic.

So far as Mr. Goulburn was concerned, the above was poetic justice. He was the minister who, in old time, told a deputation from the Astronomical Society that the Government "did not care twopence for all the science in the country." There may be some still alive who remember this: I heard it from more than one of those who were present, and are now gone. Matters are much changed. I was thirty years in office at the Astronomical Society; and, to my certain knowledge, every Government of that period, Whig and Tory, showed itself ready to help with influence when wanted, and with money whenever there was an answer for the House of Commons. The following correction subsequently appeared. Referring to the hoax about Mr. Goulburn, Messrs. C. H. and Thompson Cooper[625] have corrected an error, by stating that the election which gave rise to the hoax was that in which Messrs. Goulburn {290} and Yates Peel[626] defeated Lord Palmerston[627] and Mr. Cavendish.[628] They add that Mr. Gunning, the well-known Esquire Bedell of the University, attributed the hoax to the late Rev. R. Sheepshanks, to whom, they state, are also attributed certain clever fictitious biographies--of public men, as I understand it--which were palmed upon the editor of the Cambridge Chronicle, who never suspected their genuineness to the day of his death. Being in most confidential intercourse with Mr. Sheepshanks,[629] both at the time and all the rest of his life (twenty-five years), and never heard him allude to any such things--which were not in his line, though he had satirical power of quite another {291} kind--I feel satisfied he had nothing to do with them. I may add that others, his nearest friends, and also members of his family, never heard him allude to these hoaxes as their author, and disbelieve his authorship as much as I do myself. I say this not as imputing any blame to the true author, such hoaxes being fair election jokes in all time, but merely to put the saddle off the wrong horse, and to give one more instance of the insecurity of imputed authorship. Had Mr. Sheepshanks ever told me that he had perpetrated the hoax, I should have had no hesitation in giving it to him. I consider all clever election squibs, free from bitterness and personal imputation, as giving the multitude good channels for the vent of feelings which but for them would certainly find bad ones.

[But I now suspect that Mr. Babbage[630] had some hand in the hoax. He gives it in his "Passages, &c." and is evidently writing from memory, for he gives the wrong year. But he has given the paragraph, though not accurately, yet with such a recollection of the points as brings suspicion of the authorship upon him, perhaps in conjunction with D. B.[631] Both were on Cavendish's committee. Mr. Babbage adds, that "late one evening a cab drove up in hot haste to the office of the Morning Post, delivered the copy as coming from Mr. Goulburn's committee, and at the same time ordered fifty extra copies of the Post to be sent next morning to their committee-room." I think the man--the only one I ever heard of--who knew all about the cab and the extra copies must have known more.]

ON M. DEMONVILLE

Demonville.--A Frenchman's Christian name is his own secret, unless there be two of the surname. M. Demonville is a very good instance of the difference between a {292} French and English discoverer. In England there is a public to listen to discoveries in mathematical subjects made without mathematics: a public which will hear, and wonder, and think it possible that the pretensions of the discoverer have some foundation. The unnoticed man may possibly be right: and the old country-town reputation which I once heard of, attaching to a man who "had written a book about the signs of the zodiac which all the philosophers in London could not answer," is fame as far as it goes. Accordingly, we have plenty of discoverers who, even in astronomy, pronounce the learned in error because of mathematics. In France, beyond the sphere of influence of the Academy of Sciences, there is no one to cast a thought upon the matter: all who take the least interest repose entire faith in the Institute. Hence the French discoverer turns all his thoughts to the Institute, and looks for his only hearing in that quarter. He therefore throws no slur upon the means of knowledge, but would say, with M. Demonville: "A l'égard de M. Poisson,[632] j'envie loyalement la millième partie de ses connaissances mathématiques, pour prouver mon systême d'astronomie aux plus incrédules."[633] This system is that the only bodies of our system are the earth, the sun, and the moon; all the others being illusions, caused by reflection of the sun and moon from the ice of the polar regions. In mathematics, addition and subtraction are for men; multiplication and division, which are in truth creation and destruction, are prerogatives of deity. But nothing multiplied by nothing is one. M. Demonville obtained an introduction to William the Fourth, who desired the opinion of the Royal Society upon his system: the {293} answer was very brief. The King was quite right; so was the Society: the fault lay with those who advised His Majesty on a matter they knew nothing about. The writings of M. Demonville in my possession are as follows.[634] The dates--which were only on covers torn off in binding--were about 1831-34:

Petit cours d'astronomie[635] followed by Sur l'unité mathématique.--Principes de la physique de la création implicitement admis dans la notice sur le tonnerre par M. Arago.--Question de longitude sur mer.[636]--Vrai système du monde[637] (pp. 92). Same title, four pages, small type. Same title, four pages, addressed to the British Association. Same title, four pages, addressed to M. Mathieu. Same title, four pages, on M. Bouvard's report.--Résumé de la physique de la création; troisième partie du vrai système du monde.[638]

PARSEY'S PARADOX

The quadrature of the circle discovered, by Arthur Parsey,[639] author of the 'art of miniature painting.' Submitted to the consideration of the Royal Society, on whose protection the author humbly throws himself. London, 1832, 8vo.

Mr. Parsey was an artist, who also made himself conspicuous by a new view of perspective. Seeing that the sides of a tower, for instance, would appear to meet in a point if the tower were high enough, he thought that these sides ought to slope to one another in the picture. On this {294} theory he published a small work, of which I have not the title, with a Grecian temple in the frontispiece, stated, if I remember rightly, to be the first picture which had ever been drawn in true perspective. Of course the building looked very Egyptian, with its sloping sides. The answer to his notion is easy enough. What is called the picture is not the picture from which the mind takes its perception; that picture is on the retina. The intermediate picture, as it may be called--the human artist's work--is itself seen perspectively. If the tower were so high that the sides, though parallel, appeared to meet in a point, the picture must also be so high that the picture-sides, though parallel, would appear to meet in a point. I never saw this answer given, though I have seen and heard the remarks of artists on Mr. Parsey's work. I am inclined to think it is commonly supposed that the artist's picture is the representation which comes before the mind: this is not true; we might as well say the same of the object itself. In July 1831, reading an article on squaring the circle, and finding that there was a difficulty, he set to work, got a light denied to all mathematicians in--some would say through--a crack, and advertised in the Times that he had done the trick. He then prepared this work, in which, those who read it will see how, he showed that 3.14159... should be 3.0625. He might have found out his error by stepping a draughtsman's circle with the compasses.

Perspective has not had many paradoxes. The only other one I remember is that of a writer on perspective, whose name I forget, and whose four pages I do not possess. He circulated remarks on my notes on the subject, published in the Athenæum, in which he denies that the stereographic projection is a case of perspective, the reason being that the whole hemisphere makes too large a picture for the eye conveniently to grasp at once. That is to say, it is no perspective because there is too much perspective. {295}

ON A COUPLE OF GEOMETRIES

Principles of Geometry familiarly illustrated. By the Rev. W. Ritchie,[640] LL.D. London, 1833, 12mo.

A new Exposition of the system of Euclid's Elements, being an attempt to establish his work on a different basis. By Alfred Day,[641] LL.D. London, 1839, 12mo.

These works belong to a small class which have the peculiarity of insisting that in the general propositions of geometry a proposition gives its converse: that "Every B is A" follows from "Every A is B." Dr. Ritchie says, "If it be proved that the equality of two of the angles of a triangle depends essentially upon the equality of the opposite sides, it follows that the equality of opposite sides depends essentially on the equality of the angles." Dr. Day puts it as follows:

"That the converses of Euclid, so called, where no particular limitation is specified or implied in the leading proposition, more than in the converse, must be necessarily true; for as by the nature of the reasoning the leading proposition must be universally true, should the converse be not so, it cannot be so universally, but has at least all the exceptions conveyed in the leading proposition, and the case is therefore unadapted to geometric reasoning; or, what is the same thing, by the very nature of geometric reasoning, the particular exceptions to the extended converse must be identical with some one or other of the cases under the universal affirmative proposition with which we set forth, which is absurd."

{296}

On this I cannot help transferring to my reader the words of the Pacha when he orders the bastinado,--May it do you good! A rational study of logic is much wanted to show many mathematicians, of all degrees of proficiency, that there is nothing in the reasoning of mathematics which differs from other reasoning. Dr. Day repeated his argument in A Treatise on Proportion, London, 1840, 8vo. Dr. Ritchie was a very clear-headed man.

He published, in 1818, a work on arithmetic, with rational explanations. This was too early for such an improvement, and nearly the whole of his excellent work was sold as waste paper. His elementary introduction to the Differential Calculus was drawn up while he was learning the subject late in life. Books of this sort are often very effective on points of difficulty.

NEWTON AGAIN OBLITERATED

Letter to the Royal Astronomical Society in refutation of Mistaken Notions held in common, by the Society, and by all the Newtonian philosophers. By Capt. Forman,[642] R.N. Shepton-Mallet, 1833, 8vo.

Capt. Forman wrote against the whole system of gravitation, and got no notice. He then wrote to Lord Brougham, Sir J. Herschel, and others I suppose, desiring them to procure notice of his books in the reviews: this not being acceded to, he wrote (in print) to Lord John Russell[643] to complain of their "dishonest" conduct. He then sent a manuscript letter to the Astronomical Society, inviting controversy: he was answered by a recommendation to study {297} dynamics. The above pamphlet was the consequence, in which, calling the Council of the Society "craven dunghill cocks," he set them right about their doctrines. From all I can learn, the life of a worthy man and a creditable officer was completely embittered by his want of power to see that no person is bound in reason to enter into controversy with every one who chooses to invite him to the field. This mistake is not peculiar to philosophers, whether of orthodoxy or paradoxy; a majority of educated persons imply, by their modes of proceeding, that no one has a right to any opinion which he is not prepared to defend against all comers.

David and Goliath, or an attempt to prove that the Newtonian system of Astronomy is directly opposed to the Scriptures. By Wm. Lauder,[644] Sen., Mere, Wilts. Mere, 1833, 12mo.

Newton is Goliath; Mr. Lauder is David. David took five pebbles; Mr. Lauder takes five arguments. He expects opposition; for Paul and Jesus both met with it.

Mr. Lauder, in his comparison, seems to put himself in the divinely inspired class. This would not be a fair inference in every case; but we know not what to think when we remember that a tolerable number of cyclometers have attributed their knowledge to direct revelation. The works of this class are very scarce; I can only mention one or two from Montucla.[645] Alphonso Cano de Molina,[646] in the last century, upset all Euclid, and squared the circle upon the ruins; he found a follower, Janson, who translated him from Spanish into Latin. He declared that he believed in Euclid, until God, who humbles the proud, taught him better. One Paul Yvon, called from his estate de la Leu, a merchant at Rochelle, supported by his book-keeper, M. Pujos, and a {298} Scotchman, John Dunbar, solved the problem by divine grace, in a manner which was to convert all Jews, Infidels, etc. There seem to have been editions of his work in 1619 and 1628, and a controversial "Examen" in 1630, by Robert Sara. There was a noted discussion, in which Mydorge,[647] Hardy,[648] and others took part against de la Leu. I cannot find this name either in Lipenius[649] or Murhard,[650] and I should not have known the dates if it had not been for one of the keenest bibliographers of any time, my friend Prince Balthasar Boncompagni,[651] who is trying to find copies of the works, and has managed to find copies of the titles. In 1750, Henry Sullamar, an Englishman, squared the circle by the number of the Beast: he published a pamphlet every two or three years; but I cannot find any mention of him in English works.[652] In France, in 1753, M. de Causans,[653] of the Guards, cut a circular piece of turf, squared it, and {299} deduced original sin and the Trinity. He found out that the circle was equal to the square in which it is inscribed; and he offered a reward for detection of any error, and actually deposited 10,000 francs as earnest of 300,000. But the courts would not allow any one to recover.

SIR JOHN HERSCHEL

1834. In this year Sir John Herschel[654] set up his telescope at Feldhausen, Cape of Good Hope. He did much for astronomy, but not much for the Budget of Paradoxes. He gives me, however, the following story.

He showed a resident a remarkable blood-red star, and some little time after he heard of a sermon preached in those parts in which it was asserted that the statements of the Bible must be true, for that Sir J. H. had seen in his telescope "the very place where wicked people go."

But red is not always the color. Sir J. Herschel has in his possession a letter written to his father, Sir W. H.,[655] dated April 3, 1787, and signed "Eliza Cumyns," begging to know if any of the stars be indigo in color, "because, if there be, I think it may be deemed a strong conjectural illustration of the expression, so often used by our Saviour in the Holy Gospels, that 'the disobedient shall be cast into outer darkness'; for as the Almighty Being can doubtless confine any of his creatures, whether corporeal or spiritual, to what part of his creation He pleases, if therefore any of the stars (which are beyond all doubt so many suns to other systems) be of so dark a color as that above mentioned, they may be calculated to give the most insufferable heat to those dolorous systems dependent upon them (and to reprobate spirits placed there), without one ray of cheerful light; and may therefore be the scenes of future punishments." This letter is addressed to Dr. Heirschel at Slow. Some have placed the infernal regions inside the earth, but {300} others have filled this internal cavity--for cavity they will have--with refulgent light, and made it the abode of the blessed. It is difficult to build without knowing the number to be provided for. A friend of mine heard the following (part) dialogue between two strong Scotch Calvinists: "Noo! hoo manny d'ye thank there are of the alact on the arth at this moment?--Eh! mabbee a doozen--Hoot! mon! nae so mony as thot!"

THE NAUTICAL ALMANAC

1834. From 1769 to 1834 the Nautical Almanac was published on a plan which gradually fell behind what was wanted. In 1834 the new series began, under a new superintendent (Lieut. W. S. Stratford).[656] There had been a long scientific controversy, which would not be generally intelligible. To set some of the points before the reader, I reprint a cutting which I have by me. It is from the Nautical Magazine, but I did hear that some had an idea that it was in the Nautical Almanac itself. It certainly was not, and I feel satisfied the Lords of the Admiralty would not have permitted the insertion; they are never in advance of their age. The Almanac for 1834 was published in July 1833.

THE NEW NAUTICAL ALMANAC--Extract from the 'Primum Mobile,' and 'Milky Way Gazette.' Communicated by AEROLITH.

A meeting of the different bodies composing the Solar System was this day held at the Dragon's Tail, for the purpose of taking into consideration the alterations and amendments introduced into the New Nautical Almanac.

The honorable luminaries had been individually summoned {301} by fast-sailing comets, and there was a remarkably full attendance. Among the visitors we observed several nebulæ, and almost all the stars whose proper motions would admit of their being present.

The SUN was unanimously called to the focus. The small planets took the oaths, and their places, after a short discussion, in which it was decided that the places should be those of the Almanac itself, with leave reserved to move for corrections.

Petitions were presented from [alpha] and [delta] Ursæ Minoris, complaining of being put on daily duty, and praying for an increase of salary.--Laid on the plane of the ecliptic.

The trustees of the eccentricity[657] and inclination funds reported a balance of .00001 in the former, and a deficit of 0".009 in the latter. This announcement caused considerable surprise, and a committee was moved for, to ascertain which of the bodies had more or less than his share. After some discussion, in which the small planets offered to consent to a reduction, if necessary, the motion was carried.

The FOCAL BODY then rose to address the meeting. He remarked that the subject on which they were assembled was one of great importance to the routes and revolutions of the heavenly bodies. For himself, though a private arrangement between two of his honourable neighbours (here he looked hard at the Earth and Venus) had prevented his hitherto paying that close attention to the predictions of the Nautical Almanac which he declared he always had wished to do; yet he felt consoled by knowing that the conductors of that work had every disposition to take his peculiar circumstances into consideration. He declared that he had never passed the wires of a transit without deeply feeling his inability to adapt himself to the present state of his theory; a feeling which he was afraid had sometimes caused a slight tremor in his limb. Before {302} he sat down, he expressed a hope that honourable luminaries would refrain as much as possible from eclipsing each other, or causing mutual perturbations. Indeed, he should be very sorry to see any interruption of the harmony of the spheres.

(Applause.)

The several articles of the New Nautical Almanac were then read over without any comment; only we observed that Saturn shook his ring at every novelty, and Jupiter gave his belt a hitch, and winked at the satellites at page 21 of each month.

The MOON rose to propose a resolution. No one, he said, would be surprised at his bringing this matter forward in the way he did, when it was considered in how complete and satisfactory a manner his motions were now represented. He must own he had trembled when the Lords of the Admiralty dissolved the Board of Longitude, but his tranquillity was more than reestablished by the adoption of the new system. He did not know but that any little assistance he could give in Nautical Astronomy was becoming of less and less value every day, owing to the improvement of chronometers. But there was one thing, of which nothing could deprive him--he meant the regulation of the tides. And, perhaps, when his attention was not occupied by more than the latter, he should be able to introduce a little more regularity into the phenomena. (Here the honourable luminary gave a sort of modest libration, which convulsed the meeting with laughter.) They might laugh at his natural infirmity if they pleased, but he could assure them it arose only from the necessity he was under, when young, of watching the motions of his worthy primary. He then moved a resolution highly laudatory of the alterations which appeared in the New Nautical Almanac.

The EARTH rose, to second the motion. His honourable satellite had fully expressed his opinions on the subject. He joined his honourable friend in the focus in wishing to pay every attention to the Nautical Almanac, but, {303} really, when so important an alteration had taken place in his magnetic pole[658] (hear) and there might, for aught he knew, be a successful attempt to reach his pole of rotation, he thought he could not answer for the preservation of the precession in its present state. (Here the hon. luminary, scratching his side, exclaimed, as he sat down, "More steamboats--confound 'em!")

An honourable satellite (whose name we could not learn) proposed that the resolution should be immediately despatched, corrected for refraction, when he was called to order by the Focal Body, who reminded him that it was contrary to the moving orders of the system to take cognizance of what passed inside the atmosphere of any planet.

SATURN and PALLAS rose together. (Cries of "New member!" and the former gave way.) The latter, in a long and eloquent speech, praised the liberality with which he and his colleagues had at length been relieved from astronomical disqualifications. He thought that it was contrary to the spirit of the laws of gravitation to exclude any planet from office on account of the eccentricity or inclination of his orbit. Honourable luminaries need not talk of the want of convergency of his series. What had they to do with any private arrangements between him and the general equations of the system? (Murmurs from the opposition.) So long as he obeyed the laws of motion, to which he had that day taken a solemn oath, he would ask, were old planets, which were now so well known that nobody trusted them, to....

The FOCAL BODY said he was sorry to break the continuity of the proceedings, but he thought that remarks upon character, with a negative sign, would introduce {304} differences of too high an order. The honourable luminary must eliminate the expression which he had brought out, in finite terms, and use smaller inequalities in future. (Hear, hear.)

PALLAS explained, that he was far from meaning to reflect upon the orbital character of any planet present. He only meant to protest against being judged by any laws but those of gravitation, and the differential calculus: he thought it most unjust that astronomers should prevent the small planets from being observed, and then reproach them with the imperfections of the tables, which were the result of their own narrow-minded policy. (Cheers.)

SATURN thought that, as an old planet, he had not been treated with due respect. (Hear, from his satellites.) He had long foretold the wreck of the system from the friends of innovation. Why, he might ask, were his satellites to be excluded, when small planets, trumpery comets, which could not keep their mean distances (cries of oh! oh!), double stars, with graphical approximations, and such obscure riff-raff of the heavens (great uproar) found room enough. So help him Arithmetic, nothing could come of it, but a stoppage of all revolution. His hon. friend in the focus might smile, for he would be a gainer by such an event; but as for him (Saturn), he had something to lose, and hon. luminaries well knew that, whatever they might think under an atmosphere, above it continual revolution was the only way of preventing perpetual anarchy. As to the hon. luminary who had risen before him, he was not surprised at his remarks, for he had invariably observed that he and his colleagues allowed themselves too much latitude. The stability of the system required that they should be brought down, and he, for one, would exert all his powers of attraction to accomplish that end. If other bodies would cordially unite with him, particularly his noble friend next him, than whom no luminary possessed greater weight--

JUPITER rose to order. He conceived his noble friend {305} had no right to allude to him in that manner, and was much surprised at his proposal, considering the matters which remained in dispute between them. In the present state of affairs, he would take care never to be in conjunction with his hon. neighbour one moment longer than he could help. (Cries of "Order, order, no long inequalities," during which he sat down.)

SATURN proceeded to say, that he did not know till then that a planet with a ring could affront one who had only a belt, by proposing mutual co-operation. He would now come to the subject under discussion. He should think meanly of his hon. colleagues if they consented to bestow their approbation upon a mere astronomical production. Had they forgotten that they once were considered the arbiters of fate, and the prognosticators of man's destiny? What had lost them that proud position? Was it not the infernal march of intellect, which, after having turned the earth topsy-turvy, was now disturbing the very universe? For himself (others might do as they pleased), but he stuck to the venerable Partridge,[659] and the Stationers' Company, and trusted that they would outlive infidels and anarchists, whether of Astronomical or Diffusion of Knowledge Societies. (Cries of oh! oh!)

MARS said he had been told, for he must confess he had not seen the work, that the places of the planets were given for Sundays. This, he must be allowed to say, was an indecorum he had not expected; and he was convinced the

Lords of the Admiralty had given no orders to that effect. He hoped this point would be considered in the measure which had been introduced in another place, and that some {306} one would move that the prohibition against travelling on Sundays extend to the heavenly as well as earthly bodies.

Several of the stars here declared, that they had been much annoyed by being observed on Sunday evenings, during the hours of divine service.

The room was then cleared for a division, but we are unable to state what took place. Several comets-at-arms were sent for, and we heard rumors of a personal collision having taken place between two luminaries in opposition. We were afterwards told that the resolution was carried by a majority, and the luminaries elongated at 2 h. 15 m. 33,41 s. sidereal time.

* * * It is reported, but we hope without foundation, that Saturn, and several other discontented planets, have accepted an invitation from Sirius to join his system, on the most liberal appointments. We believe the report to have originated in nothing more than the discovery of the annual parallax of Sirius from the orbit of Saturn; but we may safely assure our readers that no steps have as yet been taken to open any communication.

We are also happy to state, that there is no truth in the rumor of the laws of gravitation being about to be repealed. We have traced this report, and find it originated with a gentleman living near Bath (Captain Forman, R.N),[660] whose name we forbear to mention.

A great excitement has been observed among the nebulæ, visible to the earth's southern hemisphere, particularly among those which have not yet been discovered from thence. We are at a loss to conjecture the cause, but we shall not fail to report to our readers the news of any movement which may take place. (Sir J. Herschel's visit. He could just see this before he went out.)

{307}

WOODLEY'S DIVINE SYSTEM.

A Treatise on the Divine System of the Universe, by Captain Woodley, R.N.,[661] and as demonstrated by his Universal Time-piece, and universal method of determining a ship's longitude by the apparent true place of the moon; with an introduction refuting the solar system of Copernicus, the Newtonian philosophy, and mathematics. 1834.[662] 8vo.

Description of the Universal Time-piece. (4pp. 12mo.)

I think this divine system was published several years before, and was republished with an introduction in 1834.[663] Capt. Woodley was very sure that the earth does not move: he pointed out to me, in a conversation I had with him, something--I forget what--in the motion of the Great Bear, visible to any eye, which could not possibly be if the earth moved. He was exceedingly ignorant, as the following quotation from his account of the usual opinion will show:

"The north pole of the Earth's axis deserts, they say, the north star or pole of the Heavens, at the rate of 1° in 71¾ years.... The fact is, nothing can be more certain than that the Stars have not changed their latitudes or declinations one degree in the last 71¾ years."

This is a strong specimen of a class of men by whom all accessible persons who have made any name in science are hunted. It is a pity that they cannot be admitted into scientific societies, and allowed fairly to state their cases, and stand quiet cross-examination, being kept in their answers very close to the questions, and the answers written down. I am perfectly satisfied that if one meeting in the year were devoted to the hearing of those who chose to come forward on such conditions, much good would be done. But I strongly suspect few would come forward {308} at first, and none in a little while: and I have had some experience of the method I recommend, privately tried. Capt. Woodley was proposed, a little after 1834, as a Fellow of the Astronomical Society; and, not caring whether he moved the sun or the earth, or both--I could not have stood neither--I signed the proposal. I always had a sneaking kindness for paradoxers, such a one, perhaps, as Petit André had for his lambs, as he called them. There was so little feeling against his opinions, that he only failed by a fraction of a ball. Had I myself voted, he would have been elected; but being engaged in conversation, and not having heard the slightest objection to him, I did not think it worth while to cross the room for the purpose. I regretted this at the time, but had I known how ignorant he was I should not have supported him. Probably those who voted against him knew more of his book than I did.

I remember no other instance of exclusion from a scientific society on the ground of opinion, even if this be one; of which it may be that ignorance had more to do with it than paradoxy. Mr. Frend,[664] a strong anti-Newtonian, was a Fellow of the Astronomical Society, and for some years in the Council. Lieut. Kerigan[665] was elected to the Royal Society at a time when his proposers must have known that his immediate object was to put F.R.S. on the title-page of a work against the tides. To give all I know, I may add that the editor of some very ignorant bombast about the "forehead of the solar sky," who did not know the difference between Bailly[666] and Baily,[667] received hints which induced him to withdraw his proposal for election into the Astronomical Society. But this was an act of kindness; {309} for if he had seen Mr. Baily in the chair, with his head on, he might have been political historian enough to faint away.

De la formation des Corps. Par Paul Laurent.[668] Nancy, 1834, 8vo.

Atoms, and ether, and ovules or eggs, which are planets, and their eggs, which are satellites. These speculators can create worlds, in which they cannot be refuted; but none of them dare attack the problem of a grain of wheat, and its passage from a seed to a plant, bearing scores of seeds like what it was itself.

ON JOHN FLAMSTEED

An account of the Rev. John Flamsteed,[669] the First Astronomer-Royal.... By Francis Baily,[670] Esq. London, 1835, 4to.

Supplement, London, 1837, 4to.

My friend Francis Baily was a paradoxer: he brought forward things counter to universal opinion. That Newton was impeccable in every point was the national creed; and failings of temper and conduct would have been utterly disbelieved, if the paradox had not come supported by very unusual evidence. Anybody who impeached Newton on existing evidence might as well have been squaring the circle, for any attention he would have got.

About this book I will tell a story. It was published by the Admiralty for distribution; and the distribution was entrusted to Mr. Baily. On the eve of its appearance, rumors of its extraordinary revelations got about, and persons of influence applied to the Admiralty for copies. The Lords were in a difficulty: but on looking at the list they saw names, as they {310} thought, which were so obscure that they had a right to assume Mr. Baily had included persons who had no claim to such a compliment as presentation from the Admiralty. The Secretary requested Mr. Baily to call upon him. "Mr. Baily, my Lords are inclined to think that some of the persons in this list are perhaps not of that note which would justify their Lordships in presenting this work."--"To whom does your observation apply, Mr. Secretary?"--"Well, now, let us examine the list; let me see; now,--now,--now,--come!--here's Gauss[671]--who's Gauss?"--"Gauss, Mr. Secretary, is the oldest mathematician now living, and is generally thought to be the greatest."--"O-o-oh! Well, Mr. Baily, we will see about it, and I will write you a letter." The letter expressed their Lordships' perfect satisfaction with the list.

There was a controversy about the revelations made in this work; but as the eccentric anomalies took no part in it, there is nothing for my purpose. The following valentine from Mrs. Flamsteed,[672] which I found among Baily's papers, illustrates some of the points:

"3 Astronomers' Row, Paradise: February 14, 1836.

"Dear Sir,--I suppose you hardly expected to receive a letter from me, dated from this place; but the truth is, a gentleman from our street was appointed guardian angel to the American Treaty, in which there is some astronomical question about boundaries. He has got leave to go back to fetch some instruments which he left behind, and I take this opportunity of making your acquaintance. That America has become a wonderful place since I was down among you; you have no idea how grand the fire at New York {311} looked up here. Poor dear Mr. Flamsteed does not know I am writing a letter to a gentleman on Valentine's day; he is walked out with Sir Isaac Newton (they are pretty good friends now, though they do squabble a little sometimes) and Sir William Herschel, to see a new nebula. Sir Isaac says he can't make out at all how it is managed; and I am sure I cannot help him. I never bothered my head about those things down below, and I don't intend to begin here.

"I have just received the news of your having written a book about my poor dear man. It's a chance that I heard it at all; for the truth is, the scientific gentlemen are somehow or other become so wicked, and go so little to church, that very few of them are considered fit company for this place. If it had not been for Dr. Brinkley,[673] who came here of course, I should not have heard about it. He seems a nice man, but is not yet used to our ways.

As to Mr. Halley,[674] he is of course not here; which is lucky for him, for Mr. Flamsteed swore the moment he caught him in a place where there are no magistrates, he would make a sacrifice of him to heavenly truth. It was very generous in Mr. F. not appearing against Sir Isaac when he came up, for I am told that if he had, Sir Isaac would not have been allowed to come in at all. I should have been sorry for that, for he is a companionable man enough, only holds his head rather higher than he should do. I met him the other day walking with Mr. Whiston,[675] and disputing about the deluge. 'Well, Mrs. Flamsteed,' says he, 'does old Poke-the-Stars understand gravitation yet?' Now you must know that is rather a sore point with poor dear Mr. Flamsteed. He says that Sir Isaac is as crochetty about the moon as ever; and as to {312} what some people say about what has been done since his time, he says he should like to see somebody who knows something about it of himself. For it is very singular that none of the people who have carried on Sir Isaac's notions have been allowed to come here.

"I hope you have not forgotten to tell how badly Sir Isaac used Mr. Flamsteed about that book. I have never quite forgiven him; as for Mr. Flamsteed, he says that as long as he does not come for observations, he does not care about it, and that he will never trust him with any papers again as long as he lives. I shall never forget what a rage he came home in when Sir Isaac had called him a puppy. He struck the stairs all the way up with his crutch, and said puppy at every step, and all the evening, as soon as ever a star appeared in the telescope, he called it puppy. I could not think what was the matter, and when I asked, he only called me puppy.

"I shall be very glad to see you if you come our way. Pray keep up some appearances, and go to church a little. St. Peter is always uncommonly civil to astronomers, and indeed to all scientific persons, and never bothers them with many questions. If they can make anything out of the case, he is sure to let them in. Indeed, he says, it is perfectly out of the question expecting a mathematician to be as religious as an apostle, but that it is as much as his place is worth to let in the greater number of those who come. So try if you cannot manage it, for I am very curious to know whether you found all the letters. I remain, dear sir, your faithful servant, "MARGARET FLAMSTEED.

Francis Baily, Esq.

"P.S. Mr. Flamsteed has come in, and says he left Sir Isaac riding cockhorse upon the nebula, and poring over it as if it were a book. He has brought in his old acquaintance Ozanam,[676] who says that it was always his maxim on {313} earth, that 'il appartient aux docteurs de Sorbonne de disputer, au Pape de prononcer, et au mathématicien d'aller en Paradis en ligne perpendiculaire.'"[677]

ON STEVIN.

The Secretary of the Admiralty was completely extinguished. I can recall but two instances of demolition as complete, though no doubt there are many others. The first is in Simon Stevin[678] and M. Dumortier. Nieuport, 1845, 12mo.

M. Dumortier was a member of the Academy of Brussels: there was a discussion, I believe, about a national Pantheon for Belgium. The name of Stevinus suggested itself as naturally as that of Newton to an Englishman; probably no Belgian is better known to foreigners as illustrious in science. Stevinus is great in the Mécanique Analytique of Lagrange;[679] Stevinus is great in the Tristram Shandy of Sterne. M. Dumortier, who believed that not one Belgian in a thousand knew Stevinus, and who confesses with ironical shame that he was not the odd man, protested against placing the statue of an obscure man in the Pantheon, to give foreigners the notion that Belgium could show nothing greater. The work above named is a slashing retort: any one who knows the history of science ever so little may imagine what a dressing was given, by mere extract from foreign writers. The tract is a letter signed J. du Fan, but this is a pseudonym of Mr. Van de Weyer.[680] The Academician says Stevinus was a man who was not {314} without merit for the time at which he lived: Sir! is the answer, he was as much before his own time as you are behind yours. How came a man who had never heard of Stevinus to be a member of the Brussels Academy?

The second story was told me by Mr. Crabb Robinson,[681] who was long connected with the Times, and intimately acquainted with Mr. W***.[682] When W*** was an undergraduate at Cambridge, taking a walk, he came to a stile, on which sat a bumpkin who did not make way for him: the gown in that day looked down on the town. "Why do you not make way for a gentleman?"--"Eh?"--"Yes, why do you not move? You deserve a good hiding, and you shall get it if you don't take care!" The bumpkin raised his muscular figure on its feet, patted his menacer on the head, and said, very quietly,--"Young man! I'm Cribb."[683] W*** seized the great pugilist's hand, and shook it warmly, got him to his own rooms in college, collected some friends, and had a symposium which lasted until the large end of the small hours.

FINLEYSON AS A PARADOXER.

God's Creation of the Universe as it is, in support of the Scriptures. By Mr. Finleyson.[684] Sixth Edition, 1835, 8vo.

{315}

This writer, by his own account, succeeded in delivering the famous Lieut. Richard Brothers[685] from the lunatic asylum, and tending him, not as a keeper but as a disciple, till he died. Brothers was, by his own account, the nephew of the Almighty, and Finleyson ought to have been the nephew of Brothers. For Napoleon came to him in a vision, with a broken sword and an arrow in his side, beseeching help: Finleyson pulled out the arrow, but refused to give a new sword; whereby poor Napoleon, though he got off with life, lost the battle of Waterloo. This story was written to the Duke of Wellington, ending with "I pulled out the arrow, but left the broken sword. Your Grace can supply the rest, and what followed is amply recorded in history." The book contains a long account of applications to Government to do three things: to pay 2,000l. for care taken of Brothers, to pay 10,000l. for discovery of the longitude, and to prohibit the teaching of the Newtonian system, which makes God a liar. The successive administrations were threatened that they would have to turn out if they refused, which, it is remarked, came to pass in every case. I have heard of a joke of Lord Macaulay, that the House of Commons must be the Beast of the Revelations, since 658 members, with the officers necessary for the action of the House, make 666. Macaulay read most things, and the greater part of the rest: so that he might be suspected of having appropriated as a joke one of Finleyson's serious points--"I wrote Earl Grey[686] upon the 13th of July, 1831, informing him that his Reform {316} Bill could not be carried, as it reduced the members below the present amount of 658, which, with the eight principal clerks or officers of the House, make the number 666." But a witness has informed me that Macaulay's joke was made in his hearing a great many years before the Reform Bill was proposed; in fact, when both were students at Cambridge. Earl Grey was, according to Finleyson, a descendant of Uriah the Hittite. For a specimen of Lieut.

Brothers, this book would be worth picking up. Perhaps a specimen of the Lieutenant's poetry may be acceptable: Brothers loquitur, remember:

"Jerusalem ! Jerusalem! shall be built again! More rich, more grand then ever; And through it shall Jordan flow!(!) My people's favourite river.

There I'll erect a splendid throne, And build on the wasted place; To fulfil my ancient covenant To King David and his race. * * * * * * "Euphrates' stream shall flow with ships, And also my wedded Nile; And on my coast shall cities rise, Each one distant but a mile. * * * * * * "My friends the Russians on the north With Persees and Arabs round, Do show the limits of my land, Here! Here! then I mark the ground."

ON THEOLOGICAL PARADOXERS

Among the paradoxers are some of the theologians who in their own organs of the press venture to criticise science. These may hold their ground when they confine themselves to the geology of long past periods and to general cosmogony: for it is the tug of Greek against Greek; and both sides deal much in what is grand when called hypothesis, petty when called supposition. And very often they are not conspicuous when they venture upon things within knowledge; {317} wrong, but not quite wrong enough for a Budget of Paradoxes. One case, however, is destined to live, as an instance of a school which finds writers, editors, and readers. The double stars have been seen from the seventeenth century, and diligently observed by many from the time of Wm. Herschel, who first devoted continuous attention to them. The year 1836 was that of a remarkable triumph of astronomical prediction. The theory of gravitation had been applied to the motion of binary stars about each other, in elliptic orbits, and in that year the two stars of [gamma] Virginis, as had been predicted should happen within a few years of that time--for years are small quantities in such long revolutions--the two stars came to their nearest: in fact, they appeared to be one as much with the telescope as without it. This remarkable turning-point of the history of a long and widely-known branch of astronomy was followed by an article in the Church of England Quarterly Review for April 1837, written against the Useful Knowledge Society. The notion that there are any such things as double stars is (p. 460) implied to be imposture or delusion, as in the following extract. I suspect that I myself am the Sidrophel, and that my companion to the maps of the stars, written for the Society and published in 1836, is the work to which the writer refers:

"We have forgotten the name of that Sidrophel who lately discovered that the fixed stars were not single stars, but appear in the heavens like soles at Billingsgate, in pairs; while a second astronomer, under the influence of that competition in trade which the political economists tell us is so advantageous to the public, professes to show us, through his superior telescope, that the apparently single stars are really three. Before such wondrous mandarins of science, how continually must homunculi like ourselves keep in the background, lest we come between the wind and their nobility."

If the homunculus who wrote this be still above ground, {318} how devoutly must he hope he may be able to keep in the background! But the chief blame falls on the editor. The title of the article is:

"The new school of superficial pantology; a speech intended to be delivered before a defunct Mechanics' Institute. By Swallow Swift, late M.P. for the Borough of Cockney-Cloud, Witsbury: reprinted Balloon Island, Bubble year, month Ventose. Long live Charlatan!"

As a rule, orthodox theologians should avoid humor, a weapon which all history shows to be very difficult to employ in favor of establishment, and which, nine times out of ten, leaves its wielder fighting on the side of heterodoxy. Theological argument, when not enlivened by bigotry, is seldom worse than narcotic: but theological fun, when not covert heresy, is almost always sialagogue. The article in question is a craze, which no editor should have admitted, except after severe inspection by qualified persons. The author of this wit committed a mistake which occurs now and then in old satire, the confusion between himself and the party aimed at. He ought to be reviewing this fictitious book, but every now and then the article becomes the book itself; not by quotation, but by the writer forgetting that he is not Mr. Swallow Swift, but his reviewer. In fact he and Mr. S. Swift had each had a dose of the Devil's Elixir. A novel so called, published about forty years ago, proceeds upon a legend of this kind. If two parties both drink of the elixir, their identities get curiously intermingled; each turns up in the character of the other throughout the three volumes, without having his ideas clear as to whether he be himself or the other.

There is a similar confusion in the answer made to the famous Epistolæ Obscurorum Virorum:[687] it is headed Lamentationes Obscurorum Virorum.[688] {319} This is not a retort of the writer, throwing back the imputation: the obscure men who had been satirized are themselves made, by name, to wince under the disapprobation which the Pope had expressed at the satire upon themselves.

Of course the book here reviewed is a transparent forgery. But I do not know how often it may have happened that the book, in the journals which always put a title at the head, may have been written after the review.

About the year 1830 a friend showed me the proof of an article of his on the malt tax, for the next number of the Edinburgh Review. Nothing was wanting except the title of the book reviewed; I asked what it was. He sat down, and wrote as follows at the head, "The Maltster's Guide (pp. 124)," and said that would do as well as anything.

But I myself, it will be remarked, have employed such humor as I can command "in favor of establishment." What it is worth I am not to judge; as usual in such cases, those who are of my cabal pronounce it good, but cyclometers and other paradoxers either call it very poor, or commend it as sheer buffoonery. Be it one or the other, I observe that all the effective ridicule is, in this subject, on the side of establishment. This is partly due to the difficulty of quizzing plain and sober demonstration; but so much, if not more, to the ignorance of the paradoxers. For that which cannot be ridiculed, can be turned into ridicule by those who know how. But by the time a person is deep enough in negative quantities, and impossible quantities, to be able to satirize them, he is caught, and being inclined to become a user, shrinks from being an abuser. Imagine a person with a gift of ridicule, and knowledge enough, trying his hand on the junction of the assertions which he will find in various books of algebra. First, that a negative quantity has no logarithm; secondly, that a {320} negative quantity has no square root; thirdly, that the first non-existent is to the second as the circumference of a circle to its diameter. One great reason of the allowance of such unsound modes of expression is the confidence felt by the writers that [root]-1 and log(-1) will make their way, however inaccurately described. I heartily wish that the cyclometers had knowledge enough to attack the weak points of algebraical diction: they would soon work a beneficial change.[689]

AN EARLY METEOROLOGIST.

Recueil de ma vie, mes ouvrages et mes pensées. Par Thomas Ignace Marie Forster.[690] Brussels, 1836, 12mo.

Mr. Forster, an Englishman settled at Bruges, was an observer in many subjects, but especially in meteorology. He communicated to the Astronomical Society, in 1848, the information that, in the registers kept by his grandfather, his father, and himself, beginning in 1767, new moon on Saturday was followed, nineteen times out of twenty, by twenty days of rain and wind. This statement being published in the Athenæum, a cluster of correspondents averred that the belief is common among seamen, in all parts of the world, and among landsmen too. Some one quoted a distich:

"Saturday's moon and Sunday's full Never were fine and never wull."

{321} Another brought forward:

"If a Saturday's moon Comes once in seven years it comes too soon."

Mr. Forster did not say he was aware of the proverbial character of the phenomenon. He was a very eccentric man. He treated his dogs as friends, and buried them with ceremony. He quarrelled with the curé of his parish, who remarked that he could not take his dogs to heaven with him. I will go nowhere, said he, where I cannot take my dog. He was a sincere Catholic: but there is a point beyond which even churches have no influence.

The following is some account of the announcement of 1849. The Athenæum (Feb. 17), giving an account of the meeting of the Astronomical Society in December, 1858, says:

"Dr. Forster of Bruges, who is well known as a meteorologist, made a communication at which our readers will stare: he declares that by journals of the weather kept by his grandfather, father, and himself, ever since 1767, to the present time, whenever the new moon has fallen on a Saturday, the following twenty days have been wet and windy, in nineteen cases out of twenty. In spite of our friend Zadkiel[691] and the others who declare that we would smother every truth that does not happen to agree with us, we are glad to see that the Society had the sense to publish this communication, coming, as it does, from a veteran observer, and one whose love of truth is undoubted. It must be that the fact is so set down in the journals, because Dr. Forster says it: and whether it be only a fact of the journals, or one of the heavens, can soon be tried. The new moon of March next, falls on Saturday the 24th, at 2 in the afternoon. We shall certainly look out."

{322}

The following appeared in the number of March 31:

"The first Saturday Moon since Dr. Forster's announcement came off a week ago. We had previously received a number of letters from different correspondents--all to the effect that the notion of new moon on Saturday bringing wet weather is one of widely extended currency. One correspondent (who gives his name) states that he has constantly heard it at sea, and among the farmers and peasantry in Scotland, Ireland, and the North of England. He proceeds thus: 'Since 1826, nineteen years of the time I have spent in a seafaring life. I have constantly observed, though unable to account for, the phenomenon. I have also heard the stormy qualities of a Saturday's moon remarked by American, French, and Spanish seamen; and, still more distant, a Chinese pilot, who was once doing duty on board my vessel seemed to be perfectly cognizant of the fact.' So that it seems we have, in giving currency to what we only knew as a very curious communication from an earnest meteorologist, been repeating what is common enough among sailors and farmers. Another correspondent affirms that the thing is most devoutly believed in by seamen; who would as soon sail on a Friday as be in the Channel after a Saturday moon.--After a tolerable course of dry weather, there was some snow, accompanied by wind on Saturday last, here in London; there were also heavy louring clouds. Sunday was cloudy and cold, with a little rain; Monday was louring, Tuesday unsettled; Wednesday quite overclouded, with rain in the morning. The present occasion shows only a general change of weather with a tendency towards rain. If Dr. Forster's theory be true, it is decidedly one of the minor instances, as far as London weather is concerned.--It will take a good deal of evidence to make us believe in the omen of a Saturday Moon. But, as we have said of the Poughkeepsie Seer, the thing is very curious whether true or false. Whence comes this universal proverb--and a hundred others--while the meteorological observer {323} cannot, when he puts down a long series of results, detect any weather cycles at all? One of our correspondents wrote us something of a lecture for encouraging, he said, the notion that names could influence the weather. He mistakes the question. If there be any weather cycles depending on the moon, it is possible that one of them may be so related to the week cycle of seven days, as to show recurrences which are of the kind stated, or any other. For example, we know that if the new moon of March fall on a Saturday in this year, it will most probably fall on a Saturday nineteen years hence. This is not connected with the spelling of Saturday--but with the connection between the motions of the sun and moon. Nothing but the Moon can settle the question--and we are willing to wait on her for further information. If the adage be true, then the philosopher has missed what lies before his eyes; if false, then the world can be led by the nose in spite of the eyes.

Both these things happen sometimes; and we are willing to take whichever of the two solutions is borne out by future facts. In the mean time, we announce the next Saturday Moon for the 18th of August."

How many coincidences are required to establish a law of connection? It depends on the way in which the mind views the matter in question. Many of the paradoxers are quite set up by a very few instances. I will now tell a story about myself, and then ask them a question.

So far as instances can prove a law, the following is proved: no failure has occurred. Let a clergyman be known to me, whether by personal acquaintance or correspondence, or by being frequently brought before me by those with whom I am connected in private life: that clergyman does not, except in few cases, become a bishop; but if he become a bishop, he is sure, first or last, to become an arch-bishop. This has happened in every case. As follows:

1. My last schoolmaster, a former Fellow of Oriel, was {324} a very intimate college friend of Richard Whately[692], a younger man. Struck by his friend's talents, he used to talk of him perpetually, and predict his future eminence. Before I was sixteen, and before Whately had even given his Bampton Lectures, I was very familiar with his name, and some of his sayings. I need not say that he became Archbishop of Dublin.

2. When I was a child, a first cousin of John Bird Sumner[693] married a sister of my mother. I cannot remember the time when I first heard his name, but it was made very familiar to me. In time he became Bishop of Chester, and then, Archbishop of Canterbury. My reader may say that Dr. C. R. Sumner,[694] Bishop of Winchester, has just as good a claim: but it is not so: those connected with me had more knowledge of Dr. J. B. Sumner;[695] and said nothing, or next to nothing, of the other. Rumor says that the Bishop of Winchester has declined an Archbishopric: if so, my rule is a rule of gradations.

3. Thomas Musgrave,[696] Fellow of Trinity College, Cambridge, was Dean of the college when I was an undergraduate: this brought me into connection with him, he giving impositions for not going to chapel, I writing them out according. We had also friendly intercourse in after life; I forgiving, he probably forgetting. Honest Tom {325} Musgrave, as he used to be called, became Bishop of Hereford, and Archbishop of York.

4. About the time when I went to Cambridge, I heard a great deal about Mr. C. T. Longley,[697] of Christchurch, from a cousin of my own of the same college, long since deceased, who spoke of him much, and most affectionately. Dr. Longley passed from Durham to York, and thence to Canterbury. I cannot quite make out the two Archbishoprics; I do not remember any other private channel through which the name came to me: perhaps Dr. Longley, having two strings to his bow, would have been one archbishop if I had never heard of him.

5. When Dr. Wm. Thomson[698] was appointed to the see of Gloucester in 1861, he and I had been correspondents on the subject of logic--on which we had both written--for about fourteen years. On his elevation I wrote to him, giving the preceding instances, and informing him that he would certainly be an Archbishop. The case was a strong one, and the law acted rapidly; for Dr. Thomson's elevation to the see of York took place in 1862.

Here are five cases; and there is no opposing instance. I have searched the almanacs since 1828, and can find no instance of a Bishop not finally Archbishop of whom I had known through private sources, direct or indirect. Now what do my paradoxers say? Is this a pre-established harmony, or a chain of coincidences? And how many instances will it require to establish a law?[699]

{326}

THE HERSCHEL HOAX.

Some account of the great astronomical discoveries lately made by Sir John Herschel at the Cape of Good Hope. Second Edition. London, 12mo. 1836.

This is a curious hoax, evidently written by a person versed in astronomy and clever at introducing probable circumstances and undesigned coincidences.[700] It first appeared in a newspaper. It makes Sir J. Herschel discover men, animals, etc. in the moon, of which much detail is given.

There seems to have been a French edition, the original, and English editions in America, whence the work came into Britain: but whether the French was published in America or at Paris I do not know. There is no doubt that it was produced in the United States, by M. Nicollet,[701] an astronomer, once of Paris, and a fugitive of some kind. About him I have heard two stories. First that he fled to America with funds not his own, and that this book was a mere device to raise the wind. Secondly, that he was a protégé of Laplace, and of the Polignac party, and also an outspoken man. That after the revolution he was so obnoxious to the republican party that he judged it prudent to quit France; which he did in debt, leaving money for his creditors, but not enough, with M. Bouvard. In America he connected himself with an assurance office. {327} The moon-story was written, and sent to France, chiefly with the intention of entrapping M. Arago, Nicollet's especial foe, into the belief of it. And those who narrate this version of the story wind up by saying that M. Arago was entrapped, and circulated the wonders through Paris, until a letter from Nicollet to M. Bouvard[702] explained the hoax. I have no personal knowledge of either story: but as the poor man had to endure the first, it is but right that the second should be told with it.

SOME MORE METEOROLOGY.

The Weather Almanac for the Year 1838. By P. Murphy,[703] Esq., M.N.S.

By M. N. S. is meant member of no society.. This almanac bears on the title-page two recommendations. The Morning Post calls it one of the most important-if-true publications of our generation. The Times says: "If the basis of his theory prove sound, and its principles be sanctioned by a more extended experience, it is not too much to say that the importance of the discovery is equal to that of the longitude." Cautious journalist! Three times that of the longitude would have been too little to say. That the landsman might predict the weather of all the year, at its beginning, Jack would cheerfully give up astronomical longitude--the problem--altogether, and fall back on chronometers with the older Ls, lead, latitude, and look-out, applied to dead-reckoning. Mr. Murphy attempted to give the weather day by day: thus the first seven days of March {328} bore Changeable; Rain; Rain; Rain-wind; Changeable; Fair; Changeable. To aim at such precision as to put a fair day between two changeable ones by weather theory was going very near the wind and weather too. Murphy opened the year with cold and frost; and the weather did the same. But Murphy, opposite to Saturday, January 20, put down "Fair, Probable lowest degree of winter temperature." When this Saturday came, it was not merely the probably coldest of 1838, but certainly the coldest of many consecutive years.

Without knowing anything of Murphy, I felt it prudent to cover my nose with my glove as I walked the street at eight in the morning. The fortune of the Almanac was made. Nobody waited to see whether the future would dement the prophecy: the shop was beset in a manner which brought the police to keep order; and it was said that the Almanac for 1838 was a gain of 5,000l. to the owners. It very soon appeared that this was only a lucky hit: the weather-prophet had a modified reputation for a few years; and is now no more heard of. A work of his will presently appear in the list. THE GREAT PYRAMIDS.

Letter from Alexandria on the evidence of the practical application of the quadrature of the circle in the great pyramids of Gizeh. By H. C. Agnew,[704] Esq. London, 1838, 4to.

{329}

Mr. Agnew detects proportions which he thinks were suggested by those of the circumference and diameter of a circle.

THE MATHEMATICS OF A CREED

The creed of St. Athanasius proved by a mathematical parallel. Before you censure, condemn, or approve; read, examine, and understand. E. B. REVILO.[705] London, 1839, 8vo.

This author really believed himself, and was in earnest. He is not the only person who has written nonsense by confounding the mathematical infinite (of quantity) with what speculators now more correctly express by the unlimited, the unconditioned, or the absolute. This tract is worth preserving, as the extreme case of a particular kind. The following is a specimen. Infinity being represented by [infinity], as usual, and f, s, g, being finite integers, the three Persons are denoted by [infinity]^{f}, (m [infinity])^{s}, [infinity]^{g}, the finite fraction m representing human nature, as opposed to [infinity]. The clauses of the Creed are then given with their mathematical parallels. I extract a couple:

"But the Godhead of the Father, of the Son, and of the Holy Ghost, is all one: the glory equal, the Majesty co-eternal.

"It has been shown that [infinity]^f, [infinity]^g, and (m [infinity])^s, together, are but [infinity], and that each is [infinity], and any magnitude in existence represented by [infinity] always was and always will be: for it cannot be made, or destroyed, and yet exists.

{330}

"Equal to the Father, as touching his Godhead: and inferior to the Father, touching his Manhood."

"(m [infinity])^s is equal to [infinity]^f as touching [infinity], but inferior to [infinity]^f as touching m: because m is not infinite."

I might have passed this over, as beneath even my present subject, but for the way in which I became acquainted with it. A bookseller, not the publisher, handed it to me over his counter: one who had published mathematical works. He said, with an air of important communication, Have you seen this, Sir! In reply, I recommended him to show it to my friend Mr.----, for whom he had published mathematics. Educated men, used to books and to the converse of learned men, look with mysterious wonder on such productions as this: for which reason I have made a quotation which many will judge had better have been omitted. But it would have been an imposition on the public if I were, omitting this and some other uses of the Bible and Common Prayer, to pretend that I had given a true picture of my school.

[Since the publication of the above, it has been stated that the author is Mr. Oliver Byrne, the author of the Dual Arithmetic mentioned further on: E. B. Revilo seems to be obviously a reversal.]

LOGIC HAS NO PARADOXERS

Old and new logic contrasted: being an attempt to elucidate, for ordinary comprehension, how Lord Bacon delivered the human mind from its 2,000 years' enslavement under Aristotle. By Justin Brenan.[706] London, 1839, 12mo.

Logic, though the other exact science, has not had the sort of assailants who have clustered about mathematics. There is a sect which disputes the utility of logic, but there are no special points, like the quadrature of the circle, which {331} excite dispute among those who admit other things. The old story about Aristotle having one logic to trammel us, and Bacon another to set us free,--always laughed at by those who really knew either Aristotle or Bacon,--now begins to be understood by a large section of the educated world. The author of this tract connects the old logic with the indecencies of the classical writers, and the new with moral purity: he appeals to women, who, "when they see plainly the demoralizing tendency of syllogistic logic, they will no doubt exert their powerful influence against it, and support the Baconian method." This is the only work against logic which I can introduce, but it is a rare one, I mean in contents. I quote the author's idea of a syllogism:

"The basis of this system is the syllogism. This is a form of couching the substance of your argument or investigation into one short line or sentence--then corroborating or supporting it in another, and drawing your conclusion or proof in a third."

On this definition he gives an example, as follows: "Every sin deserves death," the substance of the "argument or investigation." Then comes, "Every unlawful wish is a sin," which "corroborates or supports" the preceding: and, lastly, "therefore every unlawful wish deserves death," which is the "conclusion or proof." We learn, also, that "sometimes the first is called the premises (sic), and sometimes the first premiss"; as also that "the first is sometimes called the proposition, or subject, or affirmative, and the next the predicate, and sometimes the middle term." To which is added, with a mark of exclamation at the end, "but in analyzing the syllogism, there is a middle term, and a predicate too, in each of the lines!" It is clear that Aristotle never enslaved this mind.

I have said that logic has no paradoxers, but I was speaking of old time. This science has slept until our own day: Hamilton[707] says there has been "no progress made in {332} the general development of the syllogism since the time of Aristotle; and in regard to the few partial improvements, the professed historians seem altogether ignorant." But in our time, the paradoxer, the opponent of common opinion, has appeared in this field. I do not refer to Prof. Boole,[708] who is not a paradoxer, but a discoverer: his system could neither oppose nor support common opinion, for its grounds were not in the conception of any one. I speak especially of two others, who fought like cat and dog: one was dogmatical, the other categorical. The first was Hamilton himself--Sir William Hamilton of Edinburgh, the metaphysician, not Sir William Rowan Hamilton[709] of Dublin, the mathematician, a combination of peculiar genius with unprecedented learning, erudite in all he could want except mathematics, for which he had no turn, and in which he had not even a schoolboy's knowledge, thanks to the Oxford of his younger day. The other was the author of this work, so fully described in Hamilton's writings that there is no occasion to describe him here. I shall try to say a few words in common language about the paradoxers.

Hamilton's great paradox was the quantification of the predicate; a fearful phrase, easily explained. We all know that when we say "Men are animals," a form wholly unquantified in phrase, we speak of all men, but not of all animals: it is some or all, some may be all for aught the proposition says.

This some-may-be-all-for-aught-we-say, or not-none, is the logician's some. One would suppose {333} that "all men are some animals," would have been the logical phrase in all time: but the predicate never was quantified.

The few who alluded to the possibility of such a thing found reasons for not adopting it over and above the great reason, that Aristotle did not adopt it.

For Aristotle never ruled in physics or metaphysics in the old time with near so much of absolute sway as he has ruled in logic down to our own time. The logicians knew that in the proposition "all men are animals" the "animal" is not universal, but particular yet no one dared to say that all men are some animals, and to invent the phrase, "some animals are all men" until Hamilton leaped the ditch, and not only completed a system of enunciation, but applied it to syllogism.

My own case is as peculiar as his: I have proposed to introduce mathematical thought into logic to an extent which makes the old stagers cry:

"St. Aristotle! what wild notions! Serve a ne exeat regno[710] on him!"

Hard upon twenty years ago, a friend and opponent who stands high in these matters, and who is not nearly such a sectary of Aristotle and establishment as most, wrote to me as follows: "It is said that next to the man who forms the taste of the nation, the greatest genius is the man who corrupts it. I mean therefore no disrespect, but very much the reverse, when I say that I have hitherto always considered you as a great logical heresiarch." Coleridge says he thinks that it was Sir Joshua Reynolds who made the remark: which, to copy a bull I once heard, I cannot deny, because I was not there when he said it. My friend did not call me to repentance and reconciliation with the church: I think he had a guess that I was a reprobate sinner. My offences at that time were but small: I went on spinning syllogism systems, all alien from the common logic, until I had six, the initial letters of which, put together, from the {334} names I gave before I saw what they would make, bar all repentance by the words RUE NOT! leaving to the followers of the old school the comfortable option of placing the letters thus:

TRUE? NO!

It should however be stated that the question is not about absolute truth or falsehood. No one denies that anything I call an inference is an inference: they say that my alterations are extra-logical; that they are material, not formal; and that logic is a formal science.

The distinction between material and formal is easily made, where the usual perversions are not required. A form is an empty machine, such as "Every X is Y"; it may be supplied with matter, as in "Every man is animal." The logicians will not see that their formal proposition, "Every X is Y," is material in three points, the degree of assertion, the quantity of the proposition, and the copula. The purely formal proposition is "There is the probability [alpha] that X stands in the relation L to Y." The time will come when it will be regretted that logic went without paradoxers for two thousand years: and when much that has been said on the distinction of form and matter will breed jokes.

I give one instance of one mood of each of the systems, in the order of the letters first written above.

Relative.--In this system the formal relation is taken, that is, the copula may be any whatever. As a material instance, in which the relations are those of consanguinity (of men understood), take the following: X is the brother of Y; X is not the uncle of Z; therefore, Z is not the child of Y. The discussion of relation, and of the objections to the extension, is in the Cambridge Transactions, Vol. X, Part 2; a crabbed conglomerate.

Undecided.--In this system one premise, and want of power over another, infer want of power over a conclusion. {335} As "Some men are not capable of tracing consequences; we cannot be sure that there are beings responsible for consequences who are incapable of tracing consequences; therefore, we cannot be sure that all men are responsible for the consequences of their actions."

Exemplar.--This, long after it suggested itself to me as a means of correcting a defect in Hamilton's system, I saw to be the very system of Aristotle himself, though his followers have drifted into another. It makes its subject and predicate examples, thus: Any one man is an animal; any one animal is a mortal; therefore, any one man is a mortal.

Numerical.--Suppose 100 Ys to exist: then if 70 Xs be Ys, and 40 Zs be Ys, it follows that 10 Xs (at least) are Zs. Hamilton, whose mind could not generalize on symbols, saw that the word most would come under this system, and admitted, as valid, such a syllogism as "most Ys are Xs; most Ys are Zs; therefore, some Xs are Zs."

Onymatic.--This is the ordinary system much enlarged in propositional forms. It is fully discussed in my Syllabus of Logic.

Transposed.--In this syllogism the quantity in one premise is transposed into the other. As, some Xs are not Ys; for every X there is a Y which is Z; therefore, some Zs are not Xs.

Sir William Hamilton of Edinburgh was one of the best friends and allies I ever had. When I first began to publish speculation on this subject, he introduced me to the logical world as having plagiarized from him. This drew their attention: a mathematician might have written about logic under forms which had something of mathematical look long enough before the Aristotelians would have troubled themselves with him: as was done by John Bernoulli,[711] {336} James Bernoulli,[712] Lambert,[713] and Gergonne;[714] who, when our discussion began, were not known even to omnilegent Hamilton. He retracted his accusation of wilful theft in a manly way when he found it untenable; but on this point he wavered a little, and was convinced to the last that I had taken his principle unconsciously. He thought I had done the same with Ploucquet[715] and Lambert. It was his pet notion that I did not understand the commonest principles of logic, that I did not always know the difference between the middle term of a syllogism and its conclusion. It went against his grain to imagine that a mathematician could be a logician. So long as he took me to be riding my own hobby, he laughed consumedly: but when he thought he could make out that I was mounted behind Ploucquet or Lambert, the current ran thus: "It would indeed have been little short of a miracle had he, ignorant even of the common principles of logic, been able of himself to rise to generalization so lofty and so accurate as are supposed in the peculiar doctrines of both the rival logicians, Lambert and Ploucquet--how useless soever these may in practice prove to be." All this has been sufficiently discussed elsewhere: "but, masters, remember that I am an ass."

I know that I never saw Lambert's work until after all Hamilton supposed me to have taken was written: he himself, who read almost everything, knew nothing about it until after I did. I cannot prove what I say about my knowledge of Lambert: but the means of doing it may turn up. For, by the casual turning up of an old letter, I have {337} found the means of clearing myself as to Ploucquet. Hamilton assumed that (unconsciously) I took from Ploucquet the notion of a logical notation in which the symbol of the conclusion is seen in the joint symbols of the premises. For example, in my own fashion I write down (.) (.), two symbols of premises. By these symbols I see that there is a valid conclusion, and that it may be written in symbol by striking out the two middle parentheses, which gives (. .) and reading the two negative dots as an affirmative. And so I see in (.) (.) that ( ) is the conclusion. This, in full, is the perception that "all are either Xs or Ys" and "all are either Ys or Zs" necessitates "some Xs are Zs." Now in Ploucquet's book of 1763, is found, "Deleatur in præmissis medius; id quod restat indicat conclusionem."[716] In the paper in which I explain my symbols--which are altogether different from Ploucquet's--there is found "Erase the symbols of the middle term; the remaining symbols show the inference." There is very great likeness: and I would have excused Hamilton for his notion if he had fairly given reference to the part of the book in which his quotation was found. For I had shown in my Formal Logic what part of Ploucquet's book I had used: and a fair disputant would either have strengthened his point by showing that I had been at his part of the book, or allowed me the advantage of it being apparent that I had not given evidence of having seen that part of the book. My good friend, though an honest man, was sometimes unwilling to allow due advantage to controversial opponents.

But to my point. The only work of Ploucquet I ever saw was lent me by my friend Dr. Logan,[717] with whom I have often corresponded on logic, etc. I chanced (in 1865) {338} to turn up the letter which he sent me (Sept. 12, 1847) with the book. Part of it runs thus: "I congratulate you on your success in your logical researches [that is, in asking for the book, I had described some results]. Since the reading of your first paper I have been satisfied as to the possibility of inventing a logical notation in which the rationale of the inference is contained in the symbol, though I never attempted to verify it [what I communicated, then, satisfied the writer that I had done and communicated what he, from my previous paper, suspected to be practicable]. I send you Ploucquet's dissertation....'

It now being manifest that I cannot be souring grapes which have been taken from me, I will say what I never said in print before. There is not the slightest merit in making the symbols of the premises yield that of the conclusion by erasure: the thing must do itself in every system which symbolises quantities. For in every syllogism (except the inverted Bramantip of the Aristotelians) the conclusion is manifest in this way without symbols. This Bramantip destroys system in the Aristotelian lot: and circumstances which I have pointed out destroy it in Hamilton's own collection. But in that enlargement of the reputed Aristotelian system which I have called onymatic, and in that correction of Hamilton's system which I have called exemplar, the rule of erasure is universal, and may be seen without symbols.

Our first controversy was in 1846. In 1847, in my Formal Logic, I gave him back a little satire for satire, just to show, as I stated, that I could employ ridicule if I pleased. He was so offended with the appendix in which this was contained, that he would not accept the copy of the book I sent him, but returned it. Copies of controversial works, sent from opponent to opponent, are not presents, in the usual sense: it was a marked success to make him angry enough to forget this. It had some effect however: during the rest of his life I wished to avoid provocation; for I {339} could not feel sure that excitement might not produce consequences. I allowed his slashing account of me in the Discussions to pass unanswered: and before that, when he proposed to open a controversy in the Athenæum upon my second Cambridge paper, I merely deferred the dispute until the next edition of my Formal Logic. I cannot expect the account in the Discussions to amuse an unconcerned reader as much as it amused myself: but for a cut-and-thrust, might-and-main, tooth-and-nail, hammer-and-tongs assault, I can particularly recommend it. I never knew, until I read it, how much I should enjoy a thundering onslought on myself, done with racy insolence by a master hand, to whom my good genius had whispered Ita feri ut se sentiat emori.[718] Since that time I have, as the Irishman said, become "dry moulded for want of a bating." Some of my paradoxers have done their best: but theirs is mere twopenny--"small swipes," as Peter Peebles said. Brandy for heroes! I hope a reviewer or two will have mercy on me, and will give me as good discipline as Strafford would have given Hampden and his set: "much beholden," said he, "should they be to any one that should thoroughly take pains with them in that kind"--meaning objective flagellation. And I shall be the same to any one who will serve me so--but in a literary and periodical sense: my corporeal cuticle is as thin as my neighbors'.

Sir W. H. was suffering under local paralysis before our controversy commenced: and though his mind was quite unaffected, a retort of as downright a character as the attack might have produced serious effect upon a person who had shown himself sensible of ridicule. Had a second attack of his disorder followed an answer from me, I should have been held to have caused it: though, looking at Hamilton's genial love of combat, I strongly suspected that a retort in kind

{340}

"Would cheer his heart, and warm his blood, And make him fight, and do him good."

But I could not venture to risk it. So all I did, in reply to the article in the Discussions, was to write to him the following note: which, as illustrating an etiquette of controversy, I insert.

"I beg to acknowledge and thank you for.... It is necessary that I should say a word on my retention of this work, with reference to your return of the copy of my Formal Logic, which I presented to you on its publication: a return made on the ground of your disapproval of the account of our controversy which that work contained. According to my view of the subject, any one whose dealing with the author of a book is specially attacked in it, has a right to expect from the author that part of the book in which the attack is made, together with so much of the remaining part as is fairly context. And I hold that the acceptance by the party assailed of such work or part of a work does not imply any amount of approval of the contents, or of want of disapproval. On this principle (though I am not prepared to add the word alone) I forwarded to you the whole of my work on Formal Logic and my second Cambridge Memoir. And on this principle I should have held you wanting in due regard to my literary rights if you had not forwarded to me your asterisked pages, with all else that was necessary to a full understanding of their scope and meaning, so far as the contents of the book would furnish it. For the remaining portion, which it would be a hundred pities to separate from the pages in which I am directly concerned, I am your debtor on another principle; and shall be glad to remain so if you will allow me to make a feint of balancing the account by the offer of two small works on subjects as little connected with our discussion as the Epistolæ Obscurorum Virorum, or the Lutheran dispute. I trust that by accepting my Opuscula you will enable me to avoid the {341} use of the knife, and leave me to cut you up with the pen as occasion shall serve, I remain, etc. (April 21, 1852)."

I received polite thanks, but not a word about the body of the letter: my argument, I suppose, was admitted.

SOME DOGGEREL AND COUNTER DOGGEREL

I find among my miscellaneous papers the following jeu d'esprit, or jeu de bêtise,[719] whichever the reader pleases--I care not--intended, before I saw ground for abstaining, to have, as the phrase is, come in somehow. I think I could manage to bring anything into anything: certainly into a Budget of Paradoxes. Sir W. H. rather piqued himself upon some caniculars, or doggerel verses, which he had put together in memoriam [technicam] of the way in which A E I O are used in logic: he added U, Y, for the addition of meet, etc., to the system. I took the liberty of concocting some counter-doggerel, just to show that a mathematician may have architectonic power as well as a metaphysician.

DOGGEREL. BY SIR W. HAMILTON. A it affirms of this, these, all, Whilst E denies of any; I it affirms (whilst O denies) Of some (or few, or many).

Thus A affirms, as E denies, And definitely either; Thus I affirms, as O denies, And definitely neither.

A half, left semidefinite, Is worthy of its score; U, then, affirms, as Y denies, This, neither less nor more.

Indefinito-definites, I, UI, YO, last we come; {342} And this affirms, as that denies Of more, most (half, plus, some).

COUNTER DOGGEREL. BY PROF. DE MORGAN. (1847.) Great A affirms of all; Sir William does so too: When the subject is "my suspicion," And the predicate "must be true."

Great E denies of all; Sir William of all but one: When he speaks about this present time, And of those who in logic have done.

Great I takes up but some; Sir William! my dear soul! Why then in all your writings, Does "Great I" fill[720] the whole!

Great O says some are not; Sir William's readers catch, That some (modern) Athens is not without An Aristotle to match.

"A half, left semi-definite, Is worthy of its score:" This looked very much like balderdash, And neither less nor more.

It puzzled me like anything; In fact, it puzzled me worse: Isn't schoolman's logic hard enough, Without being in Sibyl's verse?

{343} At last, thinks I, 'tis German; And I'll try it with some beer! The landlord asked what bothered me so, And at once he made it clear.

It's half-and-half, the gentleman means; Don't you see he talks of score? That's the bit of memorandum That we chalk behind the door.

Semi-definite's outlandish; But I see, in half a squint, That he speaks of the lubbers who call for a quart, When they can't manage more than a pint.

Now I'll read it into English, And then you'll answer me this: If it isn't good logic all the world round, I should like to know what is?

When you call for a pot of half-and-half, If you're lost to sense of shame, You may leave it semi-definite, But you pay for it all just the same. * * * *
* *

I am unspeakably comforted when I look over the above in remembering that the question is not whether it be Pindaric or Horatian, but whether the copy be as good as the original. And I say it is: and will take no denial.

Long live--long will live--the glad memory of William Hamilton, Good, Learned, Acute, and Disputatious! He fought upon principle: the motto of his book is:

"Truth, like a torch, the more it's shook it shines."

There is something in this; but metaphors, like puddings, quarrels, rivers, and arguments, always have two sides to them. For instance, "Truth, like a torch, the more it's shook it shines; But those who want to use it, hold it steady. They shake the flame who like a glare to gaze at, They keep it still who want a light to see by."

{344}

ANOTHER THEORY OF PARALLELS

Theory of Parallels. The proof of Euclid's axiom looked for in the properties of the Equiangular Spiral. By Lieut-Col. G. Perronet Thompson.[721] The same, second edition, revised and corrected. The same, third edition, shortened, and freed from dependence on the theory of limits. The same, fourth edition, ditto, ditto. All London, 1840, 8vo.

To explain these editions it should be noted that General Thompson rapidly modified his notions, and republished his tracts accordingly.

SOME PRIMITIVE DARWINISM

Vestiges of the Natural History of Creation.[722] London, 1840, 12mo.

This is the first edition of this celebrated work. Its form is a case of the theory: the book is an undeniable duodecimo, but the size of its paper gives it the look of not the smallest of octavos. Does not this illustrate the law of development, the gradation of families, the transference of species, and so on? If so, I claim the discovery of this esoteric testimony of the book to its own contents; I defy any one to point out the reviewer who has mentioned it. The work itself is described by its author as "the first attempt to connect the natural sciences into a history of creation." The attempt was commenced, and has been carried on, both with marked talent, and will be continued. Great advantage will result: at the worst we are but in the alchemy of some new chemistry, or the astrology of some new astronomy. Perhaps it would be as well not to be too sure on the matter, until we have an antidote to possible consequences as exhibited under another theory, on which {345} it is as reasonable to speculate as on that of the Vestiges. I met long ago with a splendid player on the guitar, who assured me, and was confirmed by his friends, that he never practised, except in thought, and did not possess an instrument: he kept his fingers acting in his mind, until they got their habits; and thus he learnt the most difficult novelties of execution. Now what if this should be a minor segment of a higher law? What if, by constantly thinking of ourselves as descended from primeval monkeys, we should--if it be true--actually get our tails again? What if the first man who was detected with such an appendage should be obliged to confess himself the author of the Vestiges--a person yet unknown--who would naturally get the start of his species by having had the earliest habit of thinking on the matter? I confess I never hear a man of note talk fluently about it without a curious glance at his proportions, to see whether there may be ground to conjecture that he may have more of "mortal coil" than others, in anaxyridical concealment. I do not feel sure that even a paternal love for his theory would induce him, in the case I am supposing, to exhibit himself at the British Association, With a hole behind which his tail peeped through.

The first sentence of this book (1840) is a cast of the log, which shows our rate of progress. "It is familiar knowledge that the earth which we inhabit is a globe of somewhat less than 8,000 miles in diameter, being one of a series of eleven which revolve at different distances around the sun." The eleven! Not to mention the Iscariot which Le Verrier and Adams calculated into existence, there is more than a septuagint of new planetoids.

ON RELIGIOUS INSURANCE

The Constitution and Rules of the Ancient and Universal 'Benefit Society' established by Jesus Christ, exhibited, and its advantages and claims maintained, against all Modern and {346} merely Human Institutions of the kind: A Letter very respectfully addressed to the Rev. James Everett,[723] and occasioned by certain remarks made by him, in a speech to the Members of the 'Wesleyan Centenary Institute' Benefit Society. Dated York, Dec. 7, 1840. By Thomas Smith.[724] 12mo, (pp. 8.)

The Wesleyan minister addressed had advocated provision against old age, etc.: the writer declares all private provision un-Christian. After decent maintenance and relief of family claims of indigence, he holds that all the rest is to go to the "Benefit Society," of which he draws up the rules, in technical form, with chapters of "Officers," "Contributors" etc., from the Acts of the Apostles, etc., and some of the early Fathers. He holds that a Christian may not "make a private provision against the contingencies of the future": and that the great "Benefit Society" is the divinely-ordained recipient of all the surplus of his income; capital, beyond what is necessary for business, he is to have none. A real good speculator shuts his eyes by instinct, when opening them would not serve the purpose: he has the vizor of the Irish fairy tale, which fell of itself over the eyes of the wearer the moment he turned them upon the enchanted light which would have destroyed him if he had caught sight of it. "Whiles it remained, was it not thine own? and after it was sold, was it (the purchase-money) not in thine own power?" would have been awkward to quote, and accordingly nothing is stated except the well-known result, which is rule 3, cap. 5, "Prevention of Abuses." By putting his principles together, the author can be made, logically, to mean that the successors of the apostles should put to death all contributors who are detected in not paying their full premiums.

{347}

I have known one or two cases in which policy-holders have surrendered their policies through having arrived at a conviction that direct provision is unlawful. So far as I could make it out, these parties did not think it unlawful to lay by out of income, except when this was done in a manner which involved calculation of death-chances. It is singular they did not see that the entrance of chance of death was the entrance of the very principle of the benefit society described in the Acts of the Apostles. The family of the one who died young received more in proportion to premiums paid than the family of one who died old. Every one who understands life assurance sees that--bonus apart--the difference between an assurance office and a savings bank consists in the adoption, pro tanto, of the principle of community of goods. In the original constitution of the oldest assurance office, the Amicable Society, the plan with which they started was nothing but this: persons of all ages under forty-five paid one common premium, and the proceeds were divided among the representatives of those who died within the year.

THE TWO OLD PARADOXES AGAIN

[I omitted from its proper place a manuscript quadrature (3.1416 exactly) addressed to an eminent mathematician, dated in 1842 from the debtor's ward of a country gaol. The unfortunate speculator says, "I have labored many years to find the precise ratio." I have heard of several cases in which squaring the circle has produced an inability to square accounts. I remind those who feel a kind of inspiration to employ native genius upon difficulties, without gradual progression from elements, that the call is one which becomes stronger and stronger, and may lead, as it has led, to abandonment of the duties of life, and all the consequences.] {348}

1842. Provisional Prospectus of the Double Acting Rotary Engine Company. Also Mechanic's Magazine, March 26, 1842.

Perpetual motion by a drum with one vertical half in mercury, the other in a vacuum: the drum, I suppose, working round forever to find an easy position. Steam to be superseded: steam and electricity convulsions of nature never intended by Providence for the use of man. The price of the present engines, as old iron, will buy new engines that will work without fuel and at no expense. Guaranteed by the Count de Predaval,[725] the discoverer. I was to have been a Director, but my name got no further than ink, and not so far as official notification of the honor, partly owing to my having communicated to the Mechanic's Magazine information privately given to me, which gave premature publicity, and knocked up the plan.

An Exposition of the Nature, Force, Action, and other properties of Gravitation on the Planets. London, 1842, 12mo.

An Investigation of the principles of the Rules for determining the Measures of the Areas and Circumferences of Circular Plane Surfaces ... London, 1844, 8vo.

These are anonymous; but the author (whom I believe to be Mr. Denison,[726] presently noted) is described as author of a new system of mathematics, and also of mechanics. He had need have both, for he shows that the line which has a square equal to a given circle, has a cube equal to the sphere on the same diameter: that is, in old mathematics, the diameter is to the circumference as 9 to 16! Again, admitting that the velocities of planets in circular orbits are inversely as the square roots of their distances, that is, admitting Kepler's law, he manages to prove that gravitation is inversely as the square root of the distance: and suspects magnetism of doing the difference between this and Newton's law. {349} Magnetism and electricity are, in physics, the member of parliament and the cabman--at every man's bidding, as Henry Warburton[727] said.

The above is an outrageous quadrature. In the preceding year, 1841, was published what I suppose at first to be a Maori quadrature, by Maccook. But I get it from a cutting out of some French periodical, and I incline to think that it must be by a Mr. McCook. He makes [pi] to be 2 + 2[root](8[root]2 - 11).

THE DUPLICATION PROBLEM

Refutation of a Pamphlet written by the Rev. John Mackey, R.C.P.,[728] entitled "A method of making a cube double of a cube, founded on the principles of elementary geometry," wherein his principles are proved erroneous, and the required solution not yet obtained. By Robert Murphy.[729] Mallow, 1824, 12mo.

This refutation was the production of an Irish boy of eighteen years old, self-educated in mathematics, the son of a shoemaker at Mallow. He died in 1843, leaving a name which is well known among mathematicians. His works on the theory of equations and on electricity, and his papers in the Cambridge Transactions, are all of high genius. The only account of him which I know of is that which I wrote for the Supplement of the Penny Cyclopædia. He was thrown by his talents into a good income at Cambridge, with no social training except penury, and very little intellectual training except mathematics. He fell into dissipation, and his scientific career was almost arrested: but he had great good in him, to my knowledge. A sentence in {350} a letter from the late Dean Peacock[730] to me--giving some advice about the means of serving Murphy--sets out the old case: "Murphy is a man whose special education is in advance of his general; and such men are almost always difficult subjects to manage." This article having been omitted in its proper place, I put it at 1843, the date of Murphy's death.

A NEW VALUE OF [pi].

The Invisible Universe disclosed; or, the real Plan and Government of the Universe. By Henry Coleman Johnson, Esq. London, 1843, 8vo.

The book opens abruptly with:

"First demonstration. Concerning the centre: showing that, because the centre is an innermost point at an equal distance between two extreme points of a right line, and from every two relative and opposite intermediate points, it is composed of the two extreme internal points of each half of the line; each extreme internal point attracting towards itself all parts of that half to which it belongs...."

Of course the circle is squared: and the circumference is 3-1/21 diameters. SOME MODERN ASTROLOGY.

Combination of the Zodiacal and Cometical Systems. Printed for the London Society, Exeter Hall. Price Sixpence. (n. d. 1843.)

What this London Society was, or the "combination," did not appear. There was a remarkable comet in 1843, the tail of which was at first confounded with what is called the zodiacal light. This nicely-printed little tract, evidently got up with less care for expense than is usual in such works, brings together all the announcements of the astronomers, and adds a short head and tail piece, which I shall quote entire. As the announcements are very ordinary {351} astronomy, the reader will be able to detect, if detection be possible, what is the meaning and force of the "Combination of the Zodiacal and Cometical Systems":

"Premonition. It has pleased the AUTHOR of CREATION to cause (to His human and reasoning Creatures of this generation, by a 'combined' appearance in His Zodiacal and Cometical system) a 'warning Crisis' of universal concernment to this our GLOBE. It is this 'Crisis' that has so generally 'ROUSED' at this moment the 'nations throughout the Earth' that no equal interest has ever before been excited by MAN; unless it be in that caused by the 'PAGAN-TEMPLE IN ROME,' which is recorded by the elder Pliny, 'Nat. Hist.' i. 23. iii. 3. HARDOUIN."

After the accounts given by the unperceiving astronomers, comes what follows:

"Such has been (hitherto) the only object discerned by the 'Wise of this World,' in this twofold union of the 'Zodiacal' and 'Cometical' systems: yet it is nevertheless a most 'Thrilling Warning,' to all the inhabitants of this precarious and transitory EARTH. We have no authorized intimation or reasonable prospective contemplation, of 'current time' beyond a year 1860, of the present century; or rather, except 'the interval which may now remain from the present year 1843, to a year 1860' ([Greek: hêmeras HEXÊKONTA]--'threescore or sixty days'--'I have appointed each "DAY" for a "YEAR,"' Ezek. iv. 6): and we know, from our 'common experience,' how speedily such a measure of time will pass away.

"No words can be 'more explicit' than these of OUR BLESSED LORD: viz. 'THIS GOSPEL of the Kingdom shall be preached in ALL the EARTH, for a Witness to ALL NATIONS; AND THEN, shall the END COME.' The 'next 18 years' must therefore supply the interval of the 'special Episcopal forerunners.' (Matt. xxiv. 14.)

"See the 'JEWISH INTELLIGENCER' of the present month (April), p. 153, for the 'Debates in Parliament,' respecting {352} the BISHOP OF JERUSALEM, viz. Dr. Bowring,[731] Mr. Hume,[732] Sir R. Inglis,[733] Sir R. Peel,[734] Viscount Palmerston.[735]"

I have quoted this at length, to show the awful threats which were published at a time of some little excitement about the phenomenon, under the name of the London Society. The assumption of a corporate appearance is a very unfair trick: and there are junctures at which harm might be done by it.

THE NUMBER OF THE BEAST

Wealth the name and number of the Beast, 666, in the Book of Revelation. [by John Taylor.[736]] London, 1844, 8vo.

Whether Junius or the Beast be the more difficult to identify, must be referred to Mr. Taylor, the only person who has attempted both. His cogent argument on the political secret is not unworthily matched in his treatment of the theological riddle. He sees the solution in [Greek: euporia], which occurs in the Acts of the Apostles as the word for wealth in one of its most disgusting forms, and makes 666 in the most straightforward way. This explanation has as good a chance as any other. The work contains a general {353} attempt at explanation of the Apocalypse, and some history of opinion on the subject. It has not the prolixity which is so common a fault of apocalyptic commentators.

A practical Treatise on Eclipses ... with remarks on the anomalies of the present Theory of the Tides. By T. Kerigan,[737] F.R.S. 1844, 8vo.

Containing also a refutation of the theory of the tides, and afterwards increased by a supplement, "Additional facts and arguments against the theory of the tides," in answer to a short notice in the Athenæum journal. Mr. Kerigan was a lieutenant in the Navy: he obtained admission to the Royal Society just before the publication of his book.

A new theory of Gravitation. By Joseph Denison,[738] Esq. London, 1844, 12mo.

Commentaries on the Principia. By the author of 'A new theory of Gravitation.' London, 1846, 8vo.

Honor to the speculator who can be put in his proper place by one sentence, be that place where it may.

"But we have shown that the velocities are inversely as the square roots of the mean distances from the sun; wherefore, by equality of ratios, the forces of the sun's gravitation upon them are also inversely as the square roots of their distances from the sun."

EASTER DAY PARADOXERS.

In the years 1818 and 1845 the full moon fell on Easter Day, having been particularly directed to fall before it in the act for the change of style and in the English missals and prayer-books of all time: perhaps it would be more correct to say that Easter Day was directed to fall after the full moon; "but the principle is the same." No explanation was given in 1818, but Easter was kept by the tables, {354} in defiance of the rule, and of several protests. A chronological panic was beginning in December 1844, which was stopped by the Times newspaper printing extracts from an article of mine in the Companion to the Almanac for 1845, which had then just appeared. No one had guessed the true reason, which is that the thing called the moon in the Gregorian Calendar is not the moon of the heavens, but a fictitious imitation put wrong on purpose, as will presently appear, partly to keep Easter out of the way of the Jews' Passover, partly for convenience of calculation. The apparent error happens but rarely; and all the work will perhaps have to be gone over next time. I now give two bits of paradox.

Some theologians were angry at this explanation. A review called the Christian Observer (of which Christianity I do not know) got up a crushing article against me. I did not look at it, feeling sure that an article on such a subject which appeared on January 1, 1845, against a publication made in December 1844, must be a second-hand job. But some years afterwards (Sept. 10, 1850), the reviews, etc. having been just placed at the disposal of readers in the old reading-room of the Museum, I made a tour of inspection, came upon my critic on his perch, and took a look at him. I was very glad to remember this, for, though expecting only second-hand, yet even of this there is good and bad; and I expected to find some hints in the good second-hand of a respectable clerical publication. I read on, therefore, attentively, but not long: I soon came to the information that some additions to Delambre's[739] statement of the rule for finding Easter, belonging to distant years, had been made by Sir Harris Nicolas![740] Now as I myself furnished my friend Sir H. N. with Delambre's digest of {355} Clavius's[741] rule, which I translated out of algebra into common language for the purpose, I was pretty sure this was the ignorant reading of a person to whom Sir H. N. was the highest arithmetical authority on the subject. A person pretending to chronology, without being able to distinguish the historical points--so clearly as they stand out--in which Sir H. N. speaks with authority, from the arithmetical points of pure reckoning on which he does not pretend to do more than directly repeat others, must be as fit to talk about the construction of Easter Tables as the Spanish are to talk French. I need hardly say that the additions for distant years are as much from Clavius as the rest: my reviewer was not deep enough in his subject to know that Clavius made and published, from his rules, the full table up to A.D. 5000, for all the movable feasts of every year! I gave only a glance at the rest: I found I was either knave or fool, with a leaning to the second opinion; and I came away satisfied that my critic was either ignoramus or novice, with a leaning to the first. I afterwards found an ambiguity of expression in Sir H. N.'s account--whether his or mine I could not tell--which might mislead a novice or content an ignoramus, but would have been properly read or further inquired into by a competent person.

The second case is this. Shortly after the publication of my article, a gentleman called at my house, and, finding I was not at home, sent up his card--with a stylish west-end club on it--to my wife, begging for a few words on pressing business. With many well-expressed apologies, he stated that he had been alarmed by hearing that Prof. De M. had an intention of altering Easter next year. Mrs. De M. kept her countenance, and assured him that I had no such intention, and further, that she greatly doubted my having the power to do it. Was she quite sure? his authority was very good: fresh assurances given. He was greatly relieved, for he had some horses training for after Easter, which {356} would not be ready to run if it were altered the wrong way. A doubt comes over him: would Mrs. De M., in the event of her being mistaken, give him the very earliest information?

Promise given; profusion of thanks; more apologies; and departure.

Now, candid reader!--or uncandid either!--which most deserves to be laughed at? A public instructor, who undertakes to settle for the world whether a reader of Clavius, the constructor of the Gregorian Calendar, is fool or knave, upon information derived from a compiler--in this matter--of his own day; or a gentleman of horse and dog associations, who, misapprehending something which he heard about a current topic, infers that the reader of Clavius had the ear of the Government on a proposed alteration. I suppose the querist had heard some one say, perhaps, that the day ought to be set right, and some one else remark that I might be consulted, as the only person who had discussed the matter from the original source of the Calendar.

To give a better chance of the explanation being at once produced, next time the real full moon and Easter Day shall fall together, I insert here a summary which was printed in the Irish Prayer-book of the Ecclesiastical Society. If the amusement given by paradoxers should prevent a useless discussion some years hence, I and the paradoxers shall have done a little good between us--at any rate, I have done my best to keep the heavy weight afloat by tying bladders to it. I think the next occurrence will be in 1875.

EASTER DAY

In the years 1818 and 1845, Easter Day, as given by the rules in 24 Geo. II cap. 23. (known as the act for the change of style) contradicted the precept given in the preliminary explanations. The precept is as follows:

"Easter Day, on which the rest" of the moveable feasts "depend, is always the First Sunday after the Full Moon, which happens upon or next after the Twenty-first Day of {357} March; and if the Full Moon happens upon a Sunday, Easter Day is the Sunday after."

But in 1818 and 1845, the full moon fell on a Sunday, and yet the rules gave that same Sunday for Easter Day. Much discussion was produced by this circumstance in 1818: but a repetition of it in 1845 was nearly altogether prevented by a timely[742] reference to the intention of those who conducted the Gregorian reformation of the Calendar. Nevertheless, seeing that the apparent error of the Calendar is due to the precept in the Act of Parliament, which is both erroneous and insufficient, and that the difficulty will recur so often as Easter Day falls on the day of full moon, it may be advisable to select from the two articles cited in the note such of their conclusions and rules, without proof or controversy, as will enable the reader to understand the main points of the Easter question, and, should he desire it, to calculate for himself the Easter of the old or new style, for any given year.

1. In the very earliest age of Christianity, a controversy arose as to the mode of keeping Easter, some desiring to perpetuate the Passover, others to keep the festival of the Resurrection. The first afterwards obtained the name of Quartadecimans, from their Easter being always kept on the fourteenth day of the moon (Exod. xii. 18, Levit. xxiii. 5.). But though it is unquestionable that a Judaizing party existed, it is also likely that many dissented on chronological grounds. It is clear that no perfect anniversary can take place, except when the fourteenth of the moon, and with it the passover, falls on a Friday. Suppose, for instance, it falls on a Tuesday: one of three things must be {358} done. Either (which seems never to have been proposed) the crucifixion and resurrection must be celebrated on Tuesday and Sunday, with a wrong interval; or the former on Tuesday, the latter on Thursday, abandoning the first day of the week; or the former on Friday, and the latter on Sunday, abandoning the paschal commemoration of the crucifixion.

The last mode has been, as every one knows, finally adopted. The disputes of the first three centuries did not turn on any calendar questions. The Easter question was merely the symbol of the struggle between what we may call the Jewish and Gentile sects of Christians: and it nearly divided the Christian world, the Easterns, for the most part, being Quartadecimans. It is very important to note that there is no recorded dispute about a method of predicting the new moon, that is, no general dispute leading to formation of sects: there may have been difficulties, and discussions about them. The Metonic cycle, presently mentioned, must have been used by many, perhaps most, churches.

2. The question came before the Nicene Council (A.D. 325) not as an astronomical, but as a doctrinal, question: it was, in fact, this, Shall the passover[743] be treated as a part of Christianity? The Council resolved this question

in the negative, and the only information on its premises and conclusion, or either, which comes from itself, is contained in the following sentence of the synodical epistle, which epistle is preserved by Socrates[744] and Theodoret.[745] "We also send {359} you the good news concerning the unanimous consent of all in reference to the celebration of the most solemn feast of Easter, for this difference also has been made up by the assistance of your prayers: so that all the brethren in the East, who formerly celebrated this festival at the same time as the Jews, will in future conform to the Romans and to us, and to all who have of old observed our manner of celebrating Easter." This is all that can be found on the subject: none of the stories about the Council ordaining the astronomical mode of finding Easter, and introducing the Metonic cycle into ecclesiastical reckoning, have any contemporary evidence: the canons which purport to be those of the Nicene Council do not contain a word about Easter; and this is evidence, whether we suppose those canons to be genuine or spurious.

3. The astronomical dispute about a lunar cycle for the prediction of Easter either commenced, or became prominent, by the extinction of greater ones, soon after the time of the Nicene Council. Pope Innocent I[746] met with difficulty in 414. S. Leo,[747] in 454, ordained that Easter of 455 should be April 24; which is right. It is useless to record details of these disputes in a summary: the result was, that in the year 463, Pope Hilarius[748] employed Victorinus[749] of Aquitaine to correct the Calendar, and Victorinus formed a rule which lasted until the sixteenth century. He combined the Metonic cycle and the solar cycle presently described. But {360} this cycle bears the name of Dionysius Exiguus,[750] a Scythian settled at Rome, about A.D. 530, who adapted it to his new yearly reckoning, when he abandoned the era of Diocletian as a commencement, and constructed that which is now in common use.

4. With Dionysius, if not before, terminated all difference as to the mode of keeping Easter which is of historical note: the increasing defects of the Easter Cycle produced in time the remonstrance of persons versed in astronomy, among whom may be mentioned Roger Bacon,[751] Sacrobosco,[752] Cardinal Cusa,[753] Regiomontanus,[754] etc. From the middle of the sixth to that of the sixteenth century, one rule was observed.

5. The mode of applying astronomy to chronology has always involved these two principles. First, the actual position of the heavenly body is not the object of consideration, but what astronomers call its mean place, which may be described thus. Let a fictitious sun or moon move in the heavens, in such manner as to revolve among the fixed stars at an average rate, avoiding the alternate accelerations and retardations which take place in every planetary motion. Thus the fictitious (say mean) sun and moon are always very near to the real sun and moon. The ordinary clocks show time by the mean, not the real, sun: and it was always laid down that Easter depends on the opposition (or full moon) of the mean sun and moon, not of the real ones. Thus we see that, were the Calendar ever so correct {361} as to the mean moon, it would be occasionally false as to the true one: if, for instance, the opposition of the mean sun and moon took place at one second before midnight, and that of the real bodies only two seconds afterwards, the calendar day of full moon would be one day before that of the common almanacs. Here is a way in which the discussions of 1818 and 1845 might have arisen: the British legislature has defined the moon as the regulator of the paschal calendar. But this was only a part of the mistake.

6. Secondly, in the absence of perfectly accurate knowledge of the solar and lunar motion (and for convenience, even if such knowledge existed), cycles are, and always have been taken, which serve to represent those motions nearly. The famous Metonic cycle, which is introduced into ecclesiastical chronology under the name of the cycle of the golden numbers, is a period of 19 Julian[755] years. This period, in the old Calendar, was taken to contain exactly 235 lunations, or intervals between new moons, of the mean moon. Now the state of the case is:

19 average Julian years make 6939 days 18 hours.

235 average lunations make 6939 days 16 hours 31 minutes.

So that successive cycles of golden numbers, supposing the first to start right, amount to making the new moons fall too late, gradually, so that the mean moon of this cycle gains 1 hour 29 minutes in 19 years upon the mean moon of the heavens, or about a day in 300 years. When the Calendar was reformed, the calendar new moons were four days in advance of the mean moon of the heavens: so that, for instance, calendar full moon on the 18th usually meant real full moon on the 14th.

7. If the difference above had not existed, the moon of the heavens (the mean moon at least), would have returned {362} permanently to the same days of the month in 19 years; with an occasional slip arising from the unequal distribution of the leap years, of which a period contains sometimes five and sometimes four. As a general rule, the days of new and full moon in any one year would have been also the days of new and full moon of a year having 19 more units in its date. Again, if there had been no leap years, the days of the month would have returned to the same days of the week every seven years. The introduction of occasional 29ths of February disturbs this, and makes the permanent return of month days to week days occur only after 28 years. If all had been true, the lapse of 28 times 19, or 532 years, would have restored the year in every point: that is, A.D. 1, for instance, and A.D. 533, would have had the same almanac in every matter relating to week days, month days, sun, and moon (mean sun and moon at least). And on the supposition of its truth, the old system of Dionysius was framed. Its errors, are, first, that the moments of mean new moon advance too much by 1 h. 29 m. in 19 average Julian years; secondly, that the average Julian year of 365¼ days is too long by 11 m. 10 s.

8. The Council of Trent, moved by the representations made on the state of the Calendar, referred the consideration of it to the Pope. In 1577, Gregory XIII[756] submitted to the Roman Catholic Princes and Universities a plan presented to him by the representatives of Aloysius Lilius,[757] then deceased. This plan being approved of, the Pope nominated a commission to consider its details, the working member of which was the Jesuit Clavius. A short work was prepared by Clavius, descriptive of the new Calendar: this {363} was published[758] in 1582, with the Pope's bull (dated February 24, 1581) prefixed. A larger work was prepared by Clavius, containing fuller explanation, and entitled Romani Calendarii a Gregorio XIII. Pontifice Maximo restituti Explicatio. This was published at Rome in 1603, and again in the collection of the works of Clavius in 1612.

9. The following extracts from Clavius settle the question of the meaning of the term moon, as used in the Calendar:

"Who, except a few who think they are very sharp-sighted in this matter, is so blind as not to see that the 14th of the moon and the full moon are not the same things in the Church of God?... Although the Church, in finding the new moon, and from it the 14th day, uses neither the true nor the mean motion of the moon, but measures only according to the order of a cycle, it is nevertheless undeniable that the mean full moons found from astronomical tables are of the greatest use in determining the cycle which is to be preferred ... the new moons of which cycle, in order to the due celebration of Easter, should be so arranged that the 14th days of those moons, reckoning from the day of new moon inclusive, should not fall two or more days before the mean full moon, but only one day, or else on the very day itself, or not long after. And even thus far the Church need not take very great pains ... for it is sufficient that all should reckon by the 14th day of the moon in the cycle, even though sometimes it should be more than one day before or after the mean full moon.... We have taken pains that in our cycle the new moons should follow the real new moons, so that the 14th of the moon should fall either the day before the mean full moon, or on that day, or not long after; and this was done on purpose, for if the new moon of the cycle fell on the same day as the mean new moon of the {364} astronomers, it might chance that we should celebrate Easter on the same day as the Jews or the Quartadeciman heretics, which would be absurd, or else before them, which would be still more absurd."

From this it appears that Clavius continued the Calendar of his predecessors in the choice of the fourteenth day of the moon. Our legislature lays down the day of the full moon: and this mistake appears to be rather English than Protestant; for it occurs in missals published in the reign of Queen Mary.

The calendar lunation being 29½ days, the middle day is the fifteenth day, and this is and was reckoned as the day of the full moon. There is every right to presume that the original passover was a feast of the real full moon: but it is most probable that the moons were then reckoned, not from the astronomical conjunction with the sun, which nobody sees except at an eclipse, but from the day of first visibility of the new moon. In fine climates this would be the day or two days after conjunction; and the fourteenth day from that of first visibility inclusive, would very often be the day of full moon. The following is then the proper correction of the precept in the Act of Parliament:

Easter Day, on which the rest depend, is always the First Sunday after the fourteenth day of the calendar moon which happens upon or next after the Twenty-first day of March, according to the rules laid down for the construction of the Calendar; and if the fourteenth day happens upon a Sunday, Easter Day is the Sunday after.

10. Further, it appears that Clavius valued the celebration of the festival after the Jews, etc., more than astronomical correctness. He gives comparison tables which would startle a believer in the astronomical intention of his Calendar: they are to show that a calendar in which the moon is always made a day older than by him, represents the heavens better than he has done, or meant to do. But it must be observed that this diminution of the real moon's age has {365} a tendency to make the English explanation often practically accordant with the Calendar. For the fourteenth day of Clavius is generally the fifteenth day of the mean moon of the heavens, and therefore most often that of the real moon. But for this, 1818 and 1845 would not have been the only instances of our day in which the English precept would have contradicted the Calendar.

11. In the construction of the Calendar, Clavius adopted the ancient cycle of 532 years, but, we may say, without ever allowing it to run out. At certain periods, a shift is made from one part of the cycle into another. This is done whenever what should be Julian leap year is made a common year, as in 1700, 1800, 1900, 2100, etc. It is also done at certain times to correct the error of 1 h. 19 m., before referred to, in each cycle of golden numbers: Clavius, to meet his view of the amount of that error, put forward the moon's age a day 8 times in 2,500 years. As we cannot enter at full length into the explanation, we must content ourselves with giving a set of rules, independent of tables, by which the reader may find Easter for himself in any year, either by the old Calendar or the new. Any one who has much occasion to find Easters and movable feasts should procure Francoeur's[759] tables.

12. Rule for determining Easter Day of the Gregorian Calendar in any year of the new style. To the several parts {366} of the rule are annexed, by way of example, the results for the year 1849.

I. Add 1 to the given year. (1850).

II. Take the quotient of the given year divided by 4, neglecting the remainder. (462).

III. Take 16 from the centurial figures of the given year, if it can be done, and take the remainder. (2).

IV. Take the quotient of III. divided by 4, neglecting the remainder. (0).

V. From the sum of I, II, and IV., subtract III. (2310).

VI. Find the remainder of V. divided by 7. (0).

VII. Subtract VI. from 7; this is the number of the dominical letter 1 2 3 4 5 6 7 (7; dominical letter G). A B C D E F G

VIII. Divide I. by 19, the remainder (or 19, if no remainder) is the golden number. (7).

IX. From the centurial figures of the year subtract 17, divide by 25, and keep the quotient. (0).

X. Subtract IX. and 15 from the centurial figures, divide by 3, and keep the quotient. (1).

XI. To VIII. add ten times the next less number, divide by 30, and keep the remainder. (7).

XII. To XI. add X. and IV., and take away III., throwing out thirties, if any. If this give 24, change it into 25. If 25, change it into 26, whenever the golden number is greater than 11. If 0, change it into 30. Thus we have the epact, or age of the Calendar moon at the beginning of the year. (6).

When the Epact is 23, or less.

XIII. Subtract XII., the epact, from 45. (39).

XIV. Subtract the epact from 27, divide by 7, and keep the remainder, or 7, if there be no remainder. (7)

When the Epact is greater than 23.

XIII. Subtract XII., the epact, from 75.

XIV. Subtract the epact from 57, divide by 7, and keep the remainder, or 7, if there be no remainder.

XV. To XIII. add VII., the dominical number, (and 7 besides, if XIV. be greater than VII.,) and subtract XIV., the result is the day of March, or if more than 31, subtract 31, and {367} the result is the day of April, on which Easter Sunday falls. (39; Easter Day is April 8).

In the following examples, the several results leading to the final conclusion are tabulated.

== GIVEN YEAR | 1592 | 1637 | 1723 | 1853 | 2018 | 4686
--- I. | 1593 | 1638 | 1724 | 1854
| 2019 | 4687 II. | 398 | 409 | 430 | 463 | 504 | 1171 III. | --- | 0 | 1 | 2 | 4 | 30
IV. | --- | 0 | 0 | 0 | 1 | 7 V. | 1991 | 2047 | 2153 | 2315 | 2520 | 5835 VI. | 3 | 3
| 4 | 5 | 0 | 4 VII. | 4 | 4 | 3 | 2 | 7 | 3 VIII. | 16 | 4 | 14 | 11 | 5 | 13 IX. | --- | ---
| 0 | 0 | 0 | 1 X. | 0 | 0 | 0 | 1 | 1 | 10 XI. | 16 | 4 | 24 | 21 | 15 | 13 XII. | 16 | 4 |
23 | 20 | 13 |0 say 30 XIII. | 29 | 41 | 22 | 25 | 32 | 45 XIV. | 4 | 2 | 4 | 7 | 7 | 6
XV. | 29 | 43 | 28 | 27 | 32 | 49 Easter Day
|Mar.29|Apr.12|Mar.28|Mar.27|Apr.1 | Apr.18
----

13. Rule for determining Easter Day of the Antegregorian Calendar in any year of the old style. To the several parts of the rule are annexed, by way of example, the results for the year 1287. The steps are numbered to correspond with the steps of the Gregorian rule, so that it can be seen what augmentations the latter requires.

I. Set down the given year. (1287).

II. Take the quotient of the given year divided by 4, neglecting the remainder (321).

V. Take 4 more than the sum of I. and II. (1612).

VI. Find the remainder of V. divided by 7. (2).

VII. Subtract VI. from 7; this is the number of the dominical letter 1 2 3 4 5 6 7 (5; dominical letter E). A B C D E F G

VIII. Divide one more than the given year by 19, the remainder (or 19 if no remainder) is the golden number. (15).

XII. Divide 3 less than 11 times VIII. by 30; the remainder (or 30 if there be no remainder) is the epact. (12).

{368}

When the Epact is 23, or less.

XIII. Subtract XII., the epact, from 45. (33).

XIV. Subtract the epact from 27, divide by 7, and keep the remainder, or 7, if there be no remainder, (1).

When the Epact is greater than 23.

XIII. Subtract XII., the epact, from 75.

XIV. Subtract the epact from 57, divide by 7, and keep the remainder, or 7, if there be no remainder.

XV. To XIII. add VII., the dominical number, (and 7 besides if XIV. be greater than VII.,) and subtract XIV , the result is the day of March, or if more than 31, subtract 31, and the result is the day of April, on which

Easter Sunday (old style) falls. (37; Easter Day is April 6).

These rules completely represent the old and new Calendars, so far as Easter is concerned. For further explanation we must refer to the articles cited at the commencement.

The annexed is the table of new and full moons of the Gregorian Calendar, cleared of the errors made for the purpose of preventing Easter from coinciding with the Jewish Passover.

The second table (page 370) contains epacts, or ages of the moon at the beginning of the year: thus in 1913, the epact is 22, in 1868 it is 6. This table goes from 1850 to 1999: should the New Zealander not have arrived by that time, and should the churches of England and Rome then survive, the epact table may be continued from their liturgy-books The way of using the table is as follows: Take the epact of the required year, and find it in the first or last column of the first table, in line with it are seen the calendar days of new and full moon. Thus, when the epact is 17, the new and full moons of March fall on the 13th and 28th. The result is, for the most part, correct: but in a minority of cases there is an error of a day.

When this happens, the error is almost always a fraction of a day much less than twelve hours. Thus, when the table gives full moon on the 27th, and the real truth is the 28th, we may be sure it is early on the 28th.

{369}

|Jan.|Feb.|Mar.|Apr.|May |June|July|Aug.|Sep.|Oct.|Nov.|Dec.|
-- 1 | 29 | 27 | 29
| 27 | 27 | 25 | 25 | 23 | 22 | 21 | 20 | 19 | 1 | 14 | 13 | 14 | 13 | 12 | 11 | 10 | 9 |
7 | 7 | 5 | 5 | -- 2 |
28 | 26 | 28 | 26 | 26 | 24 | 24 | 22 | 21 | 20 | 19 | 18 | 2 | 13 | 12 | 13 | 12 | 11 |
10 | 9 | 8 | 6 | 6 | 4 | 4 |
-- 3 | 27 | 25 | 27
| 25 | 25 | 23 | 23 | 21 | 20 | 19 | 18 | 17 | 3 | 12 | 11 | 12 | 11 | 10 | 9 | 8 | 7 | 5 |
5 | 3 | 3 | -- 4 | 26

| 24 | 26 | 24 | 24 | 22 | 22 | 20 | 19 | 18 | 17 | 16 | 4 | 11 | 10 | 11 | 10 | 9 | 8 | 7
| 6 | 4 | 4 | 2 |2,31|
-- 5 | 25 | 23 | 25
| 23 | 23 | 21 | 21 | 19 | 18 | 17 | 16 | 15 | 5 | 10 | 9 | 10 | 9 | 8 | 7 | 6 | 5 | 3 | 3 |
1 |1,30| -- 6 | 24 |
22 | 24 | 22 | 22 | 20 | 20 | 18 | 17 | 16 | 15 | 14 | 6 | 9 | 8 | 9 | 8 | 7 | 6 | 5 | 4 | 2
|2,31| 30 | 29 | --
7 | 23 | 21 | 23 | 21 | 21 | 19 | 19 | 17 | 16 | 15 | 14 | 13 | 7 | 8 | 7 | 8 | 7 | 6 | 5 |
4 | 3 | 1 |1,30| 29 | 28 |
-- 8 | 22 | 20 | 22

| 20 | 20 | 18 | 18 | 16 | 15 | 14 | 13 | 12 | 8 | 7 | 6 | 7 | 6 | 5 | 4 | 3 |2,31| 30 | 29
| 28 | 27 | -- 9 |
21 | 19 | 21 | 19 | 19 | 17 | 17 | 15 | 14 | 13 | 12 | 11 | 9 | 6 | 5 | 6 | 5 | 4 | 3 | 2
|1,30| 29 | 28 | 27 | 26 |

-- 10 | 20 | 18 |
20 | 18 | 18 | 16 | 16 | 14 | 13 | 12 | 11 | 10 | 10 | 5 | 4 | 5 | 4 | 3 | 2 |1,31| 29 |
28 | 27 | 26 | 25 |

-- 11 | 19 | 17 |
19 | 17 | 17 | 15 | 15 | 13 | 12 | 11 | 10 | 9 | 11 | 4 | 3 | 4 | 3 | 2 |1,30| 30 | 28 |
27 | 26 | 25 | 24 |

-- 12 | 18 | 16 |
18 | 16 | 16 | 14 | 14 | 12 | 11 | 10 | 9 | 8 | 12 | 3 | 2 | 3 | 2 |1,31| 29 | 29 | 27 |
26 | 25 | 24 | 23 |

-- 13 | 17 | 15 |
17 | 15 | 15 | 13 | 13 | 11 | 10 | 9 | 8 | 7 | 13 | 2 | 1 | 2 |1,30| 30 | 28 | 28 | 26 |
25 | 24 | 23 | 22 |

-- 14 | 16 | 14 |
16 | 14 | 14 | 12 | 12 | 10 | 9 | 8 | 7 | 6 | 14 |1,31| -- |1,31| 29 | 29 | 27 | 27 | 25 |
24 | 23 | 22 | 21 |

-- 15 | 15 | 13 |
15 | 13 | 13 | 11 | 11 | 9 | 8 | 7 | 6 | 5 | 15 | 30 | 28 | 30 | 28 | 28 | 26 | 26 | 24 |
23 | 22 | 21 | 20 |

-- 16 | 14 | 12 |
14 | 12 | 12 | 10 | 10 | 8 | 7 | 6 | 5 | 4 | 16 | 29 | 27 | 29 | 27 | 27 | 25 | 25 | 23 |
22 | 21 | 20 | 19 |

-- 17 | 13 | 11 |

13 | 11 | 11 | 9 | 9 | 7 | 6 | 5 | 4 | 3 | 17 | 28 | 26 | 28 | 26 | 26 | 24 | 24 | 22 | 21 |
20 | 19 | 18 | --
18 | 12 | 10 | 12 | 10 | 10 | 8 | 8 | 6 | 5 | 4 | 3 | 2 | 18 | 27 | 25 | 27 | 25 | 25 | 23 |
23 | 21 | 20 | 19 | 18 | 17 |

-- 19 | 11 | 9 | 11
| 9 | 9 | 7 | 7 | 5 | 4 | 3 | 2 |1,31| 19 | 26 | 24 | 26 | 24 | 24 | 22 | 22 | 20 | 19 | 18
| 17 | 16 | -- 20 |
10 | 8 | 10 | 8 | 8 | 6 | 6 | 4 | 3 | 2 |1,31| 30 | 20 | 25 | 23 | 25 | 23 | 23 | 21 | 21 |
19 | 18 | 17 | 16 | 15 |

-- 21 | 9 | 7 | 9 | 7
| 7 | 5 | 5 | 3 | 2 |1,31| 29 | 29 | 21 | 24 | 22 | 24 | 22 | 22 | 20 | 20 | 18 | 17 | 16 |
15 | 14 | -- 22 | 8
| 6 | 8 | 6 | 6 | 4 | 4 | 2 |1,30| 30 | 28 | 28 | 22 | 23 | 21 | 23 | 21 | 21 | 19 | 19 |
17 | 16 | 15 | 14 | 13 |

-- 23 | 7 | 5 | 7 | 5
| 5 | 3 | 3 |1,31| 29 | 29 | 27 | 27 | 23 | 22 | 20 | 22 | 20 | 20 | 18 | 18 | 16 | 15 |
14 | 13 | 12 | --
24 | 6 | 5 | 6 | 5 | 4 | 3 | 2 |1,30| 29 | 28 | 27 | 26 | 24 | 21 | 19 | 21 | 19 | 19 | 17
| 17 | 15 | 14 | 13 | 12 | 11 |

-- 25 | 5 | 4 | 5 | 4
| 3 | 2 |1,31| 29 | 28 | 27 | 26 | 25 | 25 | 20 | 19 | 20 | 19 | 18 | 17 | 16 | 15 | 13 |
13 | 11 | 11 | --
26 | 4 | 3 | 4 | 3 | 2 |1,30| 30 | 28 | 27 | 26 | 25 | 24 | 26 | 19 | 18 | 19 | 18 | 17 |
16 | 15 | 14 | 12 | 12 | 10 | 10 |

-- 27 | 3 | 2 | 3 | 2
|1,31| 29 | 29 | 27 | 26 | 25 | 24 | 23 | 27 | 18 | 17 | 18 | 17 | 16 | 15 | 14 | 13 |

11 | 11 | 9 | 9 | ---
28 | 2 | 1 | 2 |1,30| 30 | 28 | 28 | 26 | 25 | 24 | 23 | 22 | 28 | 17 | 16 | 17 | 16 | 15
| 14 | 13 | 12 | 10 | 10 | 8 | 8 |
--- 29 |1,31| --
|1,31| 29 | 29 | 27 | 27 | 25 | 24 | 23 | 22 | 21 | 29 | 16 | 15 | 16 | 15 | 14 | 13 |
12 | 11 | 9 | 9 | 7 | 7 |
--- 30 | 30 | 28 |
30 | 28 | 28 | 26 | 26 | 24 | 23 | 22 | 21 | 20 | 30 | 15 | 14 | 15 | 14 | 13 | 12 | 11 |
10 | 8 | 8 | 6 | 6 |

|Jan. | Feb. | Mar. | Apr. | May |June | July | Aug. | Sep. | Oct. | Nov. | Dec. |

{370}

===
| 0 | 1 | 2 | 3 | 4 | 5 | 6 | 7 | 8 | 9 ---
185 | 17 | 28 | 9 | 20 | 2 | 12 | 23 | 4 | 15 | 26
--- 186 | 7 | 18 | 30 | 11 | 22 | 3 |
14 | 25 | 6 | 17 --- 187 | 28 | 9 |
20 | 1 | 12 | 23 | 4 | 15 | 26 | 7 ---
188 | 18 | 30 | 11 | 22 | 3 | 14 | 25 | 6 | 17 | 28
--- 189 | 9 | 21 | 1 | 12 | 23 | 4 |
15 | 26 | 7 | 18 --- 190 | 29 | 10 |
21 | 2 | 13 | 24 | 5 | 16 | 27 | 8 ---
191 | 19 | 30 | 11 | 22 | 3 | 14 | 26 | 6 | 17 | 29
--- 192 | 10 | 21 | 2 | 13 | 24 | 5 |
16 | 27 | 8 | 19 --- 193 | 30 | 11 |
22 | 3 | 14 | 26 | 6 | 17 | 29 | 10
--- 194 | 21 | 2 | 13 | 24 | 5 | 16 |
27 | 8 | 19 | 30 --- 195 | 11 | 22 |
3 | 14 | 26 | 6 | 17 | 29 | 10 | 21
--- 196 | 2 | 13 | 24 | 5 | 16 | 27 |
8 | 19 | 30 | 11 --- 197 | 22 | 3 |
14 | 26 | 6 | 17 | 29 | 10 | 21 | 2
--- 198 | 13 | 24 | 5 | 16 | 27 | 8 |
19 | 30 | 11 | 22 --- 199 | 3 | 14 |
26 | 6 | 17 | 29 | 10 | 21 | 2 | 13
===

For example, the year 1867. The epact is 25, and we find in the table:

J. F. M. AP. M. JU. JL. AU. S. O. N. D. New 5+ 4 5+ 4 3+ 2 1,31 29 28-
27 26 25 Full 20 19- 20 19- 18 17 16 15 13- 13 11+ 11

When the truth is the day after + is written after the date; when the day before, -. Thus, the new moon of March is on the 6th; the full moon of April is on the 18th. {371}

I now introduce a small paradox of my own; and as I am not able to prove it, I am compelled to declare that any one who shall dissent must be either very foolish or very dishonest, and will make me quite uncomfortable about the state of his soul. This being settled once for all, I proceed to say that the necessity of arriving at the truth about the assertions that the Nicene Council laid down astronomical tests led me to look at Fathers, Church histories, etc. to an extent which

I never dreamed of before. One conclusion which I arrived at was, that the Nicene Fathers had a knack of sticking to the question which many later councils could not acquire. In our own day, it is not permitted to Convocation seriously to discuss any one of the points which are bearing so hard upon their resources of defence--the cursing clauses of the Athanasian Creed, for example. And it may be collected that the prohibition arises partly from fear that there is no saying where a beginning, if allowed, would end. There seems to be a suspicion that debate, once let loose, would play up old Trent with the liturgy, and bring the whole book to book. But if any one will examine the real Nicene Creed, without the augmentation, he will admire the way in which the framers stuck to the point, and settled what they had to decide, according to their view of it. With such a presumption of good sense in their favor, it becomes easier to believe in any claim which may be made on their behalf to tact or sagacity in settling any other matter. And I strongly suspect such a claim may be made for them on the Easter question.

I collect from many little indications, both before and after the Council, that the division of the Christian world into Judaical and Gentile, though not giving rise to a sectarian distinction expressed by names, was of far greater force and meaning than historians prominently admit. I took note of many indications of this, but not notes, as it was not to my purpose. If it were so, we must admire the discretion of the Council. The Easter question was the {372} fighting ground of the struggle: the Eastern or Judaical Christians, with some varieties of usage and meaning, would have the Passover itself to be the great feast, but taken in a Christian sense; the Western or Gentile Christians, would have the commemoration of the Resurrection, connected with the Passover only by chronology. To shift the Passover in time, under its name, Pascha, without allusion to any of the force of the change, was gently cutting away the ground from under the feet of the Conservatives.

And it was done in a very quiet way: no allusion to the precise character of the change; no hint that the question was about two different festivals: "all the brethren in the East, who formerly celebrated this festival at the same time as the Jews, will in future conform to the Romans and to us." The Judaizers meant to be keeping the Passover as a Christian feast: they are gently assumed to be keeping, not the Passover, but a Christian feast; and a doctrinal decision is quietly, but efficiently, announced under the form of a chronological ordinance. Had the Council issued theses of doctrine, and excommunicated all dissentients, the rupture of the East and West would have taken place earlier by centuries than it did. The only place in which I ever saw any part of my paradox advanced, was in an article in the Examiner newspaper, towards the end of 1866, after the above was written.

A story about Christopher Clavius, the workman of the new Calendar. I chanced to pick up "Albertus Pighius Campensis de æquinoctiorum solsticiorumque inventione... Ejusdem de ratione Paschalis celebrationis, De que Restitutione ecclesiastici Kalendarii," Paris, 1520, folio.[760] On the title-page were decayed words followed by "..hristophor.. C..ii, 1556 (or 8)," the last blank not entirely erased by time, but showing the lower halves of an l and of an a, and {373} rather too much room for a v. It looked very like E Libris Christophori Clavii 1556. By the courtesy of some members of the Jesuit body in London, I procured a tracing of the signature of Clavius from Rome, and the shapes of the letters, and the modes of junction and disjunction, put the matter beyond question. Even the extra space was explained; he wrote himself Clauius. Now in 1556, Clavius was nineteen years old: it thus appears probable that the framer of the Gregorian Calendar was selected, not merely as a learned astronomer, but as one who had attended to the calendar, and to works on its reformation, from early youth. When on the subject I found reason to think that Clavius had really read this work, and taken from it a phrase or two and a notion or two. Observe the advantage of writing the baptismal name at full length.

A COUPLE OF MINOR PARADOXES.

The discovery of a general resolution of all superior finite equations, of every numerical both algebraick and transcendent form. By A. P. Vogel,[761] mathematician at Leipzick. Leipzick and London, 1845, 8vo.

This work is written in the English of a German who has not mastered the idiom: but it is always intelligible. It professes to solve equations of every degree "in a more extent sense, and till to every degree of exactness." The general solution of equations of all degrees is a vexed question, which cannot have the mysterious interest of the circle problem, and is of a comparatively modern date.[762] Mr. Vogel {374} announces a forthcoming treatise in which are resolved the "last impossibilities of pure mathematics."

Elective Polarity the Universal Agent. By Frances Barbara Burton, authoress of 'Astronomy familiarized,' 'Physical Astronomy,' &c. London, 1845, 8vo.[763]

The title gives a notion of the theory. The first sentence states, that 12,500 years ago [alpha] Lyræ was the pole-star, and attributes the immense magnitude of the now fossil animals to a star of such "polaric intensity as Vega pouring its magnetic streams through our planet." Miss Burton was a lady of property, and of very respectable acquirements, especially in Hebrew; she was eccentric in all things.

1867.--Miss Burton is revived by the writer of a book on meteorology which makes use of the planets: she is one of his leading minds.[764]

SPECULATIVE THOUGHT IN ENGLAND.

In the year 1845 the old Mathematical Society was merged in the Astronomical Society. The circle-squarers, etc., thrive more in England than in any other country: there are most weeds where there is the largest crop. Speculation, though not encouraged by our Government so much as by those of the Continent, has had, not indeed such forcing, but much wider diffusion: few tanks, but many rivulets. On this point I quote from the preface to the reprint of the work of Ramchundra,[765] which I superintended for the late Court of Directors of the East India Company.

{375}

"That sound judgment which gives men well to know what is best for them, as well as that faculty of invention which leads to development of resources and to the increase of wealth and comfort, are both materially advanced, perhaps cannot rapidly be advanced without, a great taste for pure speculation among the general mass of the people, down to the lowest of those who can read and write. England is a marked example. Many persons will be surprised at this assertion. They imagine that our country is the great instance of the refusal of all unpractical knowledge in favor of what is useful. I affirm, on the contrary, that there is no country in Europe in which there has been so wide a diffusion of speculation, theory, or what other unpractical word the reader pleases. In our country, the scientific society is always formed and maintained by the people; in every other, the scientific academy--most aptly named--has been the creation of the government, of which it has never ceased to be the nursling. In all the parts of England in which manufacturing pursuits have given the artisan some command of time, the cultivation of mathematics and other speculative studies has been, as is well known, a very frequent occupation. In no other country has the weaver at his loom bent over the Principia of Newton; in no other country has the man of weekly wages maintained his own scientific periodical. With us, since the beginning of the last century, scores upon scores--perhaps hundreds, for I am far from knowing all--of annuals have run, some their ten years, some their half-century, some their century and a half, containing questions to be answered, from which many of our examiners in the universities have culled materials for the academical contests. And these questions have always been answered, and in cases without number by the lower order of purchasers, the mechanics, the weavers, and the printers' workmen. I cannot here digress to point out the manner in which the concentration of manufactures, and the general diffusion of education, have affected the {376} state of things; I speak of the time during which the present system took its rise, and of the circumstances under which many of its most effective promoters were trained. In all this there is nothing which stands out, like the state-nourished academy, with its few great names and brilliant single achievements. This country has differed from all others in the wide diffusion of the disposition to speculate, which disposition has found its place among the ordinary habits of life, moderate in its action, healthy in its amount."

THE OLD MATHEMATICAL SOCIETY

Among the most remarkable proofs of the diffusion of speculation was the Mathematical Society, which flourished from 1717 to 1845. Its habitat was Spitalfields, and I think most of its existence was passed in Crispin Street. It was originally a plain society, belonging to the studious artisan. The members met for discussion once a week; and I believe

I am correct in saying that each man had his pipe, his pot, and his problem. One of their old rules was that, "If any member shall so far forget himself and the respect due to the Society as in the warmth of debate to threaten or offer personal violence to any other member, he shall be liable to immediate expulsion, or to pay such fine as the majority of the members present shall decide." But their great rule, printed large on the back of the title page of their last book of regulations, was "By the constitution of the Society, it is the duty of every member, if he be asked any mathematical or philosophical question by another member, to instruct him in the plainest and easiest manner he is able." We shall presently see that, in old time, the rule had a more homely form.

I have been told that De Moivre[766] was a member of this {377} Society. This I cannot verify: circumstances render it unlikely; even though the French refugees clustered in Spitalfields; many of them were of the Society, which there is some reason to think was founded by them. But Dolland,[767] Thomas Simpson,[768] Saunderson,[769] Crossley,[770] and others of known name, were certainly members. The Society gradually declined, and in 1845 was reduced to nineteen members. An arrangement was made by which sixteen of these members, who where not already in the Astronomical Society became Fellows without contribution, all the books and other property of the old Society being transferred to the new one. I was one of the committee which made the preliminary inquiries, and the reason of the decline was soon manifest. The only question which could arise was whether the members of the society of working men--for this repute still continued--were of that class of educated men who could associate with the Fellows of the Astronomical Society on terms agreeable to all parties. We found that the artisan element had been extinct for many years; there was not a man but might, as to education, manners, and position, have become a Fellow in the usual way. The fact was that life in Spitalfields had become harder: and the weaver could {378} only live from hand to mouth, and not up to the brain. The material of the old Society no longer existed.

In 1798, experimental lectures were given, a small charge for admission being taken at the door: by this hangs a tale--and a song. Many years ago, I found among papers of a deceased friend, who certainly never had anything to do with the Society, and who passed all his life far from London, a song, headed "Song sung by the Mathematical Society in London, at a dinner given Mr. Fletcher,[771] a solicitor, who had defended the Society gratis." Mr. Williams,[772] the Assistant Secretary of the Astronomical Society, formerly Secretary of the Mathematical Society, remembered that the Society had had a solicitor named Fletcher among the members. Some years elapsed before it struck me that my old friend Benjamin Gompertz,[773] who had long been a member, might have some recollection of the matter. The following is an extract of a letter from him (July 9, 1861):

"As to the Mathematical Society, of which I was a member when only 18 years of age, [Mr. G. was born in 1779], having been, contrary to the rules, elected under the age of 21. How I came to be a member of that Society--and continued so until it joined the Astronomical Society, and was then the President--was: I happened to pass a bookseller's small shop, of second-hand books, kept by a poor taylor, but a good mathematician, John Griffiths. I was very pleased to meet a mathematician, and I asked him if he would give me some lessons; and his reply was that I was more capable to teach him, but he belonged to a society of mathematicians, and he would introduce me. I accepted the offer, and I was elected, and had many scholars then to teach, as {379} one of the rules was, if a member asked for information, and applied to any one who could give it, he was obliged to give it, or fine one penny. Though I might say much with respect to the Society which would be interesting, I will for the present reply only to your question. I well knew Mr. Fletcher, who was a very clever and very scientific person. He did, as solicitor, defend an action brought by an informer against the Society--I think for 5,000l.--for giving lectures to the public in philosophical subjects [i.e., for unlicensed public exhibition with money taken at the doors]. I think the price for admission was one shilling, and we used to have, if I rightly recollect, from two to three hundred visitors. Mr. Fletcher was successful in his defence, and we got out of our trouble. There was a collection made to reward his services, but he did not accept of any reward: and I think we gave him a dinner, as you state, and enjoyed ourselves; no doubt with astronomical songs and other songs; but my recollection does not enable me to say if the astronomical song was a drinking song. I think the anxiety caused by that action was the cause of some of the members' death. [They had, no doubt, broken the law in ignorance; and by the sum named, the informer must have been present, and sued for a penalty on every shilling he could prove to have been taken]."

I by no means guarantee that the whole song I proceed to give is what was sung at the dinner: I suspect, by the completeness of the chain, that augmentations have been made. My deceased friend was just the man to add some verses, or the addition may have been made before it came into his hands, or since his decease, for the scraps containing the verses passed through several hands before they came into mine. We may, however, be pretty sure that the original is substantially contained in what is given, and that the character is therefore preserved. I have had myself to repair damages every now and then, in the way of conjectural restoration of defects caused by ill-usage. {380}

THE ASTRONOMER'S DRINKING SONG

"Whoe'er would search the starry sky, Its secrets to divine, sir, Should take his glass--I mean, should try A glass or two of wine, sir! True virtue lies in golden mean, And man must wet his clay, sir; Join these two maxims, and 'tis seen He should drink his bottle a day, sir!

"Old Archimedes, reverend sage! By trump of fame renowned, sir, Deep problems solved in every page, And the sphere's curved surface found,[774] sir: Himself he would have far outshone, And borne a wider sway, sir, Had he our modern secret known, And drank a bottle a day, sir!

"When Ptolemy,[775] now long ago, Believed the earth stood still, sir, He never would have blundered so, Had he but drunk his fill, sir: He'd then have felt[776] it circulate, And would have learnt to say, sir, The true way to investigate Is to drink your bottle a day, sir!

"Copernicus,[777] that learned wight, The glory of his nation, With draughts of wine refreshed his sight, And saw the earth's rotation; {381} Each planet then its orb described, The moon got under way, sir; These truths from nature he imbibed For he drank his bottle a day, sir!

"The noble[778] Tycho placed the stars, Each in its due location; He lost his nose[779] by spite of Mars, But that was no privation: Had he but lost his mouth, I grant He would have felt dismay, sir, Bless you! he knew what he should want To drink his bottle a day, sir!

"Cold water makes no lucky hits; On mysteries the head runs: Small drink let Kepler[780] time his wits On the regular polyhedrons: He took to wine, and it changed the chime, His genius swept away, sir, Through area varying[781] as the time At the rate of a bottle a day, sir!

"Poor Galileo,[782] forced to rat Before the Inquisition, E pur si muove[783] was the pat He gave them in addition: {382} He meant, whate'er you think you prove, The earth must go its way, sirs; Spite of your teeth I'll make it move, For I'll drink my bottle a day, sirs!

"Great Newton, who was never beat Whatever fools may think, sir; Though sometimes he forgot to eat, He never forgot to drink, sir: Descartes[784] took nought but lemonade, To conquer him was play, sir; The first advance that Newton made Was to drink his bottle a day, sir!

"D'Alembert,[785] Euler,[786] and Clairaut,[787] Though they increased our store, sir, Much further had been seen to go Had they tippled a little more, sir! Lagrange[788] gets mellow with Laplace,[789] And both are wont to say, sir, The philosophe who's not an ass Will drink his bottle a day, sir!

"Astronomers! what can avail Those who calumniate us; Experiment can never fail With such an apparatus: Let him who'd have his merits known Remember what I say, sir; Fair science shines on him alone Who drinks his bottle a day, sir!

{383} "How light we reck of those who mock By this we'll make to appear, sir, We'll dine by the sidereal[790] clock For one more bottle a year, sir: But choose which pendulum you will, You'll never make your way, sir, Unless you drink--and drink your fill,-- At least a bottle a day, sir!"

Old times are changed, old manners gone!

There is a new Mathematical Society,[791] and I am, at this present writing (1866), its first President. We are very high in the newest developments, and bid fair to take a place among the scientific establishments. Benjamin Gompertz, who was President of the old Society when it expired, was the link between the old and new body: he was a member of ours at his death. But not a drop of liquor is seen at our meetings, except a decanter of water: all our heavy is a fermentation of symbols; and we do not draw it mild.

There is no penny fine for reticence or occult science; and as to a song! not the ghost of a chance.

1826. The time may have come when the original documents connected with the discovery of Neptune may be worth revising. The following are extracts from the Athenæum of October 3 and October 17: LE VERRIER'S[792] PLANET.

We have received, at the last moment before making up for press, the following letter from Sir John Herschel,[793] {384} in reference to the matter referred to in the communication from Mr. Hind[794] given below:

"Collingwood, Oct. 1.

"In my address to the British Association assembled at Southampton, on the occasion of my resigning the chair to Sir R. Murchison,[795] I stated, among the remarkable astronomical events of the last twelvemonth, that it had added a new planet to our list,--adding, 'it has done more,--it has given us the probable prospect of the discovery of another. We see it as Columbus saw America from the shores of Spain. Its movements have been felt, trembling along the far-reaching line of our analysis, with a certainty hardly inferior to that of ocular demonstration.'--These expressions are not reported in any of the papers which profess to give an account of the proceedings, but I appeal to all present whether they were not used.

"Give me leave to state my reasons for this confidence; and, in so doing, to call attention to some facts which deserve to be put on record in the history of this noble discovery. On July 12, 1842, the late illustrious astronomer, Bessel,[796] honored me with a visit at my present residence. On the evening of that day, conversing on the great work of the planetary reductions undertaken by the Astronomer Royal[797]--then in progress, and since published,[798]--M. Bessel remarked that the motions of Uranus, as he had satisfied {385} himself by careful examination of the recorded observations, could not be accounted for by the perturbations of the known planets; and that the deviations far exceeded any possible limits of error of observation. In reply to the question, Whether the deviations in question might not be due to the action of an unknown planet?--he stated that he considered it highly probable that such was the case,--being systematic, and such as might be produced by an exterior planet. I then inquired whether he had attempted, from the indications afforded by these perturbations, to discover the position of the unknown body,--in order that 'a hue and cry' might be raised for it. From his reply, the words of which I do not call to mind, I collected that he had not then gone into that inquiry; but proposed to do so, having now completed certain works which had occupied too much of his time. And, accordingly, in a letter which I received from him after his return to Königsberg, dated November 14, 1842, he says,--'In reference to our conversation at Collingwood, I announce to you (melde ich Ihnen) that Uranus is not forgotten.' Doubtless, therefore, among his papers will be found some researches on the subject.

"The remarkable calculations of M. Le Verrier--which have pointed out, as now appears, nearly the true situation of the new planet, by resolving the inverse problem of the perturbations--if uncorroborated by repetition of the numerical calculations by another hand, or by independent investigation from another quarter, would hardly justify so strong an assurance as that conveyed by my expressions above alluded to. But it was known to me, at that time, (I will take the liberty to cite the Astronomer Royal as my authority) that a similar investigation had been independently entered into, and a conclusion as to the situation of the new planet very nearly coincident with M. Le Verrier's arrived at (in entire ignorance of his conclusions), by a young Cambridge mathematician, Mr. Adams;[799]--who will, I hope, {386} pardon this mention of his name (the matter being one of great historical moment),--and who will, doubtless, in his own good time and manner, place his calculations before the public.

"J. F. W. HERSCHEL."

Discovery of Le Verrier's Planet.

Mr. Hind announces to the Times that he has received a letter from Dr. Brünnow, of the Royal Observatory at Berlin, giving the very important information that Le Verrier's planet was found by M. Galle, on the night of September 23. "In announcing this grand discovery," he says, "I think it better to copy Dr. Brünnow's[800] letter."

"Berlin, Sept. 25.

"My dear Sir--M. Le Verrier's planet was discovered here the 23d of September, by M. Galle.[801] It is a star of the 8th magnitude, but with a diameter of two or three seconds. Here are its places:

h. m. s. R. A. Declination. Sept. 23, 12 0 14.6 M.T. 328° 19' 16.0" -13° 24'
8.2" Sept. 24, 8 54 40.9 M.T. 328° 18' 14.3" -13° 24' 29.7"

The planet is now retrograde, its motion amounting daily to four seconds of time.

"Yours most respectfully, BRÜNNOW."

"This discovery," Mr. Hind says, "may be justly considered one of the greatest triumphs of theoretical astronomy;" and he adds, in a postscript, that the planet was observed at Mr. Bishop's[802] Observatory, in the Regent's Park, {387} on Wednesday night, notwithstanding the moonlight and hazy sky. "It appears bright," he says, "and with a power of 320 I can see the disc. The following position is the result of instrumental comparisons with 33 Aquarii:

Sept. 30, at 8h. 16m. 21s. Greenwich mean time-- Right ascension of planet 21h. 52m. 47.15s. South declination 13° 27' 20"."

THE NEW PLANET.

"Cambridge Observatory, Oct. 15.

"The allusion made by Sir John Herschel, in his letter contained in the Athenæum of October 3, to the theoretical researches of Mr. Adams, respecting the newly-discovered planet, has induced me to request that you would make the following communication public. It is right that I should first say that I have Mr. Adams's permission to make the statements that follow, so far as they relate to his labors. I do not propose to enter into a detail of the steps by which Mr. Adams was led, by his spontaneous and independent researches, to a conclusion that a planet must exist more distant than Uranus. The matter is of too great historical moment not to receive a more formal record than it would be proper to give here. My immediate object is to show, while the attention of the scientific public is more particularly directed to the subject, that, with respect to this remarkable discovery, English astronomers may lay claim to some merit.

"Mr. Adams formed the resolution of trying, by calculation, to account for the anomalies in the motion of Uranus on the hypothesis of a more distant planet, when he was an undergraduate in this university, and when his exertions for the academical distinction, which he obtained in January 1843, left him no time for pursuing the research. In the course of that year, he arrived at an approximation to the position of the supposed planet; which, however, he did not consider to be worthy of confidence, on account of his not {388} having employed a sufficient number of observations of Uranus. Accordingly, he requested my intervention to obtain for him the early Greenwich observations, then in course of reduction;--which the Astronomer Royal immediately supplied, in the kindest possible manner.

This was in February, 1844. In September, 1845, Mr. Adams communicated to me values which he had obtained for the heliocentric longitude, excentricity of orbit, longitude of perihelion, and mass, of an assumed exterior planet,--deduced entirely from unaccounted-for perturbations of Uranus. The same results, somewhat corrected, he communicated, in October, to the Astronomer Royal. M. Le Verrier, in an investigation which was published in June of 1846, assigned very nearly the same heliocentric longitude for the probable position of the planet as Mr. Adams had arrived at, but gave no results respecting its mass and the form of its orbit. The coincidence as to position from two entirely independent investigations naturally inspired confidence; and the Astronomer Royal shortly after suggested the employing of the Northumberland telescope of this observatory in a systematic search after the hypothetical planet; recommending, at the same time, a definite plan of operations. I undertook to make the search,--and commenced observing on July 29. The observations were directed, in the first instance, to the part of the heavens which theory had pointed out as the most probable place of the planet; in selecting which I was guided by a paper drawn up for me by Mr. Adams. Not having hour xxi. of the Berlin star-maps--of the publication of which I was not aware--I had to proceed on the principle of comparison of observations made at intervals. On July 30, I went over a zone 9' broad, in such a manner as to include all stars to the eleventh magnitude. On August 4, I took a broader zone and recorded a place of the planet. My next observations were on August 12; when I met with a star of the eighth magnitude in the zone which I had gone over on July 30,--and which did not then {389} contain this star. Of course, this was the planet;--the place of which was, thus, recorded a second time in four days of observing. A comparison of the observations of July 30 and August 12 would, according to the principle of search which I employed, have shown me the planet. I did not make the comparison till after the detection of it at Berlin--partly because I had an impression that a much more extensive search was required to give any probability of discovery--and partly from the press of other occupation. The planet, however, was secured, and two positions of it recorded six weeks earlier here than in any other observatory,--and in a systematic search expressly undertaken for that purpose. I give now the positions of the planet on August 4 and August 12.

Greenwich mean time.

Aug. 4, 13h. 36m. 25s. {R.A. 21h. 58m. 14.70s. {N.P.D. 102° 57' 32.2"

Aug. 12, 13h. 3m. 26s. {R.A. 21h. 57m. 26.13s. {N.P.D. 103° 2' 0.2"

"From these places compared with recent observations Mr. Adams has obtained the following results:

Distance of the planet from the sun 30.05 Inclination of the orbit 1° 45' Longitude of the descending node 309° 43' Heliocentric longitude, Aug. 4 326° 39'

"The present distance from the sun is, therefore, thirty times the earth's mean distance;--which is somewhat less than the theory had indicated. The other elements of the orbit cannot be approximated to till the observations shall have been continued for a longer period.

"The part taken by Mr. Adams in the theoretical search after this planet will, perhaps, be considered to justify the suggesting of a name. With his consent, I mention Oceanus as one which may possibly receive the votes of astronomers.--I {390} have authority to state that Mr. Adams's investigations will in a short time, be published in detail.

"J. CHALLIS."[803]

ASTRONOMICAL POLICE REPORT.

"An ill-looking kind of a body, who declined to give any name, was brought before the Academy of Sciences, charged with having assaulted a gentleman of the name of Uranus in the public highway. The prosecutor was a youngish looking person, wrapped up in two or three great coats; and looked chillier than anything imaginable, except the prisoner,--whose teeth absolutely shook, all the time.

Policeman Le Verrier[804] stated that he saw the prosecutor walking along the pavement,--and sometimes turning sideways, and sometimes running up to the railings and jerking about in a strange way. Calculated that somebody must be pulling his coat, or otherwise assaulting him. It was so dark that he could not see; but thought, if he watched the direction in which the next odd move was made, he might find out something. When the time came, he set Brünnow, a constable in another division of the same force, to watch where he told him; and Brünnow caught the prisoner lurking about in the very spot,--trying to look as if he was minding his own business. Had suspected for a long time that somebody was lurking about in the neighborhood. Brünnow was then called, and deposed to his catching the prisoner as described.

M. Arago.--Was the prosecutor sober?

Le Verrier.--Lord, yes, your worship; no man who had a drop in him ever looks so cold as he did.

M. Arago.--Did you see the assault?

Le Verrier.--I can't say I did; but I told Brünnow exactly how he'd be crouched down;--just as he was.

{391}

M. Arago (to Brünnow).--Did you see the assault?

Brünnow.--No, your worship; but I caught the prisoner.

M. Arago.--How did you know there was any assault at all?

Le Verrier.--I reckoned it couldn't be otherwise, when I saw the prosecutor making those odd turns on the pavement.

M. Arago.--You reckon and you calculate! Why, you'll tell me, next, that you policemen may sit at home and find out all that's going on in the streets by arithmetic. Did you ever bring a case of this kind before me till now?

Le Verrier.--Why, you see, your worship, the police are growing cleverer and cleverer every day. We can't help it:--it grows upon us.

M. Arago.--You're getting too clever for me. What does the prosecutor know about the matter?

The prosecutor said, all he knew was that he was pulled behind by somebody several times. On being further examined, he said that he had seen the prisoner often, but did not know his name, nor how he got his living; but had understood he was called Neptune. He himself had paid rates and taxes a good many years now. Had a family of six,--two of whom got their own living.

The prisoner being called on for his defence, said that it was a quarrel. He had pushed the prosecutor--and the prosecutor had pushed him. They had known each other a long time, and were always quarreling;--he did not know why. It was their nature, he supposed. He further said, that the prosecutor had given a false account of himself;--that he went about under different names. Sometimes he was called Uranus, sometimes Herschel, and sometimes Georgium Sidus; and he had no character for regularity in the neighborhood. Indeed, he was sometimes not to be seen for a long time at once.

The prosecutor, on being asked, admitted, after a little hesitation, that he had pushed and pulled the prisoner too. {392} In the altercation which followed, it was found very difficult to make out which began:--and the worthy magistrate seemed to think they must have begun together.

M. Arago.--Prisoner, have you any family?

The prisoner declined answering that question at present. He said he thought the police might as well reckon it out whether he had or not.

M. Arago said he didn't much differ from that opinion.--He then addressed both prosecutor and prisoner; and told them that if they couldn't settle their differences without quarreling in the streets, he should certainly commit them both next time. In the meantime, he called upon both to enter into their own recognizances; and directed the police to have an eye upon both,--observing that the prisoner would be likely to want it a long time, and the prosecutor would be not a hair the worse for it."

This quib was written by a person who was among the astronomers: and it illustrates the fact that Le Verrier had sole possession of the field until Mr. Challis's letter appeared. Sir John Herschel's previous communication should have paved the way: but the wonder of the discovery drove it out of many heads. There is an excellent account of the whole matter in Professor Grant's[805] History of Physical Astronomy. The squib scandalized some grave people, who wrote severe admonitions to the editor. There are formalists who spend much time in writing propriety to journals, to which they serve as foolometers. In a letter to the Athenæum, speaking of the way in which people hawk fine terms for common things, I said that these people ought to have a new translation of the Bible, which should contain the verse "gentleman and lady, created He them." The editor was handsomely fired and brimstoned!

{393}

A NEW THEORY OF TIDES

A new theory of the tides: in which the errors of the usual theory are demonstrated; and proof shewn that the full moon is not the cause of a concomitant spring tide, but actually the cause of the neaps.... By Comm^r. Debenham,[806] R.N. London, 1846, 8vo.

The author replied to a criticism in the Athenæum, and I remember how, in a very few words, he showed that he had read nothing on the subject. The reviewer spoke of the forces of the planets (i.e., the Sun and Moon) on the ocean, on which the author remarks, "But N.B. the Sun is no planet, Mr. Critic." Had he read any of the actual investigations on the usual theory, he would have known that to this day the sun and moon continue to be called planets--though the phrase is disappearing--in speaking of the tides; the sense, of course, being the old one, wandering bodies.

A large class of the paradoxers, when they meet with something which taken in their sense is absurd, do not take the trouble to find out the intended meaning, but walk off with the words laden with their own first construction. Such men are hardly fit to walk the streets without an interpreter. I was startled for a moment, at the time when a recent happy--and more recently happier--marriage occupied the public thoughts, by seeing in a haberdasher's window, in staring large letters, an unpunctuated sentence which read itself to me as "Princess Alexandra! collar and cuff!" It immediately occurred to me that had I been any one of some scores of my paradoxers, I should, no doubt, have proceeded to raise the mob against the unscrupulous person who dared to hint to a young bride such maleficent--or at least immellificent--conduct towards her new lord.

But, as it was, certain material contexts in the shop window suggested a less {394} savage explanation. A paradoxer should not stop at reading the advertisements of Newton or Laplace; he should learn to look at the stock of goods.

I think I must have an eye for double readings, when presented: though I never guess riddles. On the day on which I first walked into the Panizzi reading room[807]--as it ought to be called--at the Museum, I began my circuit of the wall-shelves at the ladies' end: and perfectly coincided in the propriety of the Bibles and theological works being placed there. But the very first book I looked on the back of had, in flaming gold letters, the following inscription--"Blast the Antinomians!"[808] If a line had been drawn below the first word, Dr. Blast's history of the Antinomians would not have been so fearfully misinterpreted. It seems that neither the binder nor the arranger of the room had caught my reading. The book was removed before the catalogue of books of reference was printed.

AN ASTRONOMICAL PARADOXER

Two systems of astronomy: first, the Newtonian system, showing the rise and progress thereof, with a short historical account; the general theory with a variety of remarks thereon: second, the system in accordance with the Holy Scriptures, showing the rise and progress from Enoch, the seventh from Adam, the prophets, Moses, and others, in the first Testament; our Lord Jesus Christ, and his apostles, in the new or second Testament; Reeve and Muggleton, in the third and last Testament; with a variety of remarks thereon. By Isaac Frost.[809] London, 1846, 4to.

{395}

A very handsomely printed volume, with beautiful plates. Many readers who have heard of Muggletonians have never had any distinct idea of Lodowick Muggleton,[810] the inspired tailor, (1608-1698) who about 1650 received his commission from heaven, wrote a Testament, founded a sect, and descended to posterity. Of Reeve[811] less is usually said; according to Mr. Frost, he and Muggleton are the two "witnesses." I shall content myself with one specimen of Mr. Frost's science:

"I was once invited to hear read over 'Guthrie[812] on Astronomy,' and when the reading was concluded I was asked my opinion thereon; when I said, 'Doctor, it appears to me that Sir I. Newton has only given two proofs in support of his theory of the earth revolving round the sun: all the rest is assertion without any proofs.'--'What are they?' inquired the Doctor.--'Well,' I said, 'they are, first, the power of {396} attraction to keep the earth to the sun; the second is the power of repulsion, by virtue of the centrifugal motion of the earth: all the rest appears to me assertion without proof.' The Doctor considered a short time and then said, 'It certainly did appear so.' I said, 'Sir Isaac has certainly obtained the credit of completing the system, but really he has only half done his work.'--'How is that,' inquired my friend the Doctor. My reply was this: 'You will observe his system shows the earth traverses round the sun on an inclined plane; the consequence is, there are four powers required to make his system complete:

1st. The power of attraction. 2ndly. The power of repulsion. 3rdly. The power of ascending the inclined plane. 4thly. The power of descending the inclined plane.

You will thus easily see the four powers required, and Newton has only accounted for two; the work is therefore only half done.' Upon due reflection the Doctor said, 'It certainly was necessary to have these four points cleared up before the system could be said to be complete.'"

I have no doubt that Mr. Frost, and many others on my list, have really encountered doctors who could be puzzled by such stuff as this, or nearly as bad, among the votaries of existing systems, and have been encouraged thereby to print their objections. But justice requires me to say that from the words "power of repulsion by virtue of the centrifugal motion of the earth," Mr. Frost may be suspected of having something more like a notion of the much-mistaken term "centrifugal force" than many paradoxers of greater fame. The Muggletonian sect is not altogether friendless: over and above this handsome volume, the works of Reeve and Muggleton were printed, in 1832, in three quarto volumes. See Notes and Queries, 1st Series, v, 80; 3d Series, iii, 303. {397}

[The system laid down by Mr. Frost, though intended to be substantially that of Lodowick Muggleton, is not so vagarious. It is worthy of note how very different have been the fates of two contemporary paradoxers, Muggleton and George Fox.[813] They were friends and associates,[814] and commenced their careers about the same time, 1647-1650. The followers of Fox have made their sect an institution, and deserve to be called the pioneers of philanthropy. But though there must still be Muggletonians, since expensive books are published by men who take the name, no sect of that name is known to the world. Nevertheless, Fox and Muggleton are men of one type, developed by the same circumstances: it is for those who investigate such men to point out why their teachings have had fates so different. Macaulay says it was because Fox found followers of more sense than himself. True enough: but why did Fox find such followers and not Muggleton? The two were equally crazy, to all appearance: and the difference required must be sought in the doctrines themselves.

Fox was not a rational man: but the success of his sect and doctrines entitles him to a letter of alteration of the phrase which I am surprised has not become current. When Conduitt,[815] the husband of Newton's half-niece, wrote a circular to Newton's friends, just after his death, inviting them to bear their parts in a proper biography, he said, "As Sir I. Newton was a national man, I think every one ought to contribute to a work intended to do him justice." Here is the very phrase which is often wanted to signify that {398} celebrity which puts its mark, good or bad, on the national history, in a manner which cannot be asserted of many notorious or famous historical characters. Thus George Fox and Newton are both national men. Dr. Roget's[816] Thesaurus gives more than fifty synonyms--colleagues would be the better word--of "celebrated," any one of which might be applied, either in prose or poetry, to Newton or to his works, no one of which comes near to the meaning which Conduitt's adjective immediately suggests.

The truth is, that we are too monarchical to be national. We have the Queen's army, the Queen's navy, the Queen's highway, the Queen's English, etc.; nothing is national except the debt. That this remark is not new is an addition to its force; it has hardly been repeated since it was first made. It is some excuse that nation is not vernacular English: the country is our word, and country man is appropriated.]

Astronomical Aphorisms, or Theory of Nature; founded on the immutable basis of Meteoric Action. By P. Murphy,[817] Esq. London, 1847, 12mo.

This is by the framer of the Weather Almanac, who appeals to that work as corroborative of his theory of planetary temperature, years after all the world knew by experience that this meteorological theory was just as good as the others.

{399}

The conspiracy of the Bullionists as it affects the present system of the money laws. By Caleb Quotem. Birmingham, 1847, 8vo. (pp. 16).

This pamphlet is one of a class of which I know very little, in which the effects of the laws relating to this or that political bone of contention are imputed to deliberate conspiracy of one class to rob another of what the one knew ought to belong to the other. The success of such writers in believing what they have a bias to believe, would, if they knew themselves, make them think it equally likely that the inculpated classes might really believe what it is their interest to believe. The idea of a guilty understanding existing among fundholders, or landholders, or any holders, all the country over, and never detected except by bouncing pamphleteers, is a theory which should have been left for Cobbett[818] to propose, and for Apella to believe.[819]

[August, 1866. A pamphlet shows how to pay the National Debt. Advance paper to railways, etc., receivable in payment of taxes. The railways pay interest and principal in money, with which you pay your national debt, and redeem your notes. Twenty-five years of interest redeems the notes, and then the principal pays the debt. Notes to be kept up to value by penalties.]

THEISM INDEPENDENT OF REVELATION.

The Reasoner. No. 45. Edited by G.J. Holyoake.[820] Price 2d. Is there sufficient proof of the existence of God? 8vo. 1847.

This acorn of the holy oak was forwarded to me with a manuscript note, signed by the editor, on the part of the {400} "London Society of Theological Utilitarians," who say, "they trust you may be induced to give this momentous subject your consideration." The supposition that a middle-aged person, known as a student of thought on more subjects than one, had that particular subject yet to begin, is a specimen of what I will call the assumption-trick of controversy, a habit which pervades all sides of all subjects. The tract is a proof of the good policy of letting opinions find their level, without any assistance from the Court of Queen's Bench.

Twenty years earlier the thesis would have been positive, "There is sufficient proof of the non-existence of God," and bitter in its tone. As it stands, we have a moderate and respectful treatment--wrong only in making the opponent argue absurdly, as usually happens when one side invents the other--of a question in which a great many Christians have agreed with the atheist: that question being--Can the existence of God be proved independently of revelation? Many very religious persons answer this question in the negative, as well as Mr. Holyoake. And, this point being settled, all who agree in the negative separate into those who can endure scepticism, and those who cannot: the second class find their way to Christianity. This very number of The Reasoner announces the secession of one of its correspondents, and his adoption of the Christian faith. This would not have happened twenty years before: nor, had it happened, would it have been respectfully announced.

There are people who are very unfortunate in the expression of their meaning. Mr. Holyoake, in the name of the "London Society" etc., forwarded a pamphlet on the existence of God, and said that the Society trusted I "may be induced to give" the subject my "consideration." How could I know the Society was one person, who supposed I had arrived at a conclusion and wanted a "guiding word"? But so it seems it was: Mr. Holyoake, in the English {401} Leader of October 15, 1864, and in a private letter to me, writes as follows:

"The gentleman who was the author of the argument, and who asked me to send it to Mr. De Morgan, never assumed that that gentleman had 'that particular subject to begin'--on the contrary, he supposed that one whom we all knew to be eminent as a thinker had come to a conclusion upon it, and would perhaps vouchsafe a guiding word to one who was, as yet, seeking the solution of the Great Problem of Theology. I told my friend that 'Mr. De Morgan was doubtless preoccupied, and that he must be content to wait. On some day of courtesy and leisure he might have the kindness to write.' Nor was I wrong--the answer appears in your pages at the lapse of seventeen years."

I suppose Mr. Holyoake's way of putting his request was the stylus curiæ of the Society. A worthy Quaker who was sued for debt in the King's Bench was horrified to find himself charged in the declaration with detaining his creditor's money by force and arms, contrary to the peace of our Lord the King, etc. It's only the stylus curiæ, said a friend: I don't know curiæ, said the Quaker, but he shouldn't style us peace-breakers.

The notion that the non-existence of God can be proved, has died out under the light of discussion: had the only lights shone from the pulpit and the prison, so great a step would never have been made. The question now is as above. The dictum that Christianity is "part and parcel of the law of the land" is also abrogated: at the same time, and the coincidence is not an accident, it is becoming somewhat nearer the truth that the law of the land is part and parcel of Christianity. It must also be noticed that Christianity was part and parcel of the articles of war; and so was duelling. Any officer speaking against religion was to be cashiered; and any officer receiving an affront without, in the last resort, attempting to kill his opponent, was also to be cashiered. Though somewhat of a book-hunter, I {402} have never been able to ascertain the date of the collected remonstrances of the prelates in the House of Lords against this overt inculcation of murder, under the soft name of satisfaction: it is neither in Watt,[821] nor in Lowndes,[822] nor in any edition of Brunet;[823] and there is no copy in the British Museum. Was the collected edition really published?

[The publication of the above in the Athenæum has not produced reference to a single copy. The collected edition seems to be doubted. I have even met one or two persons who doubt the fact of the Bishops having remonstrated at all: but their doubt was founded on an absurd supposition, namely, that it was no business of theirs; that it was not the business of the prelates of the church in union with the state to remonstrate against the Crown commanding murder! Some say that the edition was published, but under an irrelevant title, which prevented people from knowing what it was about. Such things have happened: for example, arranged extracts from Wellington's general orders, which would have attracted attention, fell dead under the title of "Principles of War." It is surmised that the book I am looking for also contains the protests of the Reverend bench against other things besides the Thou-shalt-do-murder of the Articles (of war), and is called "First Elements of Religion" or some similar title. Time clears up all things.]

Notes

[1] See Mrs. De Morgan's Memoir of Augustus De Morgan, London, 1882, p 61.

[2] In the first edition this reference was to page 11.

[3] In the first edition this read "at page 438," the work then appearing in a single volume.

[4] "Just as it would surely have been better not to have considered it (i.e., the trinity) as a mystery, and with Cl. Kleckermann to have investigated by the aid of philosophy according to the teaching of true logic what it might be, before they determined what it was; just so would it have been better to withdraw zealously and industriously into the deepest caverns and darkest recesses of metaphysical speculations and suppositions in order to establish their opinion beyond danger from the weapons of their adversaries....

Indeed that great man so explains and demonstrates this dogma (although to theologians the word has not much charm) from the immovable foundations of philosophy, that with but few changes and additions a mind sincerely devoted to truth can desire nothing more."

[5] Mrs. Wititterly, in Nicholas Nickleby.--A. De M.

[6] The brackets mean that the paragraph is substantially from some one of the Athenæum Supplements.--S. E. De M.

[7] "It is annoying that this ingenious naturalist who has already given us more useful works and has still others in preparation, uses for this odious task, a pen dipped in gall and wormwood. It is true that many of his remarks have some foundation, and that to each error that he points out he at the same time adds its correction. But he is not always just and never fails to insult. After all, what does his book prove except that a forty-fifth part of a very useful review is not free from mistakes? Must we confuse him with those superficial writers whose liberty of body does not permit them to restrain their fruitfulness, that crowd of savants of the highest rank whose writings have adorned and still adorn the Transactions? Has he forgotten that the names of the Boyles, Newtons, Halleys, De Moivres, Hans Sloanes, etc. have been seen frequently? and that still are found those of the Wards, Bradleys, Grahams, Ellicots, Watsons, and of an author whom Mr. Hill prefers to all others, I mean Mr. Hill himself?"

[8] "Let no free man be seized or imprisoned or in any way harmed except by trial of his peers."

[9] "The master can rob, wreck and punish his slave according to his pleasure save only that he may not maim him."

[10] An Irish antiquary informs me that Virgil is mentioned in annals at A.D. 784, as "Verghil, i.e., the geometer, Abbot of Achadhbo [and Bishop of Saltzburg] died in Germany in the thirteenth year of his bishoprick." No allusion is made to his opinions; but it seems he was, by tradition, a mathematician. The Abbot of Aghabo (Queen's County) was canonized by Gregory IX, in 1233. The story of the second, or scapegoat, Virgil would be much damaged by the character given to the real bishop, if there were anything in it to dilapidate.--A. De M.

[11] "He performed many acts befitting the Papal dignity, and likewise many excellent (to be sure!) works."

[12] "After having been on the throne during ten years of pestilence."

[13] The work is the Questiones Joannis Buridani super X libros Aristotelis ad Nicomachum, curante Egidio Delfo ... Parisiis, 1489, folio. It also appeared at Paris in editions of 1499, 1513, and 1518, and at Oxford in 1637.

[14] Jean Buridan was born at Béthune about 1298, and died at Paris about 1358. He was professor of philosophy at the University of Paris and several times held the office of Rector. As a philosopher he was classed among the nominalists.

[15] So in the original.

[16] Baruch Spinoza, or Benedict de Spinoza as he later called himself, the pantheistic philosopher, excommunicated from the Jewish faith for heresy, was born at Amsterdam in 1632 and died there in 1677.

[17] Michael Scott, or Scot, was born about 1190, probably in Fifeshire, Scotland, and died about 1291. He was one of the best known savants of the court of Emperor Frederick II, and wrote upon astrology, alchemy, and the occult sciences. He was looked upon as a great magician and is mentioned among the wizards in Dante's Inferno.

"That other, round the loins So slender of his shape, was Michael Scot, Practised in every slight of magic wile." Inferno, XX.

Boccaccio also speaks of him: "It is not long since there was in this city (Florence) a great master in necromancy, who was called Michele Scotto, because he was a Scot." Decameron, Dec. Giorno.

Scott's mention of him in Canto Second of his Lay of the Last Minstrel, is well known:

"In these fair climes, it was my lot To meet the wondrous Michael Scott; A wizard of such dreaded fame, That when, in Salamanca's cave, Him listed his magic wand to wave, The bells would ring in Notre Dame!"

Sir Walter's notes upon him are of interest.

[18] These were some of the forgeries which Michel Chasles (1793-1880) was duped into buying. They purported to be a correspondence between Pascal and Newton and to show that the former had anticipated some of the discoveries of the great English physicist and mathematician. That they were forgeries was shown by Sir David Brewster in 1855.

[19] "Let the serpent also break from its appointed path."

[20] Guglielmo Brutus Icilius Timoleon Libri-Carucci della Sommaja, born at Florence in 1803; died at Fiesole in 1869. His Histoire des Sciences Mathématiques appeared at Paris in 1838, the entire first edition of volume I, save some half dozen that he had carried home, being burned on the day that the printing was completed. He was a great collector of early printed works on mathematics, and was accused of having stolen large numbers of them from other libraries. This accusation took him to London, where he bitterly attacked his accusers. There were two auction sales of his library, and a number of his books found their way into De Morgan's collection.

[21] Philo of Gadara lived in the second century B.C. He was a pupil of Sporus, who worked on the problem of the two mean proportionals.

[22] In his Histoire des Mathématiques, the first edition of which appeared in 1758. Jean Etienne Montucla was born at Lyons in 1725 and died at Versailles in 1799. He was therefore only thirty-three years old when his great work appeared. The second edition, with additions by D'Alembert, appeared in 1799-1802. He also wrote a work on the quadrature of the circle, Histoire des recherches sur la Quadrature du Cercle, which appeared in 1754.

[23] Eutocius of Ascalon was born in 480 A.D. He wrote commentaries on the first four books of the conics of Apollonius of Perga (247-222 B.C.). He also wrote on the Sphere and Cylinder and the Quadrature of the Circle, and on the two books on Equilibrium of Archimedes (287-212 B.C.)

[24] Edward Cocker was born in 1631 and died between 1671 and 1677. His famous arithmetic appeared in 1677 and went through many editions. It was written in a style that appealed to teachers, and was so popular that the expression "According to Cocker" became a household phrase. Early in the nineteenth century there was a similar saying in America, "According to Daboll," whose arithmetic had some points of analogy to that of Cocker.

Each had a well-known prototype in the ancient saying, "He reckons like Nicomachus of Gerasa."

[25] So in the original, for Barrême. François Barrême was to France what Cocker was to England. He was born at Lyons in 1640, and died at Paris in 1703. He published several arithmetics, dedicating them to his patron, Colbert. One of the best known of his works is L'arithmétique, ou le livre facile pour apprendre l'arithmétique soi-mème, 1677. The French word barême or barrême, a ready-reckoner, is derived from his name.

[26] Born at Rome, about 480 A.D.; died at Pavia, 524. Gibbon speaks of him as "the last of the Romans whom Cato or Tully could have acknowledged for their countryman." His works on arithmetic, music, and geometry were classics in the medieval schools.

[27] Johannes Campanus, of Novarra, was chaplain to Pope Urban IV (1261-1264). He was one of the early medieval translators of Euclid from the Arabic into Latin, and the first printed edition of the Elements (Venice, 1482) was from his translation. In this work he probably depended not a little upon at least two or three earlier scholars. He also wrote De computo ecclesiastico Calendarium, and De quadratura circuli.

[28] Archimedes gave 3-1/7, and 3-10/71 as the limits of the ratio of the circumference to the diameter of a circle.

[29] Friedrich W. A. Murhard was born at Cassel in 1779 and died there in 1853. His Bibliotheca Mathematica, Leipsic, 1797-1805, is ill arranged and inaccurate, but it is still a helpful bibliography. De Morgan speaks somewhere of his indebtedness to it.

[30] Abraham Gotthelf Kästner was born at Leipsic in 1719, and died at Göttingen in 1800. He was professor of mathematics and physics at Göttingen. His Geschichte der Mathematik (1796-1800) was a work of considerable merit. In the text of the Budget of Paradoxes the name appears throughout as Kastner instead of Kästner.

[31] Lucas Gauricus, or Luca Gaurico, born at Giffoni, near Naples, in 1476; died at Rome in 1558. He was an astrologer and mathematician, and was professor of mathematics at Ferrara in 1531. In 1545 he became bishop of Cività Ducale.

[32] John Couch Adams was born at Lidcot, Cornwall, in 1819, and died in 1892. He and Leverrier predicted the discovery of Neptune from the perturbations in Uranus.

[33] Urbain-Jean-Joseph Leverrier was born at Saint-Lô, Manche, in 1811, and died at Paris in 1877. It was his data respecting the perturbations of Uranus that were used by Adams and himself in locating Neptune.

[34] Joseph-Juste Scaliger, the celebrated philologist, was born at Agen in 1540, and died at Leyden in 1609. His Cyclometrica elementa, to which De Morgan refers, appeared at Leyden in 1594.

[35] The title is: In hoc libra contenta.... Introductio i geometri[=a].... Liber de quadratura circuli. Liber de cubicatione sphere. Perspectiva introductio. Carolus Bovillus, or Charles Bouvelles (Boüelles, Bouilles, Bouvel), was born at Saucourt, Picardy, about 1470, and died at Noyon about 1533. He was canon and professor of theology at Noyon. His Introductio contains considerable work on star polygons, a favorite study in the Middle Ages and early Renaissance. His work Que hoc volumine contin[=e]tur. Liber de intellectu. Liber de sensu, etc., appeared at Paris in 1509-10.

[36] Nicolaus Cusanus, Nicolaus Chrypffs or Krebs, was born at Kues on the Mosel in 1401, and died at Todi, Umbria, August 11, 1464. He held positions of honor in the church, including the bishopric of Brescia. He was made a cardinal in 1448. He wrote several works on mathematics, his Opuscula varia appearing about 1490, probably at Strasburg, but published without date or place. His Opera appeared at Paris in 1511 and again in 1514, and at Basel in 1565.

[37] Henry Stephens (born at Paris about 1528, died at Lyons in 1598) was one of the most successful printers of his day. He was known as Typographus Parisiensis, and to his press we owe some of the best works of the period.

[38] Jacobus Faber Stapulensis (Jacques le Fèvre d'Estaples) was born at Estaples, near Amiens, in 1455, and died at Nérac in 1536. He was a priest, vicar of the bishop of Meaux, lecturer on philosophy at the Collège Lemoine in Paris, and tutor to Charles, son of Francois I. He wrote on philosophy, theology, and mathematics.

[39] Claude-François Milliet de Challes was born at Chambéry in 1621, and died at Turin in 1678. He edited Euclidis Elementorum libri octo in 1660, and published a Cursus seu mundus mathematicus, which included a short history of mathematics, in 1674. He also wrote on mathematical geography.

[40] This date should be 1503, if he refers to the first edition. It is well known that this is the first encyclopedia worthy the name to appear in print. It was written by Gregorius Reisch (born at Balingen, and died at Freiburg in 1487), prior of the cloister at Freiburg and confessor to Maximilian I. The first edition appeared at Freiburg in 1503, and it passed through many editions in the sixteenth and seventeenth centuries. The title of the 1504 edition reads: Aepitoma omnis phylosophiae. alias Margarita phylosophica tractans de omni genere scibili: Cum additionibus: Quae in alijs non habentur.

[41] This is the Introductio in arithmeticam Divi S. Boetii.... Epitome rerum geometricarum ex geometrica introductio C. Bovilli. De quadratura circuli demonstratio ex Campano, that appeared without date about 1507.

[42] Born at Liverpool in 1805, and died there about 1872. He was a merchant, and in 1865 he published, at Liverpool, a work entitled The Quadrature of the Circle, or the True Ratio between the Diameter and Circumference geometrically and mathematically demonstrated. In this he gives the ratio as exactly 3-1/8.

[43] "That it would be impossible to tell him exactly, since no one had yet been able to find precisely the ratio of the circumference to the diameter."

[44] This is the Paris edition: "Parisiis: ex officina Ascensiana anno Christi ... MDXIIII," as appears by the colophon of the second volume to which De Morgan refers.

[45] Regiomontanus, or Johann Müller of Königsberg (Regiomontanus), was born at Königsberg in Franconia, June 5, 1436, and died at Rome July 6, 1476. He studied at Vienna under the great astronomer Peuerbach, and was his most famous pupil. He wrote numerous works, chiefly on astronomy. He is also known by the names Ioannes de Monte Regio, de Regiomonte, Ioannes Germanus de Regiomonte, etc.

[46] Henry Cornelius Agrippa was born at Cologne in 1486 and died either at Lyons in 1534 or at Grenoble in 1535. He was professor of theology at Cologne and also at Turin. After the publication of his De Occulta Philosophia he was imprisoned for sorcery. Both works appeared at Antwerp in 1530, and each passed through a large number of editions. A French translation appeared in Paris in 1582, and an English one in London in 1651.

[47] Nicolaus Remegius was born in Lorraine in 1554, and died at Nancy in 1600. He was a jurist and historian, and held the office of procurator general to the Duke of Lorraine.

[48] This was at the storming of the city by the British on May 4, 1799. From his having been born in India, all this appealed strongly to the interests of De Morgan.

[49] Orontius Finaeus, or Oronce Finé, was born at Briançon in 1494 and died at Paris, October 6, 1555. He was imprisoned by François I for refusing to recognize the concordat (1517). He was made professor of mathematics in the Collège Royal (later called the Collège de France) in 1532. He wrote extensively on astronomy and geometry, but was by no means a great scholar. He was a pretentious man, and his works went through several editions. His Protomathesis appeared at Paris in 1530-32. The work referred to by De Morgan is the Quadratura circuli tandem inventa & clarissime demonstrata ... Lutetiae Parisiorum, 1544, fol. In the 1556 edition of his De rebus mathematicis, hactenus desideratis, Libri IIII, published at Paris, the subtitle is: Quibus inter cætera, Circuli quadratura Centum modis, & suprà, per eundem Orontium recenter excogitatis, demonstratus, so that he kept up his efforts until his death.

[50] Johannes Buteo (Boteo, Butéon, Bateon) was born in Dauphiné c. 1485-1489, and died in a cloister in 1560 or 1564. Some writers give Charpey as the place and 1492 as the date of his birth, and state that he died at Canar in 1572. He belonged to the order of St. Anthony, and wrote chiefly on geometry, exposing the pretenses of Finaeus. His Opera geometrica appeared at Lyons in 1554, and his Logistica and De quadratura circuli libri duo at Lyons in 1559.

[51] This is the great French algebraist, François Viète (Vieta), who was born at Fontenay-le-Comte in 1540, and died at Paris, December 13, 1603. His well-known Isagoge in artem analyticam appeared at Tours in 1591.
His Opera mathematica was edited by Van Schooten in 1646.

[52] This is the De Rebus mathematicis hactenus desideratis, Libri IIII, that appeared in Paris in 1556. For the title page see Smith, D. E., Rara Arithmetica, Boston, 1908, p. 280.

[53] The title is correct except for a colon after Astronomicum. Nicolaus Raimarus Ursus was born in Henstede or Hattstede, in Dithmarschen, and died at Prague in 1599 or 1600. He was a pupil of Tycho Brahe. He also wrote De astronomis hypothesibus (1597) and Arithmetica analytica vulgo Cosa oder Algebra (1601).

[54] Born at Dôle, Franche-Comté, about 1550, died in Holland about 1600. The work to which reference is made is the Quadrature du cercle, ou manière de trouver un quarré égal au cercle donné, which appeared at Delft in 1584. Duchesne had the courage of his convictions, not only on circle-squaring but on religion as well, for he was obliged to leave France because of his conversion to Calvinism. De Morgan's statement that his real name is Van der Eycke is curious, since he was French born. The Dutch may have translated his name when he became professor at Delft, but we might equally well say, that his real name was Quercetanus or à Quercu.

[55] This was the father of Adriaan Metius (1571-1635). He was a mathematician and military engineer, and suggested the ratio 355/113 for [pi], a ratio afterwards published by his son. The ratio, then new to Europe, had long been known and used in China, having been found by Tsu
Ch'ung-chih (428-499 A.D.).

[56] This was Jost Bürgi, or Justus Byrgius, the Swiss mathematician of whom Kepler wrote in 1627: "Apices logistici Justo Byrgio multis annis ante editionem Neperianam viam præiverunt ad hos ipsissimos logarithmos." He constructed a table of antilogarithms (Arithmetische und geometrische Progress-Tabulen), but it was not published until after Napier's work appeared.

[57] Ludolphus Van Ceulen, born at Hildesheim, and died at Leyden in 1610. It was he who first carried the computation of [pi] to 35 decimal places.

[58] Jens Jenssen Dodt, van Flensburg, a Dutch historian, who died in 1847.

[59] I do not know this edition. There was one "Antverpiae apud Petrum Bellerum sub scuto Burgundiae," 4to, in 1591.

[60] Archytas of Tarentum (430-365 B.C.) who wrote on proportions, irrationals, and the duplication of the cube.

[61]The Circle Speaks. "At first a circle I was called, And was a curve around about Like lofty orbit of the sun Or rainbow arch among the clouds. A noble figure then was I-- And lacking nothing but a start, And lacking nothing but an end. But now unlovely do I seem Polluted by some angles new. This thing Archytas hath not done Nor noble sire of Icarus Nor son of thine, Iapetus. What accident or god can then Have quadrated mine area?"

The Author Replies. "By deepest mouth of Turia And lake of limpid clearness, lies A happy state not far removed From old Saguntus; farther yet A little way from Sucro town. In this place doth a poet dwell, Who oft the stars will closely scan, And always for himself doth claim What is denied to wiser men;-- An old man musing here and there And oft forgetful of himself, Not knowing how to rightly place The compasses, nor draw a line, As he doth of himself relate. This craftsman fine, in sooth it is Hath quadrated thine area."

[62] Pietro Bongo, or Petrus Bungus, was born at Bergamo, and died there in 1601. His work on the Mystery of Numbers is one of the most exhaustive and erudite ones of the mystic writers. The first edition appeared at Bergamo in 1583-84; the second, at Bergamo in 1584-85; the third, at Venice in 1585; the fourth, at Bergamo in 1590; and the fifth, which De Morgan calls the second, in 1591. Other editions, before the Paris edition to which he refers, appeared in 1599 and 1614; and the colophon of the Paris edition is dated 1617. See the editor's Rara Arithmetica, pp. 380-383.

[63] William Warburton (1698-1779), Bishop of Gloucester, whose works got him into numerous literary quarrels, being the subject of frequent satire.

[64] Thomas Galloway (1796-1851), who was professor of mathematics at Sandhurst for a time, and was later the actuary of the Amicable Life Assurance Company of London. In the latter capacity he naturally came to be associated with De Morgan.

[65] Giordano Bruno was born near Naples about 1550. He left the Dominican order to take up Calvinism, and among his publications was L'expulsion de la bête triomphante. He taught philosophy at Paris and Wittenberg, and some of his works were published in England in 1583-86. Whether or not he was roasted alive "for the maintenance and defence of the holy Church," as De Morgan states, depends upon one's religious point of view. At any rate, he was roasted as a heretic.

[66] Referring to part of his Discours de la méthode, Leyden, 1637.

[67] Bartholomew Legate, who was born in Essex about 1575. He denied the divinity of Christ and was the last heretic burned at Smithfield.

[68] Edward Wightman, born probably in Staffordshire. He was anti-Trinitarian, and claimed to be the Messiah. He was the last man burned for heresy in England.

[69] Gaspar Schopp, born at Neumarck in 1576, died at Padua in 1649; grammarian, philologist, and satirist.

[70] Konrad Ritterhusius, born at Brunswick in 1560; died at Altdorf in 1613. He was a jurist of some power.

[71] Johann Jakob Brucker, born at Augsburg in 1696, died there in 1770. He wrote on the history of philosophy (1731-36, and 1742-44).

[72] Daniel Georg Morhof, born at Wismar in 1639, died at Lübeck in 1691. He was rector of the University of Kiel, and professor of eloquence, poetry, and history.

[73] In the Histoire des Sciences Mathématiques, vol. IV, note X, pp. 416-435 of the 1841 edition.

[74] Colenso (1814-1883), missionary bishop of Natal, was one of the leaders of his day in the field of higher biblical criticism. De Morgan must have admired his mathematical works, which were not without merit.

[75] Samuel Roffey Maitland, born at London in 1792; died at Gloucester in 1866. He was an excellent linguist and a critical student of the Bible. He became librarian at Lambeth in 1838.

[76] Archbishop Howley (1766-1848) was a thorough Tory. He was one of the opponents of the Roman Catholic Relief bill, the Reform bill, and the Jewish Civil Disabilities Relief bill.

[77] We have, in America at least, almost forgotten the great stir made by Edward B. Pusey (1800-1882) in the great Oxford movement in the middle of the nineteenth century. He was professor of Hebrew at Oxford, and canon of Christ Church.

[78] That is, his Magia universalis naturae et artis sive recondita naturalium et artificialium rerum scientia, Würzburg, 1657, 4to, with editions at Bamberg in 1671, and at Frankfort in 1677. Gaspard Schott (Königshofen 1608, Würzburg 1666) was a physicist and mathematician, devoting most of his attention to the curiosities of his sciences. His type of mind must have appealed to De Morgan.

[79] Salicetti Quadratura circuli nova, perspicua, expedita, veraque tum naturalis, tum geometrica, etc., 1608.--Consideratio nova in opusculum Archimedis de circuli dimensione, etc., 1609.

[80] Melchior Adam, who died at Heidelberg in 1622, wrote a collection of biographies which was published at Heidelberg and Frankfort from 1615 to 1620.

[81] Born at Baden in 1524; died at Basel in 1583. The Erastians were related to the Zwinglians, and opposed all power of excommunication and the infliction of penalties by a church.

[82] See Acts xii. 20.

[83] Theodore de Bèse, a French theologian; born at Vezelay, in Burgundy, in 1519; died at Geneva, in 1605.

[84] Dr. Robert Lee (1804-1868) had some celebrity in De Morgan's time through his attempt to introduce music and written prayers into the service of the Scotch Presbyterian church.

[85] Born at Veringen, Hohenzollern, in 1512; died at Röteln in 1564. [86] Born at Kinnairdie, Bannfshire, in 1661; died at London in 1708. His Astronomiae Physicae et Geometriae Elementa, Oxford, 1702, was an influential work.

[87] The title was carelessly copied by De Morgan, not an unusual thing in his case. The original reads: A Plaine Discovery, of the whole Revelation of S. Iohn: set downe in two treatises ... set foorth by John Napier L. of Marchiston ... whereunto are annexed, certaine Oracles of Sibylla ... London ... 1611.

[88] I have not seen the first edition, but it seems to have appeared in Edinburgh, in 1593, with a second edition there in 1594. The 1611 edition was the third.

[89] It seems rather certain that Napier felt his theological work of greater importance than that in logarithms. He was born at Merchiston, near (now a part of) Edinburgh, in 1550, and died there in 1617, three years after the appearance of his Mirifici logarithmorum canonis descriptio.

[90] Followed, in the third edition, from which he quotes, by a comma.

[91] There was an edition published at Stettin in 1633. An English translation by P. F. Mottelay appeared at London in 1893. Gilbert (1540-1603) was physician to Queen Elizabeth and President of the College of Physicians at London. His De Magnete was the first noteworthy treatise on physics printed in England. He treated of the earth as a spherical magnet and suggested the variation and declination of the needle as a means of finding latitude at sea.

[92] The title says "ab authoris fratre collectum," although it was edited by J. Gruterus.

[93] Porta was born at Naples in 1550 and died there in 1615. He studied the subject of lenses and the theory of sight, did some work in hydraulics and agriculture, and was well known as an astrologer. His Magiae naturalis libri XX was published at Naples in 1589. The above title should read curvilineorum.

[94] Cataldi was born in 1548 and died at Bologna in 1626. He was professor of mathematics at Perugia, Florence, and Bologna, and is known in mathematics chiefly for his work in continued fractions. He was one of the scholarly men of his day.

[95] Georg Joachim Rheticus was born at Feldkirch in 1514 and died at Caschau, Hungary, in 1576. He was one of the most prominent pupils of Copernicus, his Narratio de libris revolutionum Copernici (Dantzig, 1540) having done much to make the theory of his master known.

[96] Henry Briggs, who did so much to make logarithms known, and who used the base 10, was born at Warley Wood, in Yorkshire, in 1560, and died at Oxford in 1630. He was Savilian professor of mathematics at Oxford, and his grave may still be seen there.

[97] He lived at "Reggio nella Emilia" in the 16th and 17th centuries. His Regola e modo facilissimo di quadrare il cerchio was published at Reggio in 1609.

[98] Christoph Klau (Clavius) was born at Bamberg in 1537, and died at Rome in 1612. He was a Jesuit priest and taught mathematics in the Jesuit College at Rome. He wrote a number of works on mathematics, including excellent text-books on arithmetic and algebra.

[99] Christopher Gruenberger, or Grienberger, was born at Halle in Tyrol in 1561, and died at Rome in 1636. He was, like Clavius, a Jesuit and a mathematician, and he wrote a little upon the subject of projections. His Prospectiva nova coelestis appeared at Rome in 1612.

[100] The name should, of course, be Lansbergii in the genitive, and is so in the original title. Philippus Lansbergius was born at Ghent in 1560, and died at Middelburg in 1632. He was a Protestant theologian, and was also a physician and astronomer. He was a well-known supporter of Galileo and Copernicus. His Commentationes in motum terrae diurnum et annuum appeared at Middelburg in 1630 and did much to help the new theory.

[101] I have never seen the work. It is rare.

[102] The African explorer, born in Somersetshire in 1827, died at Bath in 1864. He was the first European to cross Central Africa from north to south. He investigated the sources of the Nile.

[103] Prester (Presbyter, priest) John, the legendary Christian king whose realm, in the Middle Ages, was placed both in Asia and in Africa, is first mentioned in the chronicles of Otto of Freisingen in the 12th century. In the 14th century his kingdom was supposed to be Abyssinia.

[104] "It is a profane and barbarous nation, dirty and slovenly, who eat their meat half raw and drink mare's milk, and who use table-cloths and napkins only to wipe their hands and mouths."

[105] "The great Prester John, who is the fourth in rank, is emperor of Ethiopia and of the Abyssinians, and boasts of his descent from the race of David, as having descended from the Queen of Sheba, Queen of Ethiopia. She, having gone to Jerusalem to see the wisdom of Solomon, about the year of the world 2952, returned pregnant with a son whom they called Moylech, from whom they claim descent in a direct line. And so he glories in being the most ancient monarch in the world, saying that his empire has endured for more than three thousand years, which no other empire is able to assert. He also puts into his titles the following: 'We, the sovereign in my realms, uniquely beloved of God, pillar of the faith, sprung from the race of Judah, etc.' The boundaries of this empire touch the Red Sea and the mountains of Azuma on the east, and on the western side it is bordered by the River Nile which separates it from Nubia. To the north lies Egypt, and to the south the kingdoms of Congo and Mozambique. It extends forty degrees in length, or one thousand twenty-five leagues, from Congo or Mozambique on the south to Egypt on the north; and in width it reaches from the Nile on the west to the mountains of Azuma on the east, seven hundred twenty-five leagues, or twenty-nine degrees. This empire contains thirty large provinces, namely Medra, Gaga, Alchy, Cedalon, Mantro, Finazam, Barnaquez, Ambiam, Fungy, Angoté, Cigremaon, Gorga, Cafatez, Zastanla, Zeth, Barly, Belangana, Tygra, Gorgany, Barganaza, d'Ancut, Dargaly, Ambiacatina, Caracogly, Amara, Maon (sic), Guegiera, Bally, Dobora, and Macheda. All of these provinces are situated directly under the equinoctial line between the tropics of Capricorn and Cancer; but they are two hundred fifty leagues nearer our tropic than the other. The name of Prester John signifies Great Lord, and is not Priest [Presbyter] as many think. He has always been a Christian, but often schismatic. At the present time he is a Catholic and recognizes the Pope as sovereign pontiff. I met one of his bishops in Jerusalem, and often conversed with him through the medium of our guide. He was of grave and serious bearing, pleasant of speech, but wonderfully subtle in everything he said. He took great delight in what I had to relate concerning our beautiful ceremonies and the dignity of our prelates in their pontifical vestments. As to other matters I will only say that the Ethiopian is joyous and merry, not at all like the Tartar in the matter of filth, nor like the wretched Arab. They are refined and subtle, trusting no one, wonderfully suspicious, and very devout. They are not at all black as is commonly supposed, by which I refer to those who do not live under the equator or too near to it, for these are Moors as we shall see."

With respect to this translation it should be said that the original forms of the proper names have been preserved, although they are not those found in modern works. It should also be stated that the meaning of Prester is not the one that was generally accepted by scholars at the time the work was written, nor is it the one accepted to-day. There seems to be no doubt that the word is derived from Presbyter as stated in note 103 on page 71, since the above-mentioned chronicles of Otto, bishop of Freisingen about the middle of the twelfth century, states this fact clearly. Otto received his information from the bishop of Gabala (the Syrian Jibal) who told him the story of John, rex et sacerdos, or Presbyter John as he liked to be called. He goes on to say "Should it be asked why, with all this power and splendor, he calls himself merely 'presbyter,' this is because of his humility, and because it was not fitting for one whose server was a primate and king, whose butler an archbishop and king, whose chamberlain a bishop and king, whose master of the horse an archimandrite and king, whose chief cook an abbot and king, to be called by such titles as these."

[106] Thomas Fienus (Fyens) was born at Antwerp in 1567 and died in 1631. He was professor of medicine at Louvain. Besides the editions mentioned below, his De cometis anni 1618 appeared at Leipsic in 1656. He also wrote a Disputatio an coelum moveatur et terra quiescat, which appeared at Antwerp in 1619, and again at Leipsic in 1656.

[107] Libertus Fromondus (1587-c 1653), a Belgian theologian, dean of the College Church at Harcourt, and professor at Louvain. The name also appears as Froidmont and Froimont.

[108] L. Fromondi ... meteorologicorum libri sex.... Cui accessit T. Fieni et L. Fromondi dissertationes de cometa anni 1618.... This is from the 1670 edition. The 1619 edition was published at Antwerp. The Meteorologicorum libri VI, appeared at Antwerp in 1627. He also wrote Anti-Aristarchus sive orbis terrae immobilis liber unicus (Antwerp, 1631); Labyrrinthus sive de compositione continui liber unus, Philosophis, Mathematicis, Theologis utilis et jucundus (Antwerp, 1631) and Vesta sive Anti-Aristarchi vindex adversus Jac. Lansbergium (Philippi filium) et copernicanos (Antwerp, 1634).

[109] Snell was born at Leyden in 1591, and died there in 1626. He studied under Tycho Brahe and Kepler, and is known for Snell's law of the refraction of light. He was the first to determine the size of the earth by measuring the arc of a meridian with any fair degree of accuracy. The title should read: Willebrordi Snellii R. F. Cyclometricus, de circuli dimensione secundum Logistarum abacos, et ad Mechanicem accuratissima....

[110] Bacon was born at York House, London, in 1561, and died near Highgate, London, in 1626. His Novum Organum Scientiarum or New Method of employing the reasoning faculties in the pursuits of Truth appeared at London in 1620. He had previously published a work entitled Of the Proficience and Advancement of Learning, divine and humane (London, 1605), which again appeared in 1621. His De augmentis scientiarum Libri IX appeared at Paris in 1624, and his Historia naturalis et experimentalis de ventis at Leyden in 1638. He was successively solicitor general, attorney general, lord chancellor (1619), Baron Verulam and Viscount St. Albans. He was deprived of office and was imprisoned in the Tower of London in 1621, but was later pardoned.

[111] The Greek form, Organon, is sometimes used.

[112] James Spedding (1808-1881), fellow of Cambridge, who devoted his life to his edition of Bacon.

[113] R. Leslie Ellis (1817-1859), editor of the Cambridge Mathematical Journal. He also wrote on Roman aqueducts, on Boole's Laws of Thought, and on the formation of a Chinese dictionary.

[114] Douglas Derion Heath (1811-1897), a classical and mathematical scholar.

[115] There have been numerous editions of Bacon's complete works, including the following: Frankfort, 1665; London, 1730, 1740, 1764, 1765, 1778, 1803, 1807, 1818, 1819, 1824, 1825-36, 1857-74, 1877. The edition to which De Morgan refers is that of 1857-74, 14 vols., of which five were apparently out at the time he wrote. There were also French editions in 1800 and 1835.

[116] So in the original for Tycho Brahe.

[117] In general these men acted before Baron wrote, or at any rate, before he wrote the Novum Organum, but the statement must not be taken too literally. The dates are as follows: Copernicus, 1473-1543; Tycho Brahe, 1546-1601; Gilbert, 1540-1603; Kepler, 1571-1630; Galileo, 1564-1642; Harvey, 1578-1657. For example, Harvey's Exercitatio Anatomica de Motu Cordis et Sanguinis did not appear until 1628, and his Exercitationes de Generatione until 1651.

[118] Robert Hooke (1635-1703) studied under Robert Boyle at Oxford. He was "Curator of Experiments" to the Royal Society and its secretary, and was professor of geometry at Gresham College, London. It is true that he was "very little of a mathematician" although he wrote on the motion of the earth (1674), on helioscopes and other instruments (1675), on the rotation of Jupiter (1666), and on barometers and sails.

[119] The son of the Sir William mentioned below. He was born in 1792 and died in 1871. He wrote a treatise on light (1831) and one on astronomy (1836), and established an observatory at the Cape of Good Hope where he made observations during 1834-1838, publishing them in 1847. On his return to England he was knighted, and in 1848 was made president of the Royal Society. The title of the work to which reference is made is: A preliminary discourse on the Study of Natural Philosophy. It appeared at London in 1831.

[120] Sir William was horn at Hanover in 1738 and died at Slough, near Windsor in 1822. He discovered the planet Uranus and six satellites, besides two satellites of Saturn. He was knighted by George III.

[121] This was the work of 1836. He also published a work entitled Outlines of Astronomy in 1849.

[122] While Newton does not tell the story, he refers in the Principia (1714 edition, p. 293) to the accident caused by his cat.

[123] Marino Ghetaldi (1566-1627), whose Promotus Archimedes appeared at Rome in 1603, Nonnullae propositiones de parabola at Rome in 1603. and Apollonius redivivus at Venice in 1607. He was a nobleman and was ambassador from Venice to Rome.

[124] Simon Stevin (born at Bruges, 1548; died at the Hague, 1620). He was an engineer and a soldier, and his La Disme (1585) was the first separate treatise on the decimal fraction. The contribution referred to above is probably that on the center of gravity of three bodies (1586).

[125] Habakuk Guldin (1577-1643), who took the name Paul on his conversion to Catholicism. He became a Jesuit, and was professor of mathematics at Vienna and later at Gratz. In his Centrobaryca seu de centro gravitatis trium specierum quantitatis continuae (1635), of the edition of 1641, appears the Pappus rule for the volume of a solid formed by the revolution of a plane figure about an axis, often spoken of as Guldin's Theorem.

[126] Edward Wright was born at Graveston, Norfolkshire, in 1560, and died at London in 1615. He was a fellow of Caius College, Cambridge, and in his work entitled The correction of certain errors in Navigation (1599) he gives the principle of Mercator's projection. He translated the Portuum investigandorum ratio of Stevin in 1599.

[127] De Morgan never wrote a more suggestive sentence. Its message is not for his generation alone.

[128] The eminent French physicist, Jean Baptiste Biot (1779-1862), professor in the Collège de France. His work Sur les observatoires météorologiques appeared in 1855.

[129] George Biddell Airy (1801-1892), professor of astronomy and physics at Cambridge, and afterwards director of the Observatory at Greenwich.

[130] De Morgan would have rejoiced in the rôle played by Intuition in the mathematics of to-day, notably among the followers of Professor Klein.

[131] Colburn was the best known of the calculating boys produced in America. He was born at Cabot, Vermont, in 1804, and died at Norwich, Vermont, in 1840. Having shown remarkable skill in numbers as early as 1810, he was taken to London in 1812, whence he toured through Great Britain and to Paris. The Earl of Bristol placed him in Westminster School (1816-1819). On his return to America he became a preacher, and later a teacher of languages.

[132] The history of calculating boys is interesting. Mathieu le Coc (about 1664), a boy of Lorraine, could extract cube roots at sight at the age of eight. Tom Fuller, a Virginian slave of the eighteenth century, although illiterate, gave the number of seconds in 7 years 17 days 12 hours after only a minute and a half of thought. Jedediah Buxton, an Englishman of the eighteenth century, was studied by the Royal Society because of his remarkable powers. Ampère, the physicist, made long calculations with pebbles at the age of four. Gauss, one of the few infant prodigies to become an adult prodigy, corrected his father's payroll at the age of three. One of the most remarkable of the French calculating boys was Henri Mondeux.

He was investigated by Arago, Sturm, Cauchy, and Liouville, for the Académie des Sciences, and a report was written by Cauchy. His specialty was the solution of algebraic problems mentally. He seems to have calculated squares and cubes by a binomial formula of his own invention. He died in obscurity, but was the subject of a Biographie by Jacoby (1846). George P. Bidder, the Scotch engineer (1806-1878), was exhibited as an arithmetical prodigy at the age of ten, and did not attend school until he was twelve. Of the recent cases two deserve special mention, Inaudi and Diamandi. Jacques Inaudi (born in 1867) was investigated for the Académie in 1892 by a commission including Poincaré, Charcot, and Binet. (See the Revue des Deux Mondes, June 15, 1892, and the laboratory bulletins of the Sorbonne). He has frequently exhibited his remarkable powers in America. Périclès Diamandi was investigated by the same commission in 1893. See Alfred Binet, Psychologie des Grands Calculateurs et Joueurs d'Echecs, Paris, 1894.

[133] John Flamsteed's (1646-1719) "old white house" was the first Greenwich observatory. He was the Astronomer Royal and first head of this observatory.

[134] It seems a pity that De Morgan should not have lived to lash those of our time who are demanding only the immediately practical in mathematics. His satire would have been worth the reading against those who seek to stifle the science they pretend to foster.

[135] Ismael Bouillaud, or Boulliau, was born in 1605 and died at Paris in 1694. He was well known as an astronomer, mathematician, and jurist. He lived with De Thou at Paris, and accompanied him to Holland. He traveled extensively, and was versed in the astronomical work of the Persians and Arabs. It was in his Astronomia philolaica, opus novum (Paris, 1645) that he attacked Kepler's laws. His tables were shown to be erroneous by the fact that the solar eclipse did not take place as predicted by him in 1645.

[136] As it did, until 1892, when Airy had reached the ripe age of ninety-one.

[137] Didaci a Stunica ... In Job commentaria appeared at Toledo in 1584.

[138] "The false Pythagorean doctrine, absolutely opposed to the Holy Scriptures, concerning the mobility of the earth and the immobility of the sun."

[139] Paolo Antonio Foscarini (1580-1616), who taught theology and philosophy at Naples and Messina, was one of the first to champion the theories of Copernicus. This was in his Lettera sopra l'opinione de' Pittagorici e del Copernico, della mobilità della Terra e stabilità del Sole, e il nuovo pittagorico sistema del mondo, 4to, Naples, 1615. The condemnation of the Congregation was published in the following spring, and in the year of Foscarini's death at the early age of thirty-six.

[140] "To be wholly prohibited and condemned," because "it seeks to show that the aforesaid doctrine is consonant with truth and is not opposed to the Holy Scriptures."

[141] "As repugnant to the Holy Scriptures and to its true and Catholic interpretation (which in a Christian man cannot be tolerated in the least), he does not hesitate to treat (of his subject) 'by hypothesis', but he even adds 'as most true'!"

[142] "To the places in which he discusses not by hypothesis but by making assertions concerning the position and motion of the earth."

[143] "Copernicus. If by chance there shall be vain talkers who, although ignorant of all mathematics, yet taking it upon themselves to sit in judgment upon the subject on account of a certain passage of Scripture badly distorted for their purposes, shall have dared to criticize and censure this teaching of mine, I pay no attention to them, even to the extent of despising their judgment as rash. For it is not unknown that Lactantius, a writer of prominence in other lines although but little versed in mathematics, spoke very childishly about the form of the earth when he ridiculed those who declared that it was spherical. Hence it should not seem strange to the learned if some shall look upon us in the same way.

Mathematics is written for mathematicians, to whom these labors of ours will seem, if I mistake not, to add something even to the republic of the Church.... Emend. Here strike out everything from 'if by chance' to the words 'these labors of ours,' and adapt it thus: 'But these labors of ours.'"

[144] "Copernicus. However if we consider the matter more carefully it will be seen that the investigation is not yet completed, and therefore ought by no means to be condemned. Emend. However, if we consider the matter more

carefully it is of no consequence whether we regard the earth as existing in the center of the universe or outside of the center, so far as the solution of the phenomena of celestial movements is concerned."

[145] "The whole of this chapter may be cut out, since it avowedly treats of the earth's motion, while it refutes the reasons of the ancients proving its immobility. Nevertheless, since it seems to speak problematically, in order that it may satisfy the learned and keep intact the sequence and unity of the book let it be emended as below."

[146] "Copernicus. Therefore why do we still hesitate to concede to it motion which is by nature consistent with its form, the more so because the whole universe is moving, whose end is not and cannot be known, and not confess that there is in the sky an appearance of daily revolution, while on the earth there is the truth of it? And in like manner these things are as if Virgil's Æneas should say, 'We are borne from the harbor' ... Emend. Hence I cannot concede motion to this form, the more so because the universe would fall, whose end is not and cannot be known, and what appears in the heavens is just as if ..."

[147] "Copernicus. I also add that it would seem very absurd that motion should be ascribed to that which contains and locates, and not rather to that which is contained and located, that is the earth. Emend. I also add that it is not more difficult to ascribe motion to the contained and located, which is the earth, than to that which contains it."

[148] "Copernicus. You see, therefore, that from all these things the motion of the earth is more probable than its immobility, especially in the daily revolution which is as it were a particular property of it. Emend. Omit from 'You see' to the end of the chapter."

[149] "Copernicus. Therefore, since there is nothing to hinder the motion of the earth, it seems to me that we should consider whether it has several motions, to the end that it may be looked upon as one of the moving stars.

Emend. Therefore, since I have assumed that the earth moves, it seems to me that we should consider whether it has several motions."

[150] "Copernicus. We are not ashamed to acknowledge ... that this is preferably verified in the motion of the earth. Emend. We are not ashamed to assume ... that this is consequently verified in the motion."

[151] "Copernicus. So divine is surely this work of the Best and Greatest. Emend. Strike out these last words."
[152] This should be Cap. 11, lib. i, p. 10.

[153] "Copernicus. Demonstration of the threefold motion of the earth. Emend. On the hypothesis of the threefold motion of the earth and its demonstration."

[154] This should be Cap. 20, lib. iv, p. 122.

[155] "Copernicus. Concerning the size of these three stars, the sun, the moon and the earth. Emend. Strike out the words 'these three stars,' because the earth is not a star as Copernicus would make it."

[156] He seems to speak problematically in order to satisfy the learned.

[157] One of the Church Fathers, born about 250 A.D., and died about 330, probably at Trèves. He wrote Divinarum Institutionum Libri VII. and other controversial and didactic works against the learning and philosophy of the Greeks.

[158] Giovanni Battista Riccioli (1598-1671) taught philosophy and theology at Parma and Bologna, and was later professor of astronomy. His Almagestum novum appeared in 1651, and his Argomento fisico-matematico contro il moto diurno della terra in 1668.

[159] He was a native of Arlington, Sussex, and a pensioner of Christ's College, Cambridge. In 1603 he became a master of arts at Oxford.

[160] Straying, i.e., from the right way.

[161] "Private subjects may, in the presence of danger, defend themselves or their families against a monarch as against any malefactor, if the monarch assaults them like a bandit or a ravisher, and provided they are unable to summon the usual protection and cannot in any way escape the danger."

[162] Daniel Neal (1678-1743), an independent minister, wrote a History of the Puritans that appeared in 1732. The account may be found in the New York edition of 1843-44, vol. I, p. 271.

[163] Anthony Wood (1632-1695), whose Historia et Antiquitates Universitatis Oxoniensis (1674) and Athenae Oxoniensis (1691) are among the classics on Oxford.

[164] Part of the title, not here quoted, shows the nature of the work more clearly: "liber unicus, in quo decretum S. Congregationis S. R. E. Cardinal. an. 1616, adversus Pythagorico-Copernicanos editum defenditur."

[165] This was John Elliot Drinkwater Bethune (1801-1851), the statesman who did so much for legislative and educational reform in India. His father, John Drinkwater Bethune, wrote a history of the siege of Gibraltar.

[166] The article referred to is about thirty years old; since it appeared another has been given (Dubl. Rev., Sept. 1865) which is of much greater depth. In it will also be found the Roman view of Bishop Virgil (ante, p. 32).--A. De M.

[167] Jean Baptiste Morin (1583-1656), in his younger days physician to the Bishop of Boulogne and the Duke of Luxemburg, became in 1630 professor of mathematics at the Collège Royale. His chief contribution to the problem of the determination of longitude is his Longitudinum terrestrium et coelestium nova et hactenus optata scientia (1634). He also wrote against Copernicus in his Famosi problematis de telluris motu vel quiete hactenus optata solutio (1631), and against Lansberg in his Responsio pro telluris quiete (1634).

[168] The work appeared at Leyden in 1626, at Amsterdam in 1634, at Copenhagen in 1640 and again at Leyden in 1650. The title of the 1640 edition is Arithmeticae Libri II et Geometriae Libri VI. The work on which it is based is the Arithmeticae et Geometriae Practica, which appeared in 1611.

[169] The father's name was Adriaan, and Lalande says that it was Montucla who first made the mistake of calling him Peter, thinking that the initials P. M. stood for Petrus Metius, when in reality they stood for piae memoriae! The ratio 355/113 was known in China hundreds of years before his time. See note 55, page 52.

[170] Adrian Metius (1571-1635) was professor of medicine at the University of Franeker. His work was, however, in the domain of astronomy, and in this domain he published several treatises.

[171] The first edition was entitled: The Discovery of a World in the Moone. Or, a Discourse Tending to prove that 'tis probable there may be another habitable World in that Planet. 1638, 8vo. The fourth edition appeared in 1684. John Wilkins (1614-1672) was Warden of Wadham College, Oxford; master of Trinity, Cambridge; and, later, Bishop of Chester. He was influential in founding the Royal Society.

[172] The first edition was entitled: C. Hugenii [Greek: Kosmotheôros], sive de Terris coelestibus, earumque ornatu, conjecturae, The Hague, 1698, 4to. There were several editions. It was also translated into French (1718), and there was another English edition (1722). Huyghens (1629-1695) was one of the best mathematical physicists of his time.

[173] It is hardly necessary to say that science has made enormous advance in the chemistry of the universe since these words were written.

[174] William Whewell (1794-1866) is best known through his History of the Inductive Sciences (1837) and Philosophy of the Inductive Sciences (1840).

[175] Thomas Chalmers (1780-1847), the celebrated Scotch preacher. These discourses were delivered while he was minister in a large parish in the poorest part of Glasgow, and in them he attempted to bring science into harmony with the Bible. He was afterwards professor of moral philosophy at St. Andrew's (1823-28), and professor of theology at Edinburgh (1828). He became the leader of a schism from the Scotch Presbyterian Church,--the Free Church.

[176] That is, in Robert Watt's (1774-1819) Bibliotheca Britannica (posthumous, 1824). Nor is it given in the Dictionary of National Biography.

[177] The late Greek satirist and poet, c. 120-c. 200 A.D.

[178] François Rabelais (c. 1490-1553) the humorist who created Pantagruel (1533) and Gargantua (1532). His work as a physician and as editor of the works of Galen and Hippocrates is less popularly known.

[179] Francis Godwin (1562-1633) bishop of Llandaff and Hereford. Besides some valuable historical works he wrote The Man in the Moone, or a Discourse of a voyage thither by Domingo Gonsales, the Speed Messenger of London, 1638.

[180] Bernard Le Bovier de Fontenelle (1657-1757), historian, critic, mathematician, Secretary of the Académie des Sciences, and member of the Académie Française. His Entretien sur la pluralité des mondes appeared at Paris in 1686.

[181] Athanasius Kircher (1602-1680), Jesuit, professor of mathematics and philosophy, and later of Hebrew and Syriac, at Wurzburg; still later professor of mathematics and Hebrew at Rome. He wrote several works on physics. His collection of mathematical instruments and other antiquities became the basis of the Kircherian Museum at Rome.

[182] "Both belief and non-belief are dangerous. Hippolitus died because his stepmother was believed. Troy fell because Cassandra was not believed. Therefore the truth should be investigated long before foolish opinion can properly judge." (Prove = probe?).

[183] Jacobus Grandamicus (Jacques Grandami) was born at Nantes in 1588 and died at Paris in 1672. He was professor of theology and philosophy in the Jesuit colleges at Rennes, Tours, Rouen, and other places. He wrote several works on astronomy.

[184] "And I, if I be lifted up from the earth, will draw all men unto me." John xii. 32.

[185] Andrea Argoli (1568-1657) wrote a number of works on astronomy, and computed ephemerides from 1621 to 1700.

[186] So in the original edition of the Budget. It is Johannem Pellum in the original title. John Pell (1610 or 1611-1685) studied at Cambridge and Oxford, and was professor of mathematics at Amsterdam (1643-46) and Breda (1646-52). He left many manuscripts but published little. His name attaches by accident to an interesting equation recently studied with care by Dr. E. E. Whitford (New York, 1912).

[187] Christianus Longomontanus (Christen Longberg or Lumborg) was born in 1569 at Longberg, Jutland, and died in 1647 at Copenhagen. He was an assistant of Tycho Brahe and accepted the diurnal while denying the orbital motion of the earth. His Cyclometria e lunulis reciproce demonstrata appeared in 1612 under the name of Christen Severin, the latter being his family name. He wrote several other works on the quadrature problem, and some treatises on astronomy.

[188] The names are really pretty well known. Giles Persone de Roberval was born at Roberval near Beauvais in 1602, and died at Paris in 1675. He was professor of philosophy at the Collège Gervais at Paris, and later at the Collège Royal. He claimed to have discovered the theory of indivisibles before Cavalieri, and his work is set forth in his Traité des indivisibles which appeared posthumously in 1693.

Hobbes (1588-1679), the political and social philosopher, lived a good part of his time (1610-41) in France where he was tutor to several young noblemen, including the Cavendishes. His Leviathan (1651) is said to have influenced Spinoza, Leibnitz, and Rousseau. His Quadratura circuli, cubatio sphaerae, duplicatio cubi ... (London, 1669), Rosetum geometricum ... (London, 1671), and Lux Mathematica, censura doctrinae Wallisianae contra Rosetum Hobbesii (London, 1674) are entirely forgotten to-day. (See a further note, infra.)

Pierre de Carcavi, a native of Lyons, died at Paris in 1684. He was a member of parliament, royal librarian, and member of the Académie des Sciences. His attempt to prove the impossibility of the quadrature appeared in 1645. He was a frequent correspondent of Descartes.

Cavendish (1591-1654) was Sir (not Lord) Charles. He was, like De Morgan himself, a bibliophile in the domain of mathematics. His life was one of struggle, his term as member of parliament under Charles I being followed by gallant service in the royal army. After the war he sought refuge on the continent where he met most of the mathematicians of his day. He left a number of manuscripts on mathematics, which his widow promptly disposed of for waste paper. If De Morgan's manuscripts had been so treated we should not have had his revision of his Budget of Paradoxes.

Marin Mersenne (1588-1648), a minorite, living in the cloisters at Nevers and Paris, was one of the greatest Franciscan scholars. He edited Euclid, Apollonius, Archimedes, Theodosius, and Menelaus (Paris, 1626), translated the Mechanics of Galileo into French (1634), wrote Harmonicorum Libri XII (1636), and Cogitata physico-mathematica (1644), and taught theology and philosophy at Nevers.

Johann Adolph Tasse (Tassius) was born in 1585 and died at Hamburg in 1654. He was professor of mathematics in the Gymnasium at Hamburg, and wrote numerous works on astronomy, chronology, statics, and elementary mathematics.

Johann Ludwig, Baron von Wolzogen, seems to have been one of the early unitarians, called Fratres Polonorum because they took refuge in Poland.

Some of his works appear in the Bibliotheca Fratrum Polonorum (Amsterdam, 1656). I find no one by the name who was contributing to mathematics at this time.

Descartes is too well known to need mention in this connection.

Bonaventura Cavalieri (1598-1647) was a Jesuit, a pupil of Galileo, and professor of mathematics at Bologna. His greatest work, Geometria indivisibilibus continuorum nova quadam ratione promota, in which he makes a noteworthy step towards the calculus, appeared in 1635.

Jacob (Jacques) Golius was born at the Hague in 1596 and died at Leyden in 1667. His travels in Morocco and Asia Minor (1622-1629) gave him such knowledge of Arabic that he became professor of that language at Leyden. After Snell's death he became professor of mathematics there. He translated Arabic works on mathematics and astronomy into Latin.

[189] It would be interesting to follow up these rumors, beginning perhaps with the tomb of Archimedes. The Ludolph van Ceulen story is very likely a myth. The one about Fagnano may be such. The Bernoulli tomb does have the spiral, however (such as it is), as any one may see in the cloisters at Basel to-day.

[190] Collins (1625-1683) was secretary of the Royal Society, and was "a kind of register of all new improvements in mathematics." His office brought him into correspondence with all of the English scientists, and he was influential in the publication of various important works, including Branker's translation of the algebra by Rhonius, with notes by Pell, which was the first work to contain the present English-American symbol of division. He also helped in the publication of editions of Archimedes and Apollonius, of Kersey's Algebra, and of the works of Wallis. His profession was that of accountant and civil engineer, and he wrote three unimportant works on mathematics (one published posthumously, and the others in 1652 and 1658).

Heinrich Christian Schumacher (1780-1850) was professor of astronomy at Copenhagen and director of the observatory at Altona. His translation of Carnot's Géométrie de position (1807) brought him into personal relations with

Gauss, and the friendship was helpful to Schumacher. He was a member of many learned societies and had a large circle of acquaintances. He published numerous monographs and works on astronomy.

Gassendi (1592-1655) might well have been included by De Morgan in the group, since he knew and was a friend of most of the important mathematicians of his day. Like Mersenne, he was a minorite, but he was a friend of Galileo and Kepler, and wrote a work under the title Institutio astronomica, juxta hypotheses Copernici, Tychonis-Brahaei et Ptolemaei (1645). He taught philosophy at Aix, and was later professor of mathematics at the College Royal at Paris.

Burnet is the Bishop Gilbert Burnet (1643-1715) who was so strongly anti-Romanistic that he left England during the reign of James II and joined the ranks of the Prince of Orange. William made him bishop of Salisbury.

[191] There is some substantial basis for De Morgan's doubts as to the connection of that mirandula of his age, Sir Kenelm Digby (1603-1665), with the famous poudre de sympathie. It is true that he was just the one to prepare such a powder. A dilletante in everything,--learning, war, diplomacy, religion, letters, and science--he was the one to exploit a fraud of this nature. He was an astrologer, an alchemist, and a fabricator of tales, and well did Henry Stubbes characterize him as "the very Pliny of our age for lying." He first speaks of the powder in a lecture given at Montpellier in 1658, and in the same year he published the address at Paris under the title: Discours fait en une célèbre assemblée par le chevalier Digby .... touchant la guérison de playes par la poudre de sympathie. The London edition referred to by De Morgan also came out in 1658, and several editions followed it in England, France and Germany. But Nathaniel Highmore in his History of Generation (1651) referred to the concoction as "Talbot's Powder" some years before Digby took it up. The basis seems to have been vitriol, and it was claimed that it would heal a wound by simply being applied to a bandage taken from it.

[192] This work by Thomas Birch (1705-1766) came out in 1756-57. Birch was a voluminous writer on English history. He was a friend of Dr. Johnson and of Walpole, and he wrote a life of Robert Boyle.

[193] We know so much about John Evelyn (1620-1706) through the diary which he began at the age of eleven, that we forget his works on navigation and architecture.

[194] I suppose this was the seventh Earl of Shrewsbury (1553-1616).

[195] This is interesting in view of the modern aseptic practice of surgery and the antiseptic treatment of wounds inaugurated by the late Lord Lister.

[196] Perhaps De Morgan had not heard the bon mot of Dr. Holmes: "I firmly believe that if the whole materia medica could be sunk to the bottom of the sea, it would be all the better for mankind and all the worse for the fishes."

[197] The full title is worth giving, because it shows the mathematical interests of Hobbes, and the nature of the six dialogues: Examinatio et emendatio mathematicae hodiernae qualis explicatur in libris Johannis Wallisii geometriae professoris Saviliani in Academia Oxoniensi: distributa in sex dialogos (1. De mathematicae origine ...; 2. De principiis traditis ab Euclide; 3. De demonstratione operationum arithmeticarum ...; 4. De rationibus; 5. De angula contactus, de sectionibus coni, et arithmetica infinitorum; 6. Dimensio circuli tribus methodis demonstrata ... item cycloidis verae descriptio et proprietates aliquot.) Londini, 1660 (not 1666). For a full discussion of the controversy over the circle, see George Croom Robertson's biography of Hobbes in the eleventh edition of the Encyclopaedia Britannica.

[198] This is his Animadversions upon Mr. Hobbes' late book De principiis et ratiocinatione geometrarum, 1666, or his Hobbianae quadraturae circuli, cubationis sphaerae et duplicationis cubi confutatio, also of 1669.

[199] This is the work of 1669 referred to above.

[200] Gregoire de St. Vincent (1584-1667) published his Opus geometricum quadraturae circuli et sectionum coni at Antwerp in 1647.

[201] This appears in J. Scaligeri cyclometrica elementa duo, Lugduni Batav., 1594.

[202] Adriaen van Roomen (1561-1615) gave the value of [pi] to sixteen decimal places in his Ideae mathematicae pars prima (1593), and wrote his In Archimedis circuli dimensionem expositio & analysis in 1597.

[203] Kästner. See note 30 on page 43.

[204] Bentley (1662-1742) might have done it, for as the head of Trinity College, Cambridge, and a follower of Newton, he knew some mathematics. Erasmus (1466-1536) lived a little too early to attempt it, although his brilliant satire might have been used to good advantage against those who did try.

[205] "In grammar, to give the winds to the ships and to give the ships to the winds mean the same thing. But in geometry it is one thing to assume the circle BCD not greater than thirty-six segments BCDF, and another (to assume) the thirty-six segments BCDF not greater than the circle. The one assumption is true, the other false."

[206] The Greek scholar (1559-1614) who edited a Greek and Latin edition of Aristotle in 1590.

[207] Jacques Auguste de Thou (1553-1617), the historian and statesman.

[208] "To value Scaliger higher even when wrong, than the multitude when right."

[209] "I would rather err with Scaliger than be right with Clavius."

[210] "The perimeter of the dodecagon to be inscribed in a circle is greater than the perimeter of the circle. And the more sides a polygon to be inscribed in a circle successively has, so much the greater will the perimeter of the polygon be than the perimeter of the circle."

[211] De Morgan took, perhaps, the more delight in speaking thus of Sir William Hamilton (1788-1856) because of a spirited controversy that they had in 1847 over the theory of logic. Possibly, too, Sir William's low opinion of mathematics had its influence.

[212] Edwards (1699-1757) wrote The canons of criticism (1747) in which he gave a scathing burlesque on Warburton's Shakespeare. It went through six editions.

[213] Antoine Teissier (born in 1632) published his Eloges des hommes savants, tirés de l'histoire de M. de Thou in 1683.

[214] "He boasted without reason of having found the quadrature of the circle. The glory of this admirable discovery was reserved for Joseph Scaliger, as Scévole de St. Marthe has written."

[215] Natural and political observations mentioned in the following Index, and made upon the Bills of Mortality.... With reference to the government, religion, trade, growth, ayre, and diseases of the said city. London, 1662, 4to. The book went through several editions.

[216] Ne sutor ultra crepidam, "Let the cobbler stick to his last," as we now say.

[217] The author (1632-1695) of the Historia et Antiquitates Universitatis Oxoniensis (1674). See note 163, page 98.

[218] The mathematical guild owes Samuel Pepys (1633-1703) for something besides his famous diary (1659-1669). Not only was he president of the Royal Society (1684), but he was interested in establishing Sir William Boreman's mathematical school at Greenwich.

[219] John Graunt (1620-1674) was a draper by trade, and was a member of the Common Council of London until he lost office by turning Romanist.

Although a shopkeeper, he was elected to the Royal Society on the special recommendation of Charles II. Petty edited the fifth edition of his work, adding much to its size and value, and this may be the basis of Burnet's account of the authorship.

[220] Petty (1623-1687) was a mathematician and economist, and a friend of Pell and Sir Charles Cavendish. His survey of Ireland, made for Cromwell, was one of the first to be made on a large scale in a scientific manner. He was one of the founders of the Royal Society.

[221] The story probably arose from Graunt's recent conversion to the Roman Catholic faith.

[222] He was born in 1627 and died in 1704. He published a series of ephemerides, beginning in 1659. He was imprisoned in 1679, at the time of the "Popish Plot," and again for treason in 1690. His important astrological works are the Animal Cornatum, or the Horn'd Beast (1654) and The Nativity of the late King Charls (1659).

[223] Isaac D'Israeli (1766-1848), in his Curiosities of Literature (1791), speaking of Lilly, says: "I shall observe of this egregious astronomer, that there is in this work, so much artless narrative, and at the same time so much palpable imposture, that it is difficult to know when he is speaking what he really believes to be the truth." He goes on to say that Lilly relates that "those adepts whose characters he has drawn were the lowest miscreants of the town. Most of them had taken the air in the pillory, and others had conjured themselves up to the gallows. This seems a true statement of facts."

[224] It is difficult to estimate William Lilly (1602-1681) fairly. His Merlini Anglici ephemeris, issued annually from 1642 to 1681, brought him a great deal of money. Sir George Wharton (1617-1681) also published an almanac annually from 1641 to 1666. He tried to expose John Booker (1603-1677) by a work entitled Mercurio-Coelicio-Mastix; or, an Anti-caveat to all such, as have (heretofore) had the misfortune to be Cheated and Deluded by that Grand and Traiterous Impostor of this Rebellious Age, John Booker, 1644. Booker was "licenser of mathematical [astrological] publications," and as such he had quarrels with Lilly, Wharton, and others.

[225] See note 171 on page 100.

[226] This is the Ars Signorum, vulgo character universalis et lingua philosophica, that appeared at London in 1661, 8vo. George Dalgarno anticipated modern methods in the teaching of the deaf and dumb.

[227] See note 200 on page 110.

[228] If the hyperbola is referred to the asymptotes as axes, the area between two ordinates (x = a, x = b) is the difference of the logarithms of a and b to the base e. E.g., in the case of the hyperbola xy = 1, the area between x = a and x = 1 is log a.

[229] "On ne peut lui refuser la justice de remarquer que personne avant lui ne s'est porté dans cette recherche avec autant de génie, & même, si nous en exceptons son objet principal, avec autant de succès." Quadrature du Cercle, p. 66.

[230] The title proceeds: Seu duae mediae proportionales inter extremas datas per circulum et per infinitas hyperbolas, vel ellipses et per quamlibet exhibitae.... René Francois, Baron de Sluse (1622-1685) was canon and chancellor of Liège, and a member of the Royal Society. He also published a work on tangents (1672). The word mesolabium is from the Greek [Greek: mesolabion] or [Greek: mesolabon], an instrument invented by Eratosthenes for finding two mean proportionals.

[231] The full title has some interest: Vera circuli et hyperbolae quadratura cui accedit geometriae pars universalis inserviens quantitatum curvarum transmutationi et mensurae. Authore Jacobo Gregorio Abredonensi Scoto ... Patavii, 1667. That is, James Gregory (1638-1675) of Aberdeen (he was really born near but not in the city), a good Scot, was publishing his work down in Padua. The reason was that he had been studying in Italy, and that this was a product of his youth. He had already (1663) published his Optica promota, and it is not remarkable that his brilliancy brought him a wide circle of friends on the continent and the offer of a pension from Louis XIV. He became professor of mathematics at St

Andrews and later at Edinburgh, and invented the first successful reflecting telescope. The distinctive feature of his Vera quadratura is his use of an infinite converging series, a plan that Archimedes used with the parabola.

[232] Jean de Beaulieu wrote several works on mathematics, including La lumière de l'arithmétique (n.d.), La lumière des mathématiques (1673), Nouvelle invention d'arithmétique (1677), and some mathematical tables.

[233] A just estimate. There were several works published by Gérard Desargues (1593-1661), of which the greatest was the Brouillon Proiect (Paris, 1639). There is an excellent edition of the Oeuvres de Desargues by M. Poudra, Paris, 1864.

[234] "A certain M. de Beaugrand, a mathematician, very badly treated by Descartes, and, as it appears, rightly so."

[235] This is a very old approximation for [pi]. One of the latest pretended geometric proofs resulting in this value appeared in New York in 1910, entitled Quadrimetry (privately printed).

[236] "Copernicus, a German, made himself no less illustrious by his learned writings; and we might say of him that he stood alone and unique in the strength of his problems, if his excessive presumption had not led him to set forth in this science a proposition so absurd that it is contrary to faith and reason, namely that the circumference of a circle is fixed and immovable while the center is movable: on which geometrical principle he has declared in his astrological treatise that the sun is fixed and the earth is in motion."

[237] So in the original.

[238] Franciscus Maurolycus (1494-1575) was really the best mathematician produced by Sicily for a long period. He made Latin translations of Theodosius, Menelaus, Euclid, Apollonius, and Archimedes, and wrote on cosmography and other mathematical subjects.

[239] "Nicolaus Copernicus is also tolerated who asserted that the sun is fixed and that the earth whirls about it; and he rather deserves a whip or a lash than a reproof."

[240] "Algebra is the curious science of scholars, and particularly for a general of an army, or a captain, in order quickly to draw up an army in battle array and to number the musketeers and pikemen who compose it, without the figures of arithmetic. This science has five special figures of this kind: P means plus in commerce and pikemen in the army; M means minus, and musketeer in the art of war;... R signifies root in the measurement of a cube, and rank in the army; Q means square (French quarè, as then spelled) in both cases; C means cube in mensuration, and cavalry in arranging batallions and squadrons. As for the operations of this science, they are as follows: to add a plus and a plus, the sum will be plus; to add minus with plus, take the less from the greater and the remainder will be the sum required or the number to be found. I say this only in passing, for the benefit of those who are wholly ignorant of it."

[241] He refers to the Joannis de Beaugrand ... Geostatice, seu de vario pondere gravium secundum varia a terrae (centro) intervalla dissertatio mathematica, Paris, 1636. Pascal relates that de Beaugrand sent all of Roberval's theorems on the cycloid and Fermat's on maxima and minima to Galileo in 1638, pretending that they were his own.

[242] More (1614-1687) was a theologian, a fellow of Christ College, Cambridge, and a Christian Platonist.

[243] Matthew Hale (1609-1676) the famous jurist, wrote a number of tracts on scientific, moral, and religious subjects. These were collected and published in 1805.

[244] They might have been attributed to many a worse man than Dr. Hales (1677-1761), who was a member of the Royal Society and of the Paris Academy, and whose scheme for the ventilation of prisons reduced the mortality at the Savoy prison from one hundred to only four a year. The book to which reference is made is Vegetable Staticks or an Account of some statical experiments on the sap in Vegetables, 1727.

[245] Pleas of the Crown; or a Methodical Summary of the Principal Matters relating to the subject, 1678.

[246] Thomae Streete Astronomia Carolina, a new theory of the celestial motions, 1661. It also appeared at Nuremberg in 1705, and at London in 1710 and 1716 (Halley's editions). He wrote other works on astronomy.

[247] This was the Sir Thomas Street (1626-1696) who passed sentence of death on a Roman Catholic priest for saying mass. The priest was reprieved by the king, but in the light of the present day one would think the justice more in need of pardon. He took part in the trial of the Rye House Conspirators in 1683.

[248] Edmund Halley (1656-1742), who succeeded Wallis (1703) as Savilian professor of mathematics at Oxford, and Flamsteed (1720) as head of the Greenwich observatory. It is of interest to note that he was instrumental in getting Newton's Principia printed.

[249] Shepherd (born in 1760) was one of the most famous lawyers of his day. He was knighted in 1814 and became Attorney General in 1817.

[250] This was William Hone (1780-1842), a book publisher, who wrote satires against the government, and who was tried three times because of his parodies on the catechism, creed, and litany (illustrated by Cruikshank). He was acquitted on all of the charges.

[251] Valentinus was a Benedictine monk and was still living at Erfurt in 1413. His Currus triumphalis antimonii appeared in 1624. Synesius was Bishop of Ptolemaide, who died about 430. His works were printed at Paris in 1605. Theodor Kirckring (1640-1693) was a fellow-student of Spinoza's. Besides the commentary on Valentine he left several works on anatomy.

His commentary appeared at Amsterdam in 1671. There were several editions of the Chariot.

[252] The chief difficulty with this curious "monk-bane" etymology is its absurdity. The real origin of the word has given etymologists a good deal of trouble.

[253] Robert Boyle (1627-1691), son of "the Great Earl" (of Cork). Perhaps his best-known discovery is the law concerning the volume of gases.

[254] The real name of Eirenaeus Philalethes (born in 1622) is unknown. It may have been Childe. He claimed to have discovered the philosopher's stone in 1645. His tract in this work is The Secret of the Immortal Liquor Alkahest or Ignis-Aqua. See note 260, infra.

[255] Johann Baptist van Helmont, Herr von Merode, Royenborg etc. (1577-1644). His chemical discoveries appeared in his Ortus medicinae (1648), which went through many editions.

[256] De Morgan should have written up Francis Anthony (1550-1623), whose Panacea aurea sive tractatus duo de auro potabili (Hamburg, 1619) described a panacea that he gave for every ill. He was repeatedly imprisoned for practicing medicine without a license from the Royal College of Physicians.

[257] Bernardus Trevisanus (1406-1490), who traveled even through Barbary, Egypt, Palestine, and Persia in search of the philosopher's stone. He wrote several works on alchemy,--De Chemica (1567), De Chemico Miraculo (1583), Traité de la nature de l'oeuf des philosophes (1659), etc., all published long after his death.

[258] George Ripley (1415-1490) was an Augustinian monk, later a chamberlain of Innocent VIII, and still later a Carmelite monk. His Liber de mercuris philosophico and other tracts first appeared in Opuscula quaedam chymica (Frankfort, 1614).

[259] Besides the Opus majus, and other of the better known works of this celebrated Franciscan (1214-1294), there are numerous tracts on alchemy that appeared in the Thesaurus chymicus (Frankfort, 1603).

[260] George Starkey (1606-1665 or 1666) has special interest for American readers. He seems to have been born in the Bermudas and to have obtained the bachelor's degree in England. He then went to America and in 1646 obtained the master's degree at Harvard, apparently under the name of Stirk. He met Eirenaeus Philalethes (see note 254 above) in America and learned alchemy from him. Returning to England, he sold quack medicines there, and died in 1666 from the plague after dissecting a patient who had died of the disease. Among his works was the Liquor Alcahest, or a Discourse of that Immortal Dissolvent of Paracelsus and Helmont, which appeared (1675) some nine years after his death.

[261] Platt (1552-1611) was the son of a London brewer. Although he left a manuscript on alchemy, and wrote a book entitled Delights for Ladies to adorne their Persons (1607), he was knighted for some serious work on the chemistry of agriculture, fertilizing, brewing, and the preserving of foods, published in The Jewell House of Art and Nature (1594).

[262] "Those who wish to call a man a liar and deceiver speak of him a writer of almanacs; but those who (would call him) a scoundrel and an imposter (speak of him as) a chemist."

[263] "Trust your barque to the winds but not your body to a chemist; any breeze is safer than the faith of a chemist."

[264] Probably the Jesuit, Père Claude François Menestrier (1631-1705), a well known historian.

[265] The author was Christopher Nesse (1621-1705), a belligerent Calvinist, who wrote many controversial works and succeeded in getting excommunicated four times. One of his most virulent works was A Protestant Antidote against the Poison of Popery.

[266] John Case (c. 1660-1700) was a famous astrologer and physician. He succeeded to Lilly's practice in London. In a darkened room, wherein he kept an array of mystical apparatus, he pretended to show the credulous the ghosts of their departed relatives. Besides his astrological works he wrote one serious treatise, the Compendium Anatomicum nova methodo institutum (1695), in which he defends Harvey's theories of embryology.

[267] Marcelis (1636-after 1714) was a soap maker of Amsterdam. It is to be hoped that he made better soap than values of [pi].

[268] John Craig (died in 1731) was a Scotchman, but most of his life was spent at Cambridge reading and writing on mathematics. He endeavored to introduce the Leibnitz differential calculus into England. His mathematical works include the Methodus Figurarum ... Quadraturas determinandi (1685), Tractatus ... de Figurarum Curvilinearum Quadraturis et locis Geometricis (1693), and De Calculo Fluentium libri duo (1718).

[269] As is well known, this subject owes much to the Bernoullis. Craig's works on the calculus brought him into controversy with them. He also wrote on other subjects in which they were interested, as in his memoir On the Curve of the quickest descent (1700), On the Solid of least resistance (1700), and the Solution of Bernoulli's problem on Curves (1704).

[270] This is Samuel Lee (1783-1852), the young prodigy in languages. He was apprenticed to a carpenter at twelve and learned Greek while working at the trade. Before he was twenty-five he knew Hebrew, Chaldee, Syriac, Samaritan, Persian, and Hindustani. He later became Regius professor of Hebrew at Cambridge.

[271] "Where the devil, Master Ludovico, did you pick up such a collection?"

[272] Lord William Brounker (c. 1620-1684), the first president of the Royal Society, is best known in mathematics for his contributions to continued fractions.

[273] Horace Walpole (1717-1797) published his Catalogue of the Royal and Noble Authors of England in 1758. Since his time a number of worthy names in the domain of science in general and of mathematics in particular might be added from the peerage of England.

[274] It was written by Charles Hayes (1678-1760), a mathematician and scholar of no mean attainments. He travelled extensively, and was deputy governor of the Royal African Company. His Treatise on Fluxions (London, 1704) was the first work in English to explain Newton's calculus. He wrote a work entitled The Moon (1723) to prove that our satellite shines by its own as well as by reflected light. His Chronographia Asiatica & Aegyptica (1758) gives the results of his travels.

[275] Publick in the original.

[276] Whiston (1667-1752) succeeded Newton as Lucasian professor of mathematics at Cambridge. In 1710 he turned Arian and was expelled from the university. His work on Primitive Christianity appeared the following year. He wrote many works on astronomy and religion.

[277] Ditton (1675-1715) was, on Newton's recommendation, made Head of the mathematical school at Christ's Hospital, London. He wrote a work on fluxions (1706). His idea for finding longitude at sea was to place stations in the Atlantic to fire off bombs at regular intervals, the time between the sound and the flash giving the distance. He also corresponded with Huyghens concerning the use of chronometers for the purpose.

[278] This was John Arbuthnot (c. 1658-1735), the mathematician, physician and wit. He was intimate with Pope and Swift, and was Royal physician to Queen Anne. Besides various satires he published a translation of Huyghens's work on probabilities (1692) and a well-known treatise on ancient coins, weights, and measures (1727).

[279] Greene (1678-1730) was a very eccentric individual and was generally ridiculed by his contemporaries. In his will he directed that his body be dissected and his skeleton hung in the library of King's College, Cambridge. Unfortunately for his fame, this wish was never carried out.

[280] This was the historian, Robert Sanderson (1660-1741), who spent most of his life at Cambridge.

[281] I presume this was William Jones (1675-1749) the friend of Newton and Halley, vice-president of the Royal Society, in whose Synopsis Palmariorum Matheseos (1706) the symbol [pi] is first used for the circle ratio.

[282] This was the Geometrica solidorum, sive materiae, seu de varia compositione, progressione, rationeque velocitatum, Cambridge, 1712. The work was parodied in A Taste of Philosophical Fanaticism ... by a gentleman of the University of Gratz.

[283] The antiquary and scientist (1690-1754), president of the Royal Society, member of the Académie, friend of Newton, and authority on numismatics.

[284] She was Catherine Barton, Newton's step-niece. She married John Conduitt, master of the mint, who collected materials for a life of Newton.

A propos of Mrs. Conduitt's life of her illustrious uncle, Sir George Greenhill tells a very good story on Poincaré, the well-known French mathematician. At an address given by the latter at the International Congress of Mathematicians held in Rome in 1908 he spoke of the story of Newton and the apple as a mere fable. After the address Sir George asked him why he had done so, saying that the story was first published by Voltaire, who had heard it from Newton's niece, Mrs. Conduitt. Poincaré looked blank and said, "Newton, et la nièce de Newton, et Voltaire,--non! je ne vous comprends pas!" He had thought Sir George meant Professor Volterra of Rome, whose name in French is Voltaire, and who could not possibly have known a niece of Newton without bridging a century or so.

[285] This was the Edmund Turnor (1755-1829) who wrote the Collections for the Town and Soke of Grantham, containing authentic Memoirs of Sir Isaac Newton, from Lord Portsmouth's Manuscripts, London, 1806.

[286] It may be recalled to mind that Sir David (1781-1868) wrote a life of Newton (1855).

[287] "They are in the country. We rejoice." [288] "I am here, chatterbox, suck!"

[289] "I have been graduated! I decline!"

[290] Giovanni Castiglioni (Castillon, Castiglione), was born at Castiglione, in Tuscany, in 1708, and died at Berlin in 1791. He was professor of mathematics at Utrecht and at Berlin. He wrote on De Moivre's equations (1762), Cardan's rule (1783), and Euclid's treatment of parallels (1788-89).

[291] This was the Isaaci Newtoni, equitis aurati, opuscula mathematica, philosophica et philologica, Lausannae & Genevae, 1744.

[292] At London, 4to.
[293] "All the English attribute it to Newton."

[294] Stephen Peter Rigaud (1774-1839), Savilian professor of geometry at Oxford (1810-27) and later professor of astronomy and head of the Radcliffe Observatory. He wrote An historical Essay on first publication of Sir Isaac Newton's Principia, Oxford, 1838, and a two-volume work entitled Correspondence of Scientific Men of the 17th Century, 1841.

[295] It is no longer considered by scholars as the work of Newton.

[296] J. Edleston, the author of the Correspondence of Sir Isaac Newton and Professor Cotes, London, 1850.

[297] Palmer (1601-1647) was Master of Queen's College, Cambridge, a Puritan but not a separatist. His work, The Characters of a believing Christian, in Paradoxes and seeming contradictions, appeared in 1645.

[298] Grosart (1827-1899) was a Presbyterian clergyman. He was a great bibliophile, and issued numerous reprints of rare books.

[299] This was the year after Palmer's death. The title was, The Remaines of ... Francis Lord Verulam....; being Essays and severall Letters to severall great personages, and other pieces of various and high concernment not heretofore published, London, 1648, 4to.

[300] Shaw (1694-1763) was physician extraordinary to George II. He wrote on chemistry and medicine, and his edition of the Philosophical Works of Francis Bacon appeared at London in 1733.

[301] John Locke (1632-1704), the philosopher. This particular work appeared in 1695. There was an edition in 1834 (vol. 25 of the Sacred Classics) and one in 1836 (vol. 2 of the Christian Library).

[302] I use the word Socinian because it was so much used in Locke's time: it is used in our own day by the small fry, the unlearned clergy and their immediate followers, as a term of reproach for all Unitarians. I suspect they have a kind of liking for the word; it sounds like so sinful. The learned clergy and the higher laity know better: they know that the bulk of the modern Unitarians go farther than Socinus, and are not correctly named as his followers. The Unitarians themselves neither desire nor deserve a name which puts them one point nearer to orthodoxy than they put themselves.

That point is the doctrine that direct prayer to Jesus Christ is lawful and desirable: this Socinus held, and the modern Unitarians do not hold.

Socinus, in treating the subject in his own Institutio, an imperfect catechism which he left, lays much more stress on John xiv. 13 than on xv. 16 and xvi. 23. He is not disinclined to think that Patrem should be in the first citation, where some put it; but he says that to ask the Father in the name of the Son is nothing but praying to the Son in prayer to the Father. He labors the point with obvious wish to secure a conclusive sanction. In the Racovian Catechism, of which Faustus Socinus probably drew the first sketch, a clearer light is arrived at. The translation says: "But wherein consists the divine honor due to Christ? In adoration likewise and invocation. For we ought at all times to adore Christ, and may in our necessities address our prayers to him as often as we please; and there are many reasons to induce us to do this freely." There are some who like accuracy, even in aspersion--A. De M.

Socinus, or Fausto Paolo Sozzini (1539-1604), was an antitrinitarian who believed in prayer and homage to Christ. Leaving Italy after his views became known, he repaired to Basel, but his opinions were too extreme even for the Calvinists. He then tried Transylvania, attempting to convert to his views the antitrinitarian Bishop Dávid. The only result of his efforts was the imprisonment of Dávid and his own flight to Poland, in which country he spent the rest of his life (1579-1604). His complete works appeared first at Amsterdam in 1668, in the Bibliotheca Fratres Polonorum. The Racovian Catechism (1605) appeared after his death, but it seems to have been planned by him.

[303] "As much of faith as is necessary to salvation is contained in this article, Jesus is the Christ."

[304] Edwards (1637-1716) was a Cambridge fellow, strongly Calvinistic. He published many theological works, attacking the Arminians and Socinians. Locke and Whiston were special objects of attack.

[305] Sir I. Newton's views on points of Trinitarian Doctrine; his Articles of Faith, and the General Coincidence of his Opinions with those of J. Locke; a Selection of Authorities, with Observations, London, 1856.

[306] A Confession of the Faith, Bristol, 1752, 8vo.

[307] This was really very strange, because Laud (1573-1644), while he was Archbishop of Canterbury, forced a good deal of High Church ritual on the Puritan clergy, and even wished to compel the use of a prayer book in Scotland. It was this intolerance that led to his impeachment and execution.

[308] The name is Jonchère. He was a man of some merit, proposing (1718) an important canal in Burgundy, and publishing a work on the Découverte des longitudes estimées généralement impossible à trouver, 1734 (or 1735).

[309] Locke invented a kind of an instrument for finding longitude, and it is described in the appendix, but I can find nothing about the man. There was published some years later (London, 1751) another work of his, A new Problem to discover the longitude at sea.

[310] Baxter, concerning whom I know merely that he was a schoolmaster, starts with the assumption of this value, and deduces from it some fourteen properties relating to the circle.

[311] John, who died in 1780, was a well-known character in his way. He was a bookseller on Fleet Street, and his shop was a general rendezvous for the literary men of his time. He wrote the Memoirs of the Life and Writings of Mr. William Whiston (1749, with another edition in 1753). He was one of the first to issue regular catalogues of books with prices affixed.

[312] The name appears both as Hulls and as Hull. He was born in Gloucestershire in 1699. In 1754 he published The Art of Measuring made Easy by the help of a new Sliding Scale.

[313] Thomas Newcomen (1663-1729) invented the first practical steam engine about 1710. It was of about five and a half horse power, and was used for pumping water from coal mines. Savery had described such an engine in 1702, but Newcomen improved upon it and made it practical.

[314] The well-known benefactor of art (1787-1863). [315] The tract was again reprinted in 1860.

[316] Hulls made his experiment on the Avon, at Evesham, in 1737, having patented his machine in 1736. He had a Newcomen engine connected with six paddles. This was placed in the front of a small tow boat. The experiment was a failure.

[317] William Symington (1763-1831). In 1786 he constructed a working model of a steam road carriage. The machinery was applied to a small boat in 1788, and with such success as to be tried on a larger boat in 1789. The machinery was clumsy, however, and in 1801 he took out a new patent for the style of engine still used on paddle wheel steamers.

This engine was successfully used in 1802, on the Charlotte Dundas. Fulton (1765-1815) was on board, and so impressed Robert Livingston with the idea that the latter furnished the money to build the Clermont (1807), the beginning of successful river navigation.

[318] Louis Bertrand Castel (1688-1757), most of whose life was spent in trying to perfect his Clavecin oculaire, an instrument on the order of the harpsichord, intended to produce melodies and harmonies of color. He also wrote L'Optique des couleurs (1740) and Sur le fond de la Musique (1754).

[319] Dr. Robinson (1680-1754) was professor of physic at Trinity College, Dublin, and three times president of King and Queen's College of Physicians. In his Treatise on the Animal Economy (1732-3, with a third edition in 1738) he anticipated the discoveries of Lavoisier and Priestley on the nature of oxygen.

[320] There was another edition, published at London in 1747, 8vo.

[321] The author seems to have shot his only bolt in this work. I can find nothing about him.

[322] Quod Deus sit, mundusque ab ipso creatus fuerit in tempore, ejusque providentia gubernetur. Selecta aliquot theoremata adversos atheos, etc., Paris, 1635, 4to.

[323] The British Museum Catalogue mentions a copy of 1740, but this is possibly a misprint.

[324] This was Johann II (1710-1790), son of Johann I, who succeeded his father as professor of mathematics at Basel.

[325] Samuel Koenig (1712-1757), who studied under Johann Bernoulli I. He became professor of mathematics at Franeker (1747) and professor of philosophy at the Hague (1749).

[326] "In accordance with the hypotheses laid down in this memoir it is so evident that t must = 34, y = 1, and z = 1, that there is no need of proof or authority for it to be recognized by every one."

[327] "I subscribe to the judgment of Mr. Bernoulli as a result of these hypotheses."

[328] "It clearly appears from my present analysis and demonstration that they have already recognized and perfectly agreed to the fact that the quadrature of the circle is mathematically demonstrated."

[329] Dr. Knight (died in 1772) made some worthy contributions to the literature of the mariner's compass. As De Morgan states, he was librarian of the British Museum.

[330] Sir Anthony Panizzi (1797-1879) fled from Italy under sentence of death (1822). He became assistant (1831) and chief (1856) librarian of the British Museum, and was knighted in 1869. He began the catalogue of printed books of the Museum.

[331] Wright (1711-1786) was a physicist. He was offered the professorship of mathematics at the Imperial Academy of St. Petersburg but declined to accept it. This work is devoted chiefly to the theory of the Milky Way, the via lactea as he calls it after the manner of the older writers.

[332] Troughton (1753-1835) was one of the world's greatest instrument makers. He was apprenticed to his brother John, and the two succeeded (1770) Wright and Cole in Fleet Street. Airy called his method of graduating circles the greatest improvement ever made in instrument making. He constructed (1800) the first modern transit circle, and his instruments were used in many of the chief observatories of the world.

[333] William Simms (1793-1860) was taken into partnership by Troughton (1826) after the death of the latter's brother. The firm manufactured some well-known instruments.

[334] This was George Horne (1730-1792), fellow of Magdalen College, Oxford, vice-Chancellor of the University (1776), Dean of Canterbury (1781), and Bishop of Norwich (1790). He was a great satirist, but most of his pamphlets against men like Adam Smith, Swedenborg, and Hume, were anonymous, as in the case of this one against Newton. He was so liberal in his attitude towards the Methodists that he would not have John Wesley forbidden to preach in his diocese. He was twenty-one when this tract appeared.

[335] Martin (1704-1782) was by no means "old Benjamin Martin" when Horne wrote this pamphlet in 1749. In fact he was then only forty-five. He was a physicist and a well-known writer on scientific instruments. He also wrote Philosophia Britannica or a new and comprehensive system of the Newtonian Philosophy (1759).

[336] Jean Théophile Desaguliers, or Des Aguliers (1683-1744) was the son of a Protestant who left France after the revocation of the Edict of Nantes. He became professor of physics at Oxford, and afterwards gave lectures in London. Later he became chaplain to the Prince of Wales. He published several works on physics.

[337] Charles Hutton (1737-1823), professor of mathematics at Woolwich (1772-1807). His Mathematical Tables (1785) and Mathematical and Philosophical Dictionary (1795-1796) are well known.

[338] James Epps (1773-1839) contributed a number of memoirs on the use and corrections of instruments. He was assistant secretary of the Astronomical Society.

[339] John Hutchinson (1674-1737) was one of the first to try to reconcile the new science of geology with Genesis. He denied the Newtonian hypothesis as dangerous to religion, and because it necessitated a vacuum. He was a mystic in his interpretation of the Scriptures, and created a sect that went under the name of Hutchinsonians.

[340] John Rowning, a Lincolnshire rector, died in 1771. He wrote on physics, and published a memoir on A machine for finding the roots of equations universally (1770).

[341] It is always difficult to sanction this spelling of the name of this Jesuit father who is so often mentioned in the analytic treatment of conics. He was born in Ragusa in 1711, and the original spelling was Ru[=d]er Josip Bo[vs]kovi['c]. When he went to live in Italy, as professor of mathematics at Rome (1740) and at Pavia, the name was spelled Ruggiero Giuseppe Boscovich, although Boscovicci would seem to a foreigner more natural. His astronomical work was notable, and in his De maculis solaribus (1736) there is the first determination of the equator of a planet by observing the motion of spots on its surface. Boscovich came near having some contact with America, for he was delegated to observe in California the transit of Venus in 1755, being prevented by the dissolution of his order just at that time. He died in 1787, at Milan.

[342] James Granger (1723-1776) who wrote the Biographical History of England, London, 1769. His collection of prints was remarkable, numbering some fourteen thousand.

[343] He was curator of experiments for the Royal Society. He wrote a large number of books and monographs on physics. He died about 1713.

[344] Lee seems to have made no impression on biographers. [345] This work appeared at London in 1852.

[346] Of course this is no longer true. The most scholarly work to-day is that of Rudio, Archimedes, Huygens, Lambert, Legendre, vier Abhandlungen über die Kreismessung ... mit einer Uebersicht über die Geschichte des Problems von der Quadratur des Zirkels, von den ältesten Zeiten bis auf unsere Tage, Leipsic, 1892.

[347] Joseph Jérome le François de Lalande (1732-1807), professor of astronomy in the Collège de France (1753) and director of the Paris Observatory (1761). His writings on astronomy and his Bibliographie astronomique, avec l'histoire de l'astronomie depuis 1781 jusqu'en 1802 (Paris, 1803) are well known.

[348] De Morgan refers to his Histoire de l'Astronomie au 18e siècle, which appeared in 1827, five years after Delambre's death. Jean Baptiste Joseph Delambre (1749-1822) was a pupil of and a collaborator with Lalande, following his master as professor of astronomy in the Collège de France. His work on the measurements for the metric system is well known, and his four histories of astronomy, ancienne (1817), au moyen âge (1819), moderne (1821), and au 18e siècle (posthumous, 1827) are highly esteemed.

[349] Jean-Joseph Rive (1730-1792), a priest who left his cure under grave charges, and a quarrelsome character. His attack on Montucla was a case of the pot calling the kettle black; for while he was a brilliant writer he was a careless bibliographer.

[350] Isaac Barrow (1630-1677) was quite as well known as a theologian as he was from his Lucasian professorship of mathematics at Cambridge.

[351] "Besides we can see by this that Barrow was a poor philosopher; for he believed in the immortality of the soul and in a Divinity other than universal nature."

[352] The Récréations mathématiques et physiques (Paris, 1694) of Jacques Ozanam (1640-1717) is a work that is still highly esteemed. Among various other works he wrote a Dictionnaire mathématique ou Idée générale des mathématiques (1690) that was not without merit. The Récréations went through numerous editions (Paris, 1694, 1696, 1741, 1750, 1770, 1778, and the Montucla edition of 1790; London, 1708, the Montucla-Hutton edition of 1803 and the Riddle edition of 1840; Dublin, 1790).

[353] Hendryk van Etten, the nom de plume of Jean Leurechon (1591-1670), rector of the Jesuit college at Bar, and professor of philosophy and mathematics. He wrote on astronomy (1619) and horology (1616), and is known for his Selecta Propositiones in tota sparsim mathematica pulcherrime propositae in solemni festo SS. Ignatii et Francesci Xaverii, 1622. The book to which De Morgan refers is his Récréation mathématicque, composée de plusieurs problèmes plaisants et facetieux, Lyons, 1627, with an edition at Pont-à-Mousson, 1629. There were English editions published at London in 1633, 1653, and 1674, and Dutch editions in 1662 and 1672.

I do not understand how De Morgan happened to miss owning the work by Claude Gaspar Bachet de Meziriac (1581-1638), Problèmes plaisans et délectables, which appeared at Lyons in 1612, 8vo, with a second edition in 1624. There was a fifth edition published at Paris in 1884.

[354] His title page closes with "Paris, Chez Ch. Ant. Jombert.... M DCC LIV."

This was Charles-Antoine Jombert (1712-1784), a printer and bookseller with some taste for painting and architecture. He wrote several works and edited a number of early treatises.

[355] The late Professor Newcomb made the matter plain even to the non-mathematical mind, when he said that "ten decimal places are sufficient to give the circumference of the earth to the fraction of an inch, and thirty decimal places would give the circumference of the whole visible universe to a quantity imperceptible with the most powerful microscope."

[356] Antinewtonianismi pars prima, in qua Newtoni de coloribus systema ex propriis principiis geometrice evertitur, et nova de coloribus theoria luculentissimis experimentis demonstrantur.... Naples, 1754; pars secunda, Naples, 1756.

[357] Celestino Cominale (1722-1785) was professor of medicine at the University of Naples.

[358] The work appeared in the years from 1844 to 1849.

[359] There was a Vienna edition in 1758, 4to, and another in 1759, 4to. This edition is described on the title page as Editio Veneta prima ipso auctore praesente, et corrigente.

[360] The first edition was entitled De solis ac lunae defectibus libri V. P. Rogerii Josephi Boscovich ... cum ejusdem auctoris adnotationibus, London, 1760. It also appeared in Venice in 1761, and in French translation by the Abbé de Baruel in 1779, and was a work of considerable influence.

[361] Paulian (1722-1802) was professor of physics at the Jesuit college at Avignon. He wrote several works, the most popular of which, the Dictionnaire de physique (Avignon, 1761), went through nine editions by 1789.

[362] This is correct.

[363] Probably referring to the fact that Hill (1795-1879), who had done so much for postal reform, was secretary to the postmaster general (1846), and his name was a synonym for the post office directory.

[364] Richard Lovett (1692-1780) was a good deal of a charlatan. He claimed to have studied electrical phenomena, and in 1758 advertised that he could effect marvelous cures, especially of sore throat, by means of electricity. Before publishing the works mentioned by De Morgan he had issued others of similar character, including The Subtile Medium proved (London, 1756) and The Reviewers Reviewed (London, 1760).

[365] Jean Sylvain Bailly (1736-1793), member of the Académie française and of the Académie des sciences, first deputy elected to represent Paris in the Etats-généraux (1789), president of the first National Assembly, and mayor of Paris (1789-1791). For his vigor as mayor in keeping the peace, and for his manly defence of the Queen, he was guillotined. He was an astronomer of ability, but is best known for his histories of the science.

[366] These were the Histoire de l'Astronomie ancienne (1775), Histoire de l'Astronomie moderne (1778-1783), Histoire de l'Astronomie indienne et orientale (1787), and Lettres sur l'origine des peuples de l'Asie (1775).

[367] "The sick old man of Ferney, V., a boy of a hundred years." Voltaire was born in 1694, and hence was eighty-three at this time.

[368] In Palmézeaux's Vie de Bailly, in Bailly's Ouvrage Posthume (1810),
M. de Sales is quoted as saying that the Lettres sur l'Atlantide were sent to Voltaire and that the latter did not approve of the theory set forth.

[369] The British Museum catalogue gives two editions, 1781 and 1782.

[370] A mystic and a spiritualist. His chief work was the one mentioned here.

[371] Jacob Behmen, or Böhme (1575-1624), known as "the German theosophist," was founder of the sect of Boehmists, a cult allied to the Swedenborgians. He was given to the study of alchemy, and brought the vocabulary of the science into his mystic writings. His sect was revived in England in the eighteenth century through the efforts of William Law.

Saint-Martin translated into French two of his Latin works under the titles L'Aurore naissante, ou la Racine de la philosophie (1800), and Les trois principes de l'essence divine (1802). The originals had appeared nearly two hundred years earlier,--Aurora in 1612, and De tribus principiis in 1619.

[372] "Unknown."

[373] "Skeptical."

[374] "Man, man, man."

[375] "Men, men, men."

[376] It is interesting to read De Morgan's argument against Saint-Martin's authorship of this work. It is attributed to Saint-Martin both by the Biographie Universelle and by the British Museum Catalogue, and De Morgan says by "various catalogues and biographies."

[377] "To explain things by man and not man by things. On Errors and Truth, by a Ph.... Inc...."
[378] "If we would preserve ourselves from all illusions, and above all from the allurements of pride, by which man is so often seduced, we should never take man, but always God, for our term of comparison."

[379] "And here is found already an explanation of the numbers four and nine which caused some perplexity in the work cited above. Man is lost in passing from four to nine."

[380] Williams also took part in the preparation of some tables for the government to assist in the determination of longitude. He had published a work two years before the one here cited, on the same subject,--An entire new work and method to discover the variation of the Earth's Diameters, London, 1786.

[381] This is Gabriel Mouton (1618-1694), a vicar at Lyons, who suggested as a basis for a natural system of measures the mille, a minute of a degree of the meridian. This appeared in his Observationes diametrorum solis et lunae apparentium, meridianarumque aliquot altitudinum cum tabula declinationum solis.... Lyons, 1670.

[382] Jacques Cassini (1677-1756), one of the celebrated Cassini family of astronomers. After the death of his father he became director of the observatory at Paris. The basis for a metric unit was set forth by him in his Traité de la grandeur et de la figure de la terre, Paris, 1720. He was a prolific writer on astronomy.

[383] Alexis Jean Pierre Paucton (1732-1798). He was, for a time, professor of mathematics at Strassburg, but later (1796) held office in Paris.

His leading contribution to metrology was his Métrologie ou Traité des mesures, Paris, 1780.

[384] He was an obscure writer, born at Deptford.

[385] He was also a writer of no scientific merit, his chief contributions being religious tracts. One of his productions, however, went through many editions, even being translated into French; Three dialogues between a Minister and one of his Parishioners; on the true principles of Religion and salvation for sinners by Jesus Christ. The twentieth edition appeared at Cambridge in 1786.

[386] This was the Reflections on the Revolution in France, and on the proceedings in certain societies in London relative to that event (London, 1790) by Edmund Burke (1729-1797). Eleven editions of the work appeared the first year.

[387] Paine (1736-1809) was born in Norfolkshire, of Quaker parents. He went to America at the beginning of the Revolution and published, in January 1776, a violent pamphlet entitled Common Sense. He was a private soldier under Washington, and on his return to England after the war he published The Rights of Man. He was indicted for treason and was outlawed to France. He was elected to represent Calais at the French convention, but his plea for moderation led him perilously near the guillotine. His Age of Reason (1794) was dedicated to Washington. He returned to America in 1802 and remained there until his death.

[388] Part I appeared in 1791 and was so popular that eight editions appeared in that year. It was followed in 1792 by Part II, of which nine editions appeared in that year. Both parts were immediately republished in Paris, and there have been several subsequent editions.

[389] Mary Wollstonecraft (1759-1797) was only thirty-three when this work came out. She had already published An historical and moral View of the Origin and Progress of the French Revolution (1790), and Original Stories from Real Life (1791). She went to Paris in 1792 and remained during the Reign of Terror.

[390] Samuel Parr (1747-1827) was for a time head assistant at Harrow (1767-1771), afterwards headmaster in other schools. At the time this book was written he was vicar of Hatton, where he took private pupils (1785-1798) to the strictly limited number of seven. He was a violent Whig and a caustic writer.

[391] On Mary Wollstonecraft's return from France she married (1797) William Godwin (1756-1836). He had started as a strong Calvinistic Nonconformist minister, but had become what would now be called an anarchist, at least by conservatives. He had written an Inquiry concerning Political Justice (1793) and a novel entitled Caleb Williams, or Things as they are (1794), both of which were of a nature to attract his future wife.

[392] This child was a daughter. She became Shelley's wife, and Godwin's influence on Shelley was very marked.

[393] This was John Nichols (1745-1826), the publisher and antiquary. He edited the Gentleman's Magazine (1792-1826) and his works include the Literary Anecdotes of the Eighteenth Century (1812-1815), to which De Morgan here refers.

[394] William Bellenden, a Scotch professor at the University of Paris, who died about 1633. His textbooks are now forgotten, but Parr edited an edition of his works in 1787. The Latin preface, Praefatio ad Bellendum de Statu, was addressed to Burke, North, and Fox, and was a satire on their political opponents.

[395] As we have seen, he had been head-master before he began taking "his handful of private pupils."

[396] The story has evidently got mixed up in the telling, for Tom Sheridan (1721-1788), the great actor, was old enough to have been Dr. Parr's father. It was his son, Richard Brinsley Sheridan (1751-1816), the dramatist and politician, who was the pupil of Parr. He wrote The Rivals (1775) and The School for Scandal (1777) soon after Parr left Harrow.

[397] Horner (1785-1864) was a geologist and social reformer. He was very influential in improving the conditions of child labor.

[398] William Cobbett (1762-1835), the journalist, was a character not without interest to Americans. Born in Surrey, he went to America at the age of thirty and remained there eight years. Most of this time he was occupied as a bookseller in Philadelphia, and while thus engaged he was fined for libel against the celebrated Dr. Rush. On his return to England he edited the Weekly Political Register (1802-1835), a popular journal among the working classes. He was fined and imprisoned for two years because of his attack (1810) on military flogging, and was also (1831) prosecuted for sedition. He further showed his paradox nature by his History of the Protestant Reformation (1824-1827), an attack on the prevailing Protestant opinion. He also wrote a Life of Andrew Jackson (1834). After repeated attempts he succeeded in entering parliament, a result of the Reform Bill.

[399] Robinson (1735-1790) was a Baptist minister who wrote several theological works and a number of hymns. His work at Cambridge so offended the students that they at one time broke up the services.

[400] This work had passed through twelve editions by 1823. [401] Dyer (1755-1841), the poet and reformer, edited Robinson's Ecclesiastical Researches (1790). He was a life-long friend of Charles Lamb, and in their boyhood they were schoolmates at Christ's Hospital. His Complaints of the Poor People of England (1793) made him a worthy companion of the paradoxers above mentioned.

[402] These were John Thelwall (1764-1834) whose Politics for the People or Hogswash (1794) took its title from the fact that Burke called the people the "swinish multitude." The book resulted in sending the author to the Tower for sedition. In 1798 he gave up politics and started a school of elocution which became very famous. Thomas Hardy (1752-1832), who kept a bootmaker's shop in Piccadilly, was a fellow prisoner with Thelwall, being arrested for high treason. He was founder (1792) of The London Corresponding Society, a kind of clearing house for radical associations throughout the country. Horne Tooke was really John Horne (1736-1812), he having taken the name of his friend William Tooke in 1782. He was a radical of the radicals, and organized a number of reform societies. Among these was the Constitutional Society that voted money (1775) to assist the American revolutionists, appointing him to give the contribution to Franklin. For this he was imprisoned for a year. With his fellow rebels in the Tower in 1794, however, he was acquitted. As a

philologist he is known for his early advocacy of the study of Anglo-Saxon and Gothic, and his Diversions of Purley (1786) is still known to readers.

[403] This was the admiral, Adam Viscount Duncan (1731-1804), who defeated the Dutch off Camperdown in 1797.

[404] He was created Duke of Clarence and St. Andrews in 1789 and was Admiral of the Fleet escorting Louis XVIII on his return to France in 1814. He became Lord High Admiral in 1827, and reigned as William IV from 1830 to 1837.

[405] This was Charles Abbott (1762-1832) first Lord Tenterden. He succeeded Lord Ellenborough as Chief Justice (1818) and was raised to the peerage in 1827. He was a strong Tory and opposed the Catholic Relief Bill, the Reform Bill, and the abolition of the death penalty for forgery.

[406] Edward Law (1750-1818), first Baron Ellenborough. He was chief counsel for Warren Hastings, and his famous speech in defense of his client is well known. He became Chief Justice and was raised to the peerage in 1802. He opposed all efforts to modernize the criminal code, insisting upon the reactionary principle of new death penalties.

[407] Edmund Law (1703-1787), Bishop of Carlisle (1768), was a good deal more liberal than his son. His Considerations on the Propriety of requiring subscription to the Articles of Faith (1774) was published anonymously. In it he asserts that not even the clergy should be required to subscribe to the thirty-nine articles.

[408] Joe Miller (1684-1738), the famous Drury Lane comedian, was so illiterate that he could not have written the Joe Miller's Jests, or the Wit's Vade-Mecum that appeared the year after his death. It was often reprinted and probably contained more or less of Miller's own jokes.

[409] The sixth duke (1766-1839) was much interested in parliamentary reform. He was a member of the Society of Friends of the People. He was for fourteen years a member of parliament (1788-1802) and was later Lord Lieutenant of Ireland (1806-1807). He afterwards gave up politics and became interested in agricultural matters.

[410] George Jeffreys (c. 1648-1689), the favorite of James II, who was active in prosecuting the Rye House conspirators. He was raised to the peerage in 1684 and held the famous "bloody assize" in the following year, being made Lord Chancellor as a result. He was imprisoned in the Tower by William III and died there.

[411] The Every Day Book, forming a Complete History of the Year, Months, and Seasons, and a perpetual Key to the Almanack, 1826-1827.

[412] The first and second editions appeared in 1820. Two others followed in 1821.

[413] The three trials of W. H., for publishing three parodies; viz the late John Wilkes' Catechism, the Political Litany, and the Sinecurists Creed; on three ex-officio informations, at Guildhall, London, ... Dec. 18, 19, & 20, 1817,... London, 1818.

[414] The Political Litany appeared in 1817. [415] That is, Castlereagh's.

[416] The well-known caricaturist (1792-1878), then only twenty-nine years old.

[417] Robert Stewart (1769-1822) was second Marquis of Londonderry and Viscount Castlereagh. As Chief Secretary for Ireland he was largely instrumental in bringing about the union of Ireland and Great Britain. He was at the head of the war department during most of the Napoleonic wars, and was to a great extent responsible for the European coalition against the Emperor. He suicided in 1822.

[418] John Murray (1778-1843), the well-known London publisher. He refused to finish the publication of Don Juan, after the first five cantos, because of his Tory principles.

[419] Only the first two cantos appeared in 1819.

[420] Proclus (412-485), one of the greatest of the neo-Platonists, studied at Alexandria and taught philosophy at Athens. He left commentaries on Plato and on part of Euclid's Elements.

[421] Thomas Taylor (1758-1835), called "the Platonist," had a liking for mathematics, and was probably led by his interest in number mysticism to a study of neo-Platonism. He translated a number of works from the Latin and Greek, and wrote two works on theoretical arithmetic (1816, 1823).

[422] There was an earlier edition, 1788-89.

[423] Georgius Gemistus, or Georgius Pletho (Plethon), lived in the fourteenth and fifteenth centuries. He was a native of Constantinople, but spent most of his time in Greece. He devoted much time to the propagation of the Platonic philosophy, but also wrote on divinity, geography, and history.

[424] Hannah More (1745-1833), was, in her younger days, a friend of Burke, Reynolds, Dr. Johnson, and Garrick. At this time she wrote a number of poems and aspired to become a dramatist. Her Percy (1777), with a prologue and epilogue by Garrick, had a long run at Covent Garden. Somewhat later she came to believe that the playhouse was a grave public evil, and refused to attend the revival of her own play with Mrs. Siddons in the leading part. After 1789 she and her sisters devoted themselves to starting schools for poor children, teaching them religion and housework, but leaving them illiterate.

[425] These were issued at the rate of three each month,--a story, a ballad, and a Sunday tract. They were collected and published in one volume in 1795. It is said that two million copies were sold the first year. There were also editions in 1798, 1819, 1827, and 1836-37.

[426] That is, Dr. Johnson (1709-1784). The Rambler was published in 1750-1752, and was an imitation of Addison's Spectator.

[427] Dr. Moore, referred to below.

[428] Dr. John Moore (1729-1802), physician and novelist, is now best known for his Journal during a Residence in France from the beginning of August to the middle of December, 1792, a work quoted frequently by Carlyle in his French Revolution.

[429] Sir John Moore (1761-1809), Lieutenant General in the Napoleonic wars. He was killed in the battle of Corunna. The poem by Charles Wolfe (1791-1823), The Burial of Sir John Moore (1817), is well known.

[430] Referring to the novels of Thomas Love Peacock (1785-1866), who succeeded James Mill as chief examiner of the East India Company, and was in turn succeeded by John Stuart Mill.

[431] Frances Burney, Madame d'Arblay (1752-1840), married General d'Arblay, a French officer and companion of Lafayette, in 1793. She was only twenty-five when she acquired fame by her Evelina, or a Young Lady's Entrance into the World. Her Letters and Diaries appeared posthumously (1842-45).

[432] Henry Peter, Baron Brougham and Vaux (1778-1868), well known in politics, science, and letters. He was one of the founders of the Edinburgh Review, became Lord Chancellor in 1830, and took part with men like William Frend, De Morgan's father-in-law, in the establishing of London University. He was also one of the founders of the Society for the Diffusion of Useful Knowledge. He was always friendly to De Morgan, who entered the faculty of London University, whose work on geometry was published by the Society mentioned, and who was offered the degree of doctor of laws by the University of Edinburgh while Lord Brougham was Lord Rector. The Edinburgh honor was refused by De Morgan who said he "did not feel like an LL.D."

[433] Maria Edgeworth (1767-1849).

[434] Sydney Owenson (c. 1783-1859) married Sir Thomas Morgan, a well-known surgeon, in 1812. Her Irish stories were very popular with the patriots but were attacked by the Quarterly Review. The Wild Irish Girl (1806) went through seven editions in two years.

[435] 1775-1817.

[436] 1771-1832.

[437] The famous preacher (1732-1808). He was the first chairman of the Religious Tract Society. He is also known as one of the earliest advocates of vaccination, in his Cow-pock Inoculation vindicated and recommended from matters of fact, 1806.

[438] Sir Rowland Hill (1795-1879), the father of penny postage.

[439] Beilby Porteus (1731-1808), Bishop of Chester (1776) and Bishop of London (1787). He encouraged the Sunday-school movement and the dissemination of Hannah More's tracts. He was an active opponent of slavery, but also of Catholic emancipation.

[440] Henrietta Maria Bowdler (1754-1830), generally known as Mrs. Harriet Bowdler. She was the author of many religious tracts and poems. Her Poems and Essays (1786) were often reprinted. The story goes that on the appearance of her Sermons on the Doctrines and duties of Christianity (published anonymously), Bishop Porteus offered the author a living under the impression that it was written by a man.

[441] William Frend (1757-1841), whose daughter Sophia Elizabeth became De Morgan's wife (1837), was at one time a clergyman of the Established Church, but was converted to Unitarianism (1787). He came under De Morgan's definition of a true paradoxer, carrying on a zealous warfare for what he thought right. As a result of his Address to the Inhabitants of Cambridge (1787), and his efforts to have abrogated the requirement that candidates for the M.A. must subscribe to the thirty-nine articles, he was deprived of his tutorship in 1788. A little later he was banished (see De Morgan's statement in the text) from Cambridge because of his denunciation of the abuses of the Church and his condemnation of the liturgy. His eccentricity is seen in his declining to use negative quantities in the operations of algebra. He finally became an actuary at London and was prominent in radical associations. He was a mathematician of ability, having been second wrangler and having nearly attained the first place, and he was also an excellent scholar in Latin, Greek, and Hebrew.

[442] George Peacock (1791-1858), Fellow of Trinity College, Cambridge, Lowndean professor of astronomy, and Dean of Ely Cathedral (1839). His tomb may be seen at Ely where he spent the latter part of his life. He was one of the group that introduced the modern continental notation of the calculus into England, replacing the cumbersome notation of Newton, passing from "the dotage of fluxions to the deism of the calculus."

[443] Robert Simson (1687-1768); professor of mathematics at Glasgow. His restoration of Apollonius (1749) and his translation and restoration of Euclid (1756, and 1776--posthumous) are well known.

[444] Francis Maseres (1731-1824), a prominent lawyer. His mathematical works had some merit.

[445] These appeared annually from 1804 to 1822.

[446] Henry Gunning (1768-1854) was senior esquire bedell of Cambridge. The Reminiscences appeared in two volumes in 1854.

[447] John Singleton Copley, Baron Lyndhurst (1772-1863), the son of John Singleton Copley the portrait painter, was born in Boston. He was educated at Trinity College, Cambridge, and became a lawyer. He was made Lord Chancellor in 1827.

[448] Sir William Rough (c. 1772-1838), a lawyer and poet, became Chief Justice of Ceylon in 1836. He was knighted in 1837.

[449] Herbert Marsh, afterwards Bishop of Peterborough, a relation of my father.--S. E. De M.

He was born in 1757 and died in 1839. On the trial of Frend he publicly protested against testifying against a personal confidant, and was excused. He was one of the first of the English clergy to study modern higher criticism of the Bible, and amid much opposition he wrote numerous works on the subject. He was professor of theology at Cambridge (1707), Bishop of Llandaff (1816), and Bishop of Peterborough.

[450] George Butler (1774-1853), Headmaster of Harrow (1805-1829), Chancellor of Peterborough (1836), and Dean of Peterborough (1842).

[451] James Tate (1771-1843), Headmaster of Richmond School (1796-1833) and Canon of St. Paul's Cathedral (1833). He left several works on the classics.

[452] Francis Place (1771-1854), at first a journeyman breeches maker, and later a master tailor. He was a hundred years ahead of his time as a strike leader, but was not so successful as an agitator as he was as a tailor, since his shop in Charing Cross made him wealthy. He was a well-known radical, and it was largely due to his efforts that the law against the combinations of workmen was repealed in 1824. His chief work was The Principles of Population (1822).

[453] Speed (1552-1629) was a tailor until Grevil (Greville) made him independent of his trade. He was not only an historian of some merit, but a skilful cartographer. His maps of the counties were collected in the Theatre of the Empire of Great Britaine, 1611. About this same time he also published Genealogies recorded in Sacred Scripture, a work that had passed through thirty-two editions by 1640.

[454] The history of Great Britaine under the conquests of ye Romans, Saxons, Danes, and Normans.... London, 1611, folio. The second edition appeared in 1623; the third, to which De Morgan here refers, posthumously in 1632; and the fourth in 1650.

[455] William Nicolson (1655-1727) became Bishop of Carlisle in 1702, and Bishop of Derry in 1718. His chief work was the Historical Library (1696-1724), in the form of a collection of documents and chronicles. It was reprinted in 1736 and in 1776.

[456] Sir Fulk Grevil, or Fulke Greville (1554-1628), was a favorite of Queen Elizabeth, Chancellor of the Exchequer under James I, a patron of literature, and a friend of Sir Philip Sidney.

[457] See note 443 on page 197.

[458] See note 444 on page 197.

[459] See note 439 on page 193.

[460] Edward Waring (1736-1796) was Lucasian professor of mathematics at Cambridge. He published several works on analysis and curves. The work referred to was the Miscellanea Analytica de aequationibus algebraicis et curvarum proprietatibus, Cambridge, 1762.

[461] A Dissertation on the use of the Negative Sign in Algebra...; to which is added, Machin's Quadrature of the Circle, London, 1758.

[462] The paper was probably one on complex numbers, or possibly one on quaternions, in which direction as well as absolute value is involved.

[463] De Morgan quotes from one of the Latin editions. Descartes wrote in French, the title of his first edition being: Discours de la méthode pour bien conduire sa raison et chercher la vérité dans les sciences, plus la dioptrique, les météores et la géométrie qui sont des essais de cette méthode, Leyden, 1637, 4to.

[464] "I have observed that algebra indeed, as it is usually taught, is so restricted by definite rules and formulas of calculation, that it seems rather a confused kind of an art, by the practice of which the mind is in a certain manner disturbed and obscured, than a science by which it is cultivated and made acute."

[465] It appeared in 93 volumes, from 1758 to 1851.

[466] The principles of the doctrine of life-annuities; explained in a familiar manner ... with a variety of new tables ..., London, 1783.

[467] I suppose the one who wrote Conjectures on the physical causes of Earthquakes and Volcanoes, Dublin, 1820.

[468] Scriptores Logarithmici; or, a Collection of several curious tracts on the nature and construction of Logarithms ... together with same tracts on the Binomial Theorem ..., 6 vols., London, 1791-1807.

[469] Charles Babbage (1792-1871), whose work on the calculating machine is well known. Maseres was, it is true, ninety-two at this time, but Babbage was thirty-one instead of twenty-nine. He had already translated Lacroix's Treatise on the differential and integral calculus (1816), in collaboration with Herschel and Peacock. He was Lucasian professor of mathematics at Cambridge from 1828 to 1839.

[470] The great and new Art of weighing Vanity, or a discovery of the ignorance of the great and new artist in his pseudo-philosophical writings.

The "great and new artist" was Sinclair.

[471] George Sinclair, probably a native of East Lothian, who died in 1696. He was professor of philosophy and mathematics at Glasgow, and was one of the first to use the barometer in measuring altitudes. The work to which De Morgan refers is his Hydrostaticks (1672). He was a firm believer in evil spirits, his work on the subject going through four editions: Satan's Invisible World Discovered; or, a choice collection of modern relations, proving evidently against the Saducees and Athiests of this present age, that there are Devils, Spirits, Witches, and Apparitions, Edinburgh, 1685.

[472] This was probably William Sanders, Regent of St. Leonard's College, whose Theses philosophicae appeared in 1674, and whose Elementa geometriae came out a dozen years later.

[473] Ars nova et magna gravitatis et levitatis; sive dialogorum philosophicorum libri sex de aeris vera ac reali gravitate, Rotterdam, 1669, 4to.

[474] Volume I, Nos. 1 and 2, appeared in 1803.

[475] His daughter, Mrs. De Morgan, says in her Memoir of her husband: "My father had been second wrangler in a year in which the two highest were close together, and was, as his son-in-law afterwards described him, an exceedingly clear thinker. It is possible, as Mr. De Morgan said, that this mental clearness and directness may have caused his mathematical heresy, the rejection of the use of negative quantities in algebraical operations; and it is probable that he thus deprived himself of an instrument of work, the use of which might have led him to greater eminence in the higher branches." Memoir of Augustus De Morgan, London, 1882, p. 19.

[476] "If it is not true it is a good invention." A well-known Italian proverb.

[477] See page 86, note 132.

[478] He was born at Paris in 1713, and died there in 1765.

[479] Recherches sur les courbes à double courbure, Paris, 1731. Clairaut was then only eighteen, and was in the same year made a member of the Académie des sciences. His Elémens de géométrie appeared in 1741.

Meantime he had taken part in the measurement of a degree in Lapland (1736-1737). His Traité de la figure de la terre was published in 1741. The Academy of St. Petersburg awarded him a prize for his Théorie de la lune (1750). His various works on comets are well known, particularly his Théorie du mouvement des comètes (1760) in which he applied the "problem of three bodies" to Halley's comet as retarded by Jupiter and Saturn.

[480] Joseph Privat, Abbé de Molières (1677-1742), was a priest of the Congregation of the Oratorium. In 1723 he became a professor in the Collège de France. He was well known as an astronomer and a mathematician, and wrote in defense of Descartes's theory of vortices (1728, 1729). He also contributed to the methods of finding prime numbers (1705).

[481] "Deserves not only to be printed, but to be admired as a marvel of imagination, of understanding, and of ability."

[482] Blaise Pascal (1623-1662), the well-known French philosopher and mathematician. He lived for some time with the Port Royalists, and defended them against the Jesuits in his Provincial Letters. Among his works are the following: Essai pour les coniques (1640); Recit de la grande expérience de l'équilibre des liqueurs (1648), describing his experiment in finding altitudes by barometric readings; Histoire de la roulette (1658); Traité du triangle arithmétique (1665); Aleae geometria (1654).

[483] This proposition shows that if a hexagon is inscribed in a conic (in particular a circle) and the opposite sides are produced to meet, the three points determined by their intersections will be in the same straight line.

[484] Jacques Curabelle, Examen des Oeuvres du Sr. Desargues, Paris, 1644. He also published without date a work entitled: Foiblesse pitoyable du Sr. G. Desargues employée contre l'examen fait de ses oeuvres.

[485] See page 119, note 233.

[486] Until "this great proposition called Pascal's should see the light."

[487] The story is that his father, Etienne Pascal, did not wish him to study geometry until he was thoroughly grounded in Latin and Greek. Having heard the nature of the subject, however, he began at the age of twelve to construct figures by himself, drawing them on the floor with a piece of charcoal. When his father discovered what he was doing he was attempting to demonstrate that the sum of the angles of a triangle equals two right angles. The story is given by his sister, Mme. Perier.

[488] Sir John Wilson (1741-1793) was knighted in 1786 and became Commissioner of the Great Seal in 1792. He was a lawyer and jurist of recognized merit. He stated his theorem without proof, the first demonstration having been given by Lagrange in the Memoirs of the Berlin Academy for 1771,--Demonstration d'un théorème nouveau concernant les nombres premiers. Euler also gave a proof in his Miscellanea Analytica (1773). Fermat's works should be consulted in connection with the early history of this theorem.

[489] He wrote, in 1760, a tract in defense of Waring, a point of whose algebra had been assailed by a Dr. Powell. Waring wrote another tract of the same date.--A. De M.

William Samuel Powell (1717-1775) was at this time a fellow of St. John's College, Cambridge. In 1765 he became Vice Chancellor of the University. Waring was a Magdalene man, and while candidate for the Lucasian professorship he circulated privately his Miscellanea Analytica. Powell attacked this in his Observations on the First Chapter of a Book called Miscellanea (1760). This attack was probably in the interest of another candidate, a man of his own college (St. John's), William Ludlam.

[490] William Paley (1743-1805) was afterwards a tutor at Christ's College, Cambridge. He never contributed anything to mathematics, but his Evidences of Christianity (1794) was long considered somewhat of a classic. He also wrote Principles of Morality and Politics (1785), and Natural Theology (1802).

[491] Edward, first Baron Thurlow (1731-1806) is known to Americans because of his strong support of the Royal prerogative during the Revolution. He was a favorite of George III, and became Lord Chancellor in 1778.

[492] George Wilson Meadley (1774-1818) published his Memoirs of ... Paley in 1809. He also published Memoirs of Algernon Sidney in 1813. He was a merchant and banker, and had traveled extensively in Europe and the East. He was a convert to unitarianism, to which sect Paley had a strong leaning.

[493] Watson (1737-1816) was a strange kind of man for a bishopric. He was professor of chemistry at Cambridge (1764) at the age of twenty-seven. It was his experiments that led to the invention of the black-bulb thermometer. He is said to have saved the government £100,000 a year by his advice on the manufacture of gunpowder. Even after he became professor of divinity at Cambridge (1771) he published four volumes of Chemical Essays (vol. I, 1781). He became Bishop of Llandaff in 1782.

[494] James Adair (died in 1798) was counsel for the defense in the trial of the publishers of the Letters of Junius (1771). As King's Serjeant he assisted in prosecuting Hardy and Horne Tooke.

[495] Morgan (1750-1833) was actuary of the Equitable Assurance Society of London (1774-1830), and it was to his great abilities that the success of that company was due at a time when other corporations of similar kind were meeting with disaster. The Royal Society awarded him a medal (1783) for a paper on Probability of Survivorship. He wrote several important works on insurance and finance.

[496] Dr. Price (1723-1791) was a non-conformist minister and a writer on ethics, economics, politics, and insurance. He was a defender of the American Revolution and a personal friend of Franklin. In 1778 Congress invited him to America to assist in the financial administration of the new republic, but he declined. His famous sermon on the French Revolution is said to have inspired Burke's Reflections on the Revolution in France.

[497] Elizabeth Gurney (1780-1845), a Quaker, who married Joseph Fry (1800), a London merchant. She was the prime mover in the Association for the Improvement of the Female Prisoners in Newgate, founded in 1817. Her influence in prison reform extended throughout Europe, and she visited the prisons of many countries in her efforts to improve the conditions of penal servitude. The friendship of Mrs. Fry with the De Morgans began in 1837. Her scheme for a female benefit society proved worthless from the actuarial standpoint, and would have been disastrous to all concerned if it had been carried out, and it was therefore fortunate that De Morgan was consulted in time. Mrs. De Morgan speaks of the consultation in these words: "My husband, who was very sensitive on such points, was charmed with Mrs. Fry's voice and manner as much as by the simple self-forgetfulness with which she entered into this business; her own very uncomfortable share of it not being felt as an element in the question, as long as she could be useful in promoting good or preventing mischief. I can see her now as she came into our room, took off her little round Quaker cap, and laying it down, went at once into the matter. 'I have followed thy advice, and I think nothing further can be done in this case; but all harm is prevented.' In the following year I had an opportunity of seeing the effect of her most musical tones. I visited her at Stratford, taking my little baby and nurse with me, to consult her on some articles on prison discipline, which I had written for a periodical. The baby--three months old--was restless, and the nurse could not quiet her, neither could I entirely, until Mrs. Fry began to read something connected with the subject of my visit, when the infant, fixing her large eyes on the reader, lay listening till she fell asleep." Memoirs, p. 91.

[498] Mrs. Fry certainly believed that the writer was the old actuary of the Equitable, when she first consulted him upon the benevolent Assurance project; but we were introduced to her by our old and dear friend Lady Noel Byron, by whom she had been long known and venerated, and who referred her to Mr. De Morgan for advice. An unusual degree of confidence in, and appreciation of each other, arose on their first meeting between the two, who had so much that was externally different, and so much that was essentially alike, in their natures.--S. E. De M.

Anne Isabella Milbanke (1792-1860) married Lord Byron in 1815, when both took the additional name of Noel, her mother's name. They were separated in 1816.

[499] An obscure writer not mentioned in the ordinary biographies.

[500] Not mentioned in the ordinary biographies, and for obvious reasons. [501] "Before" and "after."

[502] On Bishop Wilkins see note 171 on page 100. [503] Provision for a journey.

[504] See note 179 on page 103.

[505] Thomas Bradwardine (1290-1349), known as Doctor Profundus, proctor and professor of theology at Oxford, and afterwards Chancellor of St. Paul's and confessor to Edward III. The English ascribed their success at Crécy to his prayers.

[506] He was consecrated Archbishop of Canterbury by the Pope at Avignon, July 13, 1349, and died of the plague at London in the same year.

[507] "One paltry little year."

[508] The title is carelessly copied, as is so frequently the case in catalogues, even of the Libri class. It should read: Arithmetica thome brauardini | | Olivier Senant | | Venum exponuntur ab Oliuiario senant in vico diui Jacobi sub signo beate Barbare sedente. The colophon reads: Explicit arithmetica speculatiua th[=o]e brauardini b[=n] reuisa et correcta a Petro sanchez Ciruelo aragonensi mathematicas leg[=e]te Parisius, [=i]pressa per Thom[=a] anguelart. There were Paris editions of 1495, 1496, 1498, s. a. (c. 1500), 1502, 1504, 1505, s. a. (c. 1510), 1512, 1530, a Valencia edition of 1503, two Wittenberg editions of 1534 and 1536, and doubtless several others. The work is not "very rare," although of course no works of that period are common. See the editor's Rara Arithmetica, page 61.

[509] This is his Tractatus de proportionibus, Paris, 1495; Venice, 1505; Vienna, 1515, with other editions.

[510] The colophon of the 1495 edition reads: Et sic explicit Geometria Thome brauardini c[=u] tractatulo de quadratura circuli bene reuisa a Petro sanchez ciruelo: operaqz Guidonis mercatoris dilig[=e]tissime impresse parisi^o in c[=a]po gaillardi. Anno d[=n]i. 1495. die. 20, maij.

This Petro Ciruelo was born in Arragon, and died in 1560 at Salamanca. He studied mathematics and philosophy at Paris, and took the doctor's degree there. He taught at the University of Alcalà and became canon of the Cathedral at Salamanca. Besides his editions of Bradwardine he wrote several works, among them the Liber arithmeticae practicae qui dicitur algorithmus (Paris, 1495) and the Cursus quatuor mathematicarum artium liberalium (Alcalà, 1516).

[511] Star polygons, a subject of considerable study in the later Middle Ages. See note 35 on page 44.

[512] "A new theory that adds lustre to the fourteenth century."

[513] There is nothing in the edition of 1495 that leads to this conclusion.

[514] The full title is: Nouvelle théorie des parallèles, avec un appendice contenant la manière de perfectionner la théorie des parallèles de A. M. Legendre. The author had no standing as a scientist.

[515] Adrien Marie Legendre (1752-1833) was one of the great mathematicians of the opening of the nineteenth century. His Eléments de géométrie (1794) had great influence on the geometry of the United States. His Essai sur la théorie des nombres (1798) is one of the classics upon the subject. The work to which Kircher refers is the Nouvelle théorie des parallèles (1803), in which the attempt is made to avoid using Euclid's postulate of parallels, the result being merely the substitution of another assumption that was even more unsatisfactory. The best presentations of the general theory are W. B. Frankland's Theories of Parallelism, Cambridge, 1910, and Engel and Stäckel's Die Theorie der

Parallellinien von Euclid bis auf Gauss, Leipsic, 1895. Legendre published a second work on the theory the year of his death, Réflexions sur ... la théorie des parallèles (1833). His other works include the Nouvelles méthodes pour la détermination des orbites des comètes (1805), in which he uses the method of least squares; the Traité des fonctions elliptiques et des intégrales (1827-1832), and the Exercises de calcul intégral (1811, 1816, 1817).

[516] Johann Joseph Ignatz von Hoffmann (1777-1866), professor of mathematics at Aschaffenburg, published his Theorie der Parallellinien in 1801. He supplemented this by his Kritik der Parallelen-Theorie in 1807, and his Das eilfte Axiom der Elemente des Euclidis neu bewiesen in 1859. He wrote other works on mathematics, but none of his contributions was of any importance.

[517] Johann Karl Friedrich Hauff (1766-1846) was successively professor of mathematics at Marburg, director of the polytechnic school at Augsburg, professor at the Gymnasium at Cologne, and professor of mathematics and physics at Ghent. The work to which Kircher refers is his memoirs on the Euclidean Theorie der Parallelen in Hindenburg's Archiv, vol. III (1799), an article of no merit in the general theory.

[518] Wenceslaus Johann Gustav Karsten (1732-1787) was professor of logic at Rostock (1758) and Butzow (1760), and later became professor of mathematics and physics at Halle. His work on parallels is the Versuch einer völlig berichtigten Theorie der Parallellinien (1779). He also wrote a work entitled Anfangsgründe der mathematischen Wissenschaften (1780), but neither of these works was more than mediocre.

[519] Johann Christoph Schwab (not Schwal) was born in 1743 and died in 1821. He was professor at the Karlsschule at Stuttgart. De Morgan's wish was met, for the catalogues give "c. fig. 8," so that it evidently had eight illustrations instead of eight volumes. He wrote several other works on the principles of geometry, none of any importance.

[520] Gaetano Rossi of Catanzaro. This was the libretto writer (1772-1855), and hence the imperfections of the work can better be condoned. De Morgan should have given a little more of the title: Solusione esatta e regolare ... del ... problema della quadratura del circolo. There was a second edition, London, 1805.

[521] This identifies Rossi, for Joséphine Grassini (1773-1850) was a well-known contralto, prima donna at Napoleon's court opera.

[522] William Spence (1783-1860) was an entomologist and economist of some standing, a fellow of the Royal Society, and one of the founders of the Entomological Society of London. The work here mentioned was a popular one, the first edition appearing in 1807, and four editions being justified in a single year. He also wrote Agriculture the Source of Britain's Wealth (1808) and Objections against the Corn Bill refuted (1815), besides a work in four volumes on entomology (1815-1826) in collaboration with William Kirby.

[523] "That used to be so, but we have changed all that." [524] "Meet the coming disease."

[525] George Douglas (or Douglass) was a Scotch writer. He got out an edition of the Elements of Euclid in 1776, with an appendix on trigonometry and a set of tables. His work on Mathematical Tables appeared in 1809, and his Art of Drawing in Perspective, from mathematical principles, in 1810.

[526] See note 443, on page 197.

[527] John Playfair (1748-1848) was professor of mathematics (1785) and natural philosophy (1805) at the University of Edinburgh. His Elements of Geometry went through many editions.

[528] "Tell Apella" was an expression current in classical Rome to indicate incredulity and to show the contempt in which the Jew was held. Horace says: Credat Judæus Apella, "Let Apella the Jew believe it." Our "Tell it to the marines," is a similar phrase.

[529] As De Morgan says two lines later, "No mistake is more common than the natural one of imagining that the"--University of Virginia is at Richmond. The fact is that it is not there, and that it did not exist in 1810. It was not

chartered until 1819, and was not opened until 1825, and then at Charlottesville. The act establishing the Central College, from which the University of Virginia developed, was passed in 1816. The Jean Wood to whom De Morgan refers was one John Wood who was born about 1775 in Scotland and who emigrated to the United States in 1800. He published a History of the Administration of J. Adams (New York, 1802) that was suppressed by Aaron Burr. This act called forth two works, a Narrative of the Suppression, by Col. Burr, of the 'History of the Administration of John Adams' (1802), in which Wood was sustained; and the Antidote to John Wood's Poison (1802), in which he was attacked. The work referred to in the "printed circular" may have been the New theory of the diurnal rotation of the earth (Richmond, Va., 1809). Wood spent the last years of his life in Richmond, Va., making county maps. He died there in 1822. A careful search through works relating to the University of Virginia fails to show that Wood had any connection with it.

[530] There seems to be nothing to add to Dobson's biography beyond what De Morgan has so deliciously set forth.

[531] "Give to each man his due."

[532] Hester Lynch Salusbury (1741-1821), the friend of Dr. Johnson, married Henry Thrale (1763), a brewer, who died in 1781. She then married Gabriel Piozzi (1784), an Italian musician. Her Anecdotes of the late Samuel Johnson (1786) and Letters to and from Samuel Johnson (1788) are well known. She also wrote numerous essays and poems.

[533] Samuel Pike (c. 1717-1773) was an independent minister, with a chapel in London and a theological school in his house. He later became a disciple of Robert Sandeman and left the Independents for the Sandemanian church (1765). The Philosophia Sacra was first published at London in 1753. De Morgan here cites the second edition.

[534] Pike had been dead over forty years when Kittle published this second edition. Kittle had already published a couple of works: King Solomon's portraiture of Old Age (Edinburgh, 1813), and Critical and Practical Lectures on the Apocalyptical Epistles to the Seven Churches of Asia Minor (London, 1814).

[535] See note 334, on page 152.

[536] William Stukely (1687-1765) was a fellow of the Royal Society and of the College of Physicians and Surgeons. He afterwards (1729) entered the Church. He was prominent as an antiquary, especially in the study of the Roman and Druidic remains of Great Britain. He was the author of numerous works, chiefly on paleography.

[537] William Jones (1726-1800), who should not be confused with his namesake who is mentioned in note 281 on page 135. He was a lifelong friend of Bishop Horne, and his vicarage at Nayland was a meeting place of an influential group of High Churchmen. Besides the Physiological Disquisitions (1781) he wrote The Catholic Doctrine of the Trinity (1756) and The Grand Analogy (1793).

[538] Robert Spearman (1703-1761) was a pupil of John Hutchinson, and not only edited his works but wrote his life. He wrote a work against the Newtonian physics, entitled An Enquiry after Philosophy and Theology (Edinburgh, 1755), besides the Letters to a Friend concerning the Septuagint Translation (Edinburgh, 1759) to which De Morgan refers.

[539] A writer of no importance, at least in the minds of British biographers.

[540] Alexander Catcott (1725-1779), a theologian and geologist, wrote not only a work on the creation (1756) but a Treatise on the Deluge (1761, with a second edition in 1768). Sir Charles Lyell considered the latter work a valuable contribution to geology.

[541] James Robertson (1714-1795), professor of Hebrew at the University of Edinburgh. Probably De Morgan refers to his Grammatica Linguae Hebrææ (Edinburgh, 1758; with a second edition in 1783). He also wrote Clavis Pentateuchi (1770).

[542] Benjamin Holloway (c. 1691-1759), a geologist and theologian. He translated Woodward's Naturalis Historia Telluris, and was introduced by Woodward to Hutchinson. The work referred to by De Morgan appeared at Oxford in two volumes in 1754.

[543] His work was The Christian plan exhibited in the interpretation of Elohim: with observations upon a few other matters relative to the same subject, Oxford, 1752, with a second edition in 1755.

[544] Duncan Forbes (1685-1747) studied Oriental languages and Civil law at Leyden. He was Lord President of the Court of Sessions (1737). He wrote a number of theological works.

[545] Should be 1756.

[546] Edward Henry Bickersteth (1825-1906), bishop of Exeter
(1885-1900); published The Rock of Ages; or scripture testimony to the one Eternal Godhead of the Father, and of the Son, and of the Holy Ghost at Hampstead in 1859. A second edition appeared at London in 1860.

[547] Thomas Sadler (1822-1891) took his Ph.D. at Erlangen in 1844, and became a Unitarian minister at Hampstead, where Bickersteth's work was published. Besides writing the Gloria Patri (1859), he edited Crabb Robinson's Diaries.

[548] This was his Virgil's Bucolics and the two first Satyrs of Juvenal, 1634.

[549] Possibly in his Twelve Questions or Arguments drawn out of Scripture, wherein the commonly received Opinion touching the Deity of the Holy Spirit is clearly and fully refuted, 1647. This was his first heretical work, and it was followed by a number of others that were written during the intervals in which the Puritan parliament allowed him out of prison. It was burned by the hangman as blasphemous. Biddle finally died in prison, unrepentant to the last.

[550] The first edition of the anonymous [Greek: Haireseôn anastasis] (by Vicars?) appeared in 1805.

[551] Possibly by Thomas Pearne (c. 1753-1827), a fellow of St. Peter's College, Cambridge, and a Unitarian minister.

[552] Thomas Wentworth, Earl of Strafford, was borne in London in 1593, and was executed there in 1641. He was privy councilor to Charles I, and was Lord Deputy of Ireland. On account of his repressive measures to uphold the absolute power of the king he was impeached by the Long Parliament and was executed for treason. The essence of his defence is in the sentence quoted by De Morgan, to which Pym replied that taken as a whole, the acts tended to show an intention to change the government, and this was in itself treason.

[553] The name assumed by a writer who professed to give a mathematical explanation of the Trinity, see farther on.--S. E. De M.

[554] Sabellius (fl. 230 A.D.) was an early Christian of Libyan origin. He taught that Father, Son, and Holy Spirit were different names for the same person.

[555] Sir Richard Phillips was born in London in 1767 (not 1768 as stated above), and died there in 1840. He was a bookseller and printer in Leicester, where he also edited a radical newspaper. He went to London to live in 1795 and started the Monthly Magazine there in 1796. Besides the works mentioned by De Morgan he wrote on law and economics.

[556] It was really eighteen months.

[557] While he was made sheriff in 1807 he was not knighted until the following year.

[558] James Mitchell (c. 1786-1844) was a London actuary, or rather a Scotch actuary living a good part of his life in London. Besides the work mentioned he compiled a Dictionary of Chemistry, Mineralogy, and Geology (1823), and wrote On the Plurality of Worlds (1813) and The Elements of Astronomy (1820).

[559] Richarda Smith, wife of Sir George Biddell Airy (see note 129, page 85) the astronomer. In 1835 Sir Robert Peel offered a pension of £300 a year to Airy, who requested that it be settled on his wife.

[560] Mary Fairfax (1780-1872) married as her second husband Dr. William Somerville. In 1826 she presented to the Royal Society a paper on The Magnetic Properties of the Violet Rays of the Solar Spectrum, which attracted much attention. It was for her Mechanism of the Heavens (1831), a popular translation of Laplace's Mécanique Céleste, that she was pensioned.

[561] Dominique François Jean Arago (1786-1853) the celebrated French astronomer and physicist.

[562] For there is a well-known series 1 + 1/2^2 + 1/3^2 + ... = [pi]^2/6. If, therefore, the given series equals 1, we have 2 = 1/6 [pi]^2 or [pi]^2 = 12, whence [pi] = 2 [root]3. But c = [pi]d, and twice the diagonal of a cube on the diameter is 2d [root]3.

[563] There was a second edition in 1821. [564] London, 1830.

[565] He was a resident of Chatham, and seems to have published no other works.

[566] Richard Whately (1787-1863) was, as a child, a calculating prodigy (see note 132, page 86), but lost the power as is usually the case with well-balanced minds. He was a fellow of Oriel College, Oxford, and in 1825 became principal of St. Alban Hall. He was a friend of Newman, Keble, and others who were interested in the religious questions of the day. He became archbishop of Dublin in 1831. He was for a long time known to students through his Logic (1826) and Rhetoric (1828).

[567] William King, D.C.L. (1663-1712), student at Christ Church, Oxford, and celebrated as a wit and scholar. His Dialogues of the Dead (1699) is a satirical attack on Bentley.

[568] Thomas Ebrington (1760-1835) was a fellow of Trinity College, Dublin, and taught divinity, mathematics, and natural philosophy there. He became provost of the college in 1811, bishop of Limerick in 1820, and bishop of Leighlin and Ferns in 1822. His edition of Euclid was reprinted a dozen times. The Reply to John Search's Considerations on the Law of Libel appeared at Dublin in 1834.

[569] Joseph Blanco White (1775-1841) was the son of an Irishman living in Spain. He was born at Seville and studied for orders there, being ordained priest in 1800. He lost his faith in the Roman Catholic Church, and gave up the ministry, escaping to England at the time of the French invasion. At London he edited Español, a patriotic journal extensively circulated in Spain, and for this service he was pensioned after the expulsion of the French. He then studied at Oriel College, Oxford, and became intimate with men like Whately, Newman, and Keble. In 1835 he became a Unitarian. Among his theological writings is his Evidences against Catholicism (1825). The "rejoinder" to which De Morgan refers consisted of two letters: The law of anti-religious Libel reconsidered (Dublin, 1834) and An Answer to some Friendly Remarks on "The Law of Anti-Religious Libel Reconsidered" (Dublin, 1834).

[570] The work was translated from the French.

[571] J. Hoëné Wronski (1778-1853) served, while yet a mere boy, as an artillery officer in Kosciusko's army (1791-1794). He was imprisoned after the battle of Maciejowice. He afterwards lived in Germany, and (after 1810) in Paris. For the bibliography of his works see S. Dickstein's article in the Bibliotheca Mathematica, vol. VI (2), page 48.

[572] Perhaps referring to his Introduction à la philosophie des mathématiques (1811).

[573] Read "equation of the."

[574] Thomas Young (1773-1829), physician and physicist, sometimes called the founder of physiological optics. He seems to have initiated the theory of color blindness that was later developed by Helmholtz. The attack referred to was because of his connection with the Board of Longitude, he having been made (1818) superintendent of the Nautical Almanac and secretary of the Board. He opposed introducing into the Nautical Almanac anything not immediately useful to navigation, and this antagonized many scientists.

[575] Isaac Milner (1750-1820) was professor of natural philosophy at Cambridge (1783) and later became, as De Morgan states, president of Queens' College (1788). In 1791 he became dean of Carlisle, and in 1798 Lucasian professor of mathematics. His chief interest was in chemistry and physics, but he contributed nothing of importance to these sciences or to mathematics.

[576] Thomas Perronet Thompson (1783-1869), fellow of Queens' College, Cambridge, saw service in Spain and India, but after 1822 lived in England. He became major general in 1854, and general in 1868. Besides some works on economics and politics he wrote a Geometry without Axioms (1830) that De Morgan includes later on in his Budget. In it Thompson endeavored to prove the parallel postulate.

[577] De Morgan's father-in-law. See note 441, page 196.

[578] Johann Friedrich Herbart (1776-1841), successor of Kant as professor of philosophy at Königsberg (1809-1833), where he established a school of pedagogy. From 1833 until his death he was professor of philosophy at Göttingen. The title of the pamphlet is: De Attentionis mensura causisque primariis. Psychologiae principia statica et mechanica exemplo illustraturus.... Regiomonti,... 1822. The formulas in question are given on pages 15 and 17, and De Morgan has omitted the preliminary steps, which are, for the first one: [beta] ([phi] - z) [delta]t = [delta]z unde [beta]t= Const / ([phi] - z). Pro t = 0 etiam z = 0; hinc [beta]t = log [phi]/([phi] - z). z = [phi] (1 - [epsilon]^{-[beta]t}); et [delta]z/[delta]t = [beta][phi][epsilon]^{-[beta]t} These are, however, quite elementary as compared with other portions of the theory.

[579] See note 371, page 168.

[580] William Law (1686-1761) was a clergyman, a fellow of Emanuel College, Cambridge, and in later life a convert to Behmen's philosophy. He was so free in his charities that the village in which he lived became so infested by beggars that he was urged by the citizens to leave. He wrote A serious call to a devout and holy life (1728).

[581] He was a curate at Cheshunt, and wrote the Spiritual voice to the Christian Church and to the Jews (London, 1760), A second warning to the world by the Spirit of Prophecy (London, 1760), and Signs of the Times; or a Voice to Babylon (London, 1773).

[582] His real name was Thomas Vaughan (1622-1666). He was a fellow of Jesus College, Oxford, taking orders, but was deprived of his living on account of drunkenness. He became a mystic philosopher and gave attention to alchemy. His works had a large circulation, particularly on the continent. He wrote Magia Adamica (London, 1650), Euphrates; or the Waters of the East (London, 1655), and The Chymist's key to shut, and to open; or the True Doctrine of Corruption and Generation (London, 1657).

[583] Emanuel Swedenborg, or Svedberg (1688-1772) the mystic. It is not commonly known to mathematicians that he was one of their guild, but he wrote on both mathematics and chemistry. Among his works are the Regelkonst eller algebra (Upsala, 1718) and the Methodus nova inveniendi longitudines locorum, terra marique, ope lunae (Amsterdam, 1721, 1727, and 1766). After 1747 he devoted his attention to mystic philosophy.

[584] Pierre Simon Laplace (1749-1827), whose Exposition du système du monde (1796) and Traité de mécanique celeste (1799) are well known.

[585] See note 117, page 76.

[586] John Dalton (1766-1844), who taught mathematics and physics at New College, Manchester (1793-1799) and was the first to state the law of the expansion of gases known by his name and that of Gay-Lussac. His New system of Chemical Philosophy (Vol. I, pt. i, 1808; pt. ii, 1810; vol. II, 1827) sets forth his atomic theory.

[587] Howison was a poet and philosopher. He lived in Edinburgh and was a friend of Sir Walter Scott. This work appeared in 1822.

[588] He was a shoemaker, born about 1765 at Haddiscoe, and his "astro-historical" lectures at Norwich attracted a good deal of attention at one time. He traced all geologic changes to differences in the inclination of the earth's axis to the plane of its orbit. Of the works mentioned by De Morgan the first appeared at Norwich in 1822-1823, and there was a second edition in 1824. The second appeared in 1824-1825. The fourth was Urania's Key to the Revelation; or the analyzation of the writings of the Jews..., and was first published at Norwich in 1823, there being a second edition at London in 1833. His books were evidently not a financial success, for Mackey died in an almshouse at Norwich.

[589] Godfrey Higgins (1773-1833), the archeologist, was interested in the history of religious beliefs and in practical sociology. He wrote Horae Sabbaticae (1826), The Celtic Druids (1827 and 1829), and Anacalypsis, an attempt to draw aside the veil of the Saitic Isis; or an Inquiry into the Origin of Languages, Nations, and Religions (posthumously published, 1836), and other works. See also page 274, infra.

[590] The work also appeared in French. Wirgman wrote, or at least began, two other works: Divarication of the New Testament into Doctrine and History; part I, The Four Gospels (London, 1830), and Mental Philosophy; part I, Grammar of the five senses; being the first step to infant education (London, 1838).

[591] He was born at Shandrum, County Limerick, and supported himself by teaching writing and arithmetic. He died in an almshouse at Cork.

[592] George Boole (1815-1864), professor of mathematics at Queens' College, Cork. His Laws of Thought (1854) was the first work on the algebra of logic.

[593] Oratio Grassi (1582-1654), the Jesuit who became famous for his controversy with Galileo over the theory of comets. Galileo ridiculed him in Il Saggiatore, although according to the modern view Grassi was the more nearly right. It is said that the latter's resentment led to the persecution of Galileo.

[594] De Morgan might have found much else for his satire in the letters of Walsh. He sought, in his Theory of Partial Functions, to substitute "partial equations" for the differential calculus. In his diary there is an entry: "Discovered the general solution of numerical equations of the fifth degree at 114 Evergreen Street, at the Cross of Evergreen, Cork, at nine o'clock in the forenoon of July 7th, 1844; exactly twenty-two years after the invention of the Geometry of Partial Equations, and the expulsion of the differential calculus from Mathematical Science."

[595] "It has been ordered, sir, it has been ordered."

[596] Bartholomew Prescot was a Liverpool accountant. De Morgan gives this correct spelling on page 278. He died after 1849. His Inverted Scheme of Copernicus appeared in Liverpool in 1822.

[597] Robert Taylor (1784-1844) had many more ups and downs than De Morgan mentions. He was a priest of the Church of England, but resigned his parish in 1818 after preaching against Christianity. He soon recanted and took another parish, but was dismissed by the Bishop almost immediately on the ground of heresy. As stated in the text, he was convicted of blasphemy in 1827 and was sentenced to a year's imprisonment, and again for two years on the same charge in 1831. He then married a woman who was rich in money and in years, and was thereupon sued for breach of promise by another woman. To escape paying the judgment that was rendered against him he fled to Tours where he took up surgery.

[598] Herbert Marsh, Bishop of Peterborough. See note 449 on page 199. [599] "Argument from the prison."

[600] Richard Carlile (1790-1843), one of the leading radicals of his time. He published Hone's parodies (see note 250, page 124) after they had been suppressed, and an edition of Thomas Paine (1818). He was repeatedly imprisoned, serving nine years in all. His continued conflict with the authorities proved a good advertisement for his bookshop.

[601] Wilhelm Ludwig Christmann (1780-1835) was a protestant clergyman and teacher of mathematics. For a while he taught under Pestalozzi. Disappointed in his ambition to be professor of mathematics at Tubingen, he became a confirmed misanthrope and is said never to have left his house during the last ten years of his life. He wrote several works: Ein Wort über Pestalozzi und Pestalozzismus (1812); Ars cossae promota (1814); Philosophia cossica (1815); Aetas argentea cossae (1819); Ueber Tradition und Schrift, Logos und Kabbala (1829), besides the one mentioned above. The word coss in the above titles was a German name for algebra, from the Italian cosa (thing), the name for the unknown quantity. It appears in English in the early name for algebra, "the cossic art."

[602] See note 174, page 101.

[603] See note 589, page 257.

[604] He seems to have written nothing else.

[605] See note 596 on page 270. The name is here spelled correctly.

[606] Joseph Jacotot (1770-1840), the father of this Fortuné Jacotot, was an infant prodigy. At nineteen he was made professor of the humanities at Dijon. He served in the army, and then became professor of mathematics at Dijon. He continued in his chair until the restoration of the Bourbons, and then fled to Louvain. It was here that he developed the method with which his name is usually connected. He wrote a Mathématiques in 1827, which went through four editions. The Epitomé is by his son, Fortuné.

[607] He wrote on educational topics and a Sacred History that went through several editions.

[608] "All is in all."

[609] "Know one thing and refer everything else to it," as it is often translated.

[610] A writer of no reputation.

[611] Sir John Lubbock (1803-1865), banker, scientist, publicist, astronomer, one of the versatile men of his time.

[612] See note 165, page 99.

[613] "Those about to die salute you."

[614] Georges Louis Leclerc Buffon (1707-1788), the well-known biologist. He also experimented with burning mirrors, his results appearing in his Invention des miroirs ardens pour brûler à une grande distance (1747). The reference here may be to his Resolution des problèmes qui regardent le jeu du franc carreau (1733). The prominence of his Histoire naturelle (36 volumes, 1749-1788) has overshadowed the credit due to him for his translation of Newton's work on Fluxions.

[615] See page 285. This article was a supplement to No. 14 in the Athenæum Budget.--A. De M.

[616] There are many similar series and products. Among the more interesting are the following:

[pi] 2·2·4·4·6·6·8... ---- = ----------------, 2 1·3·3·5·5·7·7...

[pi]-3 = 1 1 1 ------ = ----- - ----- + ----- - ..., 4 2·3·4 4·5·6 6·7·8

[pi] 1 1 1 1 1 ---- = sqrt - · (1 - --- + ----- - ----- + ----- - ...), 6 3 3·3 3^2·5 3^3·7 3^4·9

[pi] 1 1 1 1 ---- = 4 (- - ----- + ----- - ----- + ...) 4 5 3·5^3 5·5^5 7·5^7

1 1 1 - (--- - ------- + ------- - ...). 239 3·239^3 5·239^5

[617] "To a privateer, a privateer and a half."

[618] Joshua Milne (1776-1851) was actuary of the Sun Life Assurance Society. He wrote A Treatise on the Valuation of Annuities and Assurances on Lives and Survivorships; on the Construction of tables of mortality; and on the Probabilities and Expectations of Life, London, 1815. Upon the basis of the Carlisle bills of mortality of Dr. Heysham he reconstructed the mortality tables then in use and which were based upon the Northampton table of Dr. Price. His work revolutionized the actuarial science of the time. In later years he devoted his attention to natural history.

[619] See note 576, page 252. He also wrote the Theory of Parallels. The proof of Euclid's axiom looked for in the properties of the equiangular spiral (London, 1840), which went through four editions, and the Theory of Parallels. The proof that the three angles of a triangle are equal to two right angles looked for in the inflation of the sphere (London, 1853), of which there were three editions.

[620] For the latest summary, see W. B. Frankland, Theories of Parallelism, an historical critique, Cambridge, 1910.

[621] Joseph Louis Lagrange (1736-1813), author of the Mécanique analytique (1788), Théorie des functions analytiques (1797), Traité de la résolution des équations numériques de tous degrés (1798), Leçons sur le calcul des fonctions (1806), and many memoirs. Although born in Turin and spending twenty of his best years in Germany, he is commonly looked upon as the great leader of French mathematicians. The last twenty-seven years of his life were spent in Paris, and his remarkable productivity continued to the time of his death. His genius in the theory of numbers was probably never excelled except by Fermat. He received very high honors at the hands of Napoleon and was on the first staff of the Ecole polytechnique (1797).

[622] "I shall have to think it over again."

[623] Henry Goulburn (1784-1856) held various government posts. He was under-secretary for war and the colonies (1813), commissioner to negotiate peace with America (1814), chief secretary to the Lord Lieutenant of Ireland (1821), and several times Chancellor of the Exchequer. On the occasion mentioned by De Morgan he was standing for parliament, and was successful.

[624] On Drinkwater Bethune see note 165, page 99.

[625] Charles Henry Cooper (1808-1866) was a biographer and antiquary. He was town clerk of Cambridge (1849-1866) and wrote the Annals of Cambridge (1842-1853). His Memorials of Cambridge (1874) appeared after his death. Thompson Cooper was his son, and the two collaborated in the Athenae Cantabrigiensis (1858).

[626] William Yates Peel (1789-1858) was a brother of Sir Robert Peel, he whose name degenerated into the familiar title of the London "Bobby" or "Peeler." Yates Peel was a member of parliament almost continuously from 1817 to 1852. He represented Cambridge at Westminster from 1831 to 1835.

[627] Henry John Temple, third Viscount of Palmerston (1784-1865), was member for Cambridge in 1811, 1818, 1820, 1826 (defeating Goulburn), and 1830. He failed of reelection in 1831 because of his advocacy of reform. This must have been the time when Goulburn defeated him. He was Foreign Secretary (1827) and Secretary of State for Foreign Affairs (1830-1841, and 1846-1851). It is said of him that he "created Belgium, saved Portugal and Spain from absolutism, rescued Turkey from Russia and the highway to India from France." He was Prime Minister almost continuously from 1855 to 1865, a period covering the Indian Mutiny and the American Civil War.

[628] William Cavendish, seventh Duke of Devonshire (1808-1891). He was member for Cambridge from 1829 to 1831, but was defeated in 1831 because he had favored parliamentary reform. He became Earl of Burlington in 1834, and Duke of Devonshire in 1858. He was much interested in the promotion of railroads and in the iron and steel industries.

[629] Richard Sheepshanks (1794-1855) was a brother of John Sheepshanks the benefactor of art. (See note 314, p. 147.) He was a fellow of Trinity College, Cambridge, a fellow of the Royal Society and secretary of the Astronomical Society. Babbage (See note 469, p. 207) suspected him of advising against the government support of his calculating machine and attacked him severely in his Exposition of 1851, in the chapter on The Intrigues of Science. Babbage also showed that Sheepshanks got an astronomical instrument of French make through the custom house by having Troughton's (See note 332, page 152) name engraved on it.

Sheepshanks admitted this second charge, but wrote a Letter in Reply to the Calumnies of Mr. Babbage, which was published in 1854. He had a highly controversial nature.

[630] See note 469, page 207. The work referred to is Passages from the Life of a Philosopher, London, 1864.

[631] Drinkwater Bethune. See note 165, page 99.

[632] Siméon-Denis Poisson (1781-1840) was professor of calculus and mechanics at the Ecole polytechnique. He was made a baron by Napoleon, and was raised to the peerage in 1837. His chief works are the Traité de mécanìque (1811) and the Traité mathématique de la chaleur (1835).

[633] "As to M. Poisson, I really wish I had a thousandth part of his mathematical knowledge that I might prove my system to the incredulous."

[634] This list includes most of the works of Antoine-Louis-Guénard Demonville. There was also the Nouveau système du monde ... et hypothèses conformes aux expériences sur les vents, sur la lumière et sur le fluide électro-magnétique, Paris, 1830.

[635] Paris, 1835.

[636] Paris, 1833.

[637] The second part appeared in 1837. There were also editions in 1850 and 1852, and one edition appeared without date.

[638] Paris, 1842.

[639] Parsey also wrote The Art of Miniature Painting on Ivory (1831), Perspective Rectified (1836), and The Science of Vision (1840), the third being a revision of the second.

[640] William Ritchie (1790-1837) was a physicist who had studied at Paris under Biot and Gay-Lussac. He contributed several papers on electricity, heat, and elasticity, and was looked upon as a good experimenter. Besides the geometry he wrote the Principles of the Differential and Integral Calculus (1836).

[641] Alfred Day (1810-1849) was a man who was about fifty years ahead of his time in his attempt to get at the logical foundations of geometry. It is true that he laid himself open to criticism, but his work was by no means bad. He also wrote A Treatise on Harmony (1849, second edition 1885), The Rotation of the Pendulum (1851), and several works on Greek and Latin Grammar.

[642] Walter Forman wrote a number of controversial tracts. His first seems to have been A plan for improving the Revenue without adding to the burdens of the people, a letter to Canning in 1813. He also wrote A New Theory of

the Tides (1822). His Letter to Lord John Russell, on Lord Brougham's most extraordinary conduct; and another to Sir J. Herschel, on the application of Kepler's third law appeared in 1832.

[643] Lord John Russell (1792-1878) first Earl Russell, was one of the strongest supporters of the reform measures of the early Victorian period. He became prime minister in 1847, and again in 1865.

[644] Lauder seems never to have written anything else. [645] See note 22, page 40.

[646] The names of Alphonso Cano de Molina, Yvon, and Robert Sara have no standing in the history of the subject beyond what would be inferred from De Morgan's remark.

[647] Claude Mydorge (1585-1647), an intimate friend of Descartes, was a dilletante in mathematics who read much but accomplished little. His Récréations mathématiques is his chief work. Boncompagni published the "Problèmes de Mydorge" in his Bulletino.

[648] Claude Hardy was born towards the end of the 16th century and died at Paris in 1678. In 1625 he edited the Data Euclidis, publishing the Greek text with a Latin translation. He was a friend of Mydorge and Descartes, but an opponent of Fermat.

[649] That is, in the Bibliotheca Realis of Martin Lipen, or Lipenius (1630-1692), which appeared in six folio volumes, at Frankfort, 1675-1685. [650] See note 29, page 43.

[651] Baldassare Boncompagni (1821-1894) was the greatest general collector of mathematical works that ever lived, possibly excepting Libri. His magnificent library was dispersed at his death. His Bulletino (1868-1887) is one of the greatest source books on the history of mathematics that we have. He also edited the works of Leonardo of Pisa.

[652] He seems to have attracted no attention since De Morgan's search, for he is not mentioned in recent bibliographies.

[653] Joseph-Louis Vincens de Mouléon de Causans was born about the beginning of the l8th century. He was a Knight of Malta, colonel in the infantry, prince of Conti, and governor of the principality of Orange. His works on geometry are the Prospectus apologétique pour la quadrature du cercle (1753), and La vraie géométrie transcendante (1754).

[654] See note 119, page 80.

[655] See note 120, page 81.

[656] Lieut. William Samuel Stratford (1791-1853), was in active service during the Napoleonic wars but retired from the army in 1815. He was first secretary of the Astronomical Society (1820) and became superintendent of the Nautical Almanac in 1831. With Francis Baily he compiled a star catalogue, and wrote on Halley's (1835-1836) and Encke's (1838) comets.

[657] See Sir J. Herschel's Astronomy, p. 369.--A. De M.

[658] Captain Ross had just stuck a bit of brass there.--A. De M. Sir James Clark Ross (1800-1862) was a rear admiral in the British navy and an arctic and antarctic explorer of prominence. De Morgan's reference is to Ross's discovery of the magnetic pole on June 1, 1831. In 1838 he was employed by the Admiralty on a magnetic survey of the United Kingdom. He was awarded the gold medal of the geographical societies of London and Paris in 1842.

[659] John Partridge (1644-1715), the well-known astrologer and almanac maker. Although bound to a shoemaker in his early boyhood, he had acquired enough Latin at the age of eighteen to read the works of the astrologers. He then mastered Greek and Hebrew and studied medicine. In 1680 he began the publication of his almanac, the Merlinus

Liberatus, a book that acquired literary celebrity largely through the witty comments upon it by such writers as Swift and Steele.

[660] See note 642 on page 296.

[661] William Woodley also published several almanacs (1838, 1839, 1840) after his rejection by the Astronomical Society in 1834.

[662] It appeared at London.

[663] The first edition appeared in 1830, also at London. [664] See note 441, page 196.

[665] Thomas Kerigan wrote The Young Navigator's Guide to the siderial and planetary parts of Nautical Astronomy (London, 1821, second edition 1828), a work on eclipses (London, 1844), and the work on tides (London, 1847) to which De Morgan refers.

[666] Jean Sylvain Bailly, who was guillotined. See note 365, page 166. [667] See note 670, page 309.

[668] Laurent seems to have had faint glimpses of the modern theory of matter. He is, however, unknown.

[669] See note 133, page 87.

[670] Francis Baily (1774-1844) was a London stockbroker. His interest in science in general and in astronomy in particular led to his membership in the Royal Society and to his presidency of the Astronomical Society. He wrote on interest and annuities (1808), but his chief works were on astronomy.

[671] If the story is correctly told Baily must have enjoyed his statement that Gauss was "the oldest mathematician now living." As a matter of fact he was then only 58, three years the junior of Baily himself. Gauss was born in 1777 and died in 1855, and Baily was quite right in saying that he was "generally thought to be the greatest" mathematician then living.

[672] Margaret Cooke, who married Flamsteed in 1692.

[673] John Brinkley (1763-1835), senior wrangler, first Smith's prize-man (1788), Andrews professor of astronomy at Dublin, first Astronomer Royal for Ireland (1792), F.R.S. (1803), Copley medallist, president of the Royal Society and Bishop of Cloyne. His Elements of Astronomy appeared in 1808.

[674] See note 248, page 124.
[675] See note 276, page 133.

[676] See note 352, page 161.

[677] "It becomes the doctors of the Sorbonne to dispute, the Pope to decree, and the mathematician to go to Paradise on a perpendicular line."

[678] See note 124, page 83.

[679] See note 621, page 288.

[680] Sylvain van de Weyer, who was born at Louvain in 1802. He was a jurist and statesman, holding the portfolio for foreign affairs (1831-1833), and being at one time ambassador to England.

[681] Henry Crabb Robinson (1775-1867), correspondent of the Times at Altona and in the Peninsula, and later foreign editor. He was one of the founders of the Athenæum Club and of University College, London. He seems to have known pretty much every one of his day, and his posthumous Diary attracted attention when it appeared.

[682] Was this Whewell, who was at Trinity from 1812 to 1816 and became a fellow in 1817?

[683] Tom Cribb (1781-1848) the champion pugilist. He had worked as a coal porter and hence received his nickname, the Black Diamond.

[684] John Finleyson, or Finlayson, was born in Scotland in 1770 and died in London in 1854. He published a number of pamphlets that made a pretense to being scientific. Among his striking phrases and sentences are the statements that the stars were made "to amuse us in observing them"; that the earth is "not shaped like a garden turnip as the Newtonians make it," and that the stars are "oval-shaped immense masses of frozen water." The first edition of the work here mentioned appeared at London in 1830.

[685] Richard Brothers (1757-1824) was a native of Newfoundland. He went to London when he was about 30, and a little later set forth his claim to being a descendant of David, prince of the Hebrews, and ruler of the world. He was confined as a criminal lunatic in 1795 but was released in 1806.

[686] Charles Grey (1764-1845), second Earl Grey, Viscount Howick, was then Prime Minister. The Reform Bill was introduced and defeated in 1831. The following year, with the Royal guarantees to allow him to create peers, he finally carried the bill in spite of "the number of the beast."

[687] The letters of obscure men, the Epistolæ obscurorum virorum ad venerabilem virum Magistrum Ortuinum Gratium Dauentriensem, by Joannes Crotus, Ulrich von Hutten, and others appeared at Venice about 1516.

[688] The lamentations of obscure men, the Lamentationes obscurorum virorum, non prohibete per sedem Apostolicam. Epistola D. Erasmi Roterodami: quid de obscuris sentiat, by G. Ortwinus, appeared at Cologne in 1518.

[689] The criticism was timely when De Morgan wrote it. At present it would have but little force with respect to the better class of algebras.

[690] Thomas Ignatius Maria Forster (1789-1860) was more of a man than one would infer from this satire upon his theory. He was a naturalist, astronomer, and physiologist. In 1812 he published his Researches about Atmospheric Phenomena, and seven years later (July 3, 1819) he discovered a comet. With Sir Richard Phillips he founded a Meteorological Society, but it was short lived. He declined a fellowship in the Royal Society because he disapproved of certain of its rules, so that he had a recognized standing in his day. The work mentioned by De Morgan is the second edition, the first having appeared at Frankfort on the Main in 1835 under the title, Recueil des ouvrages et des pensées d'un physicien et metaphysicien.

[691] Zadkiel, whose real name was Richard James Morrison (1795-1874), was in his early years an officer in the navy. In 1831 he began the publication of the Herald of Astrology, which was continued as Zadkiel's Almanac. His name became familiar throughout Great Britain as a result.

[692] See note 566, page 246.

[693] Sumner (1780-1862) was an Eton boy. He went to King's College, Cambridge, and was elected fellow in 1801. He took many honors, and in 1807 became M.A. He was successively Canon of Durham (1820), Bishop of Chester (1828), and Archbishop of Canterbury (1848). Although he voted for the Catholic Relief Bill (1829) and the Reform Bill (1832), he opposed the removal of Jewish disabilities.

[694] Charles Richard Sumner (1790-1874) was not only Bishop of Winchester (1827), but also Bishop of Llandaff and Dean of St. Paul's, London (1826). He lost the king's favor by voting for the Catholic Relief Bill.

[695] John Bird Sumner, brother of Charles Richard.

[696] Thomas Musgrave (1788-1860) became Fellow of Trinity in 1812, and senior proctor in 1831. He was also Dean of Bristol.

[697] Charles Thomas Longley (1794-1868) was educated at Westminster School and at Christ Church, Oxford. He became M.A. in 1818 and D.D. in 1829. Besides the bishoprics mentioned he was Bishop of Ripon (1836-1856), and before that was headmaster of Harrow (1829-1836).

[698] Thomson (1819-1890) was scholar and fellow of Queen's College, Oxford. He became chaplain to the Queen in 1859.

[699] This is worthy of the statistical psychologists of the present day.

[700] The famous Moon Hoax was written by Richard Adams Locke, who was born in New York in 1800 and died in Staten Island in 1871. He was at one time editor of the Sun, and the Hoax appeared in that journal in 1835. It was reprinted in London (1836) and Germany, and was accepted seriously by most readers. It was published in book form in New York in 1852 under the title The Moon Hoax. Locke also wrote another hoax, the Lost Manuscript of Mungo Park, but it attracted relatively little attention.

[701] It is true that Jean-Nicolas Nicollet (1756-1843) was at that time in the United States, but there does not seem to be any very tangible evidence to connect him with the story. He was secretary and librarian of the Paris observatory (1817), member of the Bureau of Longitudes (1822), and teacher of mathematics in the Lycée Louis-le-Grand. Having lost his money through speculations he left France for the United States in 1831 and became connected with the government survey of the Mississippi Valley.

[702] This was Alexis Bouvard (1767-1843), who made most of the computations for Laplace's Mécanique céleste (1793). He discovered eight new comets and calculated their orbits. In his tables of Uranus (1821) he attributed certain perturbations to the presence of an undiscovered planet, but unlike Leverrier and Adams he did not follow up this clue and thus discover Neptune.

[703] Patrick Murphy (1782-1847) awoke to find himself famous because of his natural guess that there would be very cold weather on January 20, although that is generally the season of lowest temperature. It turned out that his forecasts were partly right on 168 days and very wrong on 197 days.

[704] He seems to have written nothing else. If one wishes to enter into the subject of the mathematics of the Great Pyramid there is an extensive literature awaiting him. Richard William Howard Vyse (1784-1853) published in 1840 his Operations carried on at the Pyramids of Gizeh in 1837, and in this he made a beginning of a scientific metrical study of the subject. Charles Piazzi Smyth (1819-1900), astronomer Royal for Scotland (1845-1888) was much carried away with the number mysticism of the Great Pyramid, so much so that he published in 1864 a work entitled Our Inheritance in the Great Pyramid, in which his vagaries were set forth.

Although he was then a Fellow of the Royal Society (1857), his work was so ill received that when he offered a paper on the subject it was rejected (1874) and he resigned in consequence of this action. The latest and perhaps the most scholarly of all investigators of the subject is William Matthew Flinders Petrie (born in 1853), Edwards professor of Egyptology at University College, London, whose Pyramids and Temples of Gizeh (1883) and subsequent works are justly esteemed as authorities.

[705] As De Morgan subsequently found, this name reversed becomes Oliver B...e, for Oliver Byrne, one of the odd characters among the minor mathematical writers of the middle of the last century. One of his most curious works is The first six Books of the Elements of Euclid; in which coloured diagrams and symbols are used instead of letters (1847). There is some merit in speaking of the red triangle instead of the triangle ABC, but not enough to give the method any standing. His Dual Arithmetic (1863-1867) was also a curious work.

[706] Brenan also wrote on English composition (1829), a work that went through fourteen editions by 1865; a work entitled The Foreigner's English Conjugator (1831), and a work on the national debt.

[707] See note 211, page 112.

[708] See note 592, page 261.

[709] Sir William Rowan Hamilton (1805-1865), the discoverer of quaternions (1852), was an infant prodigy, competing with Zerah Colburn as a child. He was a linguist of remarkable powers, being able, at thirteen years of age, to boast that he knew as many languages as he had lived years. When only sixteen he found an error in Laplace's Mécanique céleste. When only twenty-two he was appointed Andrews professor of astronomy, and he soon after became Astronomer Royal of Ireland. He was knighted in 1835. His earlier work was on optics, his Theory of Systems of Rays appearing in 1823. In 1827 he published a paper on the principle of Varying Action. He also wrote on dynamics.

[710] "Let him not leave the kingdom,"--a legal phrase.

[711] Probably De Morgan is referring to Johann Bernoulli III (1744-1807), who edited Lambert's Logische und philosophische Abhandlungen, Berlin, 1782. He was astronomer of the Academy of Sciences at Berlin.

[712] Jacob Bernoulli (1654-1705) was one of the two brothers who founded the famous Bernoulli family of mathematicians, the other being Johann I. His Ars conjectandi (1713), published posthumously, was the first distinct treatise on probabilities.

[713] Johann Heinrich Lambert (1728-1777) was one of the most learned men of his time. Although interested chiefly in mathematics, he wrote also on science, logic, and philosophy.

[714] Joseph Diez Gergonne (1771-1859), a soldier under Napoleon, and founder of the Annales de mathématiques (1810).

[715] Gottfried Ploucquet (1716-1790) was at first a clergyman, but afterwards became professor of logic at Tübingen.

[716] "In the premises let the middle term be omitted; what remains indicates the conclusion."

[717] Probably Sir William Edmond Logan (1789-1875), who became so interested in geology as to be placed at the head of the geological survey of Canada (1842). The University of Montreal conferred the title LL.D. upon him, and Napoleon III gave him the cross of the Legion of Honor.

[718] "So strike that he may think himself to die."

[719] "Witticism or piece of stupidity."

[720] A very truculently unjust assertion: for Sir W. was as great a setter up of some as he was a puller down of others. His writings are a congeries of praises and blames, both cruel smart, as they say in the States. But the combined instigation of prose, rhyme, and retort would send Aristides himself to Tartarus, if it were not pretty certain that Minos would grant a stet processus under the circumstances. The first two verses are exaggerations standing on a basis of truth. The fourth verse is quite true: Sir W. H. was an Edinburgh Aristotle, with the difference of ancient and modern Athens well marked, especially the perfervidum ingenium Scotorum.--A. De M.

[721] See note 576, p. 252. There was also a Theory of Parallels that differed from these, London, 1853, second edition 1856, third edition 1856.

[722] The work was written by Robert Chambers (1802-1871), the Edinburgh publisher, a friend of Scott and of many of his contemporaries in the literary field. He published the Vestiges of the Natural History of Creation in 1844, not 1840.

[723] Everett (1784-1872) was at that time a good Wesleyan, but was expelled from the ministry in 1849 for having written Wesleyan Takings and as under suspicion for having started the Fly Sheets in 1845. In 1857 he established the United Methodist Free Church.

[724] Smith was a Primitive Methodist preacher. He also wrote an Earnest Address to the Methodists (1841) and The Wealth Question (1840?).

[725] He wrote the Nouveau traité de Balistique, Paris, 1837.

[726] Joseph Denison, known to fame only through De Morgan. See also page 353.

[727] The radical (1784?-1858), advocate of the founding of London university (1826), of medical reform (1827-1834), and of the repeal of the duties on newspapers and corn, and an ardent champion of penny postage.

[728] I. e., Roman Catholic Priest.

[729] Murphy (1806-1843) showed extraordinary powers in mathematics even before the age of thirteen. He became a fellow of Caius College, Cambridge, in 1829, dean in 1831, and examiner in mathematics in London University in 1838.

[730] See note 442, page 196.

[731] Sir John Bowring (1792-1872), the linguist, writer, and traveler, member of many learned societies and a writer of high reputation in his time. His works were not, however, of genuine merit.

[732] Joseph Hume (1777-1855) served as a surgeon with the British army in India early in the nineteenth century. He returned to England in 1808 and entered parliament as a radical in 1812. He was much interested in all reform movements.

[733] Sir Robert Harry Inglis (1786-1855), a strong Tory, known for his numerous addresses in the House of Commons rather than for any real ability.

[734] Sir Robert Peel (1788-1850) began his parliamentary career in 1809 and was twice prime minister. He was prominent in most of the great reforms of his time.

[735] See note 627, page 290.

[736] John Taylor (1781-1864) was a publisher, and published several pamphlets opposed to Peel's currency measures. De Morgan refers to his work on the Junius question. This was done early in his career, and resulted in A Discovery of the author of the Letters of Junius (1813), and The Identity of Junius with a distinguished living character established (1816), this being Sir Philip Francis.

[737] See note 665, page 308.

[738] See page 348.

[739] See note 348, page 160.

[740] Sir Nicholas Harris Nicolas (1799-1848) was a reformer in various lines,--the Record Commission, the Society of Antiquaries, and the British Museum,--and his work was not without good results.

[741] See note 98, page 69.

[742] In the Companion to the Almanac for 1845 is a paper by Prof. De Morgan, "On the Ecclesiastical Calendar," the statements of which, so far as concerns the Gregorian Calendar, are taken direct from the work of Clavius, the principal agent in the arrangement of the reformed reckoning. This was followed, in the Companion to the Almanac for 1846, by a second paper, by the same author, headed "On the Earliest Printed Almanacs," much of which is written in direct supplement to the former article.--S. E. De Morgan.

[743] It may be necessary to remind some English readers that in Latin and its derived European languages, what we call Easter is called the passover (pascha). The Quartadecimans had the name on their side: a possession which often is, in this world, nine points of the law.--A. De M.

[744] Socrates Scholasticus was born at Constantinople c. 379, and died after 439. His Historia Ecclesiastica (in Greek) covers the period from Constantine the Great to about 439, and includes the Council of Nicæa. The work was printed in Paris 1544.

[745] Theodoretus or Theodoritus was born at Antioch and died about 457. He was one of the greatest divines of the fifth century, a man of learning, piety, and judicial mind, and a champion of freedom of opinion in all religious matters.

[746] He died in 417. He was a man of great energy and of high attainments.

[747] He died in 461, having reigned as pope for twenty-one years. It was he who induced Attila to spare Rome in 452.

[748] He succeeded Leo as pope in 461, and reigned for seven years.

[749] Victorinus or Victorius Marianus seems to have been born at Limoges. He was a mathematician and astronomer, and the cycle mentioned by De Morgan is one of 532 years, a combination of the Metonic cycle of 19 years with the solar cycle of 28 years. His canon was published at Antwerp in 1633 or 1634, De doctrina temporum sive commentarius in Victorii Aquitani et aliorum canones paschales.

[750] He went to Rome about 497, and died there in 540. He wrote his Liber de paschate in 525, and it was in this work that the Christian era was first used for calendar purposes.

[751] See note 259, page 126.

[752] Johannes de Sacrobosco (Holy wood), or John of Holywood. The name was often written, without regard to its etymology, Sacrobusto. He was educated at Oxford and taught in Paris until his death (1256). He did much to make the Hindu-Arabic numerals known to European scholars.

[753] See note 36, page 44.

[754] See note 45, page 48.

[755] The Julian year is a year of the Julian Calendar, in which there is leap year every fourth year. Its average length is therefore 365 days and a quarter.--A. De M.

[756] Ugo Buoncompagno (1502-1585) was elected pope in 1572.

[757] He was a Calabrian, and as early as 1552 was professor of medicine at Perugia. In 1576 his manuscript on the reform of the calendar was presented to the Roman Curia by his brother, Antonius. The manuscript was not printed and it has not been preserved.

[758] The title of this work, which is the authority on all points of the new Calendar, is Kalendarium Gregorianum Perpetuum. Cum Privilegio Summi Pontificis Et Aliorum Principum. Romæ, Ex Officina Dominici Basæ.

MDLXXXII. Cum Licentia Superiorum (quarto, pp. 60).--A. De M.

[759] Manuels-Roret. Théorie du Calendrier et collection de tous les Calendriers des Années passées et futures.... Par L. B. Francoeur,... Paris, à la librairie encyclopédique de Roret, rue Hautefeuille, 10 bis. 1842. (12mo.) In this valuable manual, the 35 possible almanacs are given at length, with such preliminary tables as will enable any one to find, by mere inspection, which almanac he is to choose for any year, whether of old or new style. [1866. I may now refer to my own Book of Almanacs, for the same purpose].--A. De M.

Louis Benjamin Francoeur (1773-1849), after holding positions in the Ecole polytechnique (1804) and the Lycée Charlemagne (1805), became professor of higher algebra in the University of Paris (1809). His Cours complet des mathématiques pures was well received, and he also wrote on mechanics, astronomy, and geodesy.

[760] Albertus Pighius, or Albert Pigghe, was born at Kempen c. 1490 and died at Utrecht in 1542. He was a mathematician and a firm defender of the faith, asserting the supremacy of the Pope and attacking both Luther and Calvin. He spent some time in Rome. His greatest work was his Hierarchiæ ecclesiasticæ assertio (1538).

[761] This was A. F. Vogel. The work was his translation from the German edition which appeared at Leipsic the same year, Entdeckung einer numerischen General-Auflösung aller höheren endlichen Gleichungen von jeder beliebigen algebraischen und transcendenten Form.

[762] The latest edition of Burnside and Panton's Theory of Equations has this brief summary of the present status of the problem: "Demonstrations have been given by Abel and Wantzel (see Serret's Cours d'Algèbre Supérieure, Art. 516) of the impossibility of resolving algebraically equations unrestricted in form, of a degree higher than the fourth. A transcendental solution, however, of the quintic has been given by M. Hermite, in a form involving elliptic integrals."

[763] There was a second edition of this work in 1846. The author's Astronomy Simplified was published in 1838, and the Thoughts on Physical Astronomy in 1840, with a second edition in 1842.

[764] This was The Science of the Weather, by several authors... edited by B., Glasgow, 1867.

[765] This was Y. Ramachandra, son of Sundara L[=a]la. He was a teacher of science in Delhi College, and the work to which De Morgan refers is A Treatise on problems of Maxima and Minima solved by Algebra, which appeared at Calcutta in 1850. De Morgan's edition was published at London nine years later.

[766] Abraham de Moivre (1667-1754), French refugee in London, poor, studying under difficulties, was a man with tastes in some respects like those of De Morgan. For one thing, he was a lover of books, and he had a good deal of interest in the theory of probabilities to which De Morgan also gave much thought. His introduction of imaginary quantities into trigonometry was an event of importance in the history of mathematics, and the theorem that bears his name, (cos [phi] + i sin [phi])^{n} = cos n[phi] + i sin n[phi], is one of the most important ones in all analysis.

[767] John Dolland (1706-1761), the silk weaver who became the greatest maker of optical instruments in his time.

[768] Thomas Simpson (1710-1761), also a weaver, taking his leisure from his loom at Spitalfields to teach mathematics. His New Treatise on Fluxions (1737) was written only two years after he began working in London, and six years later he was appointed professor of mathematics at Woolwich. He wrote many works on mathematics and Simpson's Formulas for computing trigonometric tables are still given in the text-books.

[769] Nicholas Saunderson (1682-1739), the blind mathematician. He lost his eyesight through smallpox when only a year old. At the age of 25 he began lecturing at Cambridge on the principles of the Newtonian philosophy. His Algebra, in two large volumes, was long the standard treatise on the subject.

[770] He was not in the class with the others mentioned. [771] Not known in the literature of mathematics.

[772] Probably J. Butler Williams whose Practical Geodesy appeared in 1842, with a third edition in 1855.

[773] Benjamin Gompertz (1779-1865) was debarred as a Jew from a university education. He studied mathematics privately and became president of the Mathematical Society. De Morgan knew him professionally through the fact that he was prominent in actuarial work.

[774] Referring to the contributions of Archimedes (287-212 B.C.) to the mensuration of the sphere.

[775] The famous Alexandrian astronomer (c. 87-c. 165 A.D.), author of the Almagest, a treatise founded on the works of Hipparchus.

[776] Dr. Whewell, when I communicated this song to him, started the opinion, which I had before him, that this was a very good idea, of which too little was made.--A. De M.

[777] See note 117, page 76.

[778] The common epithet of rank: nobilis Tycho, as he was a nobleman. The writer had been at history.--A. De M. See note 117, page 76.

[779] He lost it in a duel, with Manderupius Pasbergius. A contemporary, T. B. Laurus, insinuates that they fought to settle which was the best mathematician! This seems odd, but it must be remembered they fought in the dark, "in tenebris densis"; and it is a nice problem to shave off a nose in the dark, without any other harm.--A. De M. Was this T. B. Laurus Joannes Baptista Laurus or Giovanni Battista Lauro (1581-1621), the poet and writer?

[780] See note 117, page 76.

[781] Referring to Kepler's celebrated law of planetary motion. He had previously wasted his time on analogies between the planetary orbits and the polyhedrons.--A. De M.

[782] See note 117, page 76. [783] "It does move though."

[784] As great a lie as ever was told: but in 1800 a compliment to Newton without a fling at Descartes would have been held a lopsided structure.--A. De M.

[785] Jean-le-Rond D'Alembert (1717-1783), the foundling who was left on the steps of Jean-le-Rond in Paris, and who became one of the greatest mathematical physicists and astronomers of his century.

[786] Leonhard Euler (1707-1783), friend of the Bernoullis, the greatest of Swiss mathematicians, prominent in the theory of numbers, and known for discoveries in all lines of mathematics as then studied.

[787] See notes 478, 479, page 219.

[788] See note 621, page 288.

[789] See note 584, page 255.

[790] The siderial day is about four minutes short of the solar; there are 366 sidereal days in the year.--A. De M.

[791] The founding of the London Mathematical Society is discussed by Mrs. De Morgan in her Memoir (p. 281). The idea came from a conversation between her brilliant son, George Campbell De Morgan, and his friend Arthur Cowper Ranyard in 1864. The meeting of organization was held on Nov. 7, 1864, with Professor De Morgan in the chair, and the first regular meeting on January 16, 1865.

[792] See note 33, page 43.

[793] See note 119, page 80.

[794] John Russell Hind (b. 1823), the astronomer. Between 1847 and 1854 he discovered ten planetoids.

[795] Sir Roderick Impey Murchison (1792-1871), the great geologist. He was knighted in 1846 and devoted the latter part of his life to the work of the Royal Geographical Society and to the geology of Scotland.

[796] Friedrich Wilhelm Bessel (1784-1846), the astronomer and physicist. He was professor of astronomy at Königsberg.

[797] This was the Reduction of the Observations of Planets made ... from 1750 to 1830: computed ... under the superintendence of George Biddell Airy (1848). See note 129, page 85.

[798] The expense of this magnificent work was defrayed by Government grants, obtained, at the instance of the British Association, in 1833--A. De M.

[799] See note 32, page 43.

[800] Franz Friedrich Ernst Brünnow (1821-1891) was at that time or shortly before director of the observatory at Dusseldorf. He then went to Berlin and thence (1854) to Ann Arbor, Michigan. He then went to Dublin and finally became Royal Astronomer of Ireland.

[801] Johann Gottfried Galle (1812-1910), at that time connected with the Berlin observatory, and later professor of astronomy at Breslau.

[802] George Bishop (1785-1861), in whose observatory in Regent's Park important observations were made by Dawes, Hind, and Marth.

[803] James Challis (1803-1882), director of the Cambridge observatory, and successor of Airy as Plumian professor of astronomy.

[804] On Leverrier and Arago see note 33, page 43, and note 561, page 243.

[805] Robert Grant's (1814-1892) History of Physical Astronomy from the Earliest Ages to the Middle of the Nineteenth Century appeared in 1852. He was professor of astronomy and director of the observatory at Glasgow.

[806] John Debenham was more interested in religion than in astronomy. He wrote The Strait Gate; or, the true scripture doctrine of salvation clearly explained, London, 1843, and Tractatus de magis et Bethlehemæ stella et Christi in deserto tentatione, privately printed at London in 1845.

[807] More properly the Sydney Smirke reading room, since it was built from his designs.

[808] The Antinomians were followers of Johannes Agricola (1494-1566). They believed that Christians as such were released from all obligations to the Old Testament. Some went so far as to assert that, since all Christians were sanctified, they could not lose this sanctity even though they disobeyed God. The sect was prominent in England in the seventeenth century, and was transferred to New England. Here it suffered a check in the condemnation of Mrs. Ann Hutchinson (1636) by the Newton Synod.

[809] Aside from this work and his publications on Reeve and Muggleton he wrote nothing. With Joseph Frost he published A list of Books and general index to J. Reeve and L. Muggleton's works (1846), Divine Songs of the Muggletonians (1829), and the work mentioned on page 396. The works of J. Reeve and L. Muggleton (1832).

[810] About 1650 he and his cousin John Reeve (1608-1658) began to have visions. As part of their creed they taught that astronomy was opposed by the Bible. They asserted that the sun moves about the earth, and Reeve figured out that heaven was exactly six miles away. Both Muggleton and Reeve were imprisoned for their unitarian views. Muggleton wrote a Transcendant Spirituall Treatise (1652). I have before me A true Interpretation of All the Chief Texts ... of the whole Book of the Revelation of St. John.... By Lodowick Muggleton, one of the two last Commissioned Witnesses & Prophets of the onely high, immortal, glorious God, Christ Jesus (1665), in which the interpretation of the "number of the beast" occupies four pages without arriving anywhere.

[811] In 1652 he was, in a vision, named as the Lord's "last messenger," with Muggleton as his "mouth," and died six years later, probably of nervous tension resulting from his divine "illumination." He was the more spiritual of the two.

[812] William Guthrie (1708-1770) was a historian and political writer. His History of England (1744-1751) was the first attempt to base history on parliamentary records. He also wrote a General History of Scotland in 10 volumes (1767). The work to which Frost refers is the Geographical, Historical, and Commercial Grammar (1770) which contained an astronomical part by J. Ferguson. By 1827 it had passed through 24 editions.

[813] George Fox (1624-1691), founder of the Society of Friends; a mystic and a disciple of Boehme. He was eight times imprisoned for heresy.

[814] If they were friends they were literary antagonists, for Muggleton wrote against Fox The Neck of the Quakers Broken (1663), and Fox replied in 1667. Muggleton also wrote A Looking Glass for George Fox.

[815] John Conduitt (1688-1737), who married (1717) Newton's half niece, Mrs. Katherine Barton. See note 284, page 136.

[816] Probably Peter Mark Roget's (1779-1869) Thesaurus of English Words (1852) is not much used at present, but it went through 28 editions in his lifetime. Few who use the valuable work are aware that Roget was a professor of physiology at the Royal Institution (London), that he achieved his title of F. R. S. because of his work in perfecting the slide rule, and that he followed Sir John Herschel as secretary of the Royal Society.

[817] See note 703, page 327. This work went into a second edition in the year of its first publication.

[818] See note 398, page 177.

[819] See note 528, page 233.

[820] George Jacob Holyoake (1817-1906) entered into a controversial life at an early age. In 1841 he was imprisoned for six months for blasphemy. He founded and edited The Reasoner (Vols. 1-26, 1846-1861). In his later life he did much to promote cooperation among the working class.

[821] See note 176, page 102.

[822] William Thomas Lowndes (1798-1843), whose Bibliographer's Manual of English Literature, 4 vols., London, 1834 (also 1857-1864, and 1869) is a classic in its line.

[823] Jacques Charles Brunet (1780-1867), the author of the great French bibliography, the Manuel du Libraire (1810).

* * * * *

CONTEN

Printed in Great Britain
by Amazon

46840541R00120